# Body, Sound and Space in Music and Beyond: Multimodal Explorations

Body and space refer to vital and interrelated dimensions in the experience of sounds and music. Sounds have an overwhelming impact on feelings of bodily presence and inform us about the space we experience. Even in situations where visual information is artificial or blurred, such as in virtual environments or certain genres of film and computer games, sounds may shape our perceptions and lead to surprising new experiences. This book discusses recent developments in a range of interdisciplinary fields, taking into account the rapidly changing ways of experiencing sounds and music, the consequences for how we engage with sonic events in daily life and the technological advancements that offer insights into state-of-the-art methods and future perspectives. Topics range from the pleasures of being locked into the beat of the music, perception–action coupling and bodily resonance, and affordances of musical instruments, to neural processing and cross-modal experiences of space and pitch. Applications of these findings are discussed for movement sonification, room acoustics, networked performance, and for the spatial coordination of movements in dance, computer gaming and interactive artistic installations.

**Clemens Wöllner** is Professor of Systematic Musicology at the University of Hamburg, Germany. His research focuses on performance, multimodal perception and the acquisition of expert skills, employing a range of interdisciplinary methods including motion capture, eye-tracking and physiological measures. He has published widely on topics related to musical conducting, perception–action coupling, human movement, imagery and attention in pianists, empathy and research reflexivity.

# SEMPRE Studies in The Psychology of Music
Series Editors
Graham Welch, *Institute of Education, University of London, UK*
Adam Ockelford, *Roehampton University, UK*
Ian Cross, *University of Cambridge, UK*

The theme for the series is the psychology of music, broadly defined. Topics include (i) musical development at different ages, (ii) exceptional musical development in the context of special educational needs, (iii) musical cognition and context, (iv) culture, mind and music, (v) micro to macro perspectives on the impact of music on the individual (from neurological studies through to social psychology), (vi) the development of advanced performance skills and (vii) affective perspectives on musical learning. The series presents the implications of research findings for a wide readership, including user-groups (music teachers, policy makers, parents) as well as the international academic and research communities. This expansive embrace, in terms of both subject matter and intended audience (drawing on basic and applied research from across the globe), is the distinguishing feature of the series, and it serves SEMPRE's distinctive mission, which is to promote and ensure coherent and symbiotic links between education, music and psychology research.

*For a full list of recent titles, please visit https://www.routledge.com/music/series/SEMPRE*

**Creative Teaching for Creative Learning in Higher Music Education**
*Edited by Elizabeth Haddon and Pamela Burnard*

**Music, Technology and Education**
*Edited by Andrew King and Evangelos Himonides*

**Communities of Musical Practice**
*Ailbhe Kenny*

**Embodiment of Musical Creativity**
*Zvonimir Nagy*

**Listening in Action**
*Rebecca M. Rinsema*

**Music and Empathy**
*Edited by Elaine King and Caroline Waddington*

**Body, Sound and Space in Music and Beyond: Multimodal Explorations**
*Edited by Clemens Wöllner*

# Body, Sound and Space in Music and Beyond: Multimodal Explorations

**Edited by Clemens Wöllner**

LONDON AND NEW YORK

First published 2017
by Routledge
2 Park Square, Milton Park, Abingdon, Oxon OX14 4RN

and by Routledge
711 Third Avenue, New York, NY 10017

*Routledge is an imprint of the Taylor & Francis Group, an informa business*

© 2017 selection and editorial matter, Clemens Wöllner; individual chapters, the contributors.

The right of Clemens Wöllner to be identified as the author of the editorial material, and of the authors for their individual chapters, has been asserted in accordance with sections 77 and 78 of the Copyright, Designs and Patents Act 1988.

All rights reserved. No part of this book may be reprinted or reproduced or utilised in any form or by any electronic, mechanical, or other means, now known or hereafter invented, including photocopying and recording, or in any information storage or retrieval system, without permission in writing from the publishers.

*Trademark notice:* Product or corporate names may be trademarks or registered trademarks, and are used only for identification and explanation without intent to infringe.

*British Library Cataloguing in Publication Data*
A catalogue record for this book is available from the British Library

*Library of Congress Cataloging in Publication Data*
Names: Wollner, Clemens.
Title: Body, sound and space in music and beyond: multimodal explorations / edited by Clemens Wollner.
Description: Abingdon, Oxon; New York, NY: Routledge, 2017. | Series: SEMPRE studies in the psychology of music | Includes bibliographical references and index.
Identifiers: LCCN 2016051281 | ISBN 9781472485403 (hardback) | ISBN 9781315569628 (ebook)
Subjects: LCSH: Music—Psychological aspects. | Music—Performance—Psychological aspects. | Sound—Psychological aspects.
Classification: LCC ML3830 .B555 2017 | DDC 781.1/1—dc23
LC record available at https://lccn.loc.gov/2016051281

ISBN: 978-1-4724-8540-3 (hbk)
ISBN: 978-1-315-56962-8 (ebk)

Typeset in Times New Roman
by codeMantra

Bach musicological font developed by © Yo Tomita

# Contents

*List of figures*   vii
*List of tables*   ix
*Series editors' preface*   x
*Notes on contributors*   xii

1 **Introduction: structured sounds in bodily and spatial dimensions**   1
CLEMENS WÖLLNER

**PART I**
**Bodily movements, gestures and sonification**   11

2 **The empowering effects of being locked into the beat of the music**   13
MARC LEMAN, JESKA BUHMANN AND EDITH VAN DYCK

3 **Exploring music-related micromotion**   29
ALEXANDER REFSUM JENSENIUS

4 **Cross-modal experience of musical pitch as space and motion: current research and future challenges**   49
ZOHAR EITAN

5 **Gestural qualities in music and outward bodily responses**   69
CLEMENS WÖLLNER AND JESPER HOHAGEN

6 **Aesthetics of sonification: taking the subject-position**   89
PAUL VICKERS, BENNETT HOGG AND DAVID WORRALL

## PART II
## Sound design, instrumental affordances and embodied spatial perception — 111

7  Instruments, voices, bodies and spaces: towards an ecology of performance — 113
   W. LUKE WINDSOR

8  Sonic spaces in movies: audiovisual metaphors and embodied meanings in sound design — 129
   KATHRIN FAHLENBRACH

9  The colourful life of timbre spaces: timbre concepts from early ideas to meta-timbre space and beyond — 150
   CHRISTOPH REUTER AND SALEH SIDDIQ

10 'Music as fluid architecture': investigating core regions of the spatial brain — 168
   CHRISTIANE NEUHAUS

## PART III
## Presence and immersion in networked and virtual spaces — 189

11 Music as artificial environment: spatial, embodied multimodal experience — 191
   PETER LENNOX

12 Music perception and performance in virtual acoustic spaces — 211
   JUDE BRERETON

13 Space and body in sound art: artistic explorations in binaural audio augmented environments — 235
   MARTIN RUMORI

14 Embodiment and disembodiment in networked music performance — 257
   GEORG HAJDU

15 Presence through sound — 279
   MARK GRIMSHAW

*Index* — 299

# Figures

| | | |
|---|---|---|
| 2.1 | Being locked into the beat | 16 |
| 3.1 | Example plots of the X (sideways), Y (front-back) and Z (up–down) axes of the normalised position of a head marker | 34 |
| 3.2 | Two dancers and two musicians rehearsing relationships between actions and sounds at different levels | 43 |
| 4.1 | Ascending and descending melodic stimuli used in Eitan and Granot (2006) | 62 |
| 5.1 | Excerpt from Mozart's 'Laudate pueri' from *Vesperae solennes de Dominica* (K 321) | 71 |
| 5.2 | A movement graph from Truslit as presented to participants in the instruction condition (broken chord; left figure); and a movement response from a participant to Wagner's 'Elisabeth's Prayer' from *Tannhäuser* (right figure) | 79 |
| 5.3 | The melodic line of the music, amplitude, spectral flux, averaged vertical position of participants' fingers while performing the movements and mean tempo | 81 |
| 6.1 | Wittgenstein's duck/rabbit picture | 96 |
| 7.1 | 'In-line' (top left) and 'offset G' (top right) illustrate the relative position of the keys activated by the third (left key) and fourth (right key) fingers of the left hand (the hand closest to the head joint of the flute) in two alternative designs | 121 |
| 8.1 | *The Magnificant Ambersons* (Orson Welles, USA, 1942) 'self is a closed space': confrontation of self and society | 138 |
| 8.2 | *Taxi Driver* (Martin Scorsese, USA 1976), 'coping with identity crisis is a ride' | 143 |
| 9.1 | Top left: sound colour triangle with the axes brightness ('Helligkeit') and saturation ('Sättigung') applied to one single vowel quality (coloured point at 'bunt'). Bottom left: semicircle of vowels. Right: cylinder of sound colours | 155 |
| 9.2 | Timbre space with axis I (sharpness), II (spectral fluctuations) and III (attack transients) | 158 |

viii  *Figures*

| | | |
|---|---|---|
| 9.3 | Empirical meta-timbre space (EMTS): X-axis: Dimension 1, Y-axis: Dimension 2, Z-axis: Dimension 3, Colour bar: Dimension 4 | 160 |
| 10.1 | The intraparietal sulcus divides the PPC into a superior and an inferior part (SPL and IPL) | 173 |
| 10.2 | While dancing, proprioception provides the artist with information about body posture set in relation to room coordinates | 174 |
| 10.3 | Visuo-motor transformation is central while learning to play a musical instrument. During sight-reading, the right SPL and IPS are activated | 176 |
| 10.4 | Testing visuo-spatial and auditory imagery: example items of mental cube rotation and music permutation (inverse and retrograde forms) | 181 |
| 12.1 | John Crook's live array installation for studio, which transforms the room sound in real-time | 221 |
| 12.2 | Representation of the relationship between performance context features which influence changes in musical performance parameters | 224 |
| 12.3 | *Architexture 2* for unaccompanied voices, composed by Ambrose Field, performed in the ruins of St. Mary's Abbey, York | 231 |
| 13.1 | Graphic interpretation of field recordings forming the virtual sound scenery in *Parisflâneur* | 248 |
| 14.1 | Excerpt from *Aphasia* by Mark Applebaum | 269 |
| 14.2 | Georg Hajdu's adaptation of *Radio Music* uses a *radio avatar* to represent the actions of the (remote) musicians | 274 |
| 15.1 | A Kanizsa triangle | 293 |

# Tables

| | | |
|---|---|---|
| 3.1 | Average QoM values for the entire session, no-music and music conditions, and for each of the individual parts | 39 |
| 3.2 | Self-reported standstill conditions of the participants | 40 |
| 3.3 | Self-report on experience | 41 |
| 3.4 | Overview of the spatiotemporal categories developed in the Sverm project | 42 |
| 12.1 | Room acoustic parameters and subjective correlates | 215 |
| 12.2 | Overview of stage acoustic parameters and correlations with subjective impressions | 217 |
| 12.3 | Musical performance attribute groupings, musical performance attributes and objective (measurable) parameters which change according to the room acoustic conditions of the performance venue | 226 |
| 14.1 | Comparison of different network scenarios | 261 |

# Series editors' preface

The enormous growth of research that has been evidenced over the past three decades continues into the many different phenomena that are embraced under the psychology of music 'umbrella'. Growth is evidenced in new journals, books, media interest, an expansion of professional associations (regionally and nationally, such as in Southern Europe, Latin America, Asia), and with increasing and diverse opportunities for formal study, including within non-English-speaking countries. Such growth of interest is not only from psychologists and musicians, but also from colleagues working in the clinical sciences, neurosciences, therapies, in the lifelong health and well-being communities, philosophy, musicology, social psychology, ethnomusicology and education across the lifespan. As part of this global community, the Society for Education, Music and Psychology Research (SEMPRE) celebrated its 40th Anniversary in 2012 and continues to be one of the world's leading and longstanding professional associations in the field. SEMPRE is the only international society that embraces formally an interest in the psychology of music, research and education, seeking to promote knowledge at the interface between the twin social sciences of psychology and education with one of the world's most pervasive art forms, music. SEMPRE was founded in 1972 and has published the journals *Psychology of Music* since 1973 and *Research Studies in Music Education* since 2008, both now produced in partnership with SAGE (see www.sempre.org.uk), and we continue to seek new ways to reach out globally, both in print and online. This includes the launch of a new online journal *Music and Science* in 2017. We recognise that there is an ongoing need to promote the latest research findings to the widest possible audience. Through more extended publication formats, especially books, we believe that we are more likely to fulfil a key component of our mission, which is to have a distinctive and positive impact on individual and collective understanding, as well as on policy and practice internationally, both within and across our disciplinary boundaries. Hence, we welcome the strong collaborative partnership between SEMPRE and Routledge (formerly Ashgate Publishing).

The *SEMPRE Studies in The Psychology of Music* series has been designed to address this international need since its inception in 2007. The theme for the series is the psychology of music, broadly defined. Topics include (amongst others): musical development and learning at different ages; musical cognition and context; culture, mind and music; creativity, composition, and collaboration; micro to macro perspectives on the impact of music on the individual (from neurological studies through to social psychology); the development of advanced performance skills; musical behaviour and development in the context of special educational needs; and affective perspectives on musical learning. The series seeks to present the implications of research findings for a wide readership, including user-groups (music teachers, policy makers, parents and carers, music professionals working in a range of formal, non-formal and informal settings), as well as the international academic teaching and research communities and their students. A key distinguishing feature of the series is its broad focus that draws on basic and applied research from across the globe under the umbrella of SEMPRE's distinctive mission, which is to promote and ensure coherent and symbiotic links between education, music and psychology research.

We are very pleased to welcome this new research-based text that is edited by Clemens Wöllner (University of Hamburg) entitled *Body, Sound and Space in Music and Beyond: Multimodal Explorations*. The book's contents represent a wide range of current research and reflection by an exciting international team of new and established scholars. The focus is on the sense of music's inherent quality of encompassing motion – a quality that can be represented in many different ways in and through the body. We are indebted to the authors for the presentation of such a coherent and cogent text that challenges our understanding of how we experience music in contemporary society, not least in the advent of new technological media.

SEMPRE are delighted to have this book in the *SEMPRE Studies in The Psychology of Music* series, not least because its subject matter is topical, original and apposite in taking forward our understanding of the importance of music in the human condition.

Graham Welch
*UCL Institute of Education, London, UK*

Adam Ockelford
*Roehampton University, UK*

Ian Cross
*University of Cambridge, UK*

# Contributors

**Jude Brereton** is a Lecturer in Audio and Music Technology, in the Department of Electronic Engineering, University of York, UK. She is Programme Leader for the MSc in Audio and Music Technology and teaches postgraduate and undergraduate students in the areas of virtual acoustics and auralisation, music performance analysis and voice analysis and synthesis. Her research centres on the use of virtual reality technology to provide interactive acoustic environments for music performance and analysis. Other research interests include the use of spatial sound to enhance performer and listener experience, interaction and engagement, and the analysis and synthesis of the human voice. In 2008 she was winner of the British Voice Association Van Lawrence Prize for Voice Research. Before beginning her academic career she worked in arts and music administration and is still active in promoting research-inspired music and theatre performance events combining art and science for public engagement and outreach.

**Jeska Buhmann** is working as a PhD student at IPEM, Ghent University, Belgium. She obtained her master's degree at the Radboud University of Nijmegen, in the field of Language, Speech & Informatics, specialising in the prediction of intonation for single sentences with recurrent neural networks. Her research at IPEM focuses on the influence of music on walking or running movements. She studies the sonic characteristics in music that cause people to move with more vigour, resulting in larger step sizes and/or velocity. The work is part of the European BeatHealth project. Her research interests include the motivational qualities and personal preferences in music, the role of music in human movement, the role of music–movement alignment strategies, and the development of user- and task-specific playlists.

**Zohar Eitan** is Professor of Music Theory and Music Cognition at the Buchman-Mehta School of Music, Tel Aviv University, Israel. Much of Eitan's research involves empirical investigation of cross-modal and cross-domain experience in musical contexts. His recent work was published in *Cognition, Journal of Experimental Psychology: Human*

*Perception and Performance, Experimental Psychology, Music Perception, Psychology of Music, Musicae Scientiae, Empirical Musicology Review* and *Psychomusicology: Music, Mind, and Brain*. His current research project examines the cross-modal correspondences implied by Western tonality.

**Kathrin Fahlenbrach** is Professor of Film and Media Studies in the Department for Media and Communication at the University of Hamburg, Germany. Her current research focus lies in cognitive film and media theory, embodiment and moving images, and cognitive metaphors in audiovisual media. She also works on visual performances and the role of communication media in protest movements. She is author of several publications on embodied metaphors in moving images. In her book, *Audiovisuelle Metaphern. Zur Körper- und Affektästhetik in Film und Fernsehen* (2010), she introduces a theoretical framework on embodied and affective aesthetics of audiovisual metaphors in film and television. She has edited several volumes, such as most recently, *Embodied Metaphors in Film, Television, and Video Games: Cognitive Approaches* (2016). She is a board member of the Society for the Cognitive Study of the Moving Image (SCSMI).

**Mark Grimshaw** is the Obel Professor of Music at Aalborg University, Denmark, where he is Chair of the Music & Sound Knowledge Group. He has a BMus (Hons) from the University of Natal, South Africa, an MSc (Music Technology) from the University of York, UK, and the subject of his PhD, from the University of Waikato, New Zealand, was the *Acoustic Ecology of the First-Person Shooter*. Mark has published over 60 works across subjects as diverse as sound, virtuality, the Uncanny Valley and IT systems, and also writes free, open source software for virtual research environments (WIKINDX). His last two books were the anthology *The Oxford Handbook of Virtuality* (2014) and the monograph *Sonic Virtuality* co-authored with Tom Garner (2015). Mark is currently co-editing *The Oxford Handbook of Sound and Imagination* due in 2018.

**Georg Hajdu** is a composer and Professor of Composition and Music Theory at the Hamburg University of Music and Drama, Germany. In 2004, he established Germany's first master's program in multimedia composition as well as, in 2012, the Center for Microtonal Music and Multimedia (ZM4). In 2010 he was composer in residence with the Goethe Institute in Boston and visiting professor at Northeastern University, where he master-minded the first conference entirely dedicated to the Bohlen-Pierce scale. He was also involved in a number of large international projects such as CO-ME-DI-A – a European Culture 2007 project focusing on networked music performance. In addition to his compositions, which are characterised by a pluralistic attitude and have earned him several international prizes, Georg Hajdu has published articles on networked music performance, microtonality, and real-time composition and notation.

In 2016, he served as Chair of the 13th Sound and Music Computing conference in Hamburg.

**Bennett Hogg** is a composer and theorist who teaches at the School of Arts and Cultures, Newcastle University, UK. He currently leads the environmental sound art project Landscape Quartet. His academic research, published by Routledge, Oxford University Press, Cambridge Scholars Press, and Lund University Press, as well as online, focuses on embodiment and technology in music and sound studies from a broadly phenomenological perspective, and has included collaborations with Dr Paul Vickers of Northumbria University on theorising data sonification. Most recently he has been co-researcher on the FWF-funded Emotional Improvisation project, at Kunstuniversität Graz, Austria.

**Jesper Hohagen** currently works as a Research Assistant at the Institute of Systematic Musicology at the University of Hamburg, Germany. His field of research lies in Music Psychology with a special focus on studying the effects of music on movement and sports. Jesper studied musicology at the universities of Bremen and Cologne and gained experience in experimental psychology research during a visit to the Emotion & Well-Being Unit of Monash University in Melbourne, Australia. At present, he is working on his PhD, where he is researching the influence of music on sport-specific movement learning by applying real-time movement sonification based on motion capture.

**Alexander Refsum Jensenius** is Associate Professor of Music Technology in the Department of Musicology, University of Oslo, Norway. His research focuses on why music makes us move, which he explores through empirical studies using different types of motion sensing technologies. He also uses the knowledge and tools from his analytic work in the creation of new music. Then he performs on keyboard instruments, with his own interfaces for musical expression and with motion tracking technologies. Alexander studied at the University of Oslo (BA, MA, PhD) and Chalmers University of Technology, Gothenburg (MSc), and has been a visiting researcher at the University of California, Berkeley and at McGill University, Montreal.

**Marc Leman** is Methusalem Research Professor in Systematic Musicology at Ghent University, Belgium. He holds MA degrees in musicology and philosophy, and did his PhD on computer modelling of tonality perception. He has published more than 350 articles and several books on topics related to embodied music cognition, including *Embodied Music Cognition and Mediation Technology* (2007) and *The Expressive Moment: How Interaction (with Music) Shapes Human Empowerment* (2016). His lab is an international meeting place for researchers working on expressive interactions with music, using embodiment and action science as a point of departure. Marc Leman is laureate of the five-yearly FWO Excellence Award Ernest-John Solvay for Humanities (2015).

**Peter Lennox** is a Research Scientist and Senior Lecturer in Multimodal Spatial Perception and Psychoacoustics at the University of Derby, UK, and engages in research activities in human perception in artificial environments and 3-D music. His PhD thesis from the University of York was titled *The Philosophy of Perception in Artificial Auditory Environments: Spatial Sound and Music*. He engages in collaborations between industry partners, engineers, artists and psychologists, developing new musical forms and enabling technologies. He has mounted several medium-scale spatial sound installations (24–40 loudspeakers, 200–500 audience members) using ambisonics, wavefield synthesis and hybrid methods, and publishes internationally on related topics. He authored 'Spatializing sound', a chapter in *The Oxford Handbook of Computer Music and Digital Sound Culture* (2009), edited by Roger Dean.

**Christiane Neuhaus** is a Privatdozentin in the Institute of Systematic Musicology at the University of Hamburg, Germany. She gives lectures on many interdisciplinary issues, such as creativity research, memory and medical aspects and the cognitive neuroscience of music. She previously worked for seven years as a PostDoc at the Max Planck Institute of Cognitive and Brain Sciences, Leipzig. While there, she published ERP and MEG research in international peer-reviewed journals on issues such as prosody, Gestalt processing and form perception. She wrote her Habilitation thesis on *Structural listening to music* and her PhD thesis on the processing of musical scales from a cross-cultural perspective. This idea was given an award for being a 'Special Innovative Approach' at the ESCOM conference in 2003. She also has a strong background in classical music and studied piano at the Staatliche Hochschule für Musik, Detmold. She was recently invited to be a guest professor by the Eberhard Karls University Tübingen, Germany.

**Christoph Reuter** is Professor of Systematic Musicology at the University of Vienna, Austria. He has previously worked at the University of Cologne and the University of Music Franz Liszt in Weimar as well as in media and publishing houses (e.g. Schott Music International (Mainz), b.i.b. International College (Hanover), IAMP solutions (Cologne)). His research interests include musical acoustics, room acoustics and psychoacoustics, music psychology and sound analysis/synthesis (including music information retrieval (MIR)), as well as music-related internet and software projects. In addition to papers on various musicological themes and topics, he has written books about timbre perception and the auditory discrimination of instruments playing simultaneously (including a formant-based orchestration treatise), as well as a software encyclopaedia of self-playing musical instruments, simulations of eighteenth/nineteenth century musical dice games and other musicological software applications.

**Martin Rumori** is a Lecturer in Instrument Research at the University of Music and Performing Arts Graz, Austria. He works as an intermedia artist, musicologist and computer scientist, and investigates the boundaries of traditional music performance and the incorporation of digital sound and interface technology. His artistic work focuses on installation art and audio augmented environments, acousmatic sound projection and mediated acoustics using loudspeakers and headphones, often incorporating semi-narrative fragments of voice and everyday life footage.

**Saleh Siddiq** is currently a doctoral student at the Musicological Institute at the University of Vienna, Austria. He conducts his research on timbre perception within the framework of a project funded by the Anniversary Fund of the National Bank of Austria (OeNB). He also teaches psychoacoustics at the Music and Arts University of the City of Vienna (MUK) and the Austrian Optometry and Audiology Initiative (OHI). His research focus is on the acoustics and perception of timbre, music psychology, psychoacoustics, (neuro)physiology of hearing and music perception, as well as audiology and musical acoustics. Other research interests are popular music studies (blues and jazz history, theory of jazz and popular music, music production).

**Edith Van Dyck** holds a PhD in Musicology from IPEM, Ghent University, Belgium, and currently works as a postdoctoral researcher at the same institute. Since 2009, she has been focusing on action–perception coupling in musical interaction and has published several papers about the influence of music features and human emotions on music-induced movement (e.g. dance, running and walking). She is also a collaborator in BeatHealth, a project co-funded by the European Union, which aims at exploiting the link between rhythmical auditory information and movement for boosting motor performance and enhancing health and wellness.

**Paul Vickers** is Associate Professor and Reader in Computer Science at Northumbria University, UK. He teaches and carries out research in the computing domain with a particular interest in sonification, that is, how sound can be used to communicate data and information. Linked to this he looks at how the aesthetic properties of scientific artefacts affect how they may be used, that is, how people interact with them. He is especially interested in the relationship between sonification and visualisation and the role of aesthetics and listening in sonification design practice. He has published more than 60 conference papers, journal articles and book chapters and, with Bennett Hogg, co-authored the most cited paper on sonification aesthetics (source: Google Scholar). His current research projects include sonification for network situational awareness and sonification for medical imaging and diagnostics.

**W. Luke Windsor** is Associate Professor of Music Psychology in the School of Music, University of Leeds, UK, and is Deputy Dean of the Faculty of Arts, Humanities and Cultures. He has previously worked and studied at City University, London, the University of Sheffield, and at Radboud University in the Netherlands. Luke has been researching and teaching psychological, aesthetic, analytical and semiotic aspects of music since the mid-1990s. In particular, he has published on rhythm and timing in performance, the sources and modelling of musical expression, ecological approaches to the perception and production of musical performances, and musical gesture. He has supervised doctoral work on a range of music-psychological and practice-led topics, including musical improvisation. His work on acousmatic music and ecological psychology (particularly relevant here) is known and respected internationally, and his published work on the latter has been cited both within musicology and beyond.

**Clemens Wöllner** is Professor of Systematic Musicology at the University of Hamburg, Germany. After his academic education in Hanover, Sheffield, Berlin and Halle-Wittenberg, he worked at institutions in Germany and the UK, including the Royal Northern College of Music, Manchester, and the University of Bremen. His research focuses on performance, multimodal perception and the acquisition of expert skills, employing a range of interdisciplinary methods including motion capture, eyetracking and physiological measures. He is a member of SEMPRE, ESCOM and German music psychology and musicology associations, and serves on the editorial boards of *Psychology of Music* and *Musicae Scientiae*. As a former co-editor of *Music Performance Research*, he has recently co-edited a book published by Georg Olms Verlag. He has published widely on topics related to music performance, human movement, empathy and research reflexivity.

**David Worrall** is Chair of the Audio Arts and Acoustic Department, Columbia College Chicago, USA. He was the foundation Head of the Australian Centre for the Arts and Technology at the Australian National University in Canberra and a Research Scientist in sonification at the Audio Labs of Fraunhofer IIS in Erlangen, Germany. He is an award-winning composer of experimental music, ranging from instrumental compositions, polymedia, sound sculpture and sonification, and has recently been elected the President of the International Community for Auditory Display. In addition to music, David studied mathematics and philosophy and has an active interest in relationships between gesture, aesthetics and comprehension, which informs his work in the sonification of large multivariate datasets such as from stock markets and computer networks for both pragmatic monitoring and artistic expression.

# 1 Introduction
## Structured sounds in bodily and spatial dimensions

*Clemens Wöllner*

The key terms in the title of this volume address far-reaching concepts that have been investigated in music psychology and musicology for a long time. Given the wealth of research, each term would perhaps merit a book on its own. Body and space refer indeed to important and interrelated dimensions in the experience of sounds and music. Most notably, in most musical cultures and genres it is originally the human body in interaction with physical objects that produces musically meaningful sounds. Besides a richness of instruments as external objects, the human voice has long been considered to be the earliest instrument and the origin of music-making (Rousseau, 1786; Mithen, 2006). Hearing someone's voice or listening to a musical instrument playing may resonate with the listener's motor system (Sevdalis and Keller, 2014), thus enabling embodied experiences of musical sounds that some listeners even intensify by moving their body along with the music, ranging from armchair conducting to fine-tuned or frantic dancing in space with the whole body.

Recent advances in methodologies and technical devices permit researches to scrutinise these central experiential dimensions in a detail that was unthinkable a few decades ago. Real-time sound analysis and modelling, three-dimensional motion capture of body movements in high temporal and spatial resolution and immersive explorations of virtual performance spaces – to name but a few of these developments – lead to an unprecedented richness of data. The more information is gathered in diverse and specialist fields, the more there is a need for approaches that compare and coalesce the findings, and relate them to overarching theories that may reconcile apparently contrasting research perspectives. For example, physical descriptions of space and sounds may fundamentally differ from their perceptual counterparts and from meaning formation. Sound perception depends on individual psychological representations and not least basic physiological differences between the hearing systems of listeners. Moreover, there are to date no all-encompassing and meaningful approaches to capture apparently measurable facets of sound such as timbre in acoustic dimensions (see Reuter and Siddiq, this volume). In a similar vein, there are concepts of metaphorical space (e.g., the wideness of sounds), cross-modal perceptions (e.g., high and low for auditory pitches) and multimodal perceptions (e.g., visual, haptic, proprioceptive, auditory) of spatial dimensions based on Gestalt laws, all of which may differ from outer space and three-dimensional Euclidian measures (Eitan, 2013). In an early approach, Ernst Kurth (1931, p. 116) considered the experience of space as a 'central function in listening' to music and a valid psychological reality, such that even the demarcation of sound in distinct pitches should already evoke spatial images.

Experiences of sound and music, as a consequence, are genuinely multimodal by evoking vivid connections to bodily and spatial representations. Sound perceptions are not limited to afferent information via unimodal sensory receptors, but are rather experienced in the full associative power that the same sounds represent in real-life situations (cf. Clarke, 2005), resulting in the need to capture both stimulus features and representational parameters in the individual. Regarding the latter, some of the multimodal perceptions are based on higher-order cognitive associations grounded in memory processes, while other perceptions function on a more automatic level involving bodily representations that may not always be experienced in full awareness (cf. Cross, 2010). Therefore, conscious perceptions of the experiential dimensions alone may not lead to the full picture, and indirect measures have been included in research.

Investigating body, sound and space opens the field for approaches to one of music's fundamental features – its motional character with relevance for listeners, composers, theorists and performers. As David Epstein (1995, p. 101) put it, 'motion subsumes, integrates, and provides the broadest context for all other musical elements'. Characterisations of music as 'moving sonic forms' (Hanslick, 1854/1891, p. 74) or 'features of musical sounds in relation to their gestural affordance ... as trajectory shapes in time and space' (Godøy, 2010, p. 113) point to perceptions of motion qualities within music that are mediated by the human body (cf. Kurth, 1931; Truslit, 1938; Leman and Maes, 2014). Embodied approaches (e.g., Gallagher, 2005) lay stress on these mediation processes that are seen as interactions between the body and the environment. An example is the relationship between bodily reactions and the experience of being moved by music, such that the musical sounds resemble the time course of emotional responses (cf. Langer, 1942). Pratt (1931/1968, p. 203) stated that auditory characters are not emotions themselves, 'they merely sound the way moods feel'. The perceived motion of auditory characters in music may thus correspond with bodily movements, and emotional experiences of music often involve dynamic components of these movements (Epstein, 1993; Davies, 1994; see Eitan, this volume).

A further important aspect – time – could perhaps have been added to the title of the book. Music as a temporal art and, more broadly, sounds as ephemeral sonic events are already intrinsically defined by timing dimensions. Indeed, many contributions to this volume deal with the time course of sounds. The word 'beyond' in the title is chosen to include various types of music and sound experiences that are not often dealt with in musicological and music-psychological writings, such as sound installations (e.g., Licht, 2007), films or video games, for which the experience of space and body are equally important. Taking the perspectives of the creators or producers, sounds that are structured deliberately by a composer, improvising musician or sound designer are typically regarded as music. In a similar way, even sounds that are not intentionally composed can be experienced as intentional music if the listeners' memory system restructures their perception (such as, for example, in Diana Deutsch's well-known 'speech-to-song illusion'; see Deutsch, Henthorn and Lapidis, 2011).

The book may not ultimately clarify and stipulate the relationship between these key concepts, yet it is important to shed light on them every now and then, such as Kurth (1931) and other music scholars did, employing the methods available at their time. This volume provides a platform for the discussion of new developments, taking into account the rapidly changing ways of listening and experiencing sounds, recent theoretical and empirical approaches, consequences for how people engage with sound events in daily life as well as technological advancements that offer insights into state-of-the-art methods and future perspectives.

## Overview of *Body, Sound and Space in Music and Beyond*

The chapters of this volume discuss theories and recent research from a wide range of disciplines, including music psychology, composing, musicology, computer science, music theory, sound arts, acoustics and neuropsychology. Since multimodal experiences of sounds and music are not limited to the concert hall or silent listening at home, but have an impact on a great variety of activities and experiences in our daily lives, multidisciplinary approaches are necessary for capturing both the fundamental psychological processes involved and the specific experiential qualities for the individual engaging with music and sounds. Topics range from theories of pleasure in bodily imitation, bodily resonance in relation to accounts of perception–action coupling, investigations of spatial dimensions of sound in virtual environments or installations, through to neural mechanisms of space and sound processing or topics addressing the embodied perception of sonified movements and many more. By bringing together these perspectives, a great number of links between themes becomes apparent. For example, bodily experiences of sounds are often described using metaphors that reflect spatial dimensions. Sounds may have an overwhelming impact on feelings of presence and inform us about the space we experience, even in situations where visual information is artificial or blurred such as in virtual worlds, certain film genres or computer games.

*Part I: Bodily movements, gestures and sonification*

The first part of the book highlights the significance of music-inherent gestures and bodily movements for experiencing sounds and music. All chapters in this section also refer to spatial dimensions and characteristics of sound. The main perspective of the contributions is based on theories of embodied cognition and perception–action coupling.

Marc Leman, Jeska Buhmann and Edith Van Dyck investigate in Chapter 2 'The empowering effects of being locked into the beat of the music'. Based on studies carried out in their own lab and elsewhere, they describe two key mechanisms for synchronisation between beat patterns in music and human movements: predictive processing and reward processing. The first mechanism is based on dynamic interactions between the human body and auditory sound events, while the second mechanism draws on perceptions of agency leading to pleasurable feelings of reward. Both processes give rise to the sensation of empowerment when synchronising with a beat. The argument is supported by examples from a system called D-Jogger, where the phase and period of the music can be adjusted according to the human rhythm of the footsteps. This system allows various degrees of synchronisation and spontaneous movement adjustments, depending on the quality of sounds to synchronise with as well as individual characteristics of the human body.

A different look at bodily processes is taken by Alexander Refsum Jensenius in Chapter 3, who explores micromotion and microsound. In a series of experiments on 'standstill' behaviour, individuals were asked not to move at all, either while listening to music or being in silence. This approach on the boundaries between science and artistic experiences explores the tiny micromovements over time that are hardly visible, yet may tell researchers a lot about voluntary and unconscious interactions with music, sound and silence. With reminiscences to concepts of Cage, insights into bodily behaviour were gained by recording the standstill behaviour of various people including a dancer and musicians with a motion capture system. The performances reveal consistent patterns across sessions, indicating an extraordinary ability of the body to adapt to different situations. In contrast, subjective experiences of the tiny movements varied according to the sound and music. Besides the novel approach to micromotion, this chapter also explores bodily behaviour in joint situations.

Zohar Eitan approaches a key dimension of musical sound and motion in Chapter 4: pitch height and multimodal experiences of changing pitches. The cross-modal nature of many descriptions of pitch becomes evident when considering the multitude of words used to describe pitch changes, showing some similarities to descriptions of bodily states and spatial dimensions. Among them, Eitan highlights cross-modal perceptions of motion, touch and vision, and focuses on these interrelations by investigating the closeness of multimodal mappings in terms of valence and affect or static versus dynamic associations. In particular, experiences related to dynamic changes provide insight into perceptions that clearly attribute spatial and even bodily qualities to pitches. Investigating these dimensions of pitch and musical motion sheds light on fundamental questions in music cognition and theory.

In Chapter 5, Clemens Wöllner and Jesper Hohagen discuss evidence for correspondences between inner musical motion and outward bodily movement responses. Following an overview of research on the gestural quality of music, including spatiotemporal perceptions, kinaesthetic sensations and imagery, they investigated ideas of Alexander Truslit (1938), who claimed that there are dynamic changes in musical interpretations that can be perceived by listeners in an 'armchair conducting' style. In a series of studies, participants moved their arm along with original musical examples of Truslit, while their movements were recorded with a motion capture system and subsequently sonified using a parameter-mapping approach. High individual movement consistency was found across different listening conditions, comparable to Jensenius' findings (this volume). Selected sound characteristics were related to participants' spatial position data, supporting the interpretation that sound can be related to musical experiences as expressed in bodily motion.

The final chapter in this section deals with aesthetic qualities of sonification and explores human–machine interactions. Paul Vickers, Bennett Hogg and David Worrall explain the ideas, technologies and challenges of sonifying data and in particular human bodily motion. Comparable to types of visualisations that highlight otherwise unseen aspects, sonifications are used in many contexts, including arts, sports or medicine. Quite often, nevertheless, sine-wave sounds or other rather artificial sounds have been used that are not always aesthetically pleasant or effective. Investigating the aesthetics of sound qualities in sonifications is not only a highly needed endeavour, it may also provide insights into perceptions of sounds more generally, including their multimodal associations. The authors concentrate on the meaning and intentional qualities of sounds as a result or a by-product of actions, in contrast to more specific parameter-mapping approaches in sonification. In the latter, individuals may have some control over the sound quality they produce or experience with their bodies.

## *Part II: Sound design, instrumental affordances and embodied spatial perception*

The second part of the book addresses multimodal perceptions of sound in relation to spatial dimensions – from the spatial design of musical instruments and its consequences for sound production up to metaphors of sound and space. As stated above, structured sounds may be perceived as music, yet the specific quality of sounds and their relation to meaning formation and bodily experiences have largely been neglected in writings on music.

Spatial and bodily dimensions in musicians' performative actions are discussed by W. Luke Windsor in Chapter 7. Based on theories of ecological perception by Gibson (1979) as well as perception–action coupling, music performance is seen as closely related to the human body in the fields of acousmatic compositions or free improvisations, with conventional instruments and in vocal performance. A key term in this regard is the concept of 'affordances', which relate to the possibilities inherent in the instrument which may influence the musicians' actions. Two examples highlight the bodily affordances of instrument design (the Böhm flute) and bodily as well as spatial characteristics of a group performance (Barbershop chorus). Windsor argues that the performative actions of musicians are formed by cultural norms and the musicians' empirical investigations, seeking contact between the body, the instruments and the performance environment. Interpretations of the instrumental affordances and bodily processes may inform audience responses in similar ways as socially constrained norms and performance spaces.

In Chapter 8, Kathrin Fahlenbrach approaches the role of sound design and music in the creation of spatial experiences in film. Sounds have a crucial role not only for guiding the listeners' attention and expectancies, but also for memory processes and emotional responses. Based on Chion's (1994) concept of *synchresis*, combining temporal synchronisation and semantic synthesis, Fahlenbrach explores multimodal metaphors (see Eitan, this volume) that are crucial for the formation of meaning in film. In this way, the sound design of films establishes visual and acoustic Gestalts that shape perceptions of cross-modal correspondences and embodied meaning. In four case studies, spatial Gestalts are highlighted as metaphoric source domains, exemplifying both lower-level perceptual processes and the creation of more complex narrative and cultural meanings, with a specific focus on how sound may shape the perception of atmospheres and space.

Spatial dimensions of sound qualities are the starting point for Christoph Reuter and Saleh Siddiq, who describe the 'The colourful life of timbre spaces' in Chapter 9. Theoretical and empirical research on instrumental timbre generally failed to provide overarching categories for their description. Acoustical analyses alone do often not correspond with listeners' aesthetic experiences of sound. Reuter and Siddiq summarise writings from the 18th century, followed by von Helmholtz's (1877) system of the sound spectrum up to the most recent experimental approaches. 'Timbre spaces' are now a well-established paradigm to present the dimensional qualities of sound along three or more axes. Within these dimensional models, the closeness or distance of various sounds is depicted at certain points in space. Using computational methods derived from Music Information Retrieval, a meta-timbre space is suggested that overcomes some of the previous models' shortcomings and could be promising for applications in various areas dealing with sound dimensions.

Christiane Neuhaus in Chapter 10 employs the metaphor of music as 'fluid architecture' in order to describe spatial characteristics attributed to structured sounds. She highlights temporal processes in music and refers to the neural correlates of spatial imagery and perception by differentiating between the processing of egocentric (body-centred), allocentric (environment-based) and topological (object-centred) information, which are correlated with activations in the posterior parietal cortex and the hippocampus, respectively. A number of studies are discussed that provide evidence for the fundamental relationship between spatial information processing, music learning and perception as well as navigation and spatial cognitive functioning after exposure to music. By referring to spatial processes in relation to music-making, Neuhaus places the findings within a research tradition that considers bodily and spatial concepts as being fundamental for embodied cognition.

## *Part III: Presence and immersion in networked and virtual spaces*

The third part of the book presents chapters that deal with spatial and bodily perception in actual and virtual environments, pointing to some themes discussed in the previous parts of the book such as multimodality and embodied metaphoric perception, and exploring in what ways these concepts are fruitful for artistic installations and experiences.

In Chapter 11, Peter Lennox describes multimodal experiences of music that are spatial in its structure and impact. He refers to the separation of the senses specific to Western tradition of the arts, and developments in listening technology to overcome these separations, enabling virtual perceptions of space. These processes draw on multimodal sensory input rather than on limited perceptions that he describes as 'single-sense' and 'disembodied'. By focusing on problems with artificial and 'dry' recording spaces and unsatisfactory reverberation techniques, and by pointing to recent developments in surround sound, Lennox addresses both technological advances in three-dimensional sound systems and perceptual experiences and expectations of increasingly demanding listeners. Rather than passively listening to stereo sounds, listeners wish to immerse and participate in musical environments – in short, feel present in some way. Vivid spatial dimensions in music are thus vital for rich and satisfying perceptions.

Chapter 12 addresses virtual spaces for music performance and listening. Jude Brereton refers to the significance of spatial dimensions for composers, who often alter and adapt their works in order to meet the requirements of a given performance venue. Musicians, on the other hand, typically perform in different places and adapt to the sound and reverberation characteristics from rehearsal to various performance venues. Brereton discusses developments of virtual performance spaces, including acoustic manipulations and recent advances in computational techniques that allow for both realistically sounding and musically rich virtual scenes. The study of these scenes should also take into account spatial characteristics from the position of the audience, which show a high number of acoustical differences particularly in early reflections. This knowledge enables researchers and technicians to simulate venues as they are acoustically perceived from different perspectives, or the acoustical reconstruction of historical places that no longer exist. It can be expected that some of these advances in spatial dimensions of sound will also revolutionise the way people listen and move to music.

Sound installations are a good example for interactions between body and space in virtual environments, as Martin Rumori explores in Chapter 13. Following a positioning of sound art as a 'genre' in musicological discourse, he describes the technical foundations of binaural recording and binaural synthesis that are at the heart of his own installation 'Parisflâneur'. Conceived as 'Musique anecdotique', Rumori provides insights into his artistic aims and reflects research-related questions including options for evaluations. As in the chapters by Grimshaw and Lennox (this volume), immersion is an important aesthetic concept to describe the interactive experiences of the audience. These experiences can be shaped by the dependence or independence of the sounds in relation to bodily motion and spatial positioning. Although the physical space is considered to be veridical, sound installations often give rise to multimodal perceptions of space that may transport the individual away from the actual installation, comparable to the impact of virtual environments.

Georg Hajdu focuses on networked music performance in Chapter 14. He explores the consequences for bodily perception and the demands of performances for musicians not present in the same space. By briefly reviewing the history of networked performances, from first explorations in the early 1970s to his own networked performances called 'Quintet.net', Hajdu discusses central technological advancements and related aesthetical themes. In order to meet some of the demands such as audiovisual synchronisation and latency, a set of rules for music-making rather than free improvisation facilitates the coordination of the musicians' actions. In this regard, Cage's time-bracket rules were highly inspirational. Hajdu argues that musicians, especially in the early networked performances, often felt disorientated and compensated these experiences by hyperactivity or egocentrism. In order to overcome these issues, new and faster technology is developed that allows for feelings of agency and mutuality in spatial and temporal synchrony.

The feeling of 'presence through sound' is described by Mark Grimshaw in Chapter 15. An increasing number of experiences in virtual settings call for the fundamental question of how and when individuals feel present. Grimshaw reviews philosophical and neuropsychological approaches and highlights relationships with immersion, which became a key term in computer gaming research. Building on these concepts, the main part of the chapter investigates the influence of sound on perceptions of presence in gaming. 'Sonic virtuality' should strongly increase feelings of presence, which are not only tied to real settings and places, since sound has a key role in changing the perceived realism in games, while at the same time stimulating imagination and fantasies. Grimshaw presents examples for recent developments in virtual environments and computer games, in which interactions with the gamer's body further shape the way sounds are perceived. He concludes that some of the sonic concepts of perceived presence may even have consequences for real-world settings.

## Conclusions

As a whole, the goal of this volume is to elucidate the manifold facets of engaging with sound and music by taking into consideration spatial and bodily dimensions. Its contributions address philosophical and theoretical foundations and empirical research, including the perspectives of artists, musicians and designers of such experiences and the perspective of individuals perceiving sound and music in relation to their bodies and the surrounding space. Recent technological advances in the rendering of sound and music, including spatial dimensions in real and virtual environments, are highlighted. These experiences are described as multimodal perceptions and as interactions with the sounds in space as mediated by the body.

The contributions to this volume are partially based on a lecture series at the Institute of Systematic Musicology, University of Hamburg (Germany) in 2014–15. Many of the chapters combine rigorous scientific research with artistic work, enabling new and meaningful experiences in cutting-edge areas between sciences and the arts. By presenting insights from a variety of disciplines, the book shall find a wide readership, including researchers and students in music psychology and education, artists, musicians and composers intrigued by theoretical, physical, experiential qualities of sound and space, and all those interested in a combination of these vital and innovative themes of music and sound experiences.

## References

Chion, M. (1994). *Audio-vision: Sound on screen.* New York: Columbia University Press.
Clarke, E. (2005). *Ways of listening: An ecological approach to the perception of musical meaning.* Oxford: Oxford University Press.
Cross, I. (2010). Listening as covert performance. *Journal of the Royal Musical Association, 134*(1), 67–77.
Davies, S. (1994). *Musical meaning and expression.* Ithaca: Cornell University Press.
Deutsch, D., Henthorn, T., and Lapidis, R. (2011). Illusory transformation from speech to song. *Journal of the Acoustical Society of America, 129,* 2245–2252.
Eitan, Z. (2013). How pitch and loudness shape musical space and motion: New finding and persisting questions. In S.-L. Tan, A. J. Cohen, S. D. Lipscomb, and R. A. Kendall (Eds.), *The psychology of music in multimedia* (pp. 161–187). New York: Oxford University Press.

Epstein, D. (1993). On affect and musical motion. In S. Feder, R. L. Karmel, and G. H. Pollock (Eds.), *Psychoanalytic explorations in music* (pp. 91–123). Madison, CT: International Universities Press.
Epstein, D. (1995). *Shaping time: Music, the brain, and performance.* New York: Schirmer.
Gallagher, S. (2005). *How the body shapes the mind.* Oxford: Oxford University Press.
Gibson, J. J. (1979). *The ecological approach to visual perception.* Boston: Houghton Mifflin.
Godøy, R. (2010). Gestural affordances of musical sound. In R. Godøy and M. Leman (Eds.), *Musical gestures: Sound, movement, and meaning* (pp. 103–125). New York: Routledge.
Hanslick, E. (1854/1891). *Vom Musikalisch-Schönen: Ein Beitrag zur Revision der Ästhetik der Tonkunst* [On musical beauty. A contribution to a revision of the aesthetics of the art of sound]. (8th improved edition: 1891). Leipzig: Johann Ambrosius Barth.
Kurth, E. (1931). *Musikpsychologie* [Psychology of music]. Berlin: Max Hesse.
Langer, S. K. (1942). *Philosophy in a new key* (3rd ed. 1957). Cambridge, MA: Harvard University Press.
Leman, M., and Maes, P.-J. (2014). Music perception and embodied music cognition. In L. Shapiro (Ed.), *The Routledge handbook of embodied cognition* (pp. 81–89). New York: Routledge.
Licht, A. (2007). *Sound art: Beyond music, between categories* (with an introduction by J. O'Rourke). New York: Rizzoli.
Mithen, S (2006). *The singing Neanderthals: The origins of music, language, mind and body.* Cambridge, MA: Harvard University Press.
Pratt, C. C. (1931/1968). *The meaning of music: A study in psychological aesthetics.* New York: Johnson Reprint Corp.
Rousseau, J.-J. (1768). *Dictionnaire de musique.* Paris: Veuve Duchesne. Retrieved from http://www.rousseauonline.ch/pdf/rousseauonline-0068.pdf.
Sevdalis, V., and Keller, P. E. (2014). Know thy sound: Perceiving self and others in musical contexts. *Acta Psychologica, 152*, 67–74.
Sloboda, J. A. (2005). *Exploring the musical mind.* Oxford: Oxford University Press.
Truslit, A. (1938). *Gestaltung und Bewegung in der Musik: Ein tönendes Buch vom musikalischen Vortrag und seinem bewegungserlebten Gestalten und Hören* [Shape and movement in music]. Berlin-Lichtenfelde: Vieweg.
von Helmholtz, H. (1877). *Die Lehre von den Tonempfindungen als physiologische Grundlage für die Theorie der Musik* (4th ed.) [trans. A. Ellis, On the sensations of tone]. Braunschweig: Vieweg.

# Part I
# Bodily movements, gestures and sonification

# 2 The empowering effects of being locked into the beat of the music

*Marc Leman, Jeska Buhmann and Edith Van Dyck*

Human interaction with music is based on the capacity to synchronise. In this chapter, we look at the principles behind this capacity and we consider its empowering effect. Synchronisation is central to many new developments in music research that gives body and space a prominent place.

## The human capacity to synchronise

A regular rhythm in music is a strong driver for establishing a synchronised human rhythm. Typically, a human rhythm tends to go along with the musical rhythm in such a way that a salient feature of the human rhythm matches the timing of a salient feature of the musical rhythm. For example, when we tap our finger on a desk, we can match it with the timing of a metronome tick and, when we walk, we can match the cadence of our footfall with the timing of the beat of the music. Salient moments of the rhythm (tap, footfall, beat) are markers for synchronisation. The performer uses them to establish a synchronised action, while the scientist employs them in order to study this particular type of action.

But what are the underlying mechanisms behind music-to-movement synchronisation? And which effects does it generate? The goal of this chapter is to introduce and offer different views on the study of these underlying mechanisms, and to show how being locked to the beat of the music can pave the way for an overall empowerment effect, that is, the feeling that music affords energy and contributes to an increase in autonomy and self-determination. In this chapter, we present some recent theoretical and empirical work that focuses on movement rhythm such as walking, running, cycling and dancing. First, we introduce a theoretical umbrella perspective on synchronisation and embodied interaction with music. Then, we focus on some concrete studies that tell us something about the mechanisms of resonance, entrainment and emulation. Finally, we shed some light on possible empowering effects of music.

## The theory of embodied music cognition

Our starting point is the theory of embodied cognition (Leman, 2007; Leman, 2016; Leman and Maes, 2015; Leman, Nijs, Maes and Van Dyck, forthcoming), in which we developed the idea that cognition and the human body are tightly connected with each other. This theory is incorporated in a bigger enterprise aimed at giving cognition a new foundation in a broader ecological perspective (e.g., Prinz, Beisert and Herwig, 2013; Varela, Thompson and Rosch, 1992). While there is a common agreement that cognition deals with issues such as planning, reasoning and the prediction of action outcomes, using long-term memory, working memory and learning as basic ingredients for operating, it became clear that human–environment interaction (of which human–music interaction is a subset) draws heavily upon sensorimotor control mechanisms and their predictive capacity (Clark, 2015). Importantly, this interaction implies a two-way connection between sensorimotor control and environment in the sense that sensorimotor control determines movement in the environment, but environment also determines sensorimotor control (Maes, Leman, Palmer and Wanderley, 2014). This two-way connection informs cognitive states in at least three different ways, namely, through interaction, emulation, motivation.

### *Interaction*

Interaction is concerned with actions in relation to the environment, which is in this case music. Cyclic interactions can be semi-automatically controlled by means of sensorimotor predictive models in the brain that require limited cognitive resources, such as attention and short-term memory. However, at crucial moments, these cyclic interactions can inform an ongoing cognitive activity about special events. A good example is moving the foot along with the musical beat as a basic timing cue for other activities. For instance, during improvisation, one may use these foot taps to structure melody, harmony and expression. The maintenance of the foot tapping is controlled by a sensorimotor model that generates timing through ongoing interaction with the environment, which is maintained by a semi-automated cyclic process. The marker is the foot tap, which informs the higher-level cognitive system about timing. The foot tap uses movement through space as a timer. Note that this is very different from a situation in which the timing is counted. Counting musical beats indeed implies the use of cognitive resources, and this tends to interfere with other cognitive activities (Çorlu, Maes, Muller, Kochman and Leman, 2015; Maes, Wanderley and Palmer, 2015).

### *Emulation*

Here, emulations are understood as body movements that are aligned with the dynamics of the music. A straightforward example is dancing, which is a corporeal activity in which body movements are aligned in time with the music (Burger, Thompson, Luck, Saarikallio and Toiviainen, 2013, 2014; Van Dyck et al., 2013). This alignment can be driven by a choreography, serving as a model for the movement (Leman and Naveda, 2010; Naveda and

Leman, 2010). Through alignment, these models are activated along with associations of perceptual outcomes with music-driven aligned movements. Thus, musical patterns become endowed with an intentional character. Obviously, this requires time-critical and location-precise actions along with the beat. Although markers of rhythm may play an important role in the control of these actions, it is clear that emulation focuses more on the continuous aspects of the movement as a whole, rather than the discrete aspects of markers that characterise a salient moment of the movement. In that sense, emulation can be understood as an activity in which human body rhythms are spatially and temporally aligned with musical expression, using beat synchronisation as a timer.

*Motivation*

Motivation is a driver for cognitive activity. Recent work has pointed out that a potential reward is a strong motivator for interacting with music. Reward is associated with midbrain dopamine neurons whose activation reflects the degree of reward predictability (Hollerman and Schultz, 1998; Salimpoor, Zald, Zatorre, Dagher and McIntosh, 2015). Reward processing is clearly related to prediction processing and has dependencies related to arousal and physical effort (Fritz et al., 2013). Being locked to the beat involves prediction models that may generate rewarding outcomes affecting cognitive activity (Schaefer and Overy, 2015).

*Affordances*

Interaction, emulation and motivation are key concepts for understanding embodied music cognition from an ecological and interactive perspective (Leman, 2016). Yet, there is one additional aspect that is highly relevant in understanding synchronisation effects. It concerns the idea that musical patterns provide affordances for interacting and enacting (Godøy, 2010; Krueger, 2013; see Windsor, this volume). Ultimately, this means that musical structure is made in such a way that it unleashes the human disposition for synchronising and being locked to the beat. And as music is a construct of human action, the idea that music affords synchronisation should not come as a surprise. After all, tempi in music encode the tempi of human actions. Hence, when humans listen to music, it is these encoded actions in sound that again trigger human action responses. Therefore, regular beat patterns in music can be strong drivers for synchronised movement, especially when they match the sensitive human tempo range. Based on recent work in this domain (Leman, 2016), there is growing evidence in favour of the idea that this match between music and movement facilitates several effects. The most important effect, probably, is that, due to synchronised movements along with music stimuli, music becomes more predictive, apparently controllable and therefore more engaging. Moreover, synchronisation is likely to be a step towards rhythmic emulation of expression, which is a key aspect in the communication between humans and music.

## Mechanisms of being locked into the beat of music

For understanding the mechanisms of beat locking (by which we understand a perfect synchronisation of movement and beat), it is necessary to consider synchronisation in relation to entrainment. Synchronisation could be defined as the match of two rhythmic markers, either in period or in phase (Figure 2.1). Period-synchronisation takes place when the cycles of both rhythms have an equal duration. Phase-synchronisation happens when the markers of both rhythms occur at the same time. Thus, when musical beat and footfall match during every cycle, there is perfect phase-synchronisation. When they differ in time, but their period of occurrence is the same, period-synchronisation occurs but phase-synchronisation does not. Given this definition of synchronisation, entrainment can then be defined as the shift from period to phase-synchronisation. It is a dynamic principle that locks human movement into the beat of the music, causing strong empowering effects.

### *Resonance: a primitive embodied prediction system*

Studies of synchronised body movement in response to metronomes and music reveal the influence of a natural propensity, probably inborn (Honing, Bouwer and Háden, 2014), for frequencies in the vicinity of 2 Hz (Fraisse,1963; Nozaradan, Peretz, Missal and Mouraux, 2011; Nozaradan, Peretz and Mouraux, 2012; Repp and Su, 2013; Styns, van Noorden, Moelants and Leman, 2007; van Noorden and Moelants, 1999). This ability is indicative of resonances (neural or motor-based) (Large and Snyder, 2009; van Noorden and Moelants, 1999) which, from the viewpoint of interactive behaviour,

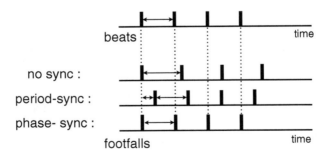

*Figure 2.1* Being locked into the beat. The upper part shows the beats, with indication of the beat period. The lower part shows the footfalls, with indication of the type of synchronisation: no synchronisation, period-synchronisation, phase-synchronisation.

have a predictive capacity, albeit limited and primitive. Depending on the damping characteristic of the resonance, external metronome ticks with a tempo in the vicinity of 2 Hz would provoke accurate phase responses in line with the periodicity of the next external ticks. Metronome tick tempi that deviate from 2 Hz would generate phase responses with small and negligible amplitudes. In other words, these resonances may serve as a primitive prediction system, but it is likely that they can be reinforced by cognitive (adaptive) predictions.

### *Entrainment: a subliminal sensorimotor principle*

Entrainment is a good example of a concept based on adaptive principles. Entrainment involves a phase-error correction mechanism (Moens and Leman, 2015; Repp and Su, 2013; Thaut, McIntosh and Hoemberg, 2014) that can be assumed to build upon the disposition of the bio-mechanical resonances. Phase-error correction is based on the prediction of the beat and the action outcome (such as a footfall on the ground at the time of the beat). However, the footfall marker may occur earlier or later than the predicted beat marker. The time difference between the two markers is the phase, which in this case is an error since it was not predicted. However, based on this error, the prediction model can be updated. Therefore, entrainment can be conceived as an updating mechanism towards more stable phase-synchronisation. Entrainment on top of a resonance means that the sensitive responsive range for beats, which occur in the vicinity of 2 Hz, gets a supplementary sensorimotor control, probably due to interaction experiences.

The study of entrainment offers an interesting way to regard the properties that are involved when interacting with a music rhythm. Several studies have indicated the ability of people to entrain their finger tapping movements to a beat, which happens spontaneously and can be executed quite accurately (Drake, Penel and Bigand, 2000; Large, Fink and Kelso, 2002; Snyder and Krumhansl, 2001; Toiviainen and Snyder, 2003) within a relatively wide range of periods from 300 to 900 ms (Parncutt, 1994; van Noorden and Moelants, 1999; see also Repp and Su, 2013, for a review).

Also, movement that requires the involvement of the entire body can be entrained with the rhythmic pulses in music, especially when that specific type of corporeal articulation contains a certain level of periodicity. People have for instance been shown to entrain their dance moves to the beat of the music and to increase their levels of entrainment when dancing in combination with increases in the sound pressure level of the beat (Toiviainen, Luck and Thompson, 2010; Van Dyck et al., 2013). Also while walking (Styns et al., 2007), running (Van Dyck et al., 2015) and cycling (Anshel and Marisi, 1978), entrainment with the pulse of the music has been demonstrated.

Entrainment can be seen as an emergent outcome of dynamic laws that operate through mediators (i.e., body parts) on interactions, whereby it is only facilitated when certain conditions are fulfilled (Schmidt and Richardson,

2008). The effect of music on repetitive endurance activities, for example, depends on the specific tempo of the musical stimulus. To illustrate, Waterhouse, Hudson and Edwards (2010) executed an experiment where participants cycled at self-chosen work rates while listening to popular music stimuli played in different tempi. The program was performed in three conditions: music was played in its original tempo, was increased by 10 per cent, or decreased by 10 per cent. Results showed that cyclists' covered distance, power and pedal cadence increased when faster music was presented, while slowing down the music tempo resulted in decreases of these measures. However, they not only worked harder with faster music but also chose to do so and enjoyed the music more when it was played at a faster tempo. Similar effects of increases in music tempo and, to a lesser extent, of boosts in the loudness of the stimulus on work output have been demonstrated for running behaviour (Edworthy and Waring, 2006; Van Dyck et al., 2015).

In addition, entrainment of one tempo (e.g., music) with another (e.g., movement) is only believed to occur when the strength of the coupling is able to overcome possible contrasts in natural movement period or tempo (von Holst, 1973). For a given coupling strength, entrainment only occurs within a specific range of period differences, reflecting the system's entrainment basin (Richardson, Marsh and Schmidt, 2005; Schmidt and Richardson, 2008). In the research by Van Dyck et al. (2015), it was checked whether a possible basin for unintentional entrainment of running cadence to music tempo could be uncovered. Recreational runners were invited to run four laps of 200 m, a task that was repeated 11 times with a short break in between each running sequence. During each first lap of a sequence, participants ran at their own preferred tempo without musical accompaniment. The registered running cadence of the first lap served as a reference for the music tempo of the second one, where music with a tempo matching the assessed cadence was played. In the last two laps, the music tempo was either increased/decreased by 3.00, 2.50, 2.00, 1.50 or 1.00 per cent or was kept stable. In general, findings of this study showed that recreational runners are able to adapt their running cadence to tempo changes in music without being instructed to do so and even without being aware of this adaptation. Evidence for an entrainment basin was discovered as well, as the degree of entrainment with the tempo of the music dropped significantly as soon as tempo increases of 2.50 per cent were introduced but also tended to drop at decreases of 3.00 per cent.

Although period- and phase-synchronisation of human movement to music has been demonstrated in several studies, it has also been shown that being able to synchronise movement tempo to a musical tempo is very personal. Leow, Parrott and Grahn (2014) revealed significant differences in period matching accuracy between groups of weak and strong beat perceivers, when instructed to synchronise their walking behaviour to music played 22.5 per cent faster than their preferred tempo. Nevertheless, no significant differences in period matching accuracy were found between walking to low-groove music and walking to high-groove music. The reason for being able to synchronise seems to sprout from personal qualities rather than from qualities inherent in the music. Additionally, Buhmann, Desmet, Moens, Van Dyck and Leman (2016) examined the phase stability or phase coherence of the footfall while walking in relation to the beat of tempo-matched music. The bimodal distribution of the phase coherence data clearly showed the presence of two processes: walking with a stable phase and walking with an unstable phase. Whether or not a walking trial was labelled as 'with stable phase' was mainly attributed to personal capabilities, rather than to sonic qualities of the song, as some participants walked with a stable phase to most of the songs and other participants hardly synchronised with any of the songs they walked to.

In recent work, technological mediators have been built that manipulate the effect of different rhythms on each other. For instance, when creating a new walking support device, 'Walk Mate', designed for patients suffering from Parkinson's disease, a human and a robot have been shown to mutually adapt and maintain stable synchronisation using a metronome as cue (Miyake, 2009). 'D-Jogger' is another example of a powerful technology for manipulating entrainment. It provides a multimodal music interface that senses the walking cadence and phase of the user and aligns the music (using a time-stretching algorithm) by manipulating the timing difference between beats and footfalls, switching songs when appropriate (Moens et al., 2014; Moens and Leman, 2015; Moens, van Noorden and Leman, 2010). As such, a person no longer needs to adapt his or her movements to a fixed beat, but the beat is automatically entrained with the gait frequency. Due to the real-time phase manipulation, a beat can even be synchronised with every single footfall, a feature that makes D-Jogger unique in its domain. This smart music player technology was originally developed for walking and running applications (e.g., Van Dyck et al., 2015; Buhman et al., 2016), but it can also be coupled with additional types of regular movement (e.g., cycling) or biological rhythms such as heart rate.

The D-Jogger system is equipped with different alignment strategies, allowing a range of coupling strengths between music and movement to occur. In a first strategy, the initial tempo of a song is adapted to the running or walking cadence, but does not start in phase. During the song, the musical tempo is continuously adapted to the movement period. In a second strategy, the initial tempo of a song is also adapted to the running or walking cadence and does not start in phase as well, but during the song, the music tempo remains stable and the subject entrains to the phase of the song. In the third strategy, again, the initial tempo of the song is adapted to the cadence, but this time also starts in phase with the movement of the exerciser. During the song, the phase remains fixed and the subject entrains to the phase of the song, while the music tempo continuously adapts to the period of the movements. In the fourth and last strategy, the initial tempo of the song is adapted to the running or walking cadence and also starts in phase. In the further course of the song, both music tempo and phase are adapted continuously according to the exerciser's cadence, as such ensuring perfect synchronisation between these two rhythms (Moens et al., 2014). Experiments bringing these different strategies into play demonstrated an apparent distinction between different modalities of entrainment: (a) finding the beat, which has been shown to be the most problematic part of entrainment; (b) keeping the beat, a more straightforward component, since a temporal scheme has been established; and (c) being in phase, an element where no entrainment is needed because the music is continuously adapted to the human rhythm. Thus, strategies that immediately lock the exerciser's movement in phase with the music are preferred, as they allow the subject to predict the beat more accurately from the beginning. In contrast, strategies that require the subject to find the beat by him- or herself are more challenging since prediction is less established and phase-correction adjustment may acquire much effort and can prove to be inaccurate (Moens and Leman, 2015).

*Dancing and walking: invoking expression*

So far we discussed entrainment in relation to the timing of the movement response. However, music can also entrain the vigour of the movement response, resulting in differences in expressivity of the movement or the amount of vigour that is used to perform a certain movement. Entrainment here means that, apart from predictive mechanisms, other mechanisms are activated to go along with the predictive mechanisms. We assume that this type of entrainment is based on the energetic content that occurs between the musical beats. This suggests that the beat locking phenomenon is connected with arousal and affective processes.

In dance movement this is typically reflected in the employment of more or less exuberant arm movements or more or less intense hip movements. During walking or running, expressivity is reflected in bigger or smaller step sizes. When people walk in synchrony with music, differences in walking velocity can only be the result of changes in step size. Rather than being influenced by music tempo, changes in step size can be attributed to the sonic characteristics (energy and pitch) in music.

In a study by Leman et al. (2013), participants were instructed to walk in synchrony with music at 130 beats per minute (bpm). This tempo, slightly above the resonance frequency of human movement (MacDougall and Moore, 2005; van Noorden and Moelants, 1999), was chosen as a result of findings by Styns et al. (2007). In this study, it was revealed that when participants were asked to synchronise their steps while walking to music at different tempi, the biggest differences in step length occurred at a walking cadence of approximately 130 steps per minute. In the study by Leman et al. (2013), participants were instructed to walk to 52 different songs. Furthermore, six metronome sequences at 130 bpm were presented at fixed, uniformly spread positions during the experiment. The average step lengths of the walking behaviour in response to music were calculated using walking behaviour in response to metronome ticks as reference step lengths. Results revealed that some music had activating qualities, increasing step size, whereas other music stimuli had relaxing qualities, actually decreasing the step size compared to the average step size of walking to a metronome.

Buhmann et al. (2016) examined the same phenomenon, but for uninstructed, spontaneous, self-paced walking. Participants had to walk for 30 minutes on an indoor track, during two blocks of 15 minutes each, and they were asked to walk as if they were going on a 30-minute walk outside. They were told that they would alternately hear music or no stimuli at all. Participants were not instructed to synchronise their steps with the music tempo, but simply walked at their own, preferred pace. Between each music stimulus presented to the participant, a 15 second period of silence was inserted. During these 15 seconds, the cadence of the participant was measured and a tempo-matching song was selected and played to the participant. A mobile D-Jogger system was used as a tool to accomplish this measurement and tempo matching. During each period of silence, this process was repeated to ensure that a participant was always presented with a music stimulus that exactly matched his or her current walking pace. In this study, the average stride length and walking velocity of the preceding silence periods were used as a neutral reference. The average stride length and walking velocity measured during the occurrence of a music stimulus were compared to the average values of the preceding silence. Results demonstrated that participants walked with a stable phase to the music stimuli in approximately half of the trials but did not do so in the other trials. However, in both cases the modulatory effect of sonic characteristics in music was unveiled; some songs increased step size and walking velocity, while other songs decreased these kinematic parameters compared to the occasions when participants were walking without auditory stimuli. The fact that this effect was also found when participants were not phase locked to the musical beat shows that invoking expression can occur independently from entrainment of the movement response.

Buhmann et al. (2016) also unveiled a significant relation between walking kinematics and the motivational aspects of music; when people walked with a higher velocity than while walking in silence, they rated the music higher according to its motivational qualities than when they walked with a lower velocity compared to walking without musical accompaniment. Although it is not clear whether motivational music causes us to increase our velocity or if an increase in velocity causes us to judge music as being more motivational, it does show that affective processing and human movement to a musical stimulus are closely linked.

In addition, the combined results of these two studies show that the capacity of music to invoke expression in our movements is independent of walking cadence, although differences in effect size have been reported. With respect to the motivational qualities, it is, however, important to stress the value of self-paced training. Williams (2008) pleads for a shift in physical activity guidelines, emphasising performance of exercise at an intensity that 'feels good' rather than at a specific prescribed intensity. This could result in a more sustainable training experience and enhanced health outcomes.

Both the studies by Leman et al. (2013) and Buhmann et al. (2016) demonstrate that 'being locked into the beat of music' is more than just a matter of synchronisation. While being synchronised and 'locked into the beat', differences in step size or walking velocity were the result of differences in sound characteristics in the music. Examples of such characteristics are energy and pitch-related features, and how these features recur over time. The sound analysis reveals the influence of tone patterns and loudness patterns in six different frequency sub-bands. They recur in subsequent intervals of two, three, four or six beats. Although the regression analysis performed in both of these studies selected different sound features to explain most of the variability in walking, results revealed that these sound features represented similar musical characteristics. The sound features showed that a binary emphasis in the music, stressing each alternating beat, has an activating effect on walking velocity and stride length, whereas a ternary emphasis distracts from a binary structure and, henceforward, has a relaxing effect on walking velocity and stride length. Also, the absence of tonal diversity, for instance in hip hop songs, where the drums and bass are most prominently present, contributed to an activating character. But this activating character could be diminished by the complexity of the rhythmic structure; the more complex a rhythm was, the more it diverted attention from the binary emphasis of the song, and this contributed to a relaxing character of the music.

The effect of different types of music on gait responses was also tested in a study by Leow et al. (2014). Kinematic parameters of walking to a metronome and to high- and low-groove music were compared to un-cued walking. This was done for two groups of participants (strong and weak beat perceivers) and at two different tempi: preferred step rate and a beat rate that was 22.5 per cent faster than the preferred tempo. For the weak beat perceivers, high-groove music elicited longer and faster steps than low-groove music, both at the preferred tempo and at the faster tempo. In the preferred tempo condition, the type of stimulus only had a significant effect on step length for weak beat perceivers. However, none of the stimuli showed a positive effect on the movement vigour. It means that neither the metronome sequences, the low-groove or the high-groove music was able to induce an increase in step length compared to the step length measured during un-cued walking.

Although high-groove music might evoke the desire to move, it might not be the optimal type of music for walking or running with more vigour. Low-groove music is typically associated with low beat salience, whereas high-groove music is associated with greater beat salience (Madison, 2006). It could be that the low-groove music used in the study by Leow et al. (2014) lacked prominent beats, therefore having a relaxing effect on step length. High-groove music, on the other hand, might have had prominent beats, but also more danceable rhythms, a typical characteristic of high-groove music. Such danceable rhythms often present themselves as syncopations by a disturbance in the regular flow of the rhythm, placing accents where they would normally not occur. However, according to the results obtained in Leman et al. (2013) and Buhmann et al. (2016), such disturbances in the regular flow of the rhythm will distract attention from the binary emphasis in the music while walking, thus having a relaxing effect on step length. A similar explanation is put forward in a study by Witek, Clarke, Wallentin, Kringelbach and Vuust (2014). Results from a web-based survey on syncopation, urge to move and experienced pleasure demonstrated that a medium degree of syncopation elicited the highest level of desire to move and was regarded as very pleasurable. An inverted U-shaped relationship between syncopation, body movement and pleasure was revealed. Also syncopation seemed to be an important structural factor in embodied and affective responses to groove.

On the subject of vigour and entrainment we can conclude that different types of music impact gait responses in different ways. The importance of musical affordances for a given task (e.g., dancing, walking, running) needs to be underlined. For each specific task one also needs to take into consideration the musical affordances that define direction (slower, faster) and the type of body movements (walking, running) targeted for change.

## Evidence in favour of empowerment

The vigour effect of being locked into the beat of music suggests that predictive mechanisms are capable of unleashing processes that have a general empowering effect. It is known that listening to music while performing exercise has empowering effects on exercise and sports activities. It raises spirits, regulates mood, increases work output, heightens arousal, induces states of higher functioning and reduces inhibitions (Karageorghis, 2008; Lucaccini and Kreit, 1972; Bood, Nijssen, van der Kamp and Roerdink, 2013). Leman (2016) argues that synchronisation and alignment with music contributes to a state of homeostasis, which is a state of being where cognitive and motivational brain mechanisms reinforce each other. Such a state can be reflected in motor activities.

Exercise that is repetitive in nature (such as walking, running, cycling, rowing) is believed to benefit mostly from music that is adapted to the tempo of the exerciser's movements. Although the psychophysical benefits of synchronous music are similar to those observed in music that is not synchronised with movement, it has been shown that the ergogenic effects consistently exceed those found in its asynchronous application; endurance can be extended and performers exercise at higher intensities when moving in synchrony with musical stimuli. It was, for instance, shown that when people are better entrained with the beat of the music, they also dance more actively (Van Dyck et al., 2013). Also when performing running tasks, either on a running track or on a treadmill, synchronous music proved to elicit faster running and longer endurance times (Simpson and Karageorghis, 2006; Terry, Karageorghis, Mecozzi Saha and D'Auria, 2012). Similar endurance benefits of synchronous music were also demonstrated for walking (Karageorghis et al., 2009) and cycling (Anshel and Marisi, 1978). It has been suggested that the empowering effect of music-to-movement alignment is due to its ability to reduce the metabolic cost of exercise by enhancing neuromuscular or metabolic efficiency (Karageorghis et al., 2009; Kenyon and Thaut, 2003). Regular corporeal patterns demand less energy to imitate, because of the lack of timely adjustments within the kinetic pattern and also because of an increased level of relaxation resulting from the precise expectancy of the forthcoming movement (Smoll and Schultz, 1982). As such, a point of reference is created that is able to attract and swiftly entrain recurring motor pattern efficiency (Kenyon and Thaut, 2003; Rossignol and Melvill-Jones, 1976). In addition, in the field of beat synchronised locomotion, the type of music for a specific task has an effect on vigour entrainment, reflected in the step size. Certain types of music, or rather certain sonic characteristics in the music have an empowering effect, both on kinematic parameters such as stride length and walking velocity and on perceived motivation (Leman et al., 2013; Buhmann et al., 2016). Moreover, when synchronisation between movement and music is acquired through the use of a system such as D-Jogger, where the runner modifies the tempo of the music through his or her own movements, the sense of agency might have an additional empowering effect. Agency, or the feeling of control, that turns co-occurrences into causes, may engage additional affective processing mechanisms related to power and satisfaction (Fritz et al., 2013). As such, the feeling of being in control over the beat could be extra rewarding to the exerciser.

## Conclusions

The human capacity to synchronise body movement with an external rhythm is remarkable. It is based on prediction mechanisms that match body movement with external rhythms. The driving factor, probably, is that being locked into the beat generates a rewarding effect due to its predictability. The rewarding effect may unleash other processes related to satisfaction and control. Especially in the social context, this effect is strong and it has been called the 'fellow feeling' effect (McNeill, 1995).

A core feature of synchronisation concerns entrainment, which implies a dynamics of adjustment. In many cases, this leads to spontaneous movement adjustments such that phase-synchronisation can be obtained. As shown above, these mechanisms not only depend on the eigen-frequency of the motor resonance, which stands in a particular relation to the frequency of the musical beat, but also on prediction and bodily alignment that connect these two rhythm frequencies. Through the manipulation of the phase and tempo of the music, it becomes possible to influence human entrainment to the beat, offering a way to reveal its principles. D-Jogger is an appropriate example of a system that enables the manipulation of spontaneous entrainment through phase and period manipulations.

The overall state of the art is that recent work on mechanisms of entrainment has provided a deeper insight in the embodied foundations of musical interactions, especially when these interactions are based on a stable beat. We know why this works, although more research about musical affordances and principles of emulation and motivation will be needed for better understanding the causal connection with empowerment processes. In Leman (2016) it is suggested that understanding musical expression emulation may be the key to unlock empowerment processes.

## References

Anshel, M. H., and Marisi, D. Q. (1978). Effects of music and rhythm on physical performance. *Research Quarterly, 49*(2), 109–113.

Bood, R. J., Nijssen, M., van der Kamp, J., and Roerdink, M. (2013). The power of auditory-motor synchronization in sports: Enhancing running performance by coupling cadence with the right beats. *PLoS One, 8*(8). doi: 10.1371/journal.pone.0070758.

Buhmann, J., Desmet, F., Moens, B., Van Dyck, E., and Leman, M. (2016). Spontaneous velocity effect of musical expression on self-paced walking. *PLoS One, 11*(5), e0154414. doi: 10.1371/journal.pone.0154414.

Burger, B., Thompson, M., Luck, G., Saarikallio, S., and Toiviainen, P. (2013). Influences of rhythm- and timbre-related musical features on characteristics of music-induced movement. *Frontiers in psychology, 4*(183). doi: 10.3389/fpsyg.2013.00183.

Burger, B., Thompson, M., Luck, G., Saarikallio, S., and Toiviainen, P. (2014). Hunting for the beat in the body: On period and phase locking in music-induced movement. *Frontiers in Human Neuroscience, 8*(903). doi: 10.3389/fnhum.2014.00903.

Clark, A. (2015). *Surfing uncertainty: Prediction, action, and the embodied mind.* Oxford: Oxford University Press.

Çorlu, M., Maes, P.-J., Muller, C., Kochman, K., and Leman, M. (2015). The impact of cognitive load on operatic singers' timing performance. *Frontiers in Psychology, 6*(429). doi: 10.3389/fpsyg.2015.00429.

Drake, C., Penel, A., and Bigand, E. (2000). Tapping in time with mechanically and expressively performed music. *Music Perception, 18*(1), 1–23.

Edworthy, J., and Waring, H. (2006). The effects of music tempo and loudness level on treadmill exercise. *Ergonomics, 49*(15), 1597–1610.

Fraisse, P. (1963). *The psychology of time.* New York: Harper and Row.

Fritz, T., Hardikar, S., Demoucron, M., Niessen, M., Demey, M., Giot, O., Li, Y., Haynes, J.-D., Villringer, A., and Leman, M. (2013). Musical agency reduces perceived exertion during strenuous physical performance. *Proceedings of the National Academy of Sciences, 110*(44), 17784–17789.

Godøy, R. (2010). Gestural affordances of musical sound. In R. Godøy and M. Leman (Eds.), *Musical gestures: Sound, movement, and meaning* (pp. 103–125). New York: Routledge.

Hollerman, J. R., and Schultz, W. (1998). Dopamine neurons report an error in the temporal prediction of reward during learning. *Nature Neuroscience, 1*(4), 304–309.

Honing, H., Bouwer, F. L., and Háden, G. P. (2014). Perceiving temporal regularity in music: The role of auditory event-related potentials (ERPs) in probing beat perception. In H. Merchant and V. de Lafuente (Eds.), *Neurobiology of interval timing* (pp. 305–323). New York: Springer.

Karageorghis, C. I. (2008). The scientific application of music in sport and exercise. In A. M. Lane (Ed.), *Sport and exercise psychology* (pp. 109–137). London: Hodder Education.

Karageorghis, C. I., Mouzourides, D., Priest, D. L., Sasso, T., Morrish, D., and Whalley, C. (2009). Psychophysical and ergogenic effects of synchronous music during treadmill walking. *Journal of Sport and Exercise Psychology, 31*(1), 18–36.

Kenyon, G. P., and Thaut, M. H. (2003). Rhythm-driven optimization of motor control. *Recent Research Developments in Biomechanics, 1,* 29–47.

Krueger, J. (2013). Affordances and the musically extended mind. *Frontiers in Psychology, 4*(1003). doi: 10.3389/fpsyg.2013.01003.

Large, E. W., Fink, P., and Kelso, J. A. (2002). Tracking simple and complex sequences. *Psychological Research, 66*(1), 3–17.

Large, E. W., and Snyder, J. S. (2009). Pulse and meter as neural resonance. *Annals of the New York Academy of Sciences, 1169*(1), 46–57.

Leman, M. (2007). *Embodied music cognition and mediation technology.* Cambridge, MA: MIT Press.

Leman, M. (2016). *The expressive moment: How interaction (with music) shapes human empowerment.* Cambridge, MA: MIT Press.

Leman, M., and Maes, P.-J. (2015). The role of embodiment in the perception of music. *Empirical Musicology Review, 9*(3–4), 236–246.

Leman, M., Moelants, D., Varewyck, M., Styns, F. van Noorden, L., and Martens, J.-P. (2013). Activating and relaxing music entrains the speed of beat synchronized walking. *PLoS One, 8*(7). doi: 10.1371/journal.pone.0067932.

Leman, M., and Naveda, L. (2010). Basic gestures as spatiotemporal reference frames for repetitive dance/music patterns in samba and charleston. *Music Perception, 28*(1), 71–91.

Leman, M., Nijs, L., Maes, P.-J., and Van Dyck, E. (forthcoming). What is embodied music cognition? In R. Bader (Ed.), *Springer handbook in Systematic Musicology.* Berlin: Springer.

Leow, L.-A., Parrott, T., and Grahn, J. A. (2014). Individual differences in beat perception affect gait responses to low- and high-groove music. *Frontiers in Human Neuroscience, 8*(811). doi: 10.3389/fnhum.2014.00811.

Lucaccini, L. F., and Kreit, L. H. (1972). Music. In W. P. Morgan (Ed.), *Ergogenic aids and muscular performance* (pp. 240–245). New York: Academic Press.

MacDougall, H. G., and Moore, S. T. (2005). Marching to the beat of the same drummer: the spontaneous tempo of human locomotion. *Journal of Applied Physiology, 99*(3), 1164–1173.

Madison, G. (2006). Experiencing groove induced by music: Consistency and phenomenology. *Music Perception, 24*(2), 201–208.

Maes, P.-J., Leman, M., Palmer, C., and Wanderley, M. M. (2014). Action-based effects on music perception. *Frontiers in Psychology, 4*(1008). doi: 10.3389/fpsyg.2013.01008.

Maes, P.-J., Wanderley, M., and Palmer, C. (2015). The role of working memory in the temporal control of discrete and continuous movements. *Experimental Brain Research, 233*(1), 263–273.

McNeill, W. H. (1995). *Keeping together in time: Dance and drill in human history.* Cambridge, MA: Harvard University Press.

Miyake, Y. (2009). Interpersonal synchronization of body motion and the Walk-Mate walking support robot. *IEEE Transactions on Robotics, 25*(3), 638–644.

Moens, B., and Leman, M. (2015). Alignment strategies for the entrainment of music and movement rhythms. *Annals of the New York Academy of Sciences, 1337*(1), 86–93.

Moens, B., Muller, C., van Noorden, L., Franěk, M., Celie, B., Boone, J, Bourgois, J., and Leman, M. (2014). Encouraging spontaneous synchronisation with D-Jogger, an adaptive music player that aligns movement and music. *PLoS One, 9*(12). doi: 10.1111/nyas.12647.

Moens, B., van Noorden, L., and Leman, M. (2010). D-jogger: Syncing music with walking. In *Proceedings of the 7th SMC conference* (pp. 451–456). Barcelona: Universidad Pompeu Fabra.

Naveda, L., and Leman, M. (2010). The spatiotemporal representation of dance and music gestures using topological gesture analysis (TGA). *Music Perception, 28*(1), 93–111.

Nozaradan, S., Peretz, I., Missal, M., and Mouraux, A. (2011). Tagging the neuronal entrainment to beat and meter. *The Journal of Neuroscience, 31*(28), 10234–10240.

Nozaradan, S., Peretz, I., and Mouraux, A. (2012). Selective neuronal entrainment to the beat and meter embedded in a musical rhythm. *The Journal of Neuroscience, 32*(49), 17572–17581.

Parncutt, R. (1994). A perceptual model of pulse salience and metrical accent in musical rhythms. *Music Perception, 11*(4), 409–464.

Prinz, W., Beisert, M., and Herwig, A. (Eds.) (2013). *Action science: Foundations of an emerging discipline.* Cambridge, MA: MIT Press.

Repp, B., and Su,Y.-H. (2013). Sensorimotor synchronization: A review of recent research (2006-2012). *Psychonomic Bulletin and Review, 20*(3), 403–452.

Richardson, M. J., Marsh, K. L., and Schmidt, R. C. (2005). Effects of visual and verbal interaction on unintentional interpersonal coordination. *Journal of Experimental Psychology: Human Perception and Performance, 31*(1), 62–79.

Rossignol, S., and Melvill-Jones, G. (1976). Audiospinal influences in man studied by the H-reflex and its possible role in rhythmic movement synchronized to sound. *Electroencephalography and Clinical Neurophysiology, 41*(1), 83–92.

Salimpoor, V., Zald, D., Zatorre, R., Dagher, A., and McIntosh, A. (2015). Predictions and the brain: How musical sounds become rewarding. *Trends in Cognitive Sciences, 19*(2), 86–91.

Schaefer, R. S., and Overy, K. (2015). Motor responses to a steady beat. *Annals of the New York Academy of Sciences, 1337*(1), 40–44.

Schmidt, R. C., and Richardson, M. J. (2008). Dynamics of interpersonal coordination. In A. Fuchs (Ed.), *Coordination: Neural, behavioral and social dynamics* (pp. 281–308). Berlin: Springer.

Simpson, S. D., and Karageorghis, C. I. (2006). The effects of synchronous music on 400-m sprint performance. *Journal of Sports Sciences, 24*(10), 1095–1102.

Smoll, F. L., and Schultz, R. W. (1982). Accuracy of motor behaviour in response to preferred and nonpreferred tempos. *Journal of Human Movement Studies, 8*, 123–138.

Snyder, J., and Krumhansl, C. L. (2001). Tapping to ragtime: Cues to pulse finding. *Music Perception, 18*(4), 455–489.

Styns, F., van Noorden, L., Moelants, D., and Leman, M. (2007). Walking on music. *Human Movement Science, 26*(5), 769–785.

Terry, P. C., Karageorghis, C. I., Mecozzi Saha, A., and D'Auria, S. (2012). Effects of synchronous music on treadmill running among elite triathletes. *Journal of Science and Medicine in Sport, 15*(1), 52–57.

Thaut, M. H., McIntosh, G. C., and Hoemberg, V. (2014). Neurobiological foundations of neurologic music therapy: Rhythmic entrainment and the motor system. *Frontiers in Psychology, 5*, 1185.

Toiviainen, P., Luck, G., and Thompson, M. (2010). Embodied meter: Hierarchical eigenmodes in music-induced movement. *Music Perception, 28*(1), 59–70.

Toiviainen, P., and Snyder, J. S. (2003). Tapping to Bach: Resonance-based modeling of pulse. *Music Perception, 21*(1), 43–80.

Van Dyck, E., Moelants, D., Demey, M., Deweppe, A., Coussement, P., and Leman, M. (2013). The impact of the bass drum on human dance movement. *Music Perception, 30*(4), 349–359.

Van Dyck, E., Moens, B., Buhmann, J., Demey, M., Coorevits, E., Dalla Bella, S., and Leman, M. (2015). Spontaneous entrainment of running cadence to music tempo. *Sports Medicine – Open, 1*(1). doi: 10.1525/mp.2013.30.4.349.

van Noorden, L., and Moelants, D. (1999). Resonance in the perception of musical pulse. *Journal of New Music Research, 28*(1), 43–66.

Varela, F. J., Thompson, E., and Rosch, E. (1992). *The embodied mind: Cognitive science and human experience.* Cambridge, MA: MIT Press.

von Holst, E. (1973). Relative coordination as a phenomenon and as a method of analysis of central nervous system function. In R. Martin (Ed.), *The collected papers of Erich von Holst: Vol. 1. The behavioral physiology of animals and man* (pp. 33–135). Coral Gables, FL: University of Miami Press.

Waterhouse, J., Hudson, P., and Edwards, B. (2010). Effects of music tempo upon submaximal cycling performance. *Scandinavian Journal of Medicine and Science in Sports, 20*(4), 662–669.

Williams, D. M. (2008). Exercise, affect, and adherence: An integrated model and a case for self-paced exercise. *Journal of Sport and Exercise Psychology, 30*(5), 471–496.

Witek, M. A. G., Clarke, E. F., Wallentin, M., Kringelbach, M. L., and Vuust, P. (2014). Syncopation, body-movement and pleasure in groove music. *PLoS One, 9*(4). doi: 10.1371/journal.pone.0094446.

# 3 Exploring music-related micromotion

*Alexander Refsum Jensenius*

As living human beings we are constantly in motion. Even when we try to stand absolutely still, our breathing, pulse and postural adjustments lead to motion at the micro-level. Such micromotion is small, but it is still possible to experience it in the body and it is also visible to others. This chapter reflects on such (un)conscious and (in)voluntary micromotion observed and experienced when one attempts to stand physically still, and how musical sound influences such micromotion.

The theoretical starting point of this chapter is that of embodied music cognition (Leman, 2008; see Leman et al., this volume), and the acknowledgement of a close relationship between body motion and musical sound in both the performance and the perception of music (Godøy and Leman, 2010). Recent decades have seen a growing interest in the study of what will be referred to as 'music-related body motion' – that is, any type of human motion carried out in a musical context. This term is used here to include the motion of both performers and perceivers, hence covering a broad range of functional motion categories, such as sound-producing, sound-modifying, sound-accompanying and communicative (see Jensenius, Wanderley, Godøy and Leman, 2010, for an overview of different types of music-related body motion).

Most studies of music-related body motion, such as summarised in Wanderley and Battier (2000), Gritten and King (2006, 2011) and Godøy and Leman (2010), have focused on fairly large-scale motion. Particularly, the many studies of different types of communicative 'gestures' in the performance and perception of music, focus on what could be referred to as *meso*-level (at a centimetre-scale) or even *macro*-level (at a metre-scale) actions. Such meso- or macro-level perspectives are prevalent also in the study of gestures in linguistics and psychology (Kendon, 2004; McNeill, 2005; Goldin-Meadow, 2003). This chapter, on the other hand, focuses on music-related micromotion, the smallest controllable and perceivable human actions, typically happening at a millimetre-scale (or smaller).

The empirical starting point of the chapter is data gathered during three phases of the artistic–scientific research project Sverm. The Norwegian word 'sverm' is quite similar to the English word 'swarm', and was chosen to symbolise the 'flocking' of markers observed in the motion capture recordings of the pilot study. In such recordings, the markers attached to the body of the people being studied move in a semi-random order, yet with a clear directionality as a group. Hence the 'swarm' may be seen as an abstraction of all the tiny actions happening in our bodies at all times. The Sverm project was a two-year-long exploration of physical standstill carried out with a group of professional artists, including composer–musicians, choreographer–dancers and a scenographer. The project culminated in a series of music/dance performances, entirely built up of micromotion and microsound. As it turned out, the Sverm project also branched into some smaller scientific sub-projects about human standstill, with the aim of answering the following questions:

1   How much do people move when standing still in silence?
2   Does the level of standstill change during the course of a standstill session?
3   Does the quantity and quality of standstill change with practice?
4   Does listening to music influence the level of standstill?

The chapter starts with a survey of related literature, followed by findings from the different phases of the Sverm project and a discussion of the elements of body, space and sound from a micromotion perspective.

**The micromotion of standstill**

The term 'standstill' will be used in this chapter to denote the act of not moving. This term is not so commonly used in the research literature on human body motion, so its usage deserves a brief explanation. In the medical literature, such as in Mulholland (1995), the word 'stillness' is often used to describe the act of standing still. Stillness, however, is clearly ambiguous in a musical context, since the word does not differentiate between the act of standing physically still and that of being silent – that is, making no sound. The same is the case for the term 'quiet standing', which is often used in the biomechanics and physiotherapy literature (Winter, 1995). Other terms commonly found in the research literature include 'immobile', 'inactive', 'motionless' and 'stationary'. These terms, however, suggest an inability to move, while we have focused on studying the motion of healthy people that are trying to stand still. As such, the term 'standstill' seems appropriate, even though it may give connotations to a traffic jam or a machine breakdown. It also effectively describes the methodological approach that is used in the project: people standing still.

Observing people standing still on the floor is a novel method in music research, but it is an approach commonly used in physiotherapy and biomechanics. In these fields the aim is to understand more about the physical and/or cognitive health of the patients, by observing the unconscious and/or involuntary micromotion of people's standstill. In the Sverm project, however, the focus was on using standstill as a method to uncover people's cognition of music, through their bodily behaviour.

Even though standstill may be new to music research, it is not new to music performance. Many musicians use physical standstill to build expectation before or after playing. A famous example is that of Michael Jackson's epic opening of the 1993 Super Bowl half-time show, during which he stood still in front of a cheering audience for 90 seconds. He brilliantly managed to build up a heightened expectation among the thousands of people in the stadium and millions watching through the TV screens, which was followed by a massive 'release' when the music began playing and he began dancing and singing. The 'lack' of performance was also used in a very different, yet related, concept in John Cage's *4'33"*. In performances of this piece the 'absence' of sound and motion of the performer leads to a heightened awareness of all types of other sounds in the performance space (Cage, 1961).

Standstill is also used in the visual arts, such as in the video works of Bill Viola (1995), who explores time-stretching his videos to such an extent that they feel like still images, albeit their slowly moving character. In dance performance, the Japanese Butoh tradition is famous for very slow-motion sequences (Kurihara, 2000). The duo Eiko and Koma, for example, have been carrying out performances in which they have been standing, sitting or lying almost still for extended periods of time (Yamada, Yamada and Yokobosky, 2000). One example is their 1998 performance installation *Breathe* in which they lay naked and still on the floor for several days. In the performance art project *Being on the beach* the participants stood still together while perceiving their surroundings (Refsum and Rimestad, 2013).

Watching others stand still, or performing standstill one your own, is interesting not because of what is not happening, but rather because of the micromotion that actually happens. As living organisms, our bodies are constantly in motion, even when trying to be still. Most such micromotion is produced unintentionally and is so small that it is barely visible at a distance. But the 'invisibility' of micromotion does not mean that it does not affect us. Rather, nuance and expressivity in music may to a great extent be conveyed and experienced through micromotion:

> As opposed to the external motor entrainment initiated by overt body motion, micro-movement might be a natural manifestation of the internal motor engagement.
> (Su and Pöppel, 2012, p. 381)

While micromotion may have not received large-scale interest so far, there are several examples of its investigation over the years. This includes the seminal work on 'microexpressions' by Ekman and Friesen (1969), which focused on how facial micromotion reveals individuals' feelings, and how this can be used to determine when someone is lying. Similarly, research on micromotion of the eyes – such as microsaccades, drifts and tremors – has shown that our eyes are always in motion (Martinez-Conde and Macknik, 2007) and that microsaccades in particular are related to our mental visualisations (Laeng and Teodorescu, 2002).

In biomechanics, standstill has been studied as an example of the 'human pendulum', since we tend to sway in a semi-random pattern as adjustments take place throughout the body (Collins and De Luca, 1994). Many of these studies focus on explaining the biomechanical nature of the swaying by using force plates to examine feet and leg activity (Winter, Patla, Prince, Ishac and Gielo-Perczak, 1998; Loram and Lakie, 2002). There are also examples of how chronobiologists study the temporal and rhythmic nature of human micromotion, with a focus on the various chronobiological cycles happening in the body (Klein, 2007).

In the world of rehabilitation, different types of slow-motion practice or standstill can be found in traditions like Feldenkrais (Feldenkrais, 1972), the Alexander Technique (Barlow, 1975), Release Technique (Johnson, 1995) and Kinetic Awareness (Saltonstall, 1988). These tools accommodate a deeper awareness or recovery from misalignments or injuries in the body, often through standstill and a focus on breathing. Similar approaches may be found in different versions of yoga and other physical meditation techniques.

## Body – space

To understand the concept of standstill and micromotion better, I teamed up with dancer-choreographer Kari Anne Vadstensvik Bjerkestrand, who has extensive experience working with different types of slow-motion practices. Together we carried out a small study in which we would explore micromotion through the act of standing still in silence for ten minutes at a time. This seemed like a good duration to work with, since ten minutes is a sufficient amount of time to get into the state of standing still, while at the same time being manageable from a practical point of view.

Together we carried out 15 standstill sessions, each ten minutes long. The sessions were done in silence, since we wanted to explore the body and its motion in space before eventually moving to investigating the influence of sound on our motion. The data collection was done using a full-body motion capture set-up of the two of us using a high-quality system from Qualisys (Oqus 300) and also recording regular video as a reference track. Each of the sessions was followed by the recording of qualitative data in the form of notes of our subjective experience of standing still.

### *Spatial distribution*

As we presented in Jensenius and Bjerkestrand (2012) and has been reported also in other studies of the 'human pendulum' (Collins and De Luca, 1994), we easily experienced how our swaying, shifting of weight, breathing and heart beating influenced our micromotion when standing still. This micromotion was also easily picked up by the motion capture system. To give an impression of what the data looks like, Figure 3.1 shows a plot of the head marker of one person's motion capture data. The two-dimensional plot in the figure can be seen as displaying a person's motion pattern from above, with the nose pointing upwards in the image. This plot shows that there is more motion in the Y plane than in the X plane, which is to be expected, since the feet stabilise the sideways motion better than the front-to-back motion. There is much less motion happening on the Z axis (up–down) than on the two other axes. This is also as expected, since a person standing still will not move very much up and down, although one may often find that a person will either tend to straighten up their back (increase height) or 'fall' together (decrease height) over time while standing still.

## *Temporal levels*

From the motion capture data we were also able to identify different temporal levels of motion. Adhering to the micro–meso–macro convention for the spatial levels mentioned in the introduction, we ended up with a similar three-level description of the observed motion in time:

- Micro: quasi-random motion happening on the scale of milliseconds. This may be caused by tiny adjustments happening throughout the joints to keep the body in balance.
- Meso: periodic motion at intervals of approximately five seconds, which most likely corresponds to respiratory patterns.
- Macro: 'spikes' or large-form changes every two to three minutes that can probably be explained by postural adjustments, or periodically larger inhalations.

Several studies have shown a 2 Hz resonance peak in human motion. For example, MacDougall and Moore (2005) found that the vertical acceleration of the head in everyday motion exhibits peaks at 2 Hz, independent of gender, age, height, weight or body mass index. A classic study on human locomotion showed that the preferred walking tempo is 120 steps per minute (2 Hz) (Murray, Drought and Kory, 1964), and other studies have shown that the sustained control of a person's position may be most efficient when carried out as a series of ballistic trajectories at a rate of 2 Hz (Loram, Gollee, Lakie and Gawthrop, 2011). These findings correspond well with studies on the perception of musical rhythm, which suggest that there is a preference for musical tempi of 120–125 beats per minute (bpm) (Moelants, 2002), while the preferred tempo of dance music is a little faster (125–130 bpm) (Moelants, 2008). We were therefore curious as to whether we would find evidence of a similar 2 Hz resonance in our standstill data. As for now, however, we have not been able to find any particular resonance at this frequency.

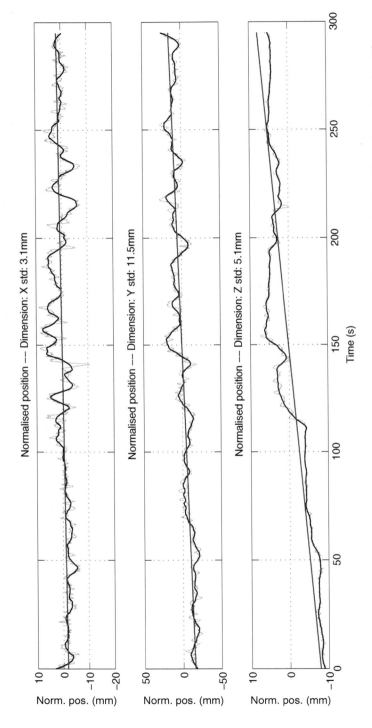

*Figure 3.1* Example plots of the X (sideways), Y (front-back) and Z (up-down) axes of the normalised position of a head marker. The grey line is the raw data; the black line results from a ten-second smoothing filter; and the red line shows the linear regression (the trend) of the dataset.

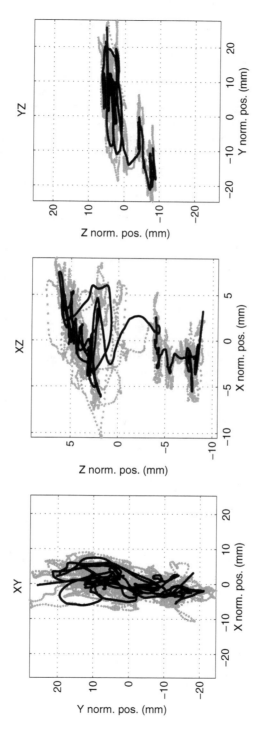

Figure 3.1 continued

## Quantity of motion

Starting out with the standstill study, we wondered about how it would feel to stand still for ten minutes at a time, and whether we would experience fatigue or boredom. It was interesting to find that it was in fact very easy to stand still for such a period of time. Most of the time it felt relaxing and at times was even exciting. Furthermore, and contrary to our expectations, we did not find any difference in the level of standstill throughout the sessions. The plots of the cumulative distance travelled are virtually linear, and the calculated slopes of the first derivative are close to 0 for all recordings. Neither could we find any difference in the standstill level based on whether we stood still for five, ten or 15 minutes. The level and shape of motion was remarkably consistent throughout all of the recordings, which may indicate that each of us has a certain level of standstill in our bodies that it is difficult to alter.

Based on the positive, interesting and, partly, surprising findings from the pilot study, we did a follow-up study, Sverm 2, in which we were joined by violinist-researcher Victoria Johnson for a year-long study of standstill and micromotion. The methodological approach was the same as for the first project: ten-minute long standstill sessions, each being motion captured, video recorded and discussed in the group (see Jensenius, Bjerkestrand, and Johnson, 2014, for details). The main difference from the first study was that we used only one, individual motion capture marker per person. In the Sverm 1 recordings we used a full-body motion capture set-up, with markers placed on all the main joints. For the analysis of the Sverm 1 data, however, we mainly focused on a marker placed on the neck, and this turned out to reveal quite a lot of the motion in the body. For Sverm 2 we therefore decided to use only one marker on the head of each person, the most extreme part of the 'swinging body'. Using only one marker per person simplified the set-up, both practically and conceptually, and still provided sufficient amounts of data for analysis.

One of the aims of Sverm 2 was to quantify the level of micromotion happening when standing still in silence, so that this base level could later be used to find how music influenced the standstill. Here we decided to calculate the 'quantity of motion' (QoM) of each motion capture marker by summing up all the differences of consecutive samples for the magnitude of its position vector – that is, the first derivative of the position:

$$QoM = \frac{1}{T}\sum_{n=2}^{N}\|p(n) - p(n-1)\|$$

where $p$ is the XYZ position vector of a marker, $N$ is the total number of samples and $T$ is the total duration of the recording. The resultant QoM is measured in millimetres per second (mm/s) and this is the feature and unit that will be used in the rest of this chapter.

Analysing 38 such ten-minute long standstill recordings showed that the individual average values for the three of us were 5.2 mm/s (SD = 1.1 mm/s), 6.4 mm/s (SD = 1.1 mm/s), and 7.3 mm/s (SD = 0.9 mm/s), respectively (Jensenius et al., 2014). The low standard deviations indicate that the results were very consistent over time, particularly considering that the recordings were done over several months, at different times of the day and with varying physical and mental tasks performed during the sessions. Also interesting was that we did not get any 'better' at standing still over time. One could have thought that we would improve our results with practice, but the findings indicate that each person may have a specific level of standstill that it is difficult to alter.

## *Physical and spatial factors influencing micromotion*

During the sessions we experimented with different physical and mental strategies to see whether they would have an effect on both the measurable and perceivable level of standstill. The most influential factors turned out to be:

- Eyes. Keeping the eyes open stabilises the body more than closing the eyes. In fact, recordings with the eyes shut would usually lead to a 1 mm/s higher average QoM.
- Knees. Locking the knees leads to lower average QoM values, as it stabilises the legs more than if the knees are open.
- Arms. Letting the arms hang straight down is the most comfortable and efficient way of standing still. Closing the arms in front of the chest may work for some, but stabilises the body less than letting them hang and may also be uncomfortable over time.
- Feet. The most stable position is to stand with the feet facing forwards and at a shoulder-width's distance. We tried many different feet positions and some of them (particularly the asymmetrical ones) made it virtually impossible to stand still for an entire ten-minute session.

In addition to testing out various types of physical strategies, we also tried to employ different mental tasks while standing still, including employing various meditation techniques, playing mental number games, imagining motion within the body and so on. We also explored how standing in various part of the lab space would influence the experience, such as standing in the middle of the room, close to a wall, and close/far from each other. Interestingly, we have not been able to find any measurable differences in the QoM from these tests. However, while the tasks and physical changes did not influence our level of standstill, these changes did have a major impact on each individual's experience of standing still, for better and for worse. Carrying out a mental exercise, for example, was a very different experience from just letting the thoughts wonder.

It was particularly interesting to find that the placement within the room had such an impact on the experience of standing still, even though it did not lead to any measurable differences. For example, the experience of standing next to a wall was clearly different from standing in the middle of the room, even when the eyes were closed. This may to a large part be based on aural differences; after all, it is easy to hear that you are standing next to a wall based on the perception of the room acoustics. But also the visual component might have had an effect, since standing closer to a wall felt like we were 'leaning' towards that wall. This knowledge about the importance of the position in space later turned out to be useful when developing the final performances of the Sverm project.

**Sound – body**

After having explored micromotion in a smaller group and over a longer period of time, we became interested in checking the validity of our findings with a larger group of people. This led to a study 'camouflaged' as the 'Norwegian Standstill Championship'. We had previously experienced that it was challenging to get volunteers for standing still in the lab, but adding a competitive element on a day with many visitors on campus turned out to be an efficient way of getting a fairly large group of people to participate. There are reports on other standstill competitions in which the aim is to stand still for a very long time (apparently up to 30 hours). We were more interested in studying the level and quality of the standstill and also the effect of music on people's micromotion.

*Procedure*

A little more than 100 participants were recruited to the study, and they took part in groups from five to 12 participants at a time. Not everyone completed the task and there were some missing/erroneous marker data, so the final dataset consisted of 77 participants, 42 male and 35 female, with an average age of 27 years (min = 16, max = 67). The participants filled out a questionnaire in which they indicated the number of hours per week spent on different music or motion-related activities:

- Listen to music: M = 19 hours per week (SD = 15 hours).
- Play/produce/compose music: M = 8 hours per week (SD = 8 hours).
- Dance: M = 2 hours per week (SD = 2 hours).
- Training/motion: M= 4 hours per week (SD = 4 hours).

The high standard deviations are due to the fact that about half of the participants were music students and professionals spending a lot of time on musical activities, while the other half had relatively little musical activity.

The task given to the participants was to stand still on the floor for six minutes in total, three minutes in silence and three minutes with music. The experiment was presented as a standstill 'championship', with an iPod Nano as the first prize. The participants knew that they were part of a research project, but they did not know anything else about the content of the study. They were free to choose their standing position.

The musical stimuli were seven excerpts of 20–40 seconds duration, ranging from slow non-rhythmic music (electronic and acoustic) to dance music (electronic dance music and salsa). The motion capture data was recorded and pre-processed in Qualisys Track Manager and the analysis was carried out in Matlab using the MoCap Toolbox (Toiviainen and Burger, 2010).

The recordings were done with a sampling rate of 100 Hz. The motion capture system was calibrated before each recording session to ensure the highest possible accuracy and precision of the data. We have previously shown that the spatial noise level of the system is much lower than that of a person standing still (Jensenius, Nymoen, Skogstad and Voldsund, 2012), and this we also checked by recording the position of a marker placed on a pole standing in the middle of the capture space throughout all the recordings.

## Results

In the Sverm project we had found QoM values in the range of 5–7 mm/s for the participants, but this was for only a few people. We were therefore eager to see if we would find a similar QoM level for a larger group of people.

As summarised in Table 3.1, we found an average QoM of 6.5 mm/s (SD = 1.6 mm/s) for the entire dataset. The best result was 3.9 mm/s (the winner) and the poorest 13.7 mm/s. These values, however, included both the no-music and music conditions, so Table 3.1 also shows a breakdown of the values in these two conditions, as well as for each of the individual music tracks (parts 2–8).

On average, participants moved slightly more to the three-minute part with music (M = 6.6 mm/s, SD = 1.9 mm/s) than to the three-minute part without music (M = 6.3 mm/s, SD = 1.4 mm/s, t(76) = –2.61, two-tailed t-test,

*Table 3.1* Average QoM values for the entire session, no-music and music conditions, and for each of the individual parts

|  | No music (3 min) | Music excerpts (3 min) | | | | | | |
|---|---|---|---|---|---|---|---|---|
| Part | 1 | 2 | 3 | 4 | 5 | 6 | 7 | 8 |
| Mean values (mm/s) | 6.5 | | | | | | | |
| Mean values (mm/s) | 6.3 | 6.6 | | | | | | |
| Mean values (mm/s) | 6.3 | 6.2 | 6.5 | 6.7 | 6.5 | 6.6 | 6.9 | 6.7 |
| Standard deviation (mm/s) | 1.4 | 1.8 | 1.9 | 1.9 | 1.7 | 1.8 | 3.8 | 2.3 |

p < 0.01). This is not a very large difference, but still shows a tendency that the musical stimuli influenced the level of standstill. The results are even clearer when looking at results for the individual stimuli, with relatively high QoM values for the electronic dance music excerpt (part 7, M = 6.9 mm/s, SD = 3,8 mm/s) and for the salsa excerpt (part 8, M = 6.7 mm/s, SD = 2.3 mm/s). As such, the results confirm the idea that 'music makes you move'. This may not be very surprising, but it is still interesting to see that even in a competitive setting during which the participants actively tried to stand still, the music had an influence on their micromotion. In future studies we will also be interested in looking at the influence of the participants' height, age, gender and music/motion background on their QoM results.

## *Self-reports*

From the Sverm studies, we knew that two of the most important factors when it comes to influencing the level of standstill, is whether one is standing with eyes open or closed and with open or locked knees. Hence the most stable position should theoretically be to stand with the eyes open and with locked knees. We did not record any data that would allow for quantifying these two conditions, but the participants did self-report on their strategies for eyes and knees, as summarised in Table 3.2.

The participants were not instructed to keep their eyes open or closed, but most people decided to keep them open during the experiment. Some participants also reflected on how they used their sight, such as:

I tried to watch a particular point all the time ...

The material does not allow for evaluating what people meant when they indicated that they had both open and locked knees. Presumably they varied during the course of the experiment, but one person also wrote in the free-text field of the questionnaire that:

I locked the left knee all the time, while the right was bent ...

There were also some that reported other types of physical strategies, such as:

I sucked my belly in ...

*Table 3.2* Self-reported standstill conditions of the participants

|  | Yes | Both | No |
|---|---|---|---|
| Eyes open? | 64 | 8 | 5 |
| Locked knees? | 35 | 32 | 10 |

*Table 3.3* Self-report on experience (1 = low, 5 = high)

|  | Mean | SD |
|---|---|---|
| How tiresome? | 2.6 | 1.0 |
| How much motion during silence? | 3.1 | 0.9 |
| How much motion during music? | 2.7 | 1.2 |

The participants were asked to self-report on how much they felt that they moved and how tiresome it was. The values, summarised in Table 3.3, indicate that they felt it was not particularly tiresome.

It is interesting to see that several of the participants wrote that they moved less during the sections with music than during the part in silence. This clearly contradicts the idea that 'music makes you move', it contradicts our QoM findings and it contradicts some of the free-text comments, such as:

> I noticed how I automatically started moving when the music started ... particularly the hip-hop.

Another had a similar observation:

> It was difficult to stand still to the 'funky music' ...

The participants were also asked to submit free-text replies on the overall experience. These were generally positive and some people even wrote that the experience had been so pleasant that they would start standing still for a few minutes every day.

## Body – sound

The scientific outcomes and the experiential knowledge gained from the first parts of the Sverm project led to the final part, Sverm 3, which was devoted to the development of a music/dance performance based on and around the concept of micromotion and microsound. After having worked analytically for several months, the group was at this stage eager to use the experiential and theoretical knowledge in artistic practice, and particularly in a truly combined music and dance constellation.

### *Spatiotemporal categories*

Throughout the rehearsals it quickly became clear that we needed a common vocabulary to systematically work with relationships between actions and sounds together in the group. Here we ended up combining the three spatial and temporal levels mentioned earlier into a set of spatiotemporal categories, as summarised in Table 3.4. The system is simple

42  *Alexander Refsum Jensenius*

*Table 3.4* Overview of the spatiotemporal categories developed in the Sverm project (approximate values)

|  | Space | Time |
|---|---|---|
| Micro | < 1 cm | < 0.5 s |
| Meso | 1–100 cm | 0.5–10 s |
| Macro | > 100 cm | > 10 s |

and is based on separating both space and time into three levels – micro, meso, macro – as presented above. Even though Table 3.4 refers to some specific number ranges for both space and time, these should be thought of only as indicative. The main point of the system is that the meso-level is used to describe what would be considered 'normal' actions and sounds, while the micro and macro levels are used to describe smaller/shorter or larger/longer actions and sounds, respectively. Of course, the interpretation of these levels is highly subjective and also context-dependent. Still the descriptions worked very well within the group, and it was also easy to introduce the system to other musicians and dancers that we occasionally worked with.

From the spatiotemporal categories we were able to create a 'matrix' from which we could also come up with combinations of the different levels. For example, a 'micro-micro action' would designate an action small in both space and time, while a 'micro-macro action' would be an action small in space but long in time. In rehearsals we systematically explored all such possible combinations of small and large, short and long actions, and everyone would easily be able to perform any type of combination spontaneously.

*Microsound*

While sound had been produced also for the exploration of actions, we next turned our attention to working specifically with sound-producing actions. Here we used the same type of matrix solution to explore different types of sounds. For example, a 'micro-micro sound' would be soft in loudness and short in time, while a 'macro-micro sound' would be very loud but short. Again, these categories are highly subjective and context-dependent, but the system still worked very well in a rehearsal context in which it was necessary to try out a number of things in rapid succession.

We found it particularly rewarding to systematically explore combinations of sounds and actions. From nature we are used to a clear causality between actions and sounds, in which the nature and quality of a sound is directly related to its sound-producing action (cf. Windsor, this volume). Since we were working between dance and music, we wanted to explore the two by 'splitting up' a sound-producing action into two parts: the action and the following sound. In that way a dancer could perform a 'sound-producing action', such as hitting in the air, which was then 'sonified' by a musician, for example through a vocal expression from the singer or violin sound from the violinist (see picture from a rehearsal in Figure 3.2). This we did using the above-mentioned matrix, testing connections between short/long and small/large actions followed by short/long and low/loud sounds. At first it appeared mainly as a miming game between the dancers and musicians, with some funny 'mickey mousing' effects in between. After getting used to this type of sonic interplay, however, we reached a level at which lots of interesting perceptual 'conflicts' were exposed, for example combinations of large/short actions followed by low/long sounds. Such combinations in some ways feel 'wrong', but many of them turned out to be aesthetically interesting, and some of them we also developed into parts of the final performance.

*Figure 3.2* Two dancers and two musicians rehearsing relationships between actions and sounds at different levels.

## Microinteraction

The above-mentioned exploration of 'unnatural' couplings between actions and sounds were performed acoustically by the dancers and musicians. Following from this we also developed a live electronics parts, through what we have called 'microinteraction' (Jensenius, forthcoming, 2017). Here we used the motion capture system (Qualisys Oqus 300) in real-time mode, tracking each of the performers in space. The data was sent to an OSC-controlled sound synthesis system and a DMX-controlled lighting system, for further electronic exploration.

For the sonic interaction we played with a number of different mapping modes, ranging from the direct mapping of marker data to sine tones to granular synthesis playback of pre-recorded sounds. The lighting was also explored fully, from motorised control of light sources based on positioning on the floor to colour transformations based on motion patterns. Perhaps the most interesting finding from these explorations was how the microinteraction worked as a 'microscope', expanding the micromotion of the performers into large-scale sound and light effects in the performance space. This was also something that would have a major impact on the final performance.

## Putting it all together in performance

The Sverm project and its various forked sub-projects culminated in a series of 45-minute long evening performances focused on 'a micro universe of dance and music'. The performance was built up of seven 'pieces' that in various ways explored the concept of standstill, micromotion and microsound. Being a minimalist project in nature, each of the 'pieces' explored only one or a few key concepts, and each of them also used the live electronic sound and lighting sparsely.

The perhaps most important challenge of the entire process was to develop a performance setting in which an audience could have a meaningful experience of watching the standstill of others. After all, to fully be able to explore the richness of such a 'micro-performance' requires some attentiveness and concentration. Through various workshop presentations and small-scale testing we found that it was necessary to start each performance with the audience members standing still themselves for a few minutes. That way they would 'calm' down, get to experience their own breathing and micromotion, and relax into a state from which they could enjoy the micromotion of the performers. So each of the performances started with the audience members coming into the space and being instructed to stand still and listen to ambient music for five minutes before sitting down. This was a very easy and efficient way of preparing the audiences for what would come.

From the performers' point of view, the main challenge was to learn how to turn the inwards-facing focus of a regular standstill session into a performance context. Here it became important to differentiate between the 'state' of standing still and the 'action' of carrying out motion at a micro-level, such as moving the finger one centimetre over the course of ten minutes (Jensenius, forthcoming). At first, it was not immediately clear whether an observer could actually spot the difference between a state and such a microaction. From the performer's perspective, however, it is quite different to walk on stage with the intention of standing still for ten minutes as compared to carrying out a 10-minute long microaction. In the end it also turned out that the focus of the performer's intention and attention was clearly visible to the audience.

The use of interactive lighting and sound was very subtle throughout the performances, but the electronics still played a crucial role. The slowly moving light and colour changes helped create transitions between the various parts of the performance, and the lighting was also the most important visual element next to the performers' bodies. Since the performers stood still most of the time, the different lighting conditions not only helped to create very different atmospheres in the performance space itself but also helped in emphasising different parts of the micromotion of the performers. The interactive sound played a similar role in creating a sonic environment ranging from the silence of the room to fully spatialised ambient sounds. Two of the pieces also contained direct mappings from micromotion to sound synthesis, during which the sound worked as the 'motion microscope' mentioned above.

We performed a total of eight 45-minute evening shows, which received both positive reviews and interesting feedback from some of the audience members that were interviewed right after the shows. One participant commented:

> I didn't know what to expect, but was curious ... at the end it felt like I had been given a massage.

Many of the audience members commented that they had enjoyed being transformed into 'another time and space'. As such, we succeeded in our aim for the performances.

## Conclusions

Summing up, this chapter has presented results from a nearly two-year-long exploration of human micromotion in the Sverm project. Combining scientific and artistic aims and methods, I worked together with a group of musicians and dancers to gain experiential knowledge of the phenomenon of micromotion in music and dance as well as develop a conceptual model for using this knowledge in artistic practice.

We found that most people move their head at around 6.5 mm/s when standing still for sustained periods of time, and that this level is consistent over individual standstill sessions as well as across different sessions. Results from the 'Norwegian Standstill Championship' confirmed that music can affect our micromotion, even though the differences are small. This was only a pilot study, however, so more systematic studies are needed to investigate more closely how (much) music influences micromotion. Here it will also be interesting to more closely study bow people's background influences their results, as well as how different musical features (rhythm, melody, loudness, spatialisation etc.) come into play.

In addition to learning more about the effects of music-induced micromotion, it will be interesting to continue exploring the field of musical microinteraction in artistic practice. We have already seen that this level of interaction may open up entirely new performance techniques, many of which give us a quite different way of exploring body, space and sound in music and dance performances.

## Acknowledgements

The Sverm project was supported by the Arts Council Norway, Norwegian Research Council, University of Oslo and Norwegian Academy of Music.

## References

Barlow, W. (1975). *Alexander-princippet*. Copenhagen: Borgen forlag.
Cage, J. (1961). *Silence: lectures and writings*. Middletown, CT: Wesleyan University Press.
Collins, J. J., and De Luca, C. J. (1994). Random walking during quiet standing. *Physical Review Letters, 73*(5), 764.
Ekman, P., and Friesen, W. V. (1969). The repertoire of nonverbal behavioral categories. *Semiotica, 1*(1), 49–98.
Feldenkrais, M. (1972). *Awareness through movement: Health exercises for personal growth*. New York: Harper and Row.
Godøy, R. I., and Leman, M. (Eds.) (2010). *Musical gestures: Sound, movement, and meaning*. New York: Routledge.
Goldin-Meadow, S. (2003). *Hearing gesture: How our hands help us think*. Cambridge, MA: Harvard University Press.
Gritten, A., and King, E. (Eds.) (2006). *Music and gesture*. Farnham: Ashgate.
Gritten, A., and King, E. (Eds.) (2011). *New perspectives on music and gesture*. Farnham: Ashgate.
Jensenius, A. R. (forthcoming). Sonic microinteraction in 'the air'. In M. Lesaffre, M. Leman and P. J. Maes (Eds.), *The Routledge companion to embodied music interaction*. New York: Routledge.
Jensenius, A. R., and Bjerkestrand, K. A. V. (2012). Exploring micromovements with motion capture and sonification. In A. L. Brooks (Ed.), *Arts and technology, revised selected papers* (pp. 100–107). Berlin: Springer.
Jensenius, A. R., Bjerkestrand, K. A. V., and Johnson, V. (2014). How still is still? Exploring human standstill for artistic applications. *International Journal of Arts and Technology, 7*(2/3), 207–222.
Jensenius, A. R., Nymoen,, K., Skogstad, S., and Voldsund, A. (2012). A study of the noise-level in two infrared marker-based motion capture systems. In *Proceedings*

*of the Sound and Music Computing Conference* (pp. 258–263). Copenhagen, Denmark.

Jensenius, A. R., Wanderley, M. M., Godøy, R. I., and Leman, M. (2010). Musical gestures: Concepts and methods in research. In R. I. Godøy and M. Leman (Eds.), *Musical gestures: Sound, movement, and meaning* (pp. 12–35). New York: Routledge.

Johnson, D. (1995). *Bone, breath & gesture: Practices of embodiment.* Berkeley, CA: North Atlantic Books.

Kendon, A. (2004). *Gesture: Visible action as utterance.* Cambridge: Cambridge University Press.

Klein, G. (2007). *Farewell to the internal clock: A contribution in the field of chronobiology.* New York: Springer.

Kurihara, N. (2000). Hijikata Tatsumi: The words of butoh. *The Drama Review, 44*(1), 10–28.

Laeng, B., and Teodorescu, D. (2002). Eye scanpaths during visual imagery reenact those of perception of the same visual scene. *Cognitive Science, 26*(2), 207–231.

Leman, M. (2008). *Embodied music cognition and mediation technology.* Cambridge, MA: MIT Press.

Loram, I., Gollee, H., Lakie, M., and Gawthrop, P. (2011). Human control of an inverted pendulum: Is continuous control necessary? Is intermittent control effective? Is intermittent control physiological? *The Journal of Physiology, 589*(2), 307–324.

Loram, I. D., and Lakie, M. (2002). Direct measurement of human ankle stiffness during quiet standing: The intrinsic mechanical stiffness is insufficient for stability. *The Journal of Physiology, 545*(3), 1041–1053.

MacDougall, H. G., and Moore, S. T. (2005). Marching to the beat of the same drummer: The spontaneous tempo of human locomotion. *Journal of Applied Physiology, 99*(3), 1164–1173.

Martinez-Conde, S., and Macknik, S. L. (2007). Windows on the mind. *Scientific American, 297*(2), 56–63.

McNeill, D. (2005). *Gesture and thought.* Chicago, IL: University of Chicago Press.

Moelants, D. (2002). Preferred tempo reconsidered. In *Proceedings of the International Conference on Music Perception & Cognition* (pp. 580–583), Sydney, Australia.

Moelants, D. (2008). Hype vs. natural tempo: a long-term study of dance music tempi. In *Proceedings of the International Conference on Music Perception & Cognition.* Sapporo, Japan.

Mulholland, T. (1995). Human EEG, behavioral stillness and biofeedback. *International Journal of Psychophysiology 19*(3), 263–279.

Murray, M. P., Drought, A. B., and Kory, R. C. (1964). Walking patterns of normal men. *The Journal of Bone & Joint Surgery, 46*(2), 335–360.

Refsum, G., and Rimestad. I. (2013). Being on the beach: Exploring sensomotoric awareness in a landscape. In S. Bergmann, I. Blindow and K. Ott (Eds.), *Aesthethics in environmental change hiking through the arts, ecology, religion and ethics of the environment* (pp. 177–201). Berlin: LIT Verlag.

Saltonstall, E. (1988). *Kinetic awareness, discovering your bodymind.* New York: Pub Center Cultural Resources.

Su, Y.-H., and Pöppel, E. (2012). Body movement enhances the extraction of temporal structures in auditory sequences. *Psychological Research, 76*(3), 373–382.

Toiviainen, P., and Burger, B. (2010). *MoCap Toolbox manual*. Technical report, University of Jyväskylä.

Viola, B. (1995). *Reasons for knocking at an empty house: writings 1973–1994*. Cambridge, MA: MIT Press.

Wanderley, M. M., and Battier, M. (Eds.) (2000). *Trends in gestural control of music*. Paris: IRCAM.

Winter, D. A. (1995). Human balance and posture control during standing and walking. *Gait & Posture, 3*(4), 193–214.

Winter, D., Patla, A., Prince, F., Ishac, M., and Gielo-Perczak, K. (1998). Stiffness control of balance in quiet standing. *Journal of Neurophysiology, 80*(3), 1211.

Yamada, E. O., Yamada, T. K., and Yokobosky, M. (2000). Movement as installation: Eiko and Koma in conversation with Matthew Yokobosky. *PAJ: A Journal of Performance and Art, 22*(1), 26–35.

# 4 Cross-modal experience of musical pitch as space and motion

## Current research and future challenges

*Zohar Eitan*

An impressive number of empirical studies, utilising diverse psychophysical, cognitive and neuropsychological experimental paradigms, indicate that basic auditory dimensions, such as pitch and loudness, associate perceptually and cognitively with features of other senses (see Marks, 2004; Spence, 2011; Walker, 2016, for research reviews). Increasingly, these studies suggest that such *cross-modal correspondences* (CMC) – for instance, the associations of higher pitch with higher spatial location, lighter surfaces or smaller objects – are widespread and systematic, and may automatically and subconsciously affect perception, cognition and action involving sound. Furthermore, some of these correspondences are shared cross-culturally, suggesting that factors other than language or culture-specific practices may generate them (e.g., Bremner et al., 2013; Parkinson, Kohler, Sievers and Wheatley, 2012; Sievers, Polansky, Casey and Wheatley, 2013); indeed, ethological studies suggest that some CMC observed in humans, such as the associations of pitch height with size and visual lightness, are also reflected in the behaviour of non-human species (Morton, 1994; Ludwig, Adachi and Matsuzawa, 2011).

For music research, the empirical study of CMC may hold substantial promise, elucidating the association of musical experience with human experience in other domains. Given the association of music with human motion across cultures (see Stevens, 2012, for a review of relevant cognitive research), studying the ways auditory features map onto aspects of physical space and bodily motion, such as location (e.g., up/down, far/near), size (large/small, increase/decrease), movement direction (rise/fall, approach/retreat) or speed, may be of particular interest and could enhance our conception of musical experience as an embodied domain.

Of all auditory dimensions, the associations of pitch height (and its dynamic correlate, pitch direction or contour) with aspects of space and motion are probably the most widely researched (see Eitan, 2013, for a research overview). That research, however, has mostly been conducted in rarified experimental settings, far removed from the multi-layered and dynamic contexts of music. Thus, issues pertinent to actual musical experience are left open or insufficiently discussed. This chapter, after introducing current research of the spatio-kinetic associations of auditory pitch, discusses some of these open or novel issues: how pitch CMC interact with the emotional connotations of pitch height and pitch contour; how tonality affects the CMC of pitch; and the different, sometimes contrasting ways static (high/low) and dynamic (rise/fall) pitch relationships associate with space and motion. I argue that the lacunas in understanding how pitch CMC are affected by these factors reduce the ecological validity of current CMC research for complex domains like music, and suggest some ways such lacunas may be addressed.

The first open issue presented here involves the interrelations of cross-modal and affective associations of pitch. As will be demonstrated in the following research survey (pp. 55–57), an interrelated triad of mappings underlies the cross-domain experience of pitch. Pitch maps onto non-auditory sensory dimensions like spatial height or size; pitch also associates with emotional features and dimensions; and the non-auditory sensory dimensions associated with pitch, such as spatial height, are themselves associated with emotion and affect. I will present some – as yet tentative – attempts to understand how these different types of mapping may interact in musical contexts.

A second lacuna addressed here involves the ways features of musical pitch other than 'height' may affect associations with space and motion. While CMC research involving auditory pitch has focused almost solely on mappings of pitch height or contour, pitch representation, particularly in tonal contexts, is multidimensional. For instance, pitches separated by an octave (or its multiples), though wide apart in terms of pitch height, represent the same pitch-class category. Fifth-related pitch-classes are adjacent in the circle of fifths (a measure of tonal distance widely accepted by tonal theorists), providing yet another dimension of tonal distance contrasting with the pitch height dimension. Furthermore, tonality engenders relationships of stability and tension among pitches and pitch configurations, relationships often referred to in terms of space and motion (e.g., leading tone, cadence). Many empirical studies and theoretical models explore the effects of such multidimensionality on the perception and cognition of musical pitch (for reviews see, e.g., Krumhansl, 1990, 2004), and the roles of metaphors of pitch space and motion have also been widely discussed (e.g., Johnson and Larson, 2003; Zbikowski, 2008). Yet, little is known about the ways such multidimensionality affects the associations of musical pitch with physical space and motion in perception and information processing.

Third, I discuss the spatio-kinetic associations of static (high vs. low) versus dynamic (rise vs. fall) pitch. I present studies suggesting that static and dynamic pitch relationships may imply different, even contrasting, cross-modal spatio-kinetic correspondences (for instance, the association of higher pitch with smaller objects is reversed in dynamic conditions), discuss their relevance to the embodied perception of music, and suggest how these static/dynamic dichotomies may reflect upon CMC of pitch in musical contexts.

## Cross-modal correspondences of pitch with space and motion: a brief research overview

Many empirical studies, applying diverse behavioural and neuropsychological paradigms, establish that CMC between auditory pitch and features of space and motion robustly affect perception, cognition and behaviour, often in automatic and subconscious ways. Here is a brief (and necessarily incomplete) survey of this research literature.

### *Pitch and the vertical spatial plane*

The association of pitch 'height' and spatial elevation, widely expressed in verbal metaphors as well as nonverbal symbols (e.g., Western musical notation), is not limited to such explicit, culturally ingrained representations. Rather, such correspondences often affect auditory, visual and spatial perception (and related action) implicitly, subconsciously and automatically. Thus, 'higher' pitch is actually *perceived* as emitted from a higher location in space (Cabrera, Ferguson, Tilley and Morimoto, 2005; Pratt, 1930; Roffler and Butler, 1968). Correspondingly, spatial height affects pitch estimation (Casasanto, Phillips and Boroditsky, 2003).

Experiments utilising diverse implicit measures suggest that the association of pitch and spatial height may be automatic and independent of conscious processes. When participants were asked to discriminate as rapidly as possible between high and low pitch, while ignoring high or low dots on the computer screen, congruence of pitch height and vertical position (high pitch and position, low pitch and position) resulted in improved accuracy and response time, as compared to incongruence (speeded discrimination paradigm: Ben-Artzi and Marks, 1995; Evans and Treisman, 2010; Melara and O'Brien, 1987). Similarly, when participants respond to high and low pitch by pressing a spatially high and low key, respectively, performance (accuracy and response time) is considerably better when spatial location and pitch correspond (higher response key to higher pitch) than when response keys are reversed (SMARC effect: Rusconi, Kwan, Giordano, Umilta and Butterworth, 2006). Neurophysiological data further substantiates the pitch–elevation association: In EEG measurements, incongruence of pitch and spatial elevation was related to specific ERP (Event Related Potential) components, located in areas of the brain associated with cross-modal integration (Widmann, Kujala, Tervaniemi, Kujala and Schröger, 2004).

Even stronger than the association of pitch and spatial height is its dynamic counterpart – correspondence between pitch direction and vertical movement direction (up/down). For instance, Mossbridge, Grabowecky and

Suzuki (2011) show that the direction of fundamental frequency change, rather than average or ending frequency, most strongly guides visuospatial attention, providing evidence that this dynamic cross-modal effect is perceptually based. Comparably, Hedger, Nussbaum, Lescop, Wallisch and Hoeckner (2013) report that repeated exposure to rising or falling scales shifts sensitivity to visually perceived motion in the opposite direction, also suggesting that the association of pitch direction and motion in the vertical plane may have a perceptual basis. Notably, the association of dynamic pitch and motion was corroborated by a number of infant (younger than four months) studies. Using the preferential-looking paradigm, these studies repeatedly demonstrated that rising and falling pitch affects infants' attention to rising and falling visual stimuli, respectively: hearing a rising pitch, infants tend to look at a rising visual stimulus, and hearing a falling pitch, at a falling stimulus (Dolscheid, Hunnius, Casasanto and Majid, 2014; Wagner, Winner, Cicchetti and Gardner, 1981; Walker et al., 2010).

As evidence for implicit infant and pre-natal learning is ubiquitous, these infant studies do not necessarily suggest that the tendency to associate pitch direction with spatial motion in the vertical plane is genetically 'hard-wired'. Yet, together with studies of pitch–height associations in non-Western cultures (e.g., Parkinson, Kohler, Sievers and Wheatley, 2012), they do suggest that this tendency is not generated by language or culturally specific symbols, such as musical notation. Rather, pitch–height associations, even if learned, may be implicitly acquired through statistical learning of audiospatial correlations in the natural environment (see Parise, Knorre and Ernst, 2014, for a study of such correlations).

For children and adults, the association of pitch and spatial direction seems to be strongly linked to bodily motion (see Wöllner and Hohagen, this volume). An association of pitch contour and bodily movement was manifested in children's movement responses to music (Kohn and Eitan, 2016) and when participants' motion imaginary was induced by short melodic stimuli (Eitan and Granot, 2006; Eitan and Tubul, 2010). A comparable correspondence is reported by Küssner, Tidhar, Prior and Leech-Wilkinson (2014), when adult participants reacted to changes in pitch, loudness and tempo by hand gestures. Likewise, watching rising or falling bodily gestures biased discrimination of concurrently heard pitch in the corresponding direction, suggesting that 'pitch and space have a shared representation, such that the mental representation of pitch is audiospatial in nature' (Connell, Cai and Holler, 2013, p. 124). Recent studies, combining psychophysical (speeded discrimination) and neurophysiological (fMRI) methods, reveal that the cross-modal correspondence of pitch change and physical movement activates brain areas associated with both visually perceived motion (hMT+/V5+) and speech (right intraparietal sulcus), suggesting that in adults both embodied (movement-related) and metaphorical (language-related) factors participate in pitch–height correspondences (Sadaghiani, Maier and Noppeney, 2009).

## Pitch and lateral position

A number of studies suggest an association of higher pitch with right-side position – and of lower pitch with left-side position. When children listened to pairs of sounds and were asked to represent these sounds by placing pegs on a pegboard, they tended to position higher pitches not only above lower pitches, but also to their right (Mudd, 1963). In a speeded detection experiment, where a visual target was presented at either the right or the left side of a screen, response time was significantly faster when the target's lateral position was congruent with a task-irrelevant pitch preceding it: high pitch enhanced detection of right-side visual targets, and low pitch detection of left-side targets (Stevens and Arieh, 2005). Pitch-laterality mapping also generates perceptual illusions, in which the lateral localisation of sound correlates with its pitch height (Deutsch, Hamaoui and Henthorn, 2007). Importantly, such effects were unequivocal mainly for right-handed participants, suggesting that the source of the phenomenon is 'a tendency to perceive higher tones as on the dominant side of space, i.e., the side of space that is contralateral to the dominant hemisphere' (Deutsch et al., 2007, p. 2986). Note, however, that in some experiments pitch-laterality associations were found mostly for musically trained participants, particularly pianists (Stewart, Walsh and Frith, 2004; Eitan and Granot, 2006). While this effect is clearly related to the structure of a keyboard, that structure could itself stem from a tendency to associate the dominant side of space with higher pitches.

## Pitch, distance and speed

While a well-known physical phenomenon – the *Doppler Effect* – associates increasing distance with falling pitch, participants in a music-induced imagery experiment (Eitan and Granot, 2006) actually associated pitch *rises* with increasing distance. A possible explanation for this inconsistency is the mediation of the pitch–size correspondence: distant objects leave a smaller retinal image and are thus seen as subjectively smaller; higher pitch is also associated with smaller size; thus, further away objects may be indirectly associated with higher pitch.

Experiments applying diverse paradigms and materials (single sounds, music, speech and vocalisations) also suggest pitch–speed correspondences, such that higher pitch is associated with faster movement. Sequences of auditory stimuli in a higher register are perceived as faster than low-register sequences in both speech (Feldstein and Bond, 1981) and music (Boltz, 2011; Collier and Hubbard, 2001; Eitan and Timmers, 2010). Correspondingly, listeners' tempo preferences in music are affected by pitch register – the higher the pitch, the faster the preferred tempo (Tamir-Ostrover and Eitan, 2015). Pitch height is also used as an icon for speed in speech intonation and expressive vocalisations. For instance, Perlman, Dale and Lupyan (2015) asked participants to create novel vocalisations communicating diverse meanings.

Vocalisations for 'fast' versus 'slow' were significantly distinguished by their average pitch height (F0). The association of pitch height and speed was also corroborated using a speeded discrimination paradigm (Walker and Smith, 1984), suggesting that this correspondence may be automatic and subconscious.

Some studies also found comparable associations between pitch direction and speed change, as ascending pitch sequences were associated with faster or increasing tempi or even perceived as faster than comparable descending sequences (Boltz, 2011; Collier and Hubbard, 2001). This relationship, however, is not equivocal. For instance, in music-induced imagery experiments, both rising and falling melodies have been associated with acceleration (Eitan and Granot, 2006; Eitan and Tubul, 2010), a 'directional asymmetry' effect further discussed below.

### *Pitch and physical size*

Higher pitch is associated with smaller physical size, a deeply rooted correspondence possibly due to the correlation of the two features in everyday experience. Pitch–size correspondences were established by several behavioural paradigms examining implicit effects: congruence of visual size with pitch affected size estimation (Gallace and Spence, 2006), speeded discrimination of visual size (Evans and Treisman, 2010) and JNDs (just noticeable differences) for both temporal order and spatial location (Parise and Spence, 2009). Comparably, in experiments based on the Stroop paradigm, participants reacted faster to the word 'large' when accompanied by a low (50 Hz) pitch, and to the word 'small' when accompanied by a high (5500 Hz) pitch (Walker and Smith, 1984). In musical contexts, participants rated the metaphors 'small' as appropriate for high-register music, and 'large' as more appropriate for lower-register music (Eitan and Timmers, 2010; Eitan, Schupak, Gotler and Marks, 2012). Neurophysiological correlates of the pitch–size correspondence were also found, using a combination of behavioural methods and brain imaging (EEG and TMS), by Bien, ten Oever, Goebel and Sack (2011).

Importantly, pitch–size associations seem to emerge very early in life, possibly due to the correlation of object size and its associated sounds in early experience. In a preferential-looking experiment (Fernández-Prieto, Navarra and Pons, 2015), six-month-olds (though not younger infants) associated higher pitch with smaller visual stimuli (see also Mondloch and Maurer, 2004, for a pitch–size correspondence in three-year-old children). A comparable correspondence, between pitch and thickness, was revealed even earlier, in four-month-olds (Dolscheid et al., 2014).

Note, however, that the above studies used static auditory stimuli (a stationary pitch or a specific pitch range). When dynamic stimuli (ascending or descending pitch glides or sound sequences) were mapped onto size, pitch rise was associated with increase, rather than decrease in size (Antovic,

2009; Eitan et al., 2015; Kim and Iwamiya, 2008). I discuss this incongruity below (pp. 59–62).

*Pitch and shape*

Higher pitch is associated with angular, sharp-edged shapes, while lower pitch is associated with round shapes. This robust association, also demonstrated for speech sound (as a factor in the well-known 'Baluma-Takete' and 'Bouba-Kiki', phenomena; Köhler, 1929; Ramachandran and Hubbard, 2001), was examined both explicitly (e.g., rating the 'sharpness' of musical stimuli differing in pitch register; Eitan and Timmers, 2010; Eitan, Katz and Shen, 2010) and implicitly, affecting speeded discrimination (Marks, 1987) and JND for temporal order (Parise and Spence, 2009). Both infant and cross-cultural studies suggest that that this correspondence is not dependent on specific cultural constraints, but reflect tendencies which are either innate or or early-learned, based on environmental correlations. Thus, four-month-old infants react to pitch–shape correspondence, as established in a preferential-looking experiment (Walker et al., 2010); and the sound–shape association revealed through the Bouba-Kiki effect was widely corroborated across cultures (e.g., Bremner et al., 2013).

## Pitch, motion and emotion: an entangled triad

Pitch height and pitch direction significantly participate in the perception and expression of emotion in music. For instance, high pitch register contributes to perceived happiness and low register to sadness and fear (Eerola, Friberg and Bresin 2013; Gabrielsson and Lindström, 2013). In musical contexts (e.g., Eitan and Timmers, 2010), pitch register has also been associated with general dimensions of affect, particularly valence (evaluation) and activity (arousal). Correspondingly, pitch direction (contour) has been associated with perceived valence and arousal in music – ascending contours tend to contribute to the perception of higher arousal and positive valence (Collier and Hubbard, 2001) – though these associations are not equivocal (Gabrielsson and Lindström, 2013). An interaction of pitch register and pitch direction also participates in the perception of musical tension (Granot and Eitan, 2011).

How do the associations of pitch register and pitch contour with physical space and bodily motion, discussed above, interact with the emotional connotations of pitch? In investigating such relationships, one may want to consider a third type of correspondence: the associations of features of space and motion – particularly bodily movement – with emotion or affect. Consider, for instance, the association of spatial height or upward motion (features which, as shown above, are strongly associated with pitch height and pitch contour) with positive emotional valence. While suggested by commonplace language metaphors and idioms (e.g., feeling high/low, high-spirited), this relationship has also been corroborated by diverse empirical studies not involving language. These include research of the role of body gestures in the expression and perception of emotion (e.g., Atkinson, Dittrich, Gemmell and Young, 2004), as well as studies of embodied cognition, suggesting that motion–emotion associations involving height and vertical motion implicitly affect cognition and behaviour. For instance, Meier and Robinson (2004) demonstrated that the valence of words presented to participants affected their spatiovisual attention, such that positive words shift attention upward and negative words downward. Correspondingly, moving objects up or down enhanced recall of positive and negative episodic memories, respectively (Casasanto and Dijkstra 2010; see also Meier and Robinson, 2005). Importantly, these spatio-kinetic associations are mostly embodied – they are strongly related to movements and positions of the human body expressing, generating, or associated with specific emotions, moods or attitudes.

In interpreting cross-domain correspondences of pitch, then, three interrelated types of mappings should be considered:

1  Pitch–space: pitch maps onto non-auditory sensory dimensions, including space and motion perception.
2  Pitch–emotion: pitch also associates with emotions and affective dimensions.
3  Space–emotion: features of perceived space and motion are associated with emotion and affect, often through expressive gesture and body movement.

How do these different types of mapping interact in musical contexts? An intriguing hypothesis concerning this 'triadic' complex of mappings suggests that some cross-modal mappings are mediated, at least in musical contexts, by emotion. That is: musical features may correspond with non-auditory features since both associate with emotion in a similar way. Several recent studies of CMC in musical contexts lend this hypothesis support. Palmer, Schloss, Xu and Prado-León (2013) show, in a cross-cultural study, that listeners' colour and emotional associations of musical pieces are strongly correlated. Levitan, Charney, Schloss and Palmer (2015) found that emotion mediates correspondences between music and smell. Some support for the role of emotion in mediating CMC in music is also provided by studies indicating that the emotions associated with specific visual (Boltz, 2013; Timmers and Crook, 2014) or verbal stimuli (Weger, Meier, Robinson and Inhoff, 2007) influence the perception of music presented concurrently with these stimuli. For instance, positive or negative valence associated with words or images may enhance the perception of high and low pitches, respectively.

Furthermore, the widespread associations of expressive body movement and gesture with music (Godøy and Leman, 2010; Wöllner and Hohagen, this volume) suggest that the emotional mediation hypothesis may apply, at least in musical contexts, to correspondences between musical configurations, such as pitch and loudness contours, and bodily motion. Cross-cultural evidence supporting the role of emotion in mediating the association of musical features with features of movement is provided by Sievers et al. (2013). Their study used a model representing corresponding features of music and movement (e.g., pitch direction and vertical spatial direction) analogously to create a computer program enabling the generation of both movement patterns (animations of a moving ball) and musical sequences (monophonic melodies). Using that program, participants were asked to create either movement or musical sequences subjectively representing five basic emotions (angry, happy, peaceful, sad and scared). Results revealed that each emotion was represented by a unique combination of features; these combinations were similar for movement and music, as well as for culturally diverse groups.

A number of models have suggested that cross-domain correspondences may by underlined by conceptual, a-modal connotative dimensions, which may also carry strong emotional connotations. For instance, the three main factors revealed by Osgood's semantic differential method (Osgood, Suci and Tannenbaum, 1957), Evaluation, Potency and Activity (EPA), also underlie listeners' characterisations of pitch register in music (Eitan and Timmers, 2010). Walker (Walker, 2016; Walker, Walker and Francis, 2012) suggests that cross-sensory correspondences are based on crosstalk among the conceptual representations of aligned feature dimensions, such as thin/thick, high/low and fast/slow. The association of such dimensions with emotional features as well – itself perhaps generated by general connotative dimensions such as Osgood's EPA – may serve as a basis for correspondences of pitch, motion and emotion in musical contexts.

Nevertheless, the interrelations of pitch, motion and emotion in complex musical contexts, and particularly the ways listeners perceive and respond to such interrelationships, have hardly been explored empirically. As Eitan, Timmers and Adler (in press) demonstrate, conflicts between the emotional and cross-modal connotations of musical features (such as rising pitch) may often underlie complex connotative musical contexts, particularly when text or visual imagery are also involved. The investigation of such interactions in specific musical contexts is a challenge for both music analysis and music psychology.

## Space, motion and tonality

As noted above, the perception of musical pitch encompasses dimensions other than pitch height, particularly in tonal or modal contexts. Yet, while the perceptual and cognitive correspondences of pitch height with aspects of physical space and motion have been widely studied, hardly any empirical studies investigate whether and how other aspects of musical pitch, including octave equivalence, fifth-relationships, tonal pitch hierarchy, or perceived tension and resolution in harmonic and voice-leading progressions, systematically associate with physical space and motion in perception, cognition, imagery and action.

One reason such investigation is called for is that tonal structure and relationships have often been described or symbolically depicted in terms of space, motion and the physical forces generating movement. Basic tonal terms often allude to spatio-kinetic domains (e.g., leading tone, cadence). In tonal theory, relationships have been mapped onto basic physical forces like gravity (Rameau, 1722) or magnetism (Larson, 2004), spatial image schemas like centre/periphery (e.g., tonal centre, outside the key; Larson and Van Handel, 2005) top/bottom, or front/back (see Spitzer, 2004), or goal-oriented movement, depicted in particular by harmonic and melodic motion toward the closing tonic (Schenker, 1906). Spatial metaphors are also central to models of tonal structure and its perception (Krumhansl, 1990; Lerdahl, 2001). For instance, the interaction of pitch height and pitch chroma, generated by octave equivalence, has been depicted using a helical representation (Shepard, 1982), and perceived relationships among pitch-classes in a tonal context were modeled using a conical geometric representation (Krumhansl, 1990).

Spatial representations, of course, are applied to many domains amenable to quantitative analysis, and such applications do not necessarily imply that the perception of these domains involves mappings onto physical space or motion. Yet, the ubiquity of spatio-kinetic metaphors and symbols in the conceptualisation of tonal structure suggests that an empirical investigation of perceived spatio-kinetic correspondences of these dimensions of pitch may be worthwhile. As studies surveyed in the previous section suggest, CMC of pitch height and physical space significantly affect perception, imagery and information processing. Given the ubiquitous spatio-kinetic conceptualisation of other dimensions of music, the hypothesis that these dimensions may also map perceptually onto physical space and bodily motion merits investigation.

While empirical research has not yet directly addressed such mappings, a number of relevant investigations should be noted. A systematic mapping of scale degrees and their basic progressions onto particular affective qualities (taking into account motion/emotion associations) has been proposed (Cooke, 1959), but received only limited empirical support (Kaminska and Woolf, 2000). Huron (2006) surveyed musicians about the qualia (subjective, phenomenological qualities) of scale degrees, presenting them with scale degree names (e.g., tonic, submediant) and asking for descriptions. The leading tone, for example, was associated with instability, a pointing quality and restlessness. However, since this methodology involved querying musicians, who have often received explicit training about the expressive associations of tonal positions, it is hard to know how results would transfer to the perceptions and experience of untrained listeners or even to implicit or nonverbal responses of trained musicians.

Preliminary research of CMC of tonal stability is currently in progress at the author's lab. Experiments applied a modified version of Krumhansl's classic probe-tone technique (Krumhansl and Kessler, 1982) to investigate the association of tonal scale degrees with non-auditory features, including visual lightness (Maimon, 2016) and visually depicted emotion (Kimchi-Gross, Maimon, Eitan and Margulis, unpublished raw data). Participants (musicians and non-musicians) performed two probe-tone tasks. One was the classic goodness-of-fit task, where they rated how well each probe tone (including each of the 12 chromatic tones) fitted a tonal context; the other – a cross-modal probe tone task, in which each of the probe tones (preceded by the same tonal context) was matched to one of a series of graded visual stimuli (e.g., seven circles varying in lightness, from white to black). Results suggest systematic correspondences between tonal stability and non-auditory features: more stable probe tones were associated with lighter visual stimuli and with 'happier' facial expression.

No empirical research, however, has so far investigated whether and how tonal relationships are actually mapped by listeners – particularly non-musicians – onto physical space and motion. Would, for instance, measures of tonal 'distance' and similarity affect the mapping of pitch relationships onto spatial distance? Would tonal stability affect mappings of pitch and spatial height (e.g., by associating tonal attraction with gravity)? Addressing such questions may significantly enhance our understanding of the way music – rather than merely sound – associates with physical space and human movement.

Two approaches for an exploratory investigation of these complex issues may suggest themselves. One (demonstrated in studies described above), involves modifying experimental paradigms well-established in tonal perception research, such as the probe-tone technique, to investigate associations of tonal structure with space and motion. Another approach would apply tonal priming to experimental paradigms used to investigate spatial associations of pitch height, such as speeded discrimination (e.g., Ben-Artzi and Marks, 1995), audiospatial plotting (Mudd, 1963; Küssner et al., 2014) or music-induced imagery tasks (Eitan and Granot, 2006). Using such modified paradigms would enable controlled comparisons of context-free pitch mappings with mappings primed by specific tonal contexts. Thus, they may supply insights concerning the ways dimensions of tonal pitch space shape correspondences of musical configurations with features such as spatial distance and direction, or the speed, effort and agency involved in bodily motion.

## Paradoxical spaces: static and dynamic pitch

In investigating CMC in music, one accounts for both *static* relationships, like pitch position (high vs. low), and *dynamic* (time-varying) parameters, such as pitch direction (rise vs. fall). It is tempting to deduce the later from the former – to infer, for instance, an association of rising pitch with shrinking size from the well-established association (see above) of higher pitch with smaller size. Research in both auditory and visual perception, however, suggests that such inference is not inevitable. When dynamic stimuli are processed, intrinsically dynamic qualities (e.g., the direction of change) may affect perception and mental representation of fundamental features like the magnitude or position of a stimulus. For instance, when equal increase and decrease in sound intensity are presented, increases would be evaluated as greater than comparable decreases (Neuhoff, 1998). For pitch height, perception of and memory for pitch position are both affected by pitch direction (Freyd, Kelly and DeKay, 1990; Hubbard and Ruppel, 2013; Kelly and Freyd, 1987; Walker and Ehrenstein, 2000). Affective connotations of pitch register, such as the degree of tension associated with a high or low melodic stimulus, are also shaped by pitch direction: low-register melodies, for instance, are perceived as tenser than high-register melodies in descent, but less tense when ascending (Granot and Eitan, 2011).

Such effects suggest that static and dynamic pitch features (e.g., high pitch and rising contour) may differ in their spatial and spatio-kinetic associations. They also imply that interactions of pitch position and pitch direction may result in unexpected spatio-kinetic mappings of pitch; and indeed, research comparing CMC of static and dynamic pitch reveals some surprising results.

One cross-modal interaction which suggests striking (even paradoxical) differences between static and dynamic pitch concerns pitch and physical size. As noted above (p. 54), the association of higher pitch with smaller object size appears robust, having been established through diverse experimental paradigms. Indeed, this association may even be instrumental in non-human vocal communication, as suggested by considerable ethological research (e.g., Morton, 1994). However, a number of recent studies, involving participants varying in cultural background, musical education and age, suggest that while *higher* pitch is indeed 'smaller' than lower pitch, *rising* pitch paradoxically 'grows', rather than shrinks. For instance, Japanese participants judged ascending melodic patterns as congruent with expanding animated visual shapes (Kim and Iwamiya, 2008). Comparably, Serbian and Romanian 11-year-old children, presented with an octave leap, associated the higher pitch with the term 'big' and the lower pitch with 'small'. This contrasts with results for isolated pitches, where lower-pitched sounds were 'bigger' (Antovic, 2009). Correspondingly, in speeded classification experiments, opposite congruence effects between pitch and visual size were found for static and dynamic stimuli (Eitan et al., 2015).

This apparent paradox may suggest that different mental processes are at work in CMC of static and dynamic pitch. As Eitan (2013) suggests, for pitch and size this disparity may stem from different bases for mappings. In static stimuli, the experiential correlation between the physical size of objects and the sound they tend to produce (larger size correlates with lower pitch) may serve as a basis for association; for dynamic stimuli, a more abstract analogy between two types of increase – pitch 'rise' and physical growth – may take hold, in line with the prevailing 'up is more' conceptual metaphor (Lakoff and Johnson, 1980). Krugliak and Noppeney (2015), who also examined pitch–size correspondences via speeded classification experiments (reproducing the dynamic rise/grow and fall/shrink correspondences established in earlier experiments, while surprisingly revealing high/large and low/small correspondences in some static conditions as well), suggest that changes in observed visual size may be interpreted as distance changes, rather than as changes in the object's physical size. However, the equivocal findings concerning pitch–distance correspondences (Eitan and Granot, 2006; see above, p. 53) do not support this explanation.

Static and dynamic pitches also differ in their association with speed. As noted above, lower pitch (and, correspondingly, music in a low pitch register) is associated with slower speed, while pitch descent is associated with accelerating, rather than decelerating motion (Eitan and Granot, 2006). In this case, as with pitch–size correspondences, the associations of static and dynamic pitch with physical space and motion may stem from different experiential sources. Low pitch correlates with larger and heavier objects, themselves associated with slower speed. Descending pitch, however, may be associated with falling objects, and hence with accelerating motion, reflecting implied 'representational gravity' (Hubbard and Ruppel, 2013).

Mapping dynamic pitch onto space and motion also seems to expose relationships and effects not observed for static pitch. One such effect is *directional asymmetry*, observed when a dynamic feature associates with a spatio-kinetic quality mainly (or even exclusively) in one direction of change. When participants were asked to imagine human motions in response to brief melodic stimuli (Figure 4.1), directional asymmetries were revealed for several features (Eitan and Granot, 2006; Eitan and Tubul, 2010). While falling pitch sequences strongly evoked spatial fall in the imagery tasks, rising pitch sequences evoked spatial rise only weakly, or (for non-musicians) not at all. Furthermore, while rising pitch was associated with increasing distance, falling pitch was not associated with decreasing distance; and while rising pitch was associated with speeding up, falling pitch was not associated with slowing down. Consequentially, pitch rise may lose its association with spatial rise when combined with 'decreasing' changes in other parameters, particularly diminuendo (Eitan and Granot, 2011; Eitan and Tubul, 2010). Pitch fall, in contrast, may hinder some motion associations of other parameters: As Küssner and colleagues (2014) reveal, the tendency to react to accelerated tempo by speeded bodily motion is hindered when fall in pitch is combined with acceleration. A comparable effect was also observed in visual motion prediction tasks (Hogan, 2015).

Dynamic contexts, then, substantially alter the ways pitch associates with physical space in perception, mental representation imagery and motion response. Neither completely mapped nor fully understood, such differences present a challenge to the study of the metaphorical spaces and movements of music, the art of 'sonically moving forms' (Hanslick, 1891/1986). Investigating the asymmetries and paradoxes of dynamic pitch space may thus

*Figure 4.1* Ascending and descending melodic stimuli used in Eitan and Granot (2006).

serve as a starting point for an exploration of CMC within the rich, multivalent flux of music.

## Conclusions

This chapter reviewed a body of experimental research which reveals systematic perceptual and cognitive mappings of auditory pitch (particularly, pitch height and pitch direction) onto basic features of physical space and bodily motion. That sizeable research notwithstanding, the ways CMC function in musical contexts are still far from being fully understood. Here, I charted three issues that empirical research of CMC in music – and specifically, studying spatio-kinetic correspondences of musical features – may need to get involved with. First, the way the emotional or affective connotations of musical features (specifically, pitch) interact with the cross-modal connotations of these features; second, how aspects of pitch structure other then 'height', which are pertinent to music cognition (e.g. octave equivalence, tonal stability), may affect the associations of musical features with physical space and bodily motion; and, third, studying cross-modal mappings of both static and dynamic dimensions, and understanding their communalities and differences.

Inquiring into these issues is pertinent for an adequate understanding of how CMC affect the ways we perceive music and assign it with meanings relevant to our experience. Yet an inquiry of such issues in dynamic, multifaceted musical settings may also contribute substantially to a better understanding of how CMC are processed in other complex contexts. Music, for instance, demonstrates the interaction of bottom-up and top-down processing in ways which may be as intricate as, yet different from, those demonstrated in language processing. Thus, studying the cross-modal connotations of tonal function may illuminate the ways other higher-order, syntactic features affect cross-modal interactions. Music also evokes both expressive and descriptive connotations, applying a myriad of genres, stylistic tropes and multimedial contexts; and music features both a continuous, dynamic flux, encompassing many concurrent realms and clear 'static' distinctions, as between contrasting registers or tempi. Such characteristics may make music an ideal – though in no way simple – course for the investigation of CMC in other knotty settings, intractably shaped by human experience and culture.

## References

Antovic, M. (2009). Musical metaphors in Serbian and Romani children: An empirical study. *Metaphor and Symbol, 24*, 184–202.

Atkinson, A. P., Dittrich, W. H., Gemmell, A. J., and Young, A. W. (2004). Emotion perception from dynamic and static body expressions in point-light and full-light displays. *Perception, 33*, 717–746.

Ben-Artzi, E. and Marks, L. E. (1995). Visual-auditory interaction in speeded classification: Role of stimulus difference. *Perception & Psychophysics, 57*(8), 1151–1162.

Bien, N., ten Oever, S., Goebel, R., and Sack, A. T. (2012). The sound of size: crossmodal binding in pitch–size synesthesia: a combined TMS, EEG and psychophysics study. *NeuroImage, 59*, 663–672.

Boltz, M. G. (2011). Illusory tempo changes due to musical characteristics. *Music Perception, 28*, 367–386.

Boltz, M. (2013). Music videos and visual influences on music perception and appreciation: Should you want your MTV? In S. L. Tan, A. Cohen, S. Lipscomb and R. Kendall (Eds.), *The psychology of music in multimedia* (pp. 217–235). Oxford: Oxford University Press.

Bremner, A. J., Caparos, S., Davidoff, J., de Fockert, J., Linnell, K. J., and Spence, C. (2013). 'Bouba' and 'Kiki' in Namibia? A remote culture makes similar shape–sound matches, but different shape–taste matches to Westerners. *Cognition, 126*, 165–172.

Cabrera, D., Ferguson, S., Tilley, S., and Morimoto, M. (2005). Recent studies on the effect of signal frequency on auditory vertical localization. In *Proceedings of ICAD 05 – Eleventh Meeting of the International Conference on Auditory Display*, 6–9 July, Limerick, Ireland.

Casasanto, D., Phillips, W., and Boroditsky, L. (2003). Do we think about music in terms of space? Metaphoric representation of musical pitch. In R. Alterman and D. Kirsh (Eds.), *Proceedings of 25th annual conference of the Cognitive Science Society*, 31 July – 1 August, Boston, USA.

Casasanto, D., and Dijkstra, K. (2010). Motor action and emotional memory. *Cognition, 115*, 179–185.

Collier, W. G., and Hubbard, T. L. (2001). Judgments of happiness, brightness, speed and tempo change of auditory stimuli varying in pitch and tempo. *Psychomusicology, 17*, 36–55.

Connell, L., Cai, Z. G., and Holler, J. (2013). Do you see what I'm singing? Visuospatial movement biases pitch perception. *Brain and Cognition, 81*(1), 124–130.
Cooke, D. (1959). *The language of music.* Oxford: Oxford University Press.
Deutsch, D., Hamaoui, K., and Henthorn, T. (2007). The glissando illusion and handedness. *Neuropsychologica, 45*(13), 2981–2988.
Dolscheid, S., Hunnius, S., Casasanto, D., and Majid, A. (2014). Prelinguistic infants are sensitive to space–pitch associations found across cultures. *Psychological Science, 25,* 1256–1261.
Eerola, T., Friberg, A., and Bresin, R. (2013). Emotional expression in music: Contribution, linearity, and additivity of primary musical cues. *Frontiers in Psychology, 4*(487). Retrieved from https://doi.org/10.3389/fpsyg.2013.00487.
Eitan, Z. (2013). How pitch and loudness shape musical space and motion: New findings and persisting questions. In S. L. Tan, A. Cohen, S. Lipscomb and E. Kendall (Eds.), *The psychology of music in multimedia* (pp. 165–191). Oxford: Oxford University Press.
Eitan, Z. and Granot, R. Y. (2006). How music moves: Musical parameters and images of motion. *Music Perception, 23,* 221–247.
Eitan, Z., Katz, A. and Shen, Y. (2010). Effects of pitch register, loudness and tempo on children's use of metaphors for music. Poster presentation, *11th International Conference on Music Perception & Cognition (ICMPC11),* Seattle, WA.
Eitan, Z., Schupak, A., Gotler, A., and Marks, L. E. (2015). Lower pitch is larger, yet falling pitches shrink: Interaction of pitch change and size change in speeded discrimination. *Experimental Psychology, 61,* 273–284.
Eitan, Z., and Timmers, R. (2010). Beethoven's last piano sonata and those who follow crocodiles: Cross-domain mappings of auditory pitch in a musical context. *Cognition, 114,* 405–422.
Eitan, Z., Timmers, R., and Adler, M. (in press). Cross-modal correspondences in a Schubert song. In D. Leech-Wilkinson and H. Prior (Eds.), *Music and shape.* Oxford: Oxford University Press.
Eitan, Z., and Tubul, N. (2010). Musical parameters and children's images of motion. *Musica Scientiae, Special Issue 2010,* 89–111.
Evans, K. and Treisman, A. (2010). Natural cross-modal mappings between visual and auditory features. *Journal of Vision, 10,* 1–12.
Feldstein, S., and Bond, R. N. (1981). Perception of speech rate as function of vocal intensity and frequency. *Language and Speech, 24,* 387–395.
Fernández-Prieto, I., Navarra, J., and Pons, F. (2015). How big is this sound? Cross-modal association between pitch and size in infants. *Infant Behavior and Development, 38,* 77–81.
Freyd, J. J., Kelly, M. H., and DeKay, M. (1990). Representational momentum in memory for pitch. *Journal of Experimental Psychology: Learning, Memory, and Cognition, 16,* 1107–1117.
Gabrielsson, A., and Lindström, E. (2013). The role of structure in the musical expression of emotions. In P. N. Juslin and J. A. Sloboda (Eds.), *Handbook of music and emotion: Theory, research, applications* (pp. 367–400). Oxford: Oxford University Press.
Gallace, A., and Spence, C. (2006). Multisensory synesthetic interactions in the speeded classification of visual size. *Perception & Psychophysics, 68,* 1191–1203.
Godøy, R. I., and Leman, M. (Eds.) (2010). *Musical gestures: Sound, movement, and meaning.* New York: Routledge.

Granot, R. Y., and Eitan, Z. (2011). Musical tension and the interaction of dynamic auditory parameters. *Music Perception, 28,* 219–245.
Hanslick, E. (1891/1986). *On the musically beautiful* (G. Payzant, Trans. and Ed.). Indianapolis: Hackett.
Hedger, S. C., Nussbaum, H. C., Lescop, O., Wallisch, P., and Hoeckner, B. (2013). Music can elicit a visual motion aftereffect. *Attention, Perception, & Psychophysics, 75,* 1039–1047.
Hogan, A. C. (2015). *Distortions in predicted motion: Pitch and direction influence imagined speed for a visual object during occlusion.* Master's thesis, Victoria University, Wellington, New Zealand.
Hubbard, T. L., and Ruppel, S. E. (2013). A Fröhlich effect and representational gravity in memory for auditory pitch. *Journal of Experimental Psychology: Human Perception and Performance, 39,* 1153–1165.
Huron, D. (2006). *Sweet anticipation: Music and the psychology of expectation.* Cambridge, MA: MIT Press.
Johnson, M., and Larson, S. (2003). 'Something in the way she moves' – Metaphors of musical motion. *Metaphor and Symbol, 18,* 63–84.
Kaminska, Z., and Woolf, J. (2000). Melodic line and emotion: Cooke's theory revisited. *Psychology of Music, 28,* 133–153.
Kelly, M. H., and Freyd, J. J. (1987). Explorations of representational momentum. *Cognitive Psychology, 19,* 369–401.
Kim, K., and Iwamiya, S. (2008). Formal congruency between Telop patterns and sound effects. *Music Perception, 25,* 429–448.
Köhler, W. (1929). *Gestalt psychology.* New York: Liveright.
Kohn, D., and Eitan, Z. (2016). Moving music: Correspondences of musical parameters and movement dimensions in children's motion and verbal responses. *Music Perception, 34,* 40–55.
Krugliak, A., and Noppeney, U. (2015). Synesthetic interactions across vision and audition. *Neuropsychologia, 15,* 30170–30176.
Krumhansl, C. L. (1990). *Cognitive foundations of musical pitch.* New York: Oxford University Press.
Krumhansl, C. L. (2004). The cognition of tonality – as we know it today. *Journal of New Music Research, 33,* 253–268.
Krumhansl, C. L., and Kessler, E. J. (1982). Tracing the dynamic changes in perceived tonal organization in a spatial representation of musical keys. *Psychological Review, 89,* 334–368.
Küssner, M. B., Tidhar, D., Prior, H. M., and Leech-Wilkinson, D. (2014). Musicians are more consistent: Gestural cross-modal mappings of pitch, loudness and tempo in real-time. *Frontiers in Psychology, 5*(789).
Lakoff, G. and Johnson, M. (1980). *Metaphors we live by.* Chicago: University of Chicago Press.
Larson, S. (2004). Musical forces and melodic expectations: Comparing computer models and experimental results. *Music Perception, 21,* 457–498.
Larson, S., and Van Handel, L. (2005). Measuring musical forces. *Music Perception, 23,* 119–136.
Lerdahl, F. (2001). *Tonal pitch space.* New York: Oxford University Press.
Levitan, C. A., Charney, S. A., Schloss, K. B., and Palmer, S. E. (2015). The smell of jazz: Crossmodal correspondences between music, odor, and emotion. In D. C.

Noelle, R. Dale, A. S. Warlaumont, J. Yoshimi, T. Matlock, C. D. Jennings and P. P. Maglio (Eds.), *Proceedings of the 37th Annual Meeting of the Cognitive Science Society* (pp. 1326–1331). Austin, TX: Cognitive Science Society.

Ludwig, V. U., Adachi, I., and Matsuzawa, T. (2011). Visuoauditory mappings between high luminance and high pitch are shared by chimpanzees (Pan Troglodytes) and humans. *Proceedings of the National Academy of Sciences, 108*, 20661–20665.

Maimon, N. (2016). *Tonal stability and cross-modal correspondence.* Master's thesis, Tel Aviv University, Tel Aviv, Israel.

Marks, L. E. (1987). On cross-modal similarity: Auditory-visual interactions in speeded discrimination. *Journal of Experimental Psychology: Human Perception and Performance, 13*, 384–394.

Marks, L. E. (2004). Cross-modal interactions in speeded classification. In G. Calvert, C. Spence and B. E. Stein (Eds.), *Handbook of multisensory processes* (pp. 85–106). Cambridge, MA: MIT Press.

Meier, B. P., and Robinson, M. D. (2004). Why the sunny side is up: Associations between affect and vertical position. *Psychological Science, 15*, 243–247.

Meier, B. P. and Robinson, M. D. (2005). The metaphorical representation of affect. *Metaphor and Symbol, 20*, 239–257.

Melara, R. D., and O'Brien, T. P. (1987). Interaction between synesthetically corresponding dimensions. *Journal of Experimental Psychology: General, 116*(4), 323–336.

Mondloch, C., and Maurer, D. (2004). Do small white balls squeak? Pitch-object correspondences in young children. *Cognitive, Affective, & Behavioral Neuroscience, 4*, 133–136.

Morton, E. (1994). Sound symbolism and its role in non-human vertebrate communication. In L. Hinton, J. Nichols and J. Ohala (Eds.), *Sound symbolism* (pp. 348–365). Cambridge: Cambridge University Press.

Mossbridge, J. A., Grabowecky, M., and Suzuki, S. (2011). Changes in auditory frequency guide visual–spatial attention. *Cognition, 121*, 133–139.

Mudd, S. A. (1963). Spatial stereotypes of four dimensions of pure tone. *Journal of Experimental Psychology, 66*, 347–352.

Neuhoff, J. G. (1998). Perceptual bias for rising tones. *Nature, 395*, 123–124.

Osgood, C. E., Succi, G. J., and Tannenbaum, P. H. (1957). *The measurement of meaning.* Urbana, IL: University of Illinois Press.

Palmer, S. E., Schloss, K. B., Xu, Z., and Prado-León, L. R. (2013). Music–color associations are mediated by emotion. *Proceedings of the National Academy of Sciences, 110*, 8836–8841.

Parise, C. V., Knorre, K., and Ernst, M. O. (2014). Natural auditory scene statistics shapes human spatial hearing. *Proceedings of the National Academy of Sciences, 111*, 6104–6108.

Parise, C. V., and Spence, C. (2009). 'When birds of a feather flock together': Synesthetic correspondences modulate audiovisual integration in non-synesthetes. *PLoS One, 4*(e5664). Retrieved from http://dx.doi.org/10.1371/journal.pone.0005664.

Parkinson, C., Kohler, P. J., Sievers, B., and Wheatley, T. (2012). Associations between auditory pitch and visual elevation do not depend on language: Evidence from a remote population. *Perception, 41*, 854–861.

Perlman, M., Dale, R., and Lupyan, G. (2015). Iconicity can ground the creation of vocal symbols. *Royal Society open science, 2*(8), 150–152.

Pratt, C. C. (1930). The spatial character of high and low tones. *Journal of Experimental Psychology, 13,* 278–285.
Ramachandran, V. S., and Hubbard, E. M. (2001). Synesthesia – a window into perception, thought and language. *Journal of Consciousness Studies, 8*(12), 3–34.
Rameau, J.-P. (1722). *Traité de l'harmonie réduite à ses principes naturels.* Paris: Ballard.
Roffler, S. K., and Butler, R. A. (1968). Localization of tonal stimuli in the vertical plane. *Journal of the Acoustical Society of America, 43,* 1260–1265.
Rusconi, E., Kwan, B., Giordano, B. L., Umiltà, C., and Butterworth, B. (2006). Spatial representation of pitch height: The SMARC effect. *Cognition, 99,* 113–129.
Sadaghiani, S., Maier, J. X., and Noppeney, U. (2009). Natural, metaphoric, and linguistic auditory direction signals have distinct influences on visual motion processing. *The Journal of Neuroscience, 29,* 6490–6499.
Schenker, H. (1906). *Neue musikalische Theorien und Phantasien, vol. I Harmonielehre.* Stuttgart: J. G. Cotta'sche Buchhandlung Nachfolger.
Shepard, R. N. (1982). Structural representations of musical pitch. In Deutsch, D. (Ed.), *The psychology of music* (pp. 343–390). London: Academic Press.
Sievers, B., Polansky, L., Casey, M., and Wheatley, T. (2013). Music and movement share a dynamic structure that supports universal expressions of emotion. *Proceedings of the National Academy of Sciences, 110*(1), 70–75.
Spence, C. (2011). Crossmodal correspondences: A tutorial review. *Attention, Perception & Psychophysics, 73,* 971–995.
Spitzer, M. (2004). *Metaphor and musical thought.* Chicago: University of Chicago Press.
Stevens, C. J. (2012). Music perception and cognition: A review of recent cross-cultural research. *Topics in Cognitive Science, 4,* 653–667.
Stevens, S. T., and Arieh, Y. (2005). What you see is what you hear: The effect of auditory pitch on the detection of visual targets. Poster presentation, *76th annual meeting of the Eastern Psychological Society,* Boston, MA.
Stewart, L., Walsh, V., and Frith, U. (2004). Reading music modifies spatial mapping in pianists. *Perception & Psychophysics, 66,* 183–195.
Tamir-Ostrover, H., and Eitan, Z. (2015). Higher is faster: Pitch register and tempo preferences. *Music Perception, 33,* 179–198.
Timmers, R., and Crook, H. (2014). Affective priming in music listening: Emotions as a source of musical expectation. *Music Perception, 31,* 470–484.
Wagner, Y. S., Winner, E., Cicchetti, D., and Gardner, H. (1981). 'Metaphorical' mapping in human infants. *Child Development, 52,* 728–731.
Walker, B. N., and Ehrenstein, A. (2000). Pitch and pitch change interact in auditory displays. *Journal of Experimental Psychology: Applied, 6,* 15–30.
Walker, P. (2016). Cross-Sensory correspondences: A theoretical framework and their relevance to music. *Psychomusicology: Music, Mind, & Brain, 26,* 103–116.
Walker, P., Bremner, J. G., Mason, U., Spring, J., Mattock, K., Slater, A., and Johnson, S. P. (2010). Preverbal infants' sensitivity to synesthetic cross-modality correspondences. *Psychological Science, 21,* 21–25.
Walker, P. and Smith, S. (1984). Stroop interference based on the synesthetic qualities of auditory pitch. *Perception, 13,* 75–81.
Walker, L., Walker, P., and Francis, B. (2012). A common scheme for cross-sensory correspondences across stimulus domains. *Perception, 41,* 1186–1192.

Weger, U. W., Meier, B. P., Robinson, M. D., and Inhoff, A. W. (2007). Things are sounding up: Affective influences on auditory tone perception. *Psychonomic Bulletin & Review, 14*, 517–521.

Widmann, A., Kujala, T., Tervaniemi, M., Kujala, A., and Schröger, E. (2004). From symbols to sounds: visual symbolic information activates sound representations. *Psychophysiology, 41*, 709–715.

Zbikowski, L. (2008). Metaphor and music. In R. Gibbs (Ed.), *The Cambridge handbook on metaphor* (pp. 502–524). Cambridge: Cambridge University Press.

# 5 Gestural qualities in music and outward bodily responses

*Clemens Wöllner and Jesper Hohagen*

'I can feel the music moving through me everywhere'. This line, taken from the 2001 album *Sunshine* by the band S Club 7, belongs to the song with the chorus 'Don't stop movin', can you feel the music ...'. The lyrics refer to the strongly moving impact of music; the song's melody and rhythm, both in popular disco style, seem to imitate human movements and were also an immense success on dancefloors. The audiences were enthralled by the motion within the music and expressed it outwardly with their bodies.

In what ways does music move? Music can be described as a combination of sonic actions, as the sounding equivalent of intentional human behaviour. Musicians' body movements shape the sounds of the instruments they play, yet the perceived sonic actions in music may even exceed the relatively fast performance movements, especially when considering phrases or whole movements of a larger musical composition. These actions are occasionally visible in musicians' lower-level body sway (Clarke and Davidson, 1998; Ragert, Schroeder and Keller, 2013), in particular signifying patterns of tension and release, and listeners may in turn perceive the action quality present in the sounds on a larger temporal level. Based on cross-modal correspondences, a melodic or rhythmic pattern may similarly resemble human actions. All these sonic events can give rise to the experience of musical gestures, that is, sound patterns directly or indirectly related to intentional human motion (for overviews, see Gritten and King, 2011; Godøy and Leman, 2010).

In various Western traditions and, even more prominently, in musical cultures beyond (Baily, 1985; Clayton, Sager and Will, 2005), a great deal of music evokes motor impulses, hence is played for moving the body and for enhancing the experience of one's own actions when dancing. These actions are exerted in the three spatial dimensions in accordance with the temporally structured sounds of music. Apart from music-theoretical and practice-based approaches (e.g., Kurth, 1931; Truslit, 1938), bodily movements along with music have been studied in dance (e.g., Krumhansl and Schenck, 1997; Camurri, Lagerlöf and Volpe, 2003) or in musical conducting (e.g., Wöllner and Auhagen, 2008). On the other hand, gestural qualities of music without strong motor components and motor impulses are manifold and have been described extensively (Scruton, 1997; Clarke, 2001), pointing to more abstract movements that may not directly be addressed with outward bodily actions.

The central aim of this chapter is to discuss the relationship between gestural qualities in music and corresponding outward movements of listeners. Based on perception–action theories (Schütz-Bosbach and Prinz, 2007; Aglioti and Pazzaglia, 2010), it is argued that feeling the sounds in a kinaesthetic way should enhance experiences of music. These theories can be traced back to the mid-19th century, where early accounts propose a linkage between human feeling, thought and muscle potentials described as 'ideomotor' experiences (Lotze, 1852; Carpenter, 1852). Potentially inspired by these theories, in Ernst Kurth's (1931) *Musikpsychologie* [Psychology of Music], the experiential dimensions of motion and space are central: 'Movement energies [in music] also evoke spatial impressions' (p. 17). He believed that inner motion energies in music are veridical psychological experiences that have an analogy in outer, physical movements. Evidence from different areas of investigation is presented that supports a close mapping between music-inherent motion and bodily responses. In the following, we will describe gestural qualities of music and the contributions of musical imagery, highlighting early approaches to visualisations of musical gestures with overt bodily movements and motion trajectories. We present selected findings of our own study based on Truslit's (1938) concepts of motion and shapes in music. Recent evidence and current challenges are discussed, with a focus on sonifying actions that translate bodily movements into sounds.

## Gestures in music

While bodily movements clearly imply time-dependent changes in space that can be perceived and measured, definitions of motion that is perceptually located in the music itself are less straightforward. The idea of music-inherent motion has, nevertheless, attracted researchers and theorists for a long time (for an overview, see Repp, 1998). One reason for the many discourses around musical motion may depend on the fact that conversations about music often reach limits in the verbal repertoire for describing cross-modal motion qualities, so a richness of metaphors is employed. Musicians and listeners then also overcome the verbal limits of metaphors by using bodily gestures when describing a tonal sequence or other musical characteristics (Walker, 2000). Elements in the music that are hardly verbalisable can thus be conveyed by means of bodily gestures – posing a challenge for researchers to capture generalisable parameters in these experiences and to find clear and meaningful verbal descriptions.

Even a 'formalist' such as Hanslick employed metaphors from domains outside the one of music in his ambiguous and widely cited phrase: 'The content of music are forms moved by sound / are moving sound forms' (original 'Der Inhalt der Musik sind tönend bewegte Formen'; Hanslick, 1854/1891, p. 74). For that reason, Scruton (1997, pp. 341–342) claimed that Hanslick's theory would not be coherent in itself and 'shows that the formal organization of music can be understood only by the person who relates it, through a metaphorical perception, to the world of life and gesture'. When carefully re-examining the original writing of Hanslick, it becomes evident that he did not generally reject metaphors and indeed employed further metaphors for the description of music, but argued against some ideas of his time that music could express and depict concrete events and emotional states, which he described as subjective experiences. Is there, however, a common basis for such gestural experiences of music, apart from physical measurements of sound parameters?

Among the elements that signify gestures within music, pitch and timing appear to be most prominent. Musical parameters such as intensity, timbre and articulation may further shape motion qualities in music, yet the former two relate directly to the experience of spatial-temporal changes – the most basic definition of movements and gestures. In other words, timing refers to the temporal dimension of movements, whereas differences in pitch are typically attributed with spatial dimensions (Eitan, 2013, see Eitan, this volume). In the next sections, we will explore the characteristics of music-inherent gestures and potential kinaesthetic sensations when responding to these gestures. By doing so, we aim to relate musical and acoustic characteristics to the more subjective perception of individual listeners.

## *The spatiality of pitch*

In his book *On the Sensations of Tone*, Hermann von Helmholtz (1877/1895, p. 596f.) remarked 'that changes in pitch, which we often describe figuratively ... as moving to heights or depths, show clear similarities with motion in space' (authors' translation). Thus melodies are experienced as rising, falling or unfolding in various shapes, all of them potentially resembling human gestures. Composers often used melodic lines to characterise the movement of objects or humans. One of many examples can be found in Mozart's *Vesperae solennes* (see Figure 5.1), where he employs the pitch space to musically characterise what is said in the text. Pitch-based successions of tones such as scales, arpeggios and trills are experienced as whole moving objects or streams rather than a succession of single sound events (Gjerdingen, 1999). In this regard, Shove and Repp (1995) distinguish tonal motion based on

*Figure 5.1* Excerpt from Mozart's 'Laudate pueri' from *Vesperae solennes de Dominica* (K 321), in which he figuratively composed the long travel of the sun 'from sunrise to sunset', matching the Latin text of Psalm 113:3.

melody and harmony from rhythmic motion. Harmonic and melodic motion are related to the perceived tension and relaxation of dissonant chords and intervals resolving to consonant ones (cf. Kurth, 1931), a process considerably influenced by the listeners' 'dynamic expectancies' (Jones, 1982, p. 1). The rhythmic motion component, on the other hand, seems more directly related to the timing of human movement (Friberg and Sundberg, 1999).

A large body of experimental research on musical motion has been devoted to grouping and Gestalt principles, analysing 'apparent motion in music' (Gjerdingen, 1999, p. 141). One of the first researchers systematically applying visual Gestalt laws to auditory processes was Burtt (1927). In a series of experiments with two identical tuning fork sounds, played to participants from different spatial positions, he found that auditory illusions of motion depend on both the time interval and the distance of the two stimuli. Aspects of loudness also play a role, such that the sound appears to move towards the stimulus with higher intensity. Comparable to vision, these experiments suggest that two distinct simple sounds at different spatial positions can already lead to the perception of motion. Later approaches have primarily focused on pitch changes in apparent motion. Deutsch (1982) described the process of perceptual synthesis, where rapid sequences of separate tones are perceived as streams if the succession rate is at an appropriate level of about ten per second. In *Auditory Scene Analysis*, Bregman (1990) directly draws analogies between visual motion in space and auditory motion in pitch, for example the perception of up- and downward motion in melodies. He states that we employ both visual and auditory information in the unconscious combination and correction of information from the other sensory modality in 'scene analysis' (1990, pp. 181, 183). Apparent motion therefore occurs for both vision and audition. Bregman described how two tones differing in pitch (and, in contrast to Burtt, 1927, not in their spatial position), alternating at intermediate speed, yield to the impression of 'melodic jumps back and forth' (1990, p. 174). These tones then lead to the perception of apparent motion or, in Bregman's own words, 'stroboscopic' motion.

Taken together, distinct sound events in alternation or succession at an appropriate time interval may give rise to the perception of one single moving object or even of more complex musical gestures. These processes are based on auditory grouping such that a series of separate tones is perceived as a coherent auditory stream (Shepard, 1999). Apparent motion experiences require relatively small time intervals, and are considered as fundamental, low-level perceptual phenomena rather than higher-order cognitive processes. It remains a question for cross-cultural research to disentangle the extent to which the spatial characteristics of pitch changes are indeed based on fundamental and innate cross-modal Gestalts or acquired culturally.

### *Temporal dimensions*

Apart from spatial characteristics, gestures are defined by timing components. Motion parameters such as velocity, acceleration and jerk are fundamentally based on temporal units (e.g., measured in meters per second), signifying an object's change in position. Music has been described as an act of temporal change (de la Motte-Haber, 2000), while listening to music resembles a perception of change but not time *per se*, underlining the multi-dimensionality of musical motion and gestures. Time itself, on the other hand, 'passes by', hence is often perceived and described in motion qualities. David Epstein (1995, p. 10) describes the experiential dimension of 'integral time', which is central to experiences of motion and life, but may also give rise to individual differences in perceptions of duration. Since time cannot be perceived directly by any of our five senses, as already observed by Augustine (see Eibl, 1923), non-temporal dimensions and metaphors are needed for describing experiences of time (see also Fahlenbrach, this volume).

Timing is crucial for musical interpretations and has attracted much research in music-psychological and historical approaches to interpretations. On a macro-level, the chosen tempo is often key to a successful performance, while on a micro-level, the music's groove may to some extent depend on small timing deviations from metronomic exactitude (Witek, Clarke, Wallentin, Kringelbach and Vuust, 2014). Musical rhythm, metre, melodies and progressions of harmony all depend on time. Furthermore, music is shaped by periodicities and synchronisation processes that are also present in human locomotion, providing additional evidence for the role of timing in musical motion perceptions, or, as David Epstein (1995, p. 5) put it: 'The essence of temporal experience is movement, or motion, through time. Motion may thus be the quintessential factor in music'.

The composer B.A. Zimmermann (1974, p. 14) stated that music regulates temporal experiences by means of structured movements, leading to 'a process of inner experiences of structured time' (authors' translation). Thus motion elements in music may shape musical experiences of time (cf. Fraisse, 1974; Kurth, 1931). Other composers deliberately 'stretched' musical time by founding whole musical works on relatively short melodic or harmonic ideas. For instance, Stockhausen's grand seven-day opera circle *Licht* [Light] was constructed by expanding three interwoven melodic lines, the 'super formula', which in the original does not even span a whole page. Other composers employed similar techniques, so that the deeper underlying structure corresponds with the music perceived at the surface level.

Given the hierarchical organisation of music with its different layers of time – from large forms comprising the movements of a whole symphony to smaller structures in single phrases, up to the so-called surface structure on a note-to-note level – music offers a whole range of temporal levels in which motion can be perceived. In other words, musical time of one and the same piece may be experienced quite differently according to which layer one refers to, and time is undoubtedly experienced as moving more slowly if one focuses on larger structures. Previous research showed that listeners perceive higher metrical levels in the music they know well (Repp, 1998), and musicians synchronise themselves with higher levels as compared to nonmusicians in experimental tapping studies (Snyder and Krumhansl, 2001; Drake, Penel and Bigand, 2000).

Music may thus enable the perception of different layers of time and motion, and, when focusing on the lower layers, particularly slow motion. These different layers should also influence the experience of gestural qualities in music, which are typically not based on the surface note-to-note level. As will be shown below, attempts to 'gesturalise' music in terms of armchair conducting do not necessarily correspond with the timing of actual performance or conducting movements.

## Kinaesthetic imagery

Are there direct links between music-inherent motion and 'feeling the music' in the body as suggested earlier in the S Club 7 song? Perceiving gestural qualities in music may resonate with the listener's motor system, since certain sounds clearly signify human actions (Aglioti and Pazzaglia, 2010). Perception–action theories (Schütz-Bosbach and Prinz, 2007) highlight that presentations of motor actions and corresponding perceptions share the same codes. This overlap is independent from modality; thus perceiving motor actions is not limited to visual sensory input, and activations in motor areas can also be triggered by auditory information (Sevdalis and Keller, 2014). In other words, sounds that resemble or signify the spatial-temporal qualities of a gesture may activate representations of physical gestures, and music may stimulate motion images. Embodied cognition approaches state that listeners do indeed perceive music as mediated by their full bodies, in multimodal terms rather than as auditory-only sound events (cf. Leman and Maes, 2014). From this perspective, sonic actions are experienced in their full behavioural consequences – thus not only resembling bodily actions but directly resonating in the listeners' motor systems.

These activations are particularly strong when watching dancers, which offers visual information about the movements in addition to the sounds of the music or the dancers' bodies. Researchers recently suggested that a great deal of the fascination with dance lies in the fact that audiences empathise with the dancers and internally co-experience their movements (Calvo-Merino, Jola, Glaser and Haggard, 2008). Rudolf von Laban's (1950/1980) 'Kinetography', a notational system for capturing human movements in dance and beyond, requires the observers to feel kinaesthetically into the movements performed by others. Basic dimensions such as movement duration, movement direction and dynamic quality can thus be described in their expressive aesthetic meaning. *Laban Movement Analysis*, based on the fundamental descriptions of 'efforts' (i.e., dynamic and energetic qualities required by the body for movements in space) and 'shapes' (i.e., bodily postures and shapes in spatial dimensions) combines kinaesthetic mirroring and visual observation methods (Bartenieff and Lewis, 1980/2002), thus offering both insights into the performer's experiences as well as into potential effects on the audience. Undoubtedly these processes are also present in music as a motional art: Even when not moving along with the music overtly, listeners may imagine the movements kinaesthetically. *Laban Movement Analysis* has recently been applied to studying music performance (Broughton and Stevens, 2012), and to investigating the expressive qualities and the meaning in music as experienced by listeners moving freely to pre-recorded music (Maes, van Dyck, Lesaffre, Leman and Kroonenberg, 2014).

While research on music listeners' kinaesthetic imagery is scarce, there are a number of studies on musicians' imagery of actions. Evidence suggests that musicians recognise specific performance movements as veridical gestures when listening to sound sequences (Sundberg, 2000). Musicians further need to anticipate the sound qualities in their imagery when practising mentally (Highben and Palmer, 2004), when playing alone (Bishop, Bailes and Dean, 2013) or in an ensemble with others (Keller and Appel, 2010; Keller, 2012). Kinaesthetic imagery helps them to attain certain musical goals in terms of sound quality and to coordinate their play with those of other musicians.

Research on musical imagery has often employed methods in which selected sensory feedback modalities were deprived, to investigate their relative importance in the performance process. If musicians possess vivid imagery, according to the rationale of these methods, they should depend less on a given feedback modality. Studies indicate that kinaesthetic feedback is typically more important than auditory feedback for musicians. In particular, playing the piano without sound is more accurate in terms of timing than hearing or imagining the sound without having the fingers move on the piano keys (Highben and Palmer, 2004). In a study on imagery and mental practice (Wöllner and Williamon, 2007), pianists indicated that they employed equal amounts of kinaesthetic, visual, auditory and conceptual memory (the latter referring to the musical structure). These distributions of different memorisation modalities mirror the advice of experienced performers and educators to use a variety of approaches in learning, imagery and mental practice (Leimer and Gieseking, 1931/1998; Lehmann and Ericsson, 1998). Yet in the behavioural findings of the study (Wöllner and Williamon, 2007) the kinaesthetic component was most stable, and utterly imagined performances without kinaesthetic feedback deviated most from a normal performance that included all feedback modalities. Thus pianists had memorised the music to a great deal 'with their fingers' by means of motor imagery.

An even greater challenge for musicians is to imagine the sonic actions of others, while at the same time performing themselves, thus integrating self- and other-imagined actions as well as own auditory-motor and other auditory feedback. Keller and Appel (2010) investigated the relation between anticipatory imagery and ensemble synchronisation. Seven pairs of pianists performed duets of the classical piano literature together on MIDI instruments, either seeing or not seeing each other. Their bodily motion was recorded with an optical motion capture system. In a second session, pianists' anticipatory auditory imagery was tested with a tapping paradigm with or without auditory feedback. As a result, anticipatory imagery skills were correlated with average duo synchrony, suggesting that those pianists with good imagery were more successful in timing their ensemble play. While being in visual contact did not markedly affect results, lags in anterior-posterior body sway between duo partners was related to synchrony, indicating that the pianists also timed their performances via body motion. Alternatively, their body motion may have functioned as individual time-keeping support.

While these results cannot directly be applied to listeners, they nevertheless point to the importance of kinaesthetic components in musical imagery. Findings highlighting the robustness of imagined in relation to perceived tempi (see, e.g., Halpern, 1987) could potentially be explained by the kinaesthetic dimension in imagined body movements. It can therefore be assumed that music, comparable to dance, is to some extent experienced kinaesthetically, giving rise to the sensations of felt motion. In the following, we describe in what ways these inner experiences of motion are expressed as bodily actions.

**Bodily responses**

What are the characteristics of the bodily actions performed along with music in listening situations? Do they share structural or expressive characteristics with music-inherent motion? In the sections above, we stated that music possesses a variety of gestural qualities, some of them related to the human movements that shape the sounds of musical instruments. The performance of music indeed provides insights into the close relationship between music and movement (Shove and Repp, 1995). Clarke and Davidson (1998) identified specific head movements as expressive gestures in a pianist's performance of a Chopin Prelude; these movements could be related to structural features of the music and were consistent across a repeated performance. It would be interesting to investigate whether audience members, either based on visually observing the pianist (or other musicians) or based on the music's gestural quality, would show similar movement patterns. Listeners are generally aware of the meaning of the performer's expressive body movements (Davidson, 1995; Behne and Wöllner, 2011). Based on perception–action accounts, it can be argued that music activates close connections between auditory, visual and motor modalities in performance, imagination and perception (see above; Leman and Maes, 2014). Mappings between judgements of musical and bodily motion provide evidence in this regard; for example Friberg and Sundberg (1999) found that the aesthetic quality of final ritardandos in musical performances was related to the temporal structure in the footsteps of running dancers who came to a standstill.

Research on musical rhythm emphasises the relationship between timing features of the music and perceived motion or bodily movement (Fraisse,

1974; Clarke, 1999). A rigid rhythm may only cause foot tapping, as Shove and Repp (1995) propose, whereas movements of the whole body may depend more on the 'expressively modulated structure' (p. 78) of the music. Responses to various controlled stimuli or valid musical examples were studied in research that asked listeners to tap to music or to simple beats (for a review, see Repp and Su, 2013). Research involving motion capture (Burger, 2013; Maes et al., 2014) provided further insight into bodily responses to music. Burger and colleagues found that a prominent beat in a low-frequency range, perceived as a clear pulse, encourages listeners to dance more on the spot, thus reflecting both the influence of musical characteristics and, supposedly, the impact of listeners' expectations with certain musical styles.

Given these relationships between music and bodily motion, researches have examined whether there is an underlying physiological basis. Todd (1999) argued for an internal sense of self-motion in listeners that is induced by expressive sounds, and suggested that sensory-motor interactions and the 'acoustic sensitivity of the vestibular system' (1999, p. 118) are the force for overt movements to music. The responsiveness of the vestibular system to high-intensity low-frequency sounds was examined by Todd and Cody (2000). In this study, all ten participants showed significant neck muscle responses that were elicited by the vestibular system rather than the cochlear. There is, however, an intensity threshold for acoustical excitations of the vestibular system, which limits such automatic responses only to high-intensity stimuli of ca. 90 dB and more.

The association of music with dance is commonplace in many writings about music since the classical antique; people are used to, and enjoy, moving their bodies to music. Baily (1985, pp. 237–239) observed that 'body movement is a prominent feature in the performance of many kinds of music in Africa' and that music should not only be considered as a pure sound phenomenon but rather as a 'sonic product of action', that is, of human movements. In some cultures the performance movements when making music are perceived to be pleasurable and seem even more important than the actual sounds resulting from the movements (Cook, 1990, pp. 5–7). Apart from culture-specific research, further insight was gained from studies with infants and young children, who already show specific bodily movement patterns to music (Zentner and Eerola, 2010). Tafuri, Hawkins and Welch (2009) observed various bodily movements related to structural features of the music in seven- and eight-year-old children, and conclude that the children are capable of identifying and, through kinetic patterns, expressing different musical concepts such as duration, intensity, rhythm, intervals and cadences. These findings support various approaches of combining formal music education with rhythmic movement, as put forward by Dalcroze (see Walker, 2000). Furthermore, given the close connection between music and bodily movement, applications for the therapeutic context were developed, especially for increased body control and body awareness through music-making, dancing and free moving to music (e.g., Ockelford, 1998; for an overview, see Leins, Spintge and Thaut, 2009).

To sum up, activations of action representations when perceiving music may account for the universal association of music with dance and other movements. Bodily movements are central for the performance of music, and expressive movement patterns are in turn experienced and interpreted by listeners in an embodied way. The behavioural component involved in bodily responses is directly observable, in contrast to the different kinds of more abstract gestures that appear to be located in the music itself. There is, however, no general agreement as to whether music or specific features of the music elicit bodily movement such as 'rhythm as the source of, or motivation for, movement' (Clarke, 1999, p. 495), or whether music merely 'serves as background to the movement' and the 'physical activity [dance or physical work] is not addressed toward ... the music' itself (Krumhansl and Schenk, 1997, p. 336). In the following section, we present selected findings of a study addressing the relationship between musical gestures and bodily responses.

### *Sound and bodily motion: an empirical approach to Truslit (1938)*

Besides the abovementioned bodily responses to music in dance, there are still open questions concerning the fundamental links between movement parameters and musical characteristics. How do we intuitively express musical sounds with gestures, and what sounds may match body movements best? Alexander Truslit (1938) offered a theory of Gestalt and movement that highlights the gestural quality of musical interpretations. More specifically, he hypothesised that musicians and performers need to learn certain regularities in order to understand musical characteristics such as dynamics and agogics; in other words, to adapt the musical shape and transform it into appropriate body movements. Truslit presented movement graphs for a selection of musical pieces, assuming that these motion trajectories would be valid on an intersubjective level.

Since Repp's (1993) synopsis of these early ideas, researchers have increasingly developed methods and paradigms to study listeners' responses to music-inherent gestures. Maes et al. (2014, p. 71) asked individuals to 'translate your experience of the music into free full-body movement' by dancing along with the music. As a result, these dance movements were linked to verbal descriptions of musical expressiveness, independent from the musical background of the participants. The verbal attributions used in this study were based on *Laban Movement Analysis* (von Laban, 1950/1980) that nowadays can be complemented by 3D motion capture and kinematic movement analysis. A different approach to musical gestures was taken by Godøy, Haga and Jensenius (2006), who asked musicians and nonmusicians to play 'air-piano' while listening to sound recordings. Even without the physical impact of the instruments, gestures revealed some resemblance to the actual sound-producing movements of pianists, especially regarding the spatial position of the piano keys and the temporal information of the note onsets.

In an empirical study, we investigated Truslit's (1938) musical gestures by comparing listeners' free movements to the original sound examples with movements of the same listeners after a visual presentation of the Truslit motion curves and detailed verbal instructions (Hohagen and Wöllner, 2015). We recorded the participants' movements with an optical 3D motion capture system and analysed motion parameters in terms of velocity, acceleration, jerk and accumulated distance travelled.

Musically trained and untrained, right-handed participants put a single reflecting marker on the index finger of their right hand. First, excerpts of three selected Truslit (1938) pieces ('Celeste Aida' by Verdi, 'Gebet der Elisabeth' [Elisabeth's Prayer] from Wagner's *Tannhäuser*, 'Mondnacht' by Schumann; all 22 s long) were presented. Participants were asked to intuitively follow the melody of the music with their right arm using the three-dimensional space in front of them. In a second step, a further 7 s original Truslit piece ('broken chord in C major, staccato, bassoon') was played. While listening to the broken chord, an original figure from Truslit (1938, p. 93, see Figure 5.2, left) showing a prototypical movement trajectory was presented on a screen. Participants were instructed to follow their arm along with the music in the way they had seen on the screen. Third, after this instruction, the procedure of the first block was repeated.

We ran a two-factor (before-after instruction * musical pieces) repeated-measures analysis, comparing measures of movement parameters across the different conditions. While there were large differences in movements regarding the musical pieces, movement trajectories before and after the instruction (i.e., Blocks 1 and 3) within participants did not result in major differences. Findings revealed large differences between participants in the movement trajectories, yet showed a relatively high individual consistency of movements across trials in the repeated-measures condition. Thus for the free arm movements, individual factors of the participants were stronger in their impact on motion parameters than one might have expected in

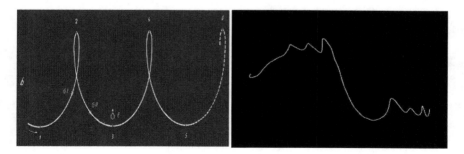

*Figure 5.2* A movement graph from Truslit as presented to participants in the instruction condition (broken chord; left figure); and a movement response from a participant to Wagner's 'Elisabeth's Prayer' from *Tannhäuser* (right figure).

comparison to the effects of the music. None of the participants had previously been familiar with Truslit's shapes, which may explain the great variety of motion responses.

### *'Elisabeth's Prayer': a short case analysis of sound and averaged motion*

While our first approach to Truslit revealed that there are large individual differences in the way people move to the musical excerpts (cf. Küssner and Caramiaux, 2015) and, perhaps not surprisingly, the prototypical graphs as suggested by Truslit were not approximated in most cases, we further analysed musical and acoustical characteristics in relation to global features of participants' gestures. Figure 5.3 presents the vocal part of an excerpt from a Wagner opera with two rising intervals and subsequently falling melodic lines. In the original recording accompanying Truslit's publication, the singer interprets these rising intervals with crescendi towards bars 2, 5 and 6, as can be seen in the oscillogram.

In order to evaluate whether the listeners' overall motion features were related to the musical interpretation, we averaged the movements of the participants in their three-dimensional positions. Cross-correlational analyses, based on smoothed values (one per second) showed highest correlations between vertical movements and musical parameters at the same time without latencies, indicating that participants to some extent anticipated the melodic progression. Pearson correlations revealed that participants raised their arms in relation to intensity ($r = .79$, $p < .001$) and spectral flux (i.e., the rapidity of changes in the spectrum, $r = .44$, $p < .05$). No such correlations were found for the other two spatial dimensions (lateral, sagittal). It should be noted that tempo was negatively related to vertical position data ($r = -.43$, $p < .05$), and changes in intensity (crescendi) in this example were related to stretched timing. Participants thus did not simply follow the rise and fall of the melodic line or fluctuations in the tempo, but rather used a combination of the various musical parameters in their gestural response to the music, with the vertical dimension being the most important spatial dimension.

### *Sonification of gestures and self-recognition*

While participants' movements were relatively consistent across conditions, we wanted to know whether they are also recognisable to them. If so, their action systems would resonate more strongly with own-produced gestures (Wöllner, 2012; cf. Sevdalis and Keller, 2014). We asked the same participants again in a further study to judge presentations of their own movements in comparison to those of others. To this end, we employed visual point-light displays of the movements, synthesiser-based movement sonifications and non-dynamic movement trajectory graphs, such as those of Truslit, in a multimodal self–other judgement paradigm. Based

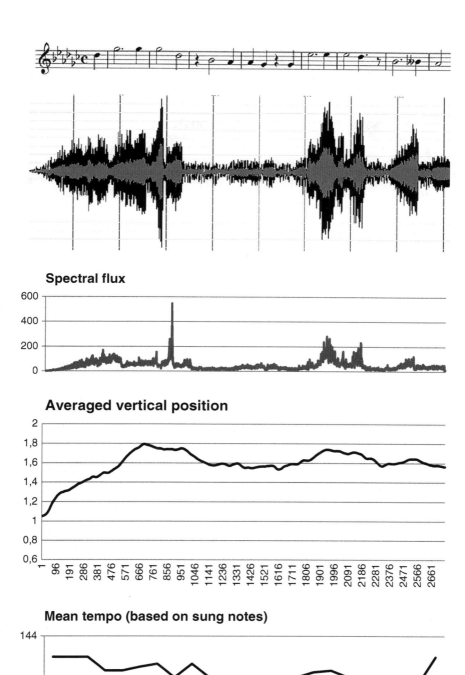

*Figure 5.3* The melodic line of the music, amplitude, spectral flux, averaged vertical position of participants' fingers while performing the movements and mean tempo. The musical notation provides an approximation and is not aligned to the acoustical and kinematic values.

on perception–action accounts, the movement sonifications should signify characteristics of participants' gestures. By indicating whether the visual or auditory movement elements had been performed by themselves or by another person, we aimed to find out whether they would kinaesthetically experience their own movements more strongly and recognise them accordingly, compared to movements of others.

Sonifications of the gestures were created. Up to now, human movement sonification was mainly applied in artistic performances (e.g., Renault, Charbonnier and Chagué, 2014) or sport and rehabilitation science (e.g., Effenberg et al., 2011; Schaffert, 2011). For the sonification of the movement data, we applied the continuous parameter-mapping method (Grond and Berger, 2011), matching the trajectory data from the index finger movements with a continuous synthesiser. More specifically, we matched the marker movement information of the y-axis with pitch, and the information of the x-axis with stereo panning. The aim of this parameter mapping was to make the matching system of movement and sound as easy as possible to understand for the participants, allowing them to respond intuitively in the self–other identification task.

Results indicated that participants were generally successful in distinguishing between their own and other individuals' movements as presented visually, but less so when evaluating the sonified movements. A reason for this result could lie in the high variance in participants' ability to transfer the information from their own movements into sounds as realised by the sonification. It might well be that this link between own movements and (artificial) sounds needs to be learned in real-time conditions and does not work for all participants in retrospective judgements.

In what ways are the findings informative regarding potential links between movement parameters and musical characteristics? Results of the second study indicated that it was difficult to comprehend the movement sonification and recognise one's own movements on the basis of sounds. Further research on sonification needs to clarify which sound characteristics are mapped with individuals' movements and subsequent kinaesthetic movement imagery in retrospective listening. These approaches would bring us a step further also in terms of aesthetical judgements of sonifications and emotional responses (cf. Vickers et al., this volume).

## Conclusions

In this chapter we addressed potential relationships between motion within music – experienced as rhythmic, melodic or harmonic motion with gestural qualities – and outer bodily responses that can be observed in listeners moving along with music. We presented evidence for fundamental psychological links between pitch and the perception of spatial change, as well as musical timing being related to temporal perceptions. As spatiotemporal changes constitute the basic characteristics of movement, music has been described as a motional art par excellence. Nevertheless, the way listeners move to music may not simply reflect these spatiotemporal characteristics, and music may express a great amount of further dynamic changes.

The most direct match between music and bodily movements lies in the kinaesthetic feeling in performance movements. Musicians internally feel the music that is played, but even nonmusicians may re-experience some of the physical energy that the musicians radiated when producing the sounds (cf. Godøy, 2010). Since sounds can signify human actions, any such associations become evident. In our own study, however, the sonification of movements did not resonate with the listeners' motor systems. The two-dimensional parameter-mapping approach may have required some online training before these motion–sound relations would have been learned and automatised. Studies of playing 'air instruments' (Godøy et al., 2006) discuss such intuitive links in the other direction: individuals can easily mimic musical performance movements while listening to the sounds of the music. The mimicry is informed either by the participants' own musical competencies or by their familiarity with the performance style, that is by having observed the play of (other) musicians.

Familiarity with the music may thus strengthen the relationship between sound and bodily movement as well as the recognition of musical gestures. Yet research on musical motion often does not take into account differences in musical preferences, the variety of listening styles or the listening situation. Generalisations across listeners seem only appropriate for basic perceptual phenomena such as pitch–space relationships (Eitan and Granot, 2006), but are clearly not evident for the ways listeners move their bodies to different types of music, which are undoubtedly influenced by the social environment or cultural traditions. In this regard, Simon Frith (1996) states:

> The relationship of 'listening' to music and 'moving' to music, is, in short, a matter of convention, as is what sort of movement to make; even a spontaneous response has to be coded as 'spontaneous' ... how free are we to move, how do we know what movement is appropriate? ... When dancing we subject our body movements to musical rules ... Movement to music seems more willed than movement without it; more thought is going into it. (p. 210)

Albeit bodily motion with music may also be 'unwilled' and is certainly not entirely determined by culture, especially for overlearned movements, it is a task for future research to investigate the musical rules that are mentioned in this quote. The answer to the questions above may lie at the heart of why music indeed moves us. While rhythmic, harmonic and melodic musical characteristics are to some extent interrelated in the perception of music, little is known, for instance, whether a relative dominance of one of these musical features leads to differences in the perception of inherent musical motion or performed bodily movements when listening to music (cf. Kurth, 1931). New technology both for the recording of body movements and for real-time sonification of motion offers novel approaches to investigate the relationships between musical gestures and bodily actions.

## References

Aglioti, S. M., and Pazzaglia, M. (2010). Representing actions through their sound. *Experimental Brain Research, 206,* 141–151.

Baily, J. (1985). Music structure and human movement. In P. Howell, I. Cross and R. West (Eds.), *Musical structure and cognition* (pp. 237–258). London: Academic Press.

Bartenieff, I., and Lewis, D. (1980/2002). *Body movement: Coping with the environment.* New York: Routledge.

Behne, K.-E., and Wöllner, C. (2011). Seeing or hearing the pianists? A synopsis of an early audiovisual perception experiment and a replication. *Musicae Scientiae, 15*(3), 324–342.

Bishop, L., Bailes, F., and Dean, R.T. (2013). Musical imagery and the planning of dynamics and articulation during performance. *Music Perception, 31,* 97–117.

Bregman, A. S. (1990). *Auditory scene analysis: the perceptual organization of sound.* Cambridge, MA: MIT Press.

Broughton, M. C., and Stevens, C. J. (2012). Analyzing expressive qualities in movement and stillness: Effort-shape analyses of solo marimbists' bodily expression. *Music Perception, 29,* 339–357.

Burger, B. (2013). *Move the way you feel: Effects of musical features, perceived emotions, and personality on music-induced movement.* PhD thesis, Department of Music, University of Jyväskylä, Finland.

Burtt, H.E. (1927). Auditory illusions of movement – a preliminary study. *Journal of Experimental Psychology, 2,* 63–75.

Calvo-Merino, B., Jola, C., Glaser, D. E., and Haggard, P. (2008). Towards a sensorimotor aesthetics of performing art. *Consciousness and Cognition, 17,* 911–922.

Camurri, A., Lagerlöf, I., and Volpe, G. (2003). Recognizing emotion from dance movement: Comparison of spectator recognition and automated techniques. *International Journal of Human-Computer Studies, 59,* 213–225.

Carpenter, W.B. (1852). On the influence of suggestion in modifying and directing muscular movement, independently of volition. *Proceedings of the Royal Institution of Great Britain, March 1852,* 147–153.

Clarke, E. F. (1999). Rhythm and timing in music. In D. Deutsch (Ed.), *The psychology of music* (2nd ed.) (pp. 473–500). New York: Academic Press.

Clarke, E. F. (2001). Meaning and the specification of motion in music. *Musicae Scientiae, 5,* 213–234.

Clarke, E. F., and Davidson, J. W. (1998). The body in performance. In W. Thomas (Ed.), *Composition–performance–reception.* Aldershot: Ashgate.

Clayton, M., Sager, R., and Will, U (2005). In time with the music: the concept of entrainment and its significance for ethnomusicology. *European Meetings in Ethnomusicology, 11,* 3–142.

Cook, N. (1990). *Music in imagination and culture.* New York: Oxford University Press.

Davidson, J. W. (1995). What does the visual information contained in music performances offer the observer? Some preliminary thoughts. In R. Steinberg (Ed.),

Music and the mind machine: The psychophysiology and psychopathology of the sense of music (pp. 105–113). Berlin: Springer.
de la Motte-Haber, H. (2000). Raum-Zeit als musikalische Dimension [Space-time as a musical dimension]. In T. Böhme and K. Mehner (Eds.), *Zeit und Raum in Musik und Bildender Kunst* (S. 31–38). Köln: Böhlau.
Deutsch, D. (1982). Grouping mechanisms in music. In D. Deutsch (Ed.), *The psychology of music* (pp. 99–134). New York: Academic Press.
Drake, C., Penel, A., and Bigand, E. (2000). Tapping in time with mechanically and expressively performed music. *Music Perception, 18*(1), 1–23.
Effenberg, A. O., Fehse, U., and Weber, A. (2011). Movement sonification: audiovisual benefits on motor learning. In B. G. Bardy, J. Lagarde and D. Mottet (Eds.), *BIO Web of Conferences. The International Conference SKILLS* (pp. 1–5). London: EDP Sciences.
Eibl, H. (1923). *Augustin und die Patristik.* [Augustinus and the patristics]. Munich: Ernst Reinhardt.
Eitan, Z. (2013). How pitch and loudness shape musical space and motion. In S.-L. Tan, A. J. Cohen, S. D. Lipscomp and R. A. Kendall (Eds.), *The psychology of music in multimedia* (pp. 165–191). Oxford: Oxford University Press.
Eitan, Z., and Granot, R.Y. (2006). How music moves: Musical parameters and images of motion. *Music Perception, 23*, 221–247.
Epstein, D. (1995). *Shaping time: Music, the brain, and performance.* New York: Schirmer.
Fraisse, P. (1974). *Psychologie du rythme.* Paris: Presses universitaires de France.
Friberg, A., and Sundberg, J. (1999). Does music performance allude to locomotion? A model of final ritardandi derived from measurements of stopping runners. *Journal of the Acoustical Society of America, 105*, 1469–1484.
Frith, S. (1996). *Performing rites. On the value of popular music.* Cambridge, MA: Harvard University Press.
Gjerdingen, R. O. (1999). Apparent motion in music. In N. Griffith and P. M. Todd (Eds.), *Musical networks. Parallel distributed perception and performance* (pp. 141–173). Cambridge, MA: MIT Press.
Godøy, R. (2010). Gestural affordances of musical sound. In R. Godøy and M. Leman (Eds.), *Musical gestures: Sound, movement, and meaning* (pp. 103–125). New York: Routledge.
Godøy, R. I., Haga, E., and Jensenius, A. R. (2006). Playing 'air instruments': Mimicry of sound-producing gestures by novices and experts. In S. Gibet, N. Courty and J.-F. Kamp (Eds.), *Gesture in human-computer interaction and simulation: 6th international gesture workshop* (pp. 256–267). Berlin: Springer.
Godøy, R. I., and Leman, M. (Eds.) (2010). *Musical gestures: sound, movement, and meaning.* New York: Routledge.
Gritten, A., and King, E. (Eds.) (2011). *New perspectives on music and gesture.* Aldershot: Ashgate.
Grond, F., and Berger, J. (2011). Parameter mapping sonification. In T. Hermann, A. Hunt, and J. G. Neuhoff (Eds.), *The sonification handbook* (pp. 363–398). Berlin: Logos.
Halpern, A. R. (1987). Perceived and imagined tempos of familiar songs. *Music Perception, 6*, 193–202.
Hanslick, E. (1854/1891). *Vom Musikalisch-Schönen. Ein Beitrag zur Revision der Ästhetik der Tonkunst* [On musical beauty]. Leipzig: Weigel.

Highben, Z., and Palmer, C. (2004). Effects of auditory and motor mental practice in memorized piano performance. *Bulletin of the Council for Research in Music Education, 159*, 58–65.

Hohagen, J. and Wöllner, C. (2015). Self–other judgements of sonified movements: Investigating Truslit's musical gestures. In *Proceedings of the Ninth Triennial Conference of the European Society for the Cognitive Sciences of Music*, 17–22 August 2015, Royal Northern College of Music, Manchester.

Jones, M. R. (1982). Music as a stimulus for psychological motion: part II. An expectancy model. *Psychomusicology, 2*, 1–13.

Keller, P. E. (2012). Mental imagery in music performance: Underlying mechanisms and potential benefits. *Annals of the New York Academy of Sciences, 1252*, 206–213.

Keller, P. E., and Appel, M. (2010). Individual differences, auditory imagery, and the coordination of body movements and sounds in musical ensembles. *Music Perception, 28*(1), 27–46.

Krumhansl, C. L., and Schenck, D. L. (1997). Can dance reflect the structural and expressive qualities of music? A perceptual experiment on Balanchine's choreography of Mozart's Divertimento No. 15. *Musicae Scientiae, 1*, 63–85.

Kurth, E. (1931). *Musikpsychologie* [Psychology of Music]. Berlin: Max Hesse.

Küssner, M. B. and Caramiaux, B. (2015). Motor invariants in gestural responses to music. In: R. Timmers, N. Dibben, Z. Eitan, R. Granot, T. Metcalfe, A. Schiavio and V. Williamson (Eds.), *Proceedings of the International Conference on the Multimodal Experience of Music*. Sheffield: HRI Online Publications. Retrieved from https://www.hrionline.ac.uk/openbook/chapter/ICMEM2015-Kussner.

Lehmann, A. C., and Ericsson, K. A. (1998). Preparation of a public piano performance: The relation between practice and performance. *Musicae Scientiae, 2*, 67–94.

Leimer, K., and Gieseking, W. (1931/1998). *Modernes Klavierspiel* [Modern Pianoplaying] (27th ed.). Mainz: Schott.

Leins, A. K., Spintge, R. and Thaut, M. (2009). Music therapy in medical and neurological rehabilitation settings. In S. Hallam, I. Cross and M. Thaut (Eds.), *The Oxford handbook of music psychology* (pp. 526–535). New York: Oxford University Press.

Leman, M., and Maes, P.-J. (2014). Music perception and embodied music cognition. In L. Shapiro (Ed.), *The Routledge handbook of embodied cognition* (pp. 81–89). New York: Routledge.

Lotze, R. H. (1852). *Medizinische Psychologie oder Physiologie der Seele* [Medical psychology or physiology of the soul]. Leipzig: Weidmannsche Buchhandlung.

Maes, P.-J., van Dyck, E., Lesaffre, M., Leman, M., and Kroonenberg, P. M. (2014). The coupling of action and perception in musical meaning formation. *Music Perception, 32*(1), 67–84.

Ockelford, A. (1998). *Music moves: Music in the education of children and young people who are visually impaired and have learning disabilities*. London: Royal National Institute for the Blind.

Ragert, M., Schroeder, T., and Keller, P. E. (2013). Knowing too little or too much: The effects of familiarity with a co-performer's part on interpersonal coordination in musical ensembles. *Frontiers in Psychology, 4*(368).

Renault, A., Charbonnier, C., and Chagué, S. (2014). 3dinmotion – a mocap based interface for real time visualisation and sonification of multi-user interactions. In *NIME International Conferences on New Interfaces for Musical Expression* (pp. 495–496).

Repp, B. H. (1993). Music as motion: A synopsis of Alexander Truslit's (1938) Gestaltung and Bewegung in der Musik. *Psychology of Music, 21*, 48–72.
Repp, B. H. (1998). Musical motion in perception and performance. In D. A. Rosenbaum and C. E. Collyer (Eds.), *Timing of behavior: Neural, psychological, and computational perspectives* (pp. 125–144). Cambridge, MA: MIT Press.
Repp, B. H., and Su, Y.-H. (2013). Sensorimotor synchronization: A review of recent research (2006–2012). *Psychonomic Bulletin and Review, 20*, 403–452.
Schaffert, N. (2011). *Sonifikation des Bootsbeschleunigungs-Zeit-Verlaufs als akustisches Feedback im Rennrudern* [Sonification of the boat acceleration time process as an acoustical feedback in rowing]. Berlin: Logos.
Schütz-Bosbach, S., and Prinz, W. (2007). Perceptual resonance: Action-induced modulation of perception. *Trends in Cognitive Sciences, 11*, 349–355.
Scruton, R. (1997). *The aesthetics of music.* Oxford: Oxford University Press.
Sevdalis, V., and Keller, P. E. (2014). Know thy sound: Perceiving self and others in musical contexts. *Acta Psychologica, 152*, 67–74.
Shepard, R. (1999). Stream segregation and ambiguity in audition. In P. R. Cook and R. Perry (Eds.), *Music, cognition, and computerized sound: An introduction to psychoacoustics* (pp. 117–127). Cambridge, MA: MIT Press.
Shove, P., and Repp, B. H. (1995). Musical motion and performance. In J. Rink (Ed.), *The practice in performance. Studies in musical interpretation* (pp. 55–83). Cambridge: Cambridge University Press.
Snyder, J., and Krumhansl, C.L. (2001). Tapping to ragtime: Cues to pulse finding. *Music Perception, 18*(4), 455–489.
Sundberg, J. (2000). Four years of research on music and motion. *Journal of New Music Research, 3*(29), 183–186.
Tafuri, J., Hawkins, E., and Welch, G. (2009). *Infant musicality. New research for educators and parents.* London: Routledge.
Todd, N. P. M. (1999). Motion in music: A neurobiological perspective. *Music Perception, 19*(1), 115–126.
Todd, N. P. McA. and Cody, F. W. (2000). Vestibular responses to loud dance music: A physiological basis of the 'rock and roll threshold'? *Journal of the Acoustical Society of America, 107*, 496–500.
Truslit, A. (1938). *Gestaltung und Bewegung in der Musik* [Shaping and motion in music]. Berlin-Lichtenfelde: Vieweg.
von Helmholtz, H. (1877/1895). On the sensations of tone as a physiological basis for the theory of music. London: Longmans, Greens & Co.
von Laban, R. (1950/1980). *The mastery of movement.* London: Macdonald & Evans.
Walker, M. E. (2000). Movement and metaphor: Towards an embodied theory of music cognition and hermeneutics. *Bulletin of the Council of Research for Music Education, 145*, 27–42.
Witek, M. A. G., Clarke, E. F., Wallentin, M., Kringelbach, M. L., and Vuust, P. (2014). Syncopation, body-movement and pleasure in groove music. *PLoS ONE, 9*(4), e94446.
Wöllner, C. (2012). Self-recognition of highly skilled actions: a study of orchestral conductors. *Consciousness and Cognition, 21*, 1311–1321.
Wöllner, C., and Auhagen, W. (2008). Perceiving conductors' expressive gestures from different visual perspectives. An exploratory continuous response study. *Music Perception, 26*, 129–143.

Wöllner, C., and Williamon, A. (2007). An exploratory study of the role of performance feedback and musical imagery in piano playing. *Research Studies in Music Education, 29*, 39–54.

Zentner, M., and Eerola, T. (2010). Rhythmic engagement with music in infancy. *Proceedings of the National Academy of Sciences, 107,* 5568–5573.

Zimmermann, B. A. (1974). *Intervall und Zeit: Aufsätze und Schriften zum Werk* (ed. by C. Bitter) [Interval and time. Essays and writings on his works]. Mainz: Schott.

# 6 Aesthetics of sonification
## Taking the subject-position

*Paul Vickers, Bennett Hogg and David Worrall*

> Experience is the result, the sign and the reward of that interaction of organism and environment which, when it is carried to the full, is a transformation of interaction into participation and communication.
> (John F. Dewey, 1934/1958, p. 22)

Sonification is a family of representational techniques under the umbrella of the more general term 'auditory display' for revealing information in data and communicating it in a non-speech aural form – sonification makes the inaudible audible. Sonification is not bound to any particular types of data and has been applied across a diverse range of domains. In all cases the purpose of sonification is to let people gain information about the phenomenon under investigation by listening to the data. Fundamentally, sonification is concerned with causation: the sounds we hear are caused by changes in data values sampled from some underlying phenomenon or domain of enquiry.

Much has been written about how data can be mapped to sound, with a taxonomy of auditory display techniques now well established in the literature. For a good coverage of the field including techniques and application domains see Hermann, Hunt and Neuhoff (2011). Broadly speaking, techniques range from the more direct processes of audification in which time series data are scaled and filtered so that their frequencies lie in a human-audible range (for example, see Dombois and Eckel, 2011; Höldrich and Vogt, 2015) to the less direct parameter mapping sonification (Grond and Berger, 2011) and model-based sonification (Hermann, 2011). In the former, data varies the parameters of an audio signal, in the latter a virtual sound-generating model (such as a mass-spring system) is excited by user interactions emitting sound which conveys information about the underlying dataset. Sonifications inhabit the same spatial environment as the user and so become part of the acoustic ecology and, thus, become part of the user's embodied experience of that environment.

A major design challenge is to create sonifications that are not only effective at communicating information but which are sufficiently engaging to engender sustained attention. Sonification may be ineffective if the rendered sound appears arbitrary to the listener in relation to the underlying data. The design task then becomes about finding a suitable fit between communicational efficacy and appropriate aesthetic character. Chris Chafe's work on the *Brain Stethoscope* is a compelling example of how it can work well (see Razavi et al., 2015, for preliminary results and http://chrischafe.net/brain-stethoscope for links to audio examples).

This brings to the fore the two related issues of listening attitudes and sonification aesthetics, both of which have recently attracted increasing attention in the sonification literature (Grond and Hermann, 2012, 2014; Tuuri and Eerola, 2012; Vickers, 2012). Until recently, commentators have tended to separate questions of aesthetics from the act of listening to sonifications, but listening's multimodal nature, its connectedness to other perceptual streams and the role that cultural understanding (through listening) plays in interpreting the sounds deployed in sonification indicates that listening must be considered as integral to the broader ecosystem of sonification aesthetics.

The matter of listening and aesthetics is a tension at the heart of sonification. At the 2015 International Conference on Auditory Display, an open discussion arose on the subject of the public understanding of sonification and the way the media portrays the field. Some delegates expressed extreme disquiet at the habit of journalists calling sonifications 'music': the music of atoms or the music of brainwaves and so forth. Researchers were concerned that such portrayals misrepresented and even devalued what they do, as though casting sonification as music cheapens it or undermines its scientific *bona fides*. The above issues raise several questions: What constitutes an aesthetics of sonification? How does our listening attitude affect how we 'read' a sonification and what we take away from it? How does the listening environment affect our experience? What part do our bodies play in the interaction?

We need an account of aesthetics that understands sonification as a real-world activity but which recognises the fact that musical experience may inform our listening as embodied and enculturated subjects. In this chapter we propose that adopting an ecological approach based upon Eric Clarke's use of the *subject-position* in musical listening (Clarke, 2005) can provide the language and tools necessary for this.

Clarke's (2005) ecological view of listening talks of perception of information where the 'information is *for* something' (p. 32). Perception falls into two categories: unproblematic perception in which the subject is able to perceive an object or event through sound, and ambiguous or degraded perception where the structure of the sound becomes salient. This view puts the aesthetic focus on sonification design squarely in terms of how listeners may perceive the phenomenon or dataset and away from the more compositional considerations (in Nancy's terminology, see Nancy, 2007) of musical structure and form. Clarke (2005, p. 91) understands perception as 'as a relationship between environmentally available information and the capacities, sensitivities, and interests of a perceiver' and observes that an 'aesthetic attitude' is defined by the relationship between music and listener.

Furthermore, one element of the

> mutualism of perceivers and their environments ... is the way in which a perceiving subject takes up a stance in relation to the objects of perception. ... The subject-position of everyday life is overwhelmingly one of transparently active engagement. But many aesthetic objects and circumstances [the latter would apply, arguably, to sonification] change this seamless state of affairs by radically limiting the perceiver's capacity to intervene in, or act upon, the immediate environment in a free-flowing manner. Under these circumstances, perceivers may become much more aware of their *perspective* on the objects of perception.
> (Clarke, 2005, pp. 124–125)

Clarke invokes the idea of *subject-position* from film theory as a middle way between 'the unconstrained relativism of reader-response theory' (Clarke, 2005, p. 93) in which the perceiver's readings of an aesthetic object are individual and unpredictable) and the structuralist idea that the objective structures of the work contain its entire meaning. This is a middle way resonant with Nancy's insistence upon the inseparability of the sensory and the compositional. The subject-position of a text circumscribes the possible responses from the reader in that although the text can be interepreted in different ways, the text imposes limits on the interpretation, avoiding the twin traps of 'infinite pluralism' and 'an essentialism which asserts a single "true" meaning' (Johnson, 1985, cited in Clarke, 2005, p. 92).

In pursuit of an aesthetics of sonification, in the following sections we expand upon the issues raised above and discuss how Clarke's ecological account may be usefully adapted to overcome these hindrances.

## Aesthetics or information?

Sonification is a representational process. Like its cousin, information visualisation, its goal is to provide access to data by constructing representations that reveal values, trends and relationships in a dataset. Visualisation is also called 'visual analytics', so sonification can be thought of as aural analytics. Research into auditory perception, especially the work of Al Bregman (Bregman, 1990), revealed that auditory perception is very sensitive to the way sound changes over time (even when those changes are very small) and that the ability to perceive sound does not require the listener to be oriented in any special way to the sound's source (Kramer et al., 1999). These features of auditory perception raised the potential for sound to be an effective communicator of information, especially fast-changing or temporal information (Kramer et al., 1999).

However, sonification occupies a richly nuanced perceptual space that is complicated by several factors. First, hearing is qualitatively different from vision in that we see objects, but we hear events (see Rosenblum, 2004).

Gaver (1988, p. 3) described this 'perception of events from the sounds they make' as 'everyday listening'. Thus, sounds are a consequence of activity: a book lying on a table emits no sound but we can still see it. If someone were to drop the book onto the table then we hear the thud of its impact. This means that any sonification conveys an implicit assumption of action or movement.

This is what makes it particularly suitable for time series data in which the differences in data values over time can be considered as signs of activity: a stock market that experiences no rise or fall is dormant. Because sound implies activity the question of what caused the sound is foregrounded and so sonification is fundamentally about causality. What caused that sound to occur? What caused that pitch to rise at that particular time? This, in turn, raises questions of embodiment which will be considered below (see also Hajdu, this volume).

The second main complicating factor is our innate tendency to adopt musical listening attitudes even when consciously taking an attitude of everyday listening, as illustrated very powerfully by Diana Deutsch with her speech-to-song illusion (see Deutsch, Lapidis and Henthorn, 2011). When editing a vocal commentary for a CD, Deutsch had the phrase 'sometimes behave so strangely' on a loop. After a number of repeated listenings the speech started to sound as though it was sung rather than spoken. When the original clip was played back the phrase 'sometimes behave so strangely' jumped out for the listener as song rather than speech.[1] In this example it is clear that once something is heard as 'musical' this experience remains embodied in the listening subject and informs subsequent listening, regardless of their intellectual understanding of what they are listening to. We can thus raise a preliminary question as to whether a complete separation of sonification and music is ever fully possible. Many sonifications contain pitched tones and regular rhythms which may – perhaps unconsciously – predispose musical listening attitudes (e.g., see Vickers and Alty, 2003). Listeners may still carry over 'musical' listening attitudes to sonifications that were never designed to be 'musical'. This in turn raises some very important considerations for sonification design and its relationship to musical aesthetics and listening. An awareness of the potential role played by aesthetics is vital because our engagement with sonification is through senses that are culturally – and therefore in part aesthetically – organised. Furthermore, insofar as listening is a transmodal activity in which senses other than just hearing are implicated, the transmodal nature of musical understanding (musical gesture, emotion, dance responses and the fact that most musical terms are also visual (high, low, bright, dark) or haptic (soft, warm, cutting, brisk) metaphors; see also Eitan, this volume) brings a set of positions in which embodiment is central, and which thus afford an entrance into investigating sonification aesthetics from the perspective of embodiment.

Supper (2015) notes that when Greg Kramer founded the International Conference on Auditory Display series in 1992, he 'was primarily a composer of electronic music who became interested in using his musical tools and skills for the exploration of complex datasets. Thus, translating data into music was not just a means to an end for him, it was an end in itself' (p. 448). From its earliest days, auditory display and sonification have been linked in one way or another to music, and because sonification *can* be thought of and experienced *as* music the question of sonification's relations with musical aesthetics arises. Sonification designers frequently express an intention to create sonifications that are 'aesthetically pleasing' without having first established what this might mean, beyond some vague sense of being 'musical' or not being annoying to listen to.

However, even if our experience of listening to sonifications is almost inescapably informed by music, aspects of music aesthetics present serious obstacles where sonification is concerned. Much of music aesthetics is predicated upon 'autonomous' music, music for its own sake. Emblematic of this is a stylised mode of concert listening that is both passive (the audience is silent and unmoving) and abstract (the music is experienced in terms of its own structure and organisation) without reference to causation. The latter point is often reinforced through acousmatic listening (Schaeffer, 1967; Windsor, 2000) (via radio, CDs, etc.) in which the sources of the musical sounds are themselves removed.

Because sonification involves both causality and signification, theorising it through the lens of acousmatic musical listening is self-defeating. In recent years a focus on the embodied nature of listening, and how this applies to musical experience, has gained currency in musicological discourse. Key to this is an understanding that listening is a culturally acquired practice which is developed through *sounding* – the sonic results of our physical interactions with the world – as much as hearing (Nancy, 2007; Smalley, 2007; Clarke, 2005). It follows that listening is transmodal in nature. As Idhe (1976/2007, p. 5) has indicated, this embodied transmodality includes technologies in ways that are particularly pertinent to sonification:

> Contemporary science is experienced as embodied in and through instruments. Instruments are the 'body' that extends and transforms the perceptions of the users of the instruments.

Smalley (2007, p. 39) notes that recent theorists have foregrounded the transmodal in terms of listening:

> Although acousmatic music may be received via a single sensory mode, this does not mean that the other senses lie dormant; in fact they spill over into sonic experience. Our sense of texture is learned through vision and touch as well as sound; our experience of the physical act of sound making involves both touch and proprioception; spectral motion, and the movement and distribution of sounds in space relate to our own experience of physical motion and cultural and natural

environments. ... sense experiences are also rooted in the physical and spatial entity of the human body, which is always at the focal centre of perception – as utterer, initiator and gestural agent, peripatetic participant, observer and auditor.

A current direction in artistic research (or practice-as-research) is where the aesthetic *qua* sensual experience is precisely the interface through which artistic practice can become 'epistemic action' (Eckel, 2013). What is more, a contemporary view that refutes the separation of sight, touch and hearing characteristic of some modernist thought (and which has been assumed in a philosophical tradition going back through Locke to the Pythagoreans) opens up genuinely new possibilities for knowledge through a more holistic and transmodal conceptualisation of the sensorium.

Sonification may be heard as music, but it is not intended to produce music as an outcome; the intended outcome of sonification is knowledge and understanding of the phenomenon under investigation. However, when Supper reports that some sonification designers 'professed to sacrifice aesthetic preferences for information content' (Supper, 2014, p. 47), who, or what determines that it must be either information *or* aesthetics? For an informed musical listener, one who has 'worked at it', and understands that music is not either structure or emotion but a weaving together of both, it is not necessary to choose one above the other (Nancy, 2007).

Clarke observed that most music does not take place in dedicated listening spaces:

> Overwhelmingly, people listen to music in a far more pragmatic and 'instrumental' manner: as a means to achieving or transforming an emotional state, as the stimulus for exercise, as a social facilitator, or as sound to fill an otherwise awkward silence.
>
> (Clarke, 2005, p. 144)

Most music encountered is not the main focus of attention. Clarke treats musical listening as *perception*, an ecological phenomenon in which an organism experiences and interacts with its environment. This is quite different from the traditional cognitivist information processing view of music aesthetics and psychoacoustics. In an ecological account of listening there is a mutualism between the information available in the environment and the 'capacities, sensitivities, and interests of a perceiver' (Clarke, 2005, p. 91) and 'every perceptual experience will bear the trace of an action component' (2005, p. 62) such as foot tapping, head nodding, body swaying, and so on. Listening becomes a very engaged activity in which the listener is aware of the space around them, how they are moving in the space, and in which causality is being sought in the events being perceived through hearing.

Such a listening practice, though able to be somewhat differentiated according to intention and situatedness, is not easily disciplined into clearly demarcated strategies. It seems almost nonsensical to imagine that something of how we listen to speech, to music, to warning signals, and so on, is not always already carried over into how we listen 'in general', including into sonification. We can, thus, move away from questions such as 'When is sonification music?' and focus on the more fruitful question: 'When is sonification *more than only* sonification?'

## Sonification as representation

A sonification can be described as an external representation of data or information, for example, communicating the state of a computer network to a network administrator. The network traffic is inherently invisible, but information visualisation and sonification can show the traffic levels visually (e.g., http://tnv.sourceforge.net) and aurally (e.g., see Worrall, 2015; and Vickers, Laing and Fairfax, in press). Both are processes of perceptualisation concerned with making hidden, invisible or complex data more accessible. In discussing the foundations of representing knowledge, Sowa (2000) describes three ways of classifying entities:

1  Phenomenal (monadic): *Wooden cube* = *Wooden* $(x) \wedge Cube$ $(x)$
2  Role type (dyadic): *mother* $(x, y)$
3  Representation: Rep $(x, y, z)$. That is, a sign $x$ represents something $y$ to agent $z$, which is consistent with C. S. Peirce's semiotics that has been used as a foundation for describing processes of perceptualisation (e.g., see Vickers, Faith and Rossiter, 2013).

In sonification we are dealing with Sowa's third type and are using 'representation' in the sense that it is applied to visualisation – in the way that a graph is a representation of a mathematical function, for instance – rather than the more complicated meanings that have accrued to 'representation' in philosophical and psychological discourse.

The situation is complicated by the fact that we can confidently assert that sonification is not *only* a causal notion. The fact the sound is produced by making use in some way of a particular dataset is not sufficient to sustain the claim that the sound represents that data. For example, the video to *House of Cards* (Radiohead, 2007) was described by its producers as a visualisation. The video is data driven in that the pictures are constructed from the data generated by laser surveying instrumentation, but what is being represented are Thom Yorke's face, landscapes and roads, not the dataset itself. *House of Cards* represents faces, objects, landscapes, and so on, while a visualisation represents facts, trends, data and information. In the case of *House of Cards* the representation of recognisable objects gets in the way of seeing the representation of the data; it is simply more legible. In the same way, a listener enculturated to hear pitched sounds in musical terms is always likely to experience that attribute of sound more vividly than the data lying behind it. Thus, there can be a tension between a sonification's perceived function and its potential status as an artwork, if the aesthetics under which it is conceptualised as art creates that tension. When 'a work represents some data then it seems that the data must, in some more substantial way be part of how the representation is properly experienced, so we somehow experience the thing in terms of what it represents' (Caddick-Bourne, 2014, personal transcript). The fact that a sonification can be heard musically, then, risks our attention being directed away from its data-informational function and towards features such as the sonic textures, the beauty of the sound and so forth.

## *Hearing-as and hearing-in*

In an attempt to explain how we read images, Wittgenstein (1953/1968, Part II, §xi) came up with the concepts of *seeing-that* and *seeing-as*. *Seeing-that* is where we see that an object in a picture is a particular object. *Seeing-as* is the phenomenon in which we see an object *as* something. For example, Wittgenstein would say that we see Figure 6.1 as a rabbit, but then we notice other aspects that allow us to see it as a duck.

Although Richard Wollheim, in *Art and Its Objects* (1968), originally argued that one primarily sees pictures and objects in pictures *as* something (*seeing-as*), he later replaced *seeing-as* with *seeing-in* as the correct explanation of representational seeing. He offers three reasons for this. First, *seeing-as* admits seeing a range of $y$s in $x$, whereas *seeing-in* also admits seeing a range of particular states of affairs of $y$ in $x$; *seeing-in* lets us see in $x$ that a woman is reading a love letter while seeing-as only lets us see $x$ as a woman. *Seeing-as* is concerned only with objects, *seeing-in* admits states of

*Figure 6.1* Wittgenstein's duck/rabbit picture. This is a public domain version of the simpler line drawing presented by Wittgenstein in his *Philosophical Investigations* (Wittgenstein, 1953/1968, p. 194).

## Aesthetics of sonification

affairs (Wollheim, 1980). Second, *seeing-as* has to meet the requirement of localisation. That is, there is some part (up to the whole) of *x* that the viewer sees as *y*. *Seeing-in*, on the other hand, requires no such localisation. The third reason (and the one for which Wollheim's theory is most well-known) is that *seeing-in* permits a twofoldness, an 'unlimited simultaneous attention to what is seen and the features of the medium', which 'seeing-as does not' (Wollheim, 1980, p. 212). That is, *seeing-in* allows one simultaneously to attend to what is represented (the object) and to the representation itself (the medium). If one looks 'at a representation as a representation, then it is ... required of me, that I attend simultaneously to object and medium' (Wollheim, 1980, p. 213), though the distribution of attention need not be equally balanced. This has importance for the way we consider listening as it affects sonification.

> Seeing-in ... is not the exercise of visual curiosity about a present object. It is the cultivation of a special kind of visual experience, which fastens upon certain objects in the environment for its furtherance. ... The cultivated experience can be, as experiences in general can be, of either of two kinds: it can be an experience of a particular, or it can be an experience of a state of affairs ... [which] can be seen in a particular [object].
>
> (Wollheim 1980, p. 223)

Moving to the sonic domain we might talk of a *hearing-as* (see Arbo, 2012), which resonates best with a notion of sonification in which the quality or aesthetic attributes of the sound 'itself' are subordinated to the efficiency with which otherwise inaccessible information is accessed. But can we ever separate that which we claim is being represented and the means or medium through which such representation is actuated?

### A musical listening attitude

This state of affairs does not seem to apply in the field of information visualisation, where the various representational tropes are recognised for what they are. Nobody suggests the makers of dendrograms or node-link diagrams have produced art. That people do not naturally label graphics as art but commonly refer to sonification as 'the music of *x*' may be, in part, due to the absence in Western culture – until very recently – of a sonic equivalent to graphic design.

Perhaps the moves to render sonification unambiguously as a scientific method, distancing it from the metaphysical associations with music, are an attempt to decontaminate it from the more subjective realms of art; a classic 'two cultures' worldview (Snow, 1959). What is it about sonification that causes such a strong reaction? Part of the answer lies, we argue, with the way we listen to the world. Unfortunately (from the scientist's viewpoint), the embodied mind seems bent on hearing musical patterns in the world around us, and this is reinforced by our describing sequences of pitched tones as melody – some avian vocal utterances are called bird song after all.

We noted above how Deutsch's speech-to-song illusion points to something about listening that is intrinsically bound up with music, though it is better to say that we naturally listen to things musically irrespective of volition. As Schaeffer noted when, in pursuit of experiments into the psychological understanding of sonic perception, he discovered the musical possibilities of looping a sound (which he termed the *sillon fermé*, the closed groove, see Demers, 2010, pp. 28–29) he, in his own words, 'stumble[d] onto music' (Rothenberg and Ulvaeus, 2013, p. 237).

Sounds always appear to have a real-world cause, whereas in visualisation the signs can be purely conventional. Because our perception of sound is as much determined by our sedimented knowledge of sound production as by the sense of hearing, we cannot bypass all that innate knowledge we have about sound in the real world, and we reach for that knowledge in our listening. Given the phenomenon of unconscious musical listening discovered by Schaeffer and rediscovered by Deutsch, regardless of whether there is any compositional intention in a sonification's design, it is possible (probable, even) that a listener will adopt some attitude of musical listening (just as journalists tend to do in their descriptions of sonification). While a musical listening attitude is not typically the intended mode of reception, it behoves the sonification designer to be cognisant of some of what is involved.

Taking this idea that we reach for a cause in listening, Peters (in terms of musical listening) says:

> an essential part of our listening experience draws on what our *own* body suggests might have gone into the making of this sound. This suggestion is an animation of the *heard*, and not, as is mostly held, the transfer of what is *seen* in a performer (imagined or real). It comes as an inkling of a *feeling*.
>
> (Peters, 2012, p. 22)

Peters uses the phenomenon of feeling within listening to categorise listening as either *abstractive* or *empathic*. Abstractive listening corresponds to Schaeffer's reduced listening and, in being disinterested in the causes of the sounds heard, leads to a disembodying of musical experience. Empathic listening is interested in 'hearing a making or a maker (concrete or imagined)'. As sonification is focused primarily on the cause of the sounds heard, an abstractive listening could only rarely be the goal of interacting with sonifications. Grond and Herman (2014, p. 45) claim this view to be in 'contradiction with other auditory display literature' invoking de Campo (2007) in whose *Sonification Design Space Map* 'the goal is to find ways to define potential sound objects, which are by definition the correlates of reduced listening' (Grond and Hermann, 2014, p. 45). De Campo stated the problem as finding:

> transformations that let structures/patterns in the data (which are not known beforehand) emerge as perceptual entities in the sound which jump to the foreground, i.e., as identifiable 'interesting audible objects'; in the electronic music field, these are called 'sound objects'.
>
> (de Campo, 2007, p. 2)

However, these auditory Gestalts that de Campo labels 'sound objects' ought more properly to be called 'sound events' (Murray Schafer's term, see Schafer, 1994, p. 131). This is because a sound object (*objet sonore*), according to Pierre Schaeffer (1967) who coined the term, is a correlate of reduced listening (as Grond and Hermann state). But this means it is a sound that is listened to independent of its cause and any referential links it might have. In his work on soundscape, Murray Schafer recognised the need to be able to listen in a referential manner and thus proposed the term 'sound event' to allow reference (signification) to be maintained. In sonification, a sound object, in the sense of Schaeffer's second acousmatic reduction, permitting abstractive listening, is of no functional value and such reductive listening has no place in sonification (Vickers, 2012): one always attends to the sounds in order to infer something about the data to which they point. As the post-structuralist philosopher Jean-Luc Nancy puts it, hearing (as opposed to *listening*) is 'above all about "hearing say" (rather than "hearing sound")' (Nancy, 2007, p. 6), but he insists that any 'musical listening worth its name can consist only in a correct combination ... the compositional and the sensory' (Nancy, 2007, pp. 63–64), where the compositional identifies the musical structures placed by the composer, and the sensory the perception of the results of those structures by the listener.

This brings us to a situation redolent of Wollheim's *seeing-as* and *seeing-in*, whereby 'hearing say' has a similar relation to the perceptual process to *seeing-as*, the reception of already existent information. For Nancy listening is altogether more active:

> If 'to hear' is to understand the sense ... to listen is to be straining toward a possible meaning, and consequently one that is not immediately accessible.
>
> (Nancy, 2007, p. 6)

If we listen to sonification (rather than just hearing it), the aesthetic cannot be excluded. The act of listening is a search for information in and of itself, the sonic aesthetic then becomes the vehicle through which such information is made available: the informational/compositional is not separate from the aesthetic/sensual. Rather than focusing efforts on a sonification that is 'aesthetically pleasing' we should instead be looking to ensure that the data becomes part of how a sonification is experienced. A sonification that sounds 'nice' but which reveals little about its dataset is less useful than one which takes some effort to listen to but which gives greater insight. Indeed, not all data values ought to sound nice: what should a rapid drop in the value of a key stock in our pension portfolio sound like? In the world around us significant events and actions usually result in a more salient sound that communicates direction, magnitude, distance and cause.

## The subject-position in sonification aesthetics

Because the sounds we listen to in sonification are used in the perception and understanding of the indicated data, any study of sonification aesthetics must go beyond the syntactic and semantic and consider the pragmatics or experiential aspects (Barrass and Vickers, 2011). Fishwick (2006, p. 21) argued that 'computing is not just about mental formalisms and algorithmic complexity; it is also about how to more effectively interface along the lines of tangible, augmented, and ubiquitous computing'. He defined 'aesthetic computing' as:

> *the application of the theory and practice of art to the field of computing.* ... Aesthetic computing relates to the following sorts of activities: (1) representing programs and data structures with customized, culturally specific notations; (2) incorporating artistic methods in typically computing-intensive activities, such as scientific visualization; (3) improving the emotional and cultural level of interaction with the computer.
> (Fishwick, 2006, p. 6; emphasis as in the original text)

Sometimes sound is intentional (e.g., the sound of the starting pistol firing to signal the start of a race). Other times sound is consequential, it is a by-product of some activity, event or action (e.g., the swooshing sound made when erasing a whiteboard). Consequential sound is used in everyday life as a carrier of information. For example, a mechanic will diagnose faults in a car engine by listening to it running (a form of auscultation). The sound generated by sonification processes is intentional but is applied to objects (data) that do not generate their own sound either intentionally or consequentially. So, sonification adds sound as a by-product with intention; it gives objects an aural identity. But this identity is imposed, contingent and acquired rather than essential, innate or necessary. Taking account of this, an imposed sound that is closer to the nature and context of the data – through attention to its aesthetic qualities – may lead to a quicker and more intuitive understanding of the phenomenon being sonified.

In parameter-mapping sonification, the properties of the data are directed to control parameters of a generated sound, thereby creating the conceptual conflation that the sound is a property of the data – a transformation of chosen properties of the data into an 'equivalent' sound structure. Where this link between sound and data is unclear, the sonification will be less successful even if the sounds themselves are judged to be pleasing. For example, consider the sonification of biological cells in a biopsy situation reported by Edwards et al. (2010). Properties of cells were used to calculate a 'badness' rating scale (indicating potential pathology), which was then mapped to ten different animal and human sounds. For example, cells with a badness score from 0 to 99 were represented by the sound of a cow mooing. Values between 100 to 199 mapped to a frog croak. The worst scores, 900 to 999, were mapped to a woman's scream. Participants in an experiment found this sonification strategy to be difficult to use, reporting it too arbitrary and not a clear linear mapping of cell properties. It is clear that the relationship between the data and the sound is weak.

In model-based sonification, the properties of the data can be explored through a variety of technological procedures with the effect of these explorations registering in sound. Rather than rendering a set of data into sound, for human perception a more embodied relationship emerges in which feedback between the operator and the system constitute the primary mode of encounter. Hermann (2011) offers several model-based sonification designs that fit well with different underlying types of dataset. The conceptual map formed when the user interacts with such designs allows for a more meaningful exploration of the data. The sonification is experienced in an embodied way: the sound results from physical interactions, and the sound itself is understood in an embodied manner as a causal event. This constellation of sound, listening and physical action is strongly congruent with what we know about the embodied nature of the listening subject.

Will Derkse describes the Benedictine practice of *lectio divina* (spiritual reading) thus: 'This is about, as it were, to tap the text from all sides and to listen to it with the stethoscope' (Derkse, 2003, p. 38). This is a good analogy for what happens during our interaction with sonification; both are a searching for meaning: meaning in the text in the former case, and meaning or information in the data in the latter. Parameter mapping sonification, because the sounds emitted are wholly controlled by the data, admits less of a direct tapping than model-based sonification. However, a parameter mapping system with interactive controls to turn on or off, up or down, sonic representations of certain data streams or data attributes still maps well to the stethoscope metaphor.

## *From a production focus to perception*

In a wide-ranging sociological account of sonification, Supper (2015, p. 442) notes that 'many projects playfully straddle the boundary between science and art' with patterns in large datasets being a justification for using sonification. Supper writes that when popular media propose that 'by merely listening to the data ... patterns and relations [in sonification] will reveal themselves' (2015, p. 442), a common misconception about sonification is rehearsed. Worrall said 'the idea that information can automatically "pop-out" of a sonification once an optimal parameter mapping of the dataset is found' (Worrall, 2009, p. 1.3) is a delusion. There is a 'false expectation that the interpretation of sonifications is a relatively straightforward and trivial problem' (Supper, 2015, p. 457). It stems, perhaps, from a bias in sonification research in favour of rendering rather than on perception that is a function of the history of sonification (see 'Sonification as representation', above) and also a site of worry over the scientific validity of sonification.

If, as Supper suggests, the focus on the discourses around sonification is on the means by which data is rendered into information, this both carries over the dominant concerns of a composerly understanding of organised sound, which is the 'how' of such organising, and relegates the perception/reception of such sounds to the margins. Worrall observed that the tools typically chosen to implement sonification:

> have been adopted or adapted from software sound-synthesis systems for music. Seminally, the Music N series ...which established the conceptual building blocks that remain in place in most music software systems, was designed to compose computer music not to soniculate abstract datasets. Such systems, including all those based on the MIDI protocol, adopted the score-and-instrument model from Western instrumental music.
>
> (Worrall, 2014, p. 54)

It can be argued that by focusing mostly on technical questions about how data can be made audible, the interpretation of the underlying data often slips into the background, which also means that the contributions of specialists in the technical aspects of the conversion weigh more heavily than the expertise of specialists in the empirical domains from which data are taken:

> Sonification researchers frequently face categorical objections that listening cannot be an objective entrance to scientific knowledge. Indeed, even in scientific disciplines dedicated to the study of sound, the usual strategy for infusing their object of study with objectivity is not to carefully listen to sounds but, rather, to turn them into images and analyze them visually. The idea that listening itself can be used as a scientific method, on the other hand, is rather controversial.
>
> (Supper, 2015, p. 449)

The unspoken problem, of course, is that sonification *on its own* is not ever going to work; it has inherited an understanding of the auditory as a hermetic sense/practice in disregard of the palpable reality of the transmodal nature of all sense perception. But there are many other modalities for music and general listening alike. The silent, stationary, detached and attentive modes of the 'classical' concert, upon which many aesthetic concerns about music are predicated, are historically and socio-economically contingent. Sonification mobilises the sense of hearing and thus the associated 'knowledges' of motion, touch, vision, proprioception, adding to the layers of sensation through which we comprehend the state of things in our immediate environment. This is a sense of hearing that is not already divided up into strategies of listening, but where each subject navigates and negotiates their way along an otherwise unbroken continuum of listening. Sound touches at a distance, but through this touching allows us to touch, like Merleau-Ponty's 'being honeyed' (Merleau-Ponty, 2004, pp. 60–61). This role of aesthetics in sonification is in the construction and development of a 'subject-position' – a way of guiding the listener through, but by deploying more than just listening. Compositional methods and tropes borrowed from music need to be assessed not in terms of their musical aesthetics but in terms of how they help the listener engage with and understand the data the sonification purports to represent.

Aesthetic computing, says Fishwick (2006, p. 6), 'involves one of two types of aesthetics applications: *analysis* and *synthesis*'. In this view, an analytic approach would evaluate sonifications 'from the perspective of classical aesthetic *qualities* such as mimesis, symmetry, parsimony, and beauty' (p. 6). A synthetic approach to sonification would:

> employ aesthetics as a means of *representation* of the artifacts. The word 'representation' is broadly defined to encompass the concepts of interaction and interface, rather than simply static presentation.
> (Fishwick, 2006, p. 6)

Up until now commentators have tended to focus on these analytic aspects of sonification aesthetics. Adopting an ecological perspective, which places the subject-position at the centre of attention, lets us regard sonification aesthetics synthetically in terms of sonification's function as representation.

Listening brings to life an experience in the body of the listener that is at once analytic, synthetic, emotional and partially internalised. This involves the intuitive, the learned and the aesthetic, with emotion, mood, social circumstance and identity. Beyond a certain point we move into the regions of ecstasy where the abandonment of unified subjectivity is imagined to lead to a sort of sublime disintegration through music (Kramer, 1997; Middleton, 2006; Poizat, 1992). If the discernment and communication of more or less precise information is required, this avenue of the aesthetic seems profoundly counter-productive.

The aesthetic nonetheless affords a way into culturally meaningful engagement with sound. Even though this sound is organised according to Western musical traditions, we can learn much that is of use for sonification from the ideological restrictions imposed on it through its inheritances from (capital M) Music; here, Music has an inside – the 'real' Music – and an outside – the avant-garde, Sound Art, Muzak, non-musical sound – music defined by its materiality, in other words. But this is not how we listen or hear, and neither need it be the touchstone against which all 'alternatives' must be tested. In contrast, John Cage made no distinction between the sounds of music and ambient sound. Robin Maconie (Maconie, 1990, quoted in Hamilton, 2007, p. 46) puts the argument this way: 'for sound to be perceived as music is an act of individual determination ... what is music to one listener may be noise to another'. The danger here is that we are thrown back into a radically relativist 'anything can mean anything to anyone', which is not only spurious in terms of real experience, but leads us nowhere by simply discounting the possibility of moving beyond such a terminal position.

If music, according to Hamilton's description, is 'a human activity grounded in the body and bodily movement and infused with human life' (Hamilton, 2007, p. 6), the popular (musicological) idea which says 'that when sounds are experienced as music they are experienced as divorced from their causes' (p. 7) must be rejected. As mentioned above, abstractive listening, in which one attends to the attributes of a sound without reference to any external object to which it may be linked, has no useful role in sonification experience. As Marc Leman says, 'the musician encodes gestures in sound, and the listener can decode particular aspects of them through corporeal imagination ... a model of musical communication in which the encoding and decoding of biomechanical energy allows the communication of intentions' (Leman, 2008, pp. 159–160). In sonification the intentions become the information contained in a dataset and the gestures become the inferred events that give rise to the sound. A sonification aesthetic that closely couples the sound to the underlying data in form and structure through an ecologically valid metaphor will allow a listener to perceive the data. They will hear events caused by the data and will use innate and learned embodied associations to interpret what they perceive.

## Conclusions

Arguments against the value of the aesthetic in sonification, or against the potential for a sonification to be an artwork, are grounded in philosophically determined positions, which at best misunderstand, at worst deliberately obfuscate, the extent to which scientific method and aesthetics express fundamentally similar ideological groundings. That is, although the claims of aesthetics rely upon subjectivity, and those of science rely upon objectivity, both are grounded in a detached, disinterested, uninvolved viewer, whose presence does not affect the object under observation. However, alternative philosophical positions that strive to take up a critical position afford ways of conceptualising the relationship between science and aesthetics which do not depend upon their radical separation. Instead, we can see how both procedures distance the perceiver from the object of their perception, in science in the interest of quantitative objectivity, in aesthetics in pursuit of qualitative experience, at the same time as relying on the perceiver's sensual perception – empirical, observable data in the case of science, sensual experience in the case of the aesthetic. Sonification needs to draw on both scientific and aesthetic methods, and now that the perspectives from studies of human perception have rendered the distinctions between science and aesthetics as less rigid, these distinctions are less reliable grounds on which to build an argument against the aesthetic having a useful role in sonification.

In relation to music aesthetics, for example, Nancy (2007) insists that musical listening acknowledges the inextricability of the sensuous and the compositional. Listening encompasses sensual experience and the discernment of information, information that might be seismic data or the pitches and durations encoded in the score of a musical work.

Just as 'the compositional' is not the exclusive knowledge of the composer or the musicologist but is accessible to the trained listener through the aesthetic (with which it is ineluctably co-present), so the sonified data is not the exclusive knowledge of the designer of the algorithm. Indeed, taking account of the perceiver of sonification rather than focusing on the means through which sonifications are produced makes it essential to understand the reception of a sonification as being, like music, an integral element in a broader, more ecosystemic network of experiences, memories, imaginings and expectations. In theory, a sonification can be anything to anyone, thus defeating its purpose as the organisation of otherwise illegible information. From everything we know about non-indexical sound, it cannot convey information as such. The aesthetic thus becomes an essential factor in sonification design, because through this it is possible to establish a subject-position for the sonification which carefully directs the listener, limits the degree to which the sound signification process can remain essentially arbitrary and thus renders considerably more effective the attempts to engage otherwise inaccessible data through sound.

The idea of a subject-position acknowledges that there is an emotional direction to our perception of sound that colours what we perceive. For sonification, the aesthetic is about trying to cultivate 'right' listening without the illusion that the sounds of a sonification are somehow an inevitable or unmediated result of the underlying data. The aesthetic enters at the point of constructing the subject-position such that a *hearing-in* becomes more probable, that is, something in the aesthetic of the sound has to match the phenomenon being revealed. It sounds so simple to say that good sonification design involves finding the right way to represent the kinds of data or facts that we wish to reveal, but the realisation of this ideal has proved problematic (e.g. Edwards et al., 2010). Recognising that there will always be an aesthetic experience when attending to a sonification, that this experience will be affected by prior knowledge and experience, and that the mind will, regardless of our volition, identify musical patterns in phrases which were not intentionally music, requires us to explicitly consider the aesthetic in our practice. Taking a subject-position stance allows us to escape the strictures of taxonomy and, instead, to focus on designing for experience, but experiences that are constrained by the scope of what the sonification designer wishes to reveal about the underlying data.

A sonification aesthetic, therefore, is not a Western concert music aesthetic. It is an experiential, ecological or perception-action aesthetic. It is concerned with events and signs (*écouter* and *comprendre*) and is not about autonomous listening *per se* (though anything *may* be listened to in that mode) but we acknowledge that in such a mode, when judged as an aesthetic object, the sonification may be deemed to be inadequate or impoverished. Sonification does not have to sound pleasant: auditory signals need to be appropriate to the task at hand, where sounding pleasant might interfere with the signal's communicative ability (e.g., warnings in the cockpit of a fighter plane).

## Note

1 For an explanation of this phenomenon together with audio examples, see http://deutsch.ucsd.edu/psychology/pages.php?i=212.

## References

Arbo, A. (2012). Typology and functions of 'hearing-as'. In A. Arbo, M. LeDu and S. Plaud (Eds.), *Wittgenstein and aesthetics: perspectives and debates* (pp. 117–128). Frankfurt: Ontos.

Barrass, S., and Vickers, P. (2011). Sonification design and aesthetics. In T. Hermann, A. D. Hunt and J. Neuhoff (Eds.), *The sonification handbook* (pp. 145–172). Berlin: Logos Verlag.

Bregman, A. S. (1990). *Auditory scene analysis: The perceptual organization of sound.* Cambridge, MA: MIT Press.

Caddick-Bourne, E. (2014). *Verbal response at hearing-in: Philosophical perspectives on sounds and sonification.* Event at University of London's Institute of Philosophy, 10 October (transcribed by the first author).

Clarke, E. F. (2005). *Ways of listening: An ecological approach to the perception of musical meaning.* Oxford: Oxford University Press.

de Campo, A. (2007). Toward a data sonification design space map. In *ICAD 2007: Proceedings of the 13th International Conference on Auditory Display* (pp. 342–347), Montréal, Canada. Canada: International Community for Auditory Display, Schulich School of Music, McGill University. Retrieved from https://smartech.gatech.edu/handle/1853/50042.

Demers, J. (2010). *Listening through the noise: The aesthetics of experimental electronic music.* New York: Oxford University Press.

Derkse, W. (2003). *The rule of benedict for beginners: Spirituality for daily life.* Collegeville, MN: Liturgical Press.

Deutsch, D., Lapidis, R., and Henthorn, T. (2011). Illusory transformation from speech to song. *Journal of the Acoustical Society of America, 129*(4), 2245–2252.

Dewey, J. F. (1934/1958). *Art as experience.* Oakville: Capricorn Books.

Dombois, F., and Eckel, G. (2011). Audification. In T. Hermann, A. D. Hunt and J. Neuhoff (Eds.), *The sonification handbook* (pp. 301–324). Berlin: Logos Verlag.

Eckel, G. (2013). Improvisation as epistemic practice. In H. Frisk and S. Österjö (Eds.), *(Re)thinking improvisation – Artistic explorations and conceptual writing* (pp. 42–47). Malmö: Academy of Music.

Edwards, A. D. N., Hunt, A., Hines, G., Jackson, V., Podvoskis, A., Roseblade, R., and Stammers, J. (2010). Sonification strategies for examination of biological cells. In E. Brazil (Ed.), *16th International Conference on Auditory Display* (pp. 193–200). Washington, DC: International Community for Auditory Display.

Fishwick, P. A. (2006). An introduction to aesthetic computing. In P. A. Fishwick (Ed.), *Aesthetic computing* (pp. 3–28). Cambridge, MA: MIT Press.

Gaver, W. W. (1988). *Everyday listening and auditory icons*. PhD thesis, University of California, San Diego.

Grond, F., and Berger, J. (2011). Parameter mapping sonification. In T. Hermann, A. D. Hunt and J. Neuhoff (Eds.), *The sonification handbook* (pp. 363–398). Berlin: Logos Verlag.

Grond, F., and Hermann, T. (2012). Aesthetic strategies in sonification. *AI & Society, 27*(2), 213–222.

Grond, F., and Hermann, T. (2014). Interactive sonification for data exploration: How listening modes and display purposes define design guidelines. *Organised Sound, 19*, 41–51.

Hamilton, A. (2007). *Aesthetics and music*. London: Continuum.

Hermann, T. (2011). Model-based sonification. In T. Hermann, A. D. Hunt and J. Neuhoff (Eds.), *The sonification handbook* (pp. 399–428). Berlin: Logos Verlag.

Hermann, T., Hunt, A. D., and Neuhoff, J., (Eds.) (2011). *The sonification handbook*. Berlin: Logos Verlag.

Höldrich, R., and Vogt, K. (2015). Augmented audification. In K. Vogt, A. Andreopoulou and V. Goudarzi (Eds.), *ICAD 15: Proceedings of the 21st International Conference on Auditory Display* (pp. 102–108). Graz, Austria: Institute of Electronic Music and Acoustics (IEM), University of Music and Performing Arts Graz (KUG).

Idhe, D. (1976/2007). *Listening and voice: Phenomenologies of sound*. New York: SUNY Press.

Kramer, G., Walker, B., Bonebright, T., Cook, P., Flowers, J. H., Miner, N., and Neuhoff, J. (1999). Sonification report: Status of thefField andrResearch agenda. ICAD/NSF. Retrieved from http://sonify.psych.gatech.edu/publications/pdfs/1999-NSF-Report.pdf.

Kramer, L. (1997). *After the lovedeath: Sexual violence and the making of culture*. Berkeley: University of California Press.

Leman, M. (2008). *Embodied musical cognition and mediation technology*. Cambridge, MA: MIT Press.

Merleau-Ponty, M. (2004). *The world of perception*. London: Routledge.

Middleton, R. (2006). *Voicing the popular: On the subjects of popular music*. New York: Routledge.

Nancy, J-L. (2007). *Listening* (Charlotte Mandell, Trans.). New York: Fordham University Press (first published in French 2002, Paris: Éditions Galilée).

Peters, D. (2012). Touch: Real, apparent, and absent – on bodily expression in electronic music. In D. Peters, G. Eckel and A. Dorschel (Eds.), *Bodily expression in electronic music: Perspectives on reclaiming performativity* (pp. 17–34). London: Routledge.

Poizat, M. (1992). *The angel's cry: Beyond the pleasure principle in opera* (Arthur Denner, Trans.). Ithaca: Cornell University Press.

Radiohead. (2007). House of cards. On *In rainbows* [CD]. London: XL Recordings. The video's project site can be found at https://github.com/dataarts/radiohead.

Razavi, B., Ehsani, P., Kamrava, M., Pekelis, L., Nangia, V., Chafe, C., and Parvizi, J. (2015). The brain stethoscope: A device that turns brain activity into sound. *Epilepsy & Behavior, 46*, 53–54.

Rosenblum, L. D. (2004). Perceiving articulatory events: Lessons for an ecological psychoacoustics. In J. G. Neuhoff (Ed.), *Ecological psychoacoustics* (pp. 219–248). London: Elsevier Academic Press.

Rothenberg, D., and Ulvaeus, M. (2013). *The book of music and nature: An anthology of sounds, words, thoughts*. Middletown, CT: Wesleyan University Press.

Schaeffer, P. (1967). *Traité des objets musicaux* (rev. ed.). Paris: Seuil.

Schafer, R. M. (1994). *Our sonic environment and the tuning of the world*. Rochester, VT: Destiny Books.

Smalley, D. (2007). Space-form and the acousmatic image. *Organised Sound, 12*, 35–58.

Snow, C. P. (1959). *The two cultures and the scientific revolution*. Cambridge: Cambridge University Press.

Sowa, J. F. (2000). *Knowledge representation: Logical, philosophical, and computational foundations*. Pacific Grove, CA: Brooks/Cole.

Supper, A. (2014). Sublime frequencies: The construction of sublime listening experiences in the sonification of scientific data. *Social Studies of Science, 44*(1), 34–58.

Supper, A. (2015). Sound information: Sonification in the age of complex data and digital audio. *Information & Culture, 50*(4), 441–464.

Tuuri, K., and Eerola, T. (2012). Formulating a revised taxonomy for modes of listening. *Journal of New Music Research, 41*(2), 137–152.

Vickers, P. (2012). Ways of listening and modes of being: Electroacoustic auditory display. *Journal of Sonic Studies, 2*(1). Retrieved from http://journal.sonicstudies.org/vol02/nr01/a04.

Vickers, P., and Alty, J. L. (2003). Siren songs and swan songs: Debugging with music. *Communications of the ACM, 46*(7), 86–92.

Vickers, P., Faith, J., and Rossiter, N. (2013). Understanding visualization: A formal approach using category theory and semiotics. *IEEE Transactions on Visualization and Computer Graphics, 19*(6), 1048–1061.

Vickers, P., Laing, C., and Fairfax, T. (in press). Sonification of a network's self-organized criticality for real-time situational awareness. *Displays*. doi: 10.1016/j.displa.2016.05.002.

Windsor, W. L. (2000). Through and around the acousmatic: The interpretation of electroacoustic sounds. In Emmerson S. (Ed.), *Music, electronic media and culture* (pp. 7–35). London: Ashgate.

Wittgenstein, L. (1953/1968). *Philosophical investigations* (G. E. M. Anscombe, Trans.) (3rd ed.). Oxford: Basil Blackwell.

Wollheim, R. (1968). *Art and its objects*. New York: Harper & Row.

Wollheim, R. (1980). Seeing-as, seeing-in, and pictorial representation. In *Art and its objects* (2nd ed.; pp. 202–226). Cambridge: Cambridge University Press.

Worrall, D. (2009). *Sonification and information: Concepts, instruments and techniques.* PhD thesis, University of Canberra.

Worrall, D. (2014). Can micro-gestural inflections be used to improve the soniculatory effectiveness of parameter mapping sonifications? *Organised Sound (Special Issue 01), 19,* 52–59.

Worrall, D. (2015). Realtime sonification and visualisation of network metadata (the NetSon project). In K. Vogt, A. Andreopoulou and V. Goudarzi (Eds.), *ICAD 15: Proceedings of the 21st International Conference on Auditory Display* (pp. 337–339). Graz, Austria: Institute of Electronic Music and Acoustics (IEM), University of Music and Performing Arts Graz (KUG).

Part II
# Sound design, instrumental affordances and embodied spatial perception

# 7 Instruments, voices, bodies and spaces
## Towards an ecology of performance

*W. Luke Windsor*

Music, whether instrumental or vocal, requires people to create vibrations in air, although much musicological study seems to prefer attending to the abstract representation of music as notated or the mental or sociological manifestations of musical events. The actions of performers, the nature of the objects they manipulate and the spaces in which they do so are not often regarded as particularly important to an understanding of musical meaning. Increasingly, however, recent work has attended in more detail to the relationships between sound and their material sources, the constraints and affordances of instruments, bodies and environments and to the ways in which perception and action are closely coupled in the reception and performance of music.

In this chapter, a framework for rethinking the ecology of performance is presented and then applied to two case studies of musical instrumental 'design'. The word design is intentionally used to highlight the deliberate organisation not of abstract musical material but of the (bio)physical materials of music: objects, people and spaces. Before approaching the musical performance in particular, the recent and growing use of ecological psychology as a theoretical construct will be introduced in relation to music and design. Following this necessary contextual preamble, I will propose a theory of musical design that first attends to the structure of musical instruments, then turns to the structures of the wider environment, to examine how these generate and curtail musical creativity.

Although there are many ways in which space and instrument design have been credited with key developments in music history, this chapter cannot review them all. It is a commonplace that architecture can be used to create spatial effects in music (as in Monteverdi's *1610 Vespers*) or that the evolution of the modern piano drove, and was driven by, the desire for dynamic contrast and range. The tendency of mainstream musicology to favour notation over sound, pitch and rhythm over colour, tends to leave such discussion of spaces and instruments on the margins; the province of early music scholars, ethnomusicologists, organologists and theorists/practitioners of electro-acoustic music. My intention here is to foreground the processes of action and perception that lead to musical meaning and to show how instruments and places play key roles in constraining and generating such meaning across all musics. In doing so this chapter provides and exemplifies an approach to spaces and sounding movement within those spaces in which these are analysed literally rather than through the metaphorical approach to spaces and gestures best exemplified by the work of Scruton (1983). One caveat should be noted here: this chapter does not engage with the manipulations of sound made available by recording or production technology, a subject dealt with elsewhere (see e.g., Windsor, 2000; Knakkergaard, 2013).

## An ecological psychology of music

Two different yet related psychological traditions (both sitting outside the mainstream of cognitive psychology) have begun to place the continuous interplay of organism and environment at the heart of musical understanding. Both confusingly have become associated with the same name: ecological psychology. Although they are related in history and in some of their theoretical ideas, they are also distinct in their outlook. Hence, I will introduce them briefly before turning to a brief review of their application to music.

### *Ecological psychology*

The first tradition requiring some explication is the ecological psychology developed by James Gibson (see, e.g., Gibson, 1979), partly in response to his dissatisfaction with theories of visual perception derived from experiments using static visual displays, and partly from his revulsion with social determinism. Although Gibson's contribution to mainstream psychology in the form of his empirical work on optic flow is acknowledged widely, his two major theoretical innovations are much less well regarded within mainstream psychology, despite their roots in his well-regarded and influential empirical work on visual perception. First, Gibson concluded that, since many phenomena of visual perception which seem to require mental processing of sensory data can instead be solved by presenting realistic stimuli in realistic situations, many perceptual processes do not require cognitive mediation. Direct perception of predictably structured information, Gibson concluded, was the way in which humans and other organisms guide their actions. A full explanation of his thinking is beyond the scope of this chapter, but his refusal to accept the dominant tendency of psychology to assume the world presents confusing and chaotic information that needs to be made sense of through computation was both out of step with a cognitive turn in psychology and felt by many to be intellectually lazy or, perhaps worse, a form of sophisticated behaviourism. Gibson's second and even more outrageous claim was that not only can we perceive the movement, size or integrity of an object without processing, but that the information we pick up from exploring it specifies its potential uses: the theory of affordance (see, e.g, Gallagher, 2009 for a discussion of the broader philosophical context for this reassessment of meaning). Gibson claimed that we can discover the affordances of many objects without internal or external symbolic knowledge, and in many cases without familiarity: a doorway affords exit; a pen writing; a wave surfing. Both the natural and designed environments present us with affordances which we pick up through exploration and become sensitive to through familiarity.

Affordances are not determined by object or subject, but through their relationship: a principle often described as mutuality. Hence, to take a musical turn, the affordances of a grand piano vary in relation to the size of the human body and our particular needs. A piano serves as a rather expensive table, a surface for leaning, a den (for an infant), a noise-making machine or indeed as a sophisticated musical tool depending on the nature of the body addressing it. To a toddler, a piano becomes a toy through which to explore sound and its relation to action; the concert pianist has developed a repertoire of actions and a degree of sensitivity which allows the piano to afford a greater range of acoustic, harmonic, rhythmic and even timbral effects. How such sensitivities develop is the subject of another chapter. The important idea here is that the piano affords a huge range of actions but is not infinite in these affordances: its size does not afford easy transportation; its construction does not afford continuous modulation of dynamics once a note is struck.

The relational fertility of affordance has been most keenly felt and applied in the theory and practice of design, stimulated by its adoption and adaptation by Norman (see e.g., Norman, 2013), although his own view of this concept has recently evolved in part to reflect a need for better distinction between potentially discoverable attributes of objects and the way in which designers call attention to these through signification. Although some have sought to integrate semiotics within ecological psychology through a broadening of the types of information by which affordance is constituted (see, e.g., Windsor, 2004), Norman prefers, for both practical and conceptual reasons, to point up the role of explicit conventional or motivated signs which direct users towards design features. His amusing discussion of doors and the ways in which poor design can make the discovery of their affordances fraught with confusion is supplemented, for example, with the more or less sophisticated ways that designers point users towards essential information and, in the worst examples, how users (and third parties) add textual signs to overcome confusion (Norman, 2013). In musical situations the gap between affordances and signifiers may not seem that apparent, partly because the affordances of a musical instrument (such as a piano) are picked up alongside implicit and explicit levels of training which reflect a shared techno-cultural milieu. A piano, as already observed, affords differently to a concert pianist than it does to either a novice on the one hand or a jazz pianist on the other. However, this analysis forgets both the relational aspect of affordances and the ways in which the layout of the piano keyboard is designed to direct the eye and hand towards particular modes of action.

In respect of the first, the relationship of key to sound, whether in terms of pitch, duration or loudness, is encoded in a predictable and freely discoverable layout. In addition, the colour, layout and size of black and white keys, encodes and signifies Western pitch organisation using a sophisticated mapping through which more distant keys on the circle of fifths from C requires the use of an increasing number of the smaller, black keys (for a parallel discussion of such mappings see Sudnow, 1978). Mooney (2011), turning to the educational implications of such a view, reminds us that the discoverability of affordances does not have a simple relationship with aesthetic potential; discovering the musically interesting and appropriate affordances of a violin requires much effort and selectivity and the most easily discovered sound may not be the most interesting.

*Eco-behavioural science*

The second type of ecological psychology, also known as eco-behavioural science, focuses upon the role of the environment in providing behaviour settings which constrain and motivate action. Although recently re-integrated with Gibson's approach by Heft (2001), the eco-behavioural tradition of Roger Barker (see, e.g., Barker, 1978) was much more explicitly driven by social psychology methods than Gibson's attention to individual acts of perception and laboratory approach. Heft usefully suggests that behaviour settings can be thought of as comprising three types of information for behaviour: topographical features, climatological properties and socio-cultural practices, and exemplifies these through analysis of a baseball game. Topographical features of a musical setting, describing the physical space and its constraints, might include the positioning and nature of stage, audience, balconies, seating and the like. These features constrain the audience and musicians and their lines of sight, also determining acoustic potentialities. Climatological features would comprise, for example, the temperature and lighting of a concert hall (see for example, Burland and Windsor, 2014, for a discussion of their non-trivial impact on musical behaviour; also see Boyle and Waterman, 2015). Socio-cultural practices are encoded within the performing spaces as well, through the kinds of means described by Small (e.g., 1988) in relation to ritualised aspects of performance in relation to space; and through the layout and affordances of people, instruments and the sounds that they make (bringing the two kinds of ecological psychology back together). It is easy to underplay or trivialise these aspects of the interaction between performing spaces and musical behaviour, and it is important to note that such interaction goes beyond accommodation to, or exploitation of, acoustic peculiarities (as described in Blesser and Salter, 2007). Later in this chapter, the mutual adaptation of space and action for aesthetic ends will be explored in a detailed example.

Ecological approaches to music perception and performance have proven attractive to a number of researchers in recent years, notably Clarke (2005).

Rather than review this contextual work in detail (see instead Windsor and de Bézenac, 2012), the following sections turn to the proposition of a theoretical framework for understanding music in ecological terms. Following on from this, two analytical examples are then offered that highlight the need for musicology to explore more candidly the means through which the 'designers' of music act to optimise the fit between actions, bodies, spaces and aesthetic ends. I will not attempt to review empirical work along these lines and would point the reader towards Boyle and Waterman (2015) for some early hints as to the form such empirical work should take.

## *Events, objects, behaviour settings and the organism*

Music, considered from an ecological standpoint, is constituted by, and arises from, the interactions between organisms (arguably only human organisms) and objects within behaviour settings, and can be analysed in two ways. The most interesting result of taking this approach is the way in which sound is considered not for itself, but as structured information about the events that result from these interactions. Sound becomes the means through which we perceive the affordances of objects. While this may seem to deny the aesthetic dimension of sound as a direct source of meaning, relegating it to a mediating and informative status, more careful consideration of this leads to a position where meaning arises through the pick-up of information about actions (see e.g., Windsor and de Bézenac, 2012).

## *The ecology of a performance*

Considered within such an ecological framework, a performance is constituted by a set of events within a particular behaviour setting and benefits from forms of analysis that consider the contributions of different sources of information to the actions and perceptions of performers and audience. Such analyses must take into account the 'designed' nature of the objects and settings (whether instrumental or environmental) and the influence of socio-cultural practices. Again, sound here is information for action, used by performers to synchronise their performances, either in acoustic or aesthetic terms, and by audiences to discover the bodily/instrumental gestures that generated those sounds. The two case studies provided later in this chapter will be used to illustrate the relational nature of performance ecology.

Performance can be described as an act of communication, by which musical intent is communicated to an audience to be decoded more or less accurately. This somewhat unidirectional view of performance, although it can be useful (see e.g., Juslin and Madison, 1999), downplays the impact of instruments, spaces and audiences on the act of performance, and portrays intentionality as internally generated; within an ecological perspective, intentionality is conceived as being an emergent property of the interactions between a musician and their surroundings (see Kugler, Shaw, Vincente and Kinsella-Shaw, 1990, for a thought-provoking analysis of intentionality in termite colonies). In the examples provided here, the properties of the musician's environment are shown to constitute non-trivial factors in the production of a performance, and the exploration of these constraints is fundamental to the aesthetics of performance. Moreover, the case studies will show how instrument designers, composers and performers work with, but also creatively adapt, the spaces in which their bodies must play, with both predicable and less predictable creative consequences.

## *Meaning: affordances and interpretation; affordances and signs*

If sound (or other sources of information) provides insufficiently detailed information about the events in a performance, then the perceptual system actively hunts for stimulus material to resolve ambiguity or becomes increasingly reliant on conscious inference, even imagination. This is where music becomes aesthetic: in the tension between the everyday perception of causation and the increasingly abstract attempts to ascribe purpose to acoustic stimulation (see Windsor, 2004). Gibson, in his few attempts to consider aesthetic perception, becomes fixated upon the way in which art reduces perception to the appreciation of surfaces for themselves: 'information as such' rather than information 'about' the world (Gibson, 1966, p. 225). Later in his book, he discusses in more detail the consequences of being presented with ambiguous or 'impoverished' information of the kind that art is so fond, whether it be a two-dimensional painting of a three dimensional scene or a seemingly abstract piano solo: 'the perceptual system hunts' for information to help resolve ambiguity and pick up enough information to act (Gibson, 1966, p. 303). This hunting, I would argue, is not turned off when we engage with aesthetic artefacts, as Gibson implies. Instead, it is the basis for our interpretation of art, as opposed to our consumption of it; and not only do we seek causation, we construct narratives in order to substantiate what is unavailable to our senses. The ways in which we discuss artistic events after the fact are often attempts to impose causality (such as a theatrical character's intention) where it was left uncertain; similarly, the re-watching or re-reading of a detective story to pick up 'clues' that had been missed is the result of this active attempt to construct meaning.

In summary, after introducing the individual and social flavours of ecological psychology personified by Gibson and Barker, and their unification in the work of Heft (2001), a view of music has been presented in which sound is viewed as information about the world. Within this approach meaning operates on a continuum between the trivial identification of causes and the construction of interpretations where the usefulness or specificity of our perceptions is challenged by ambiguity. In the next section this approach will be applied to the analysis of bodies and spaces, first at the level of body–instrument interactions, and then at the level of corporate music-making in a choral setting.

## Instruments, spaces, bodies and design

The layout and acoustics of instruments afford and constrain certain behaviours, some of which become sedimented within culture. The modern grand piano has an accepted set of techniques that do not comprise all the ways in which it can be played. 'Extended' techniques such as preparation of the strings or modes of playing that avoid the keyboard, actuating the strings directly with fingers or hammers, are less obvious consequences of the design of the piano, especially the way in which its keyboard both signifies and is driven by more common approaches to the instrument and the music for which it evolved (see above). The range of affordances of most instruments is, in fact, explored rarely by student performers once formal training begins and most improvisation is constrained more by socio-cultural practice than the physicality of the instrument. Similarly, the actual physical constraints of the piano in performance can easily be overstated: a piece such as La Monte Young's *Piano Piece for David Tudor #1* in which the piano is fed by the pianist, illustrates how relational affordances of instruments are. At root, the piano is a large object on wheels that *can* make sounds.

Of course, it is not just instruments that are designed, spaces for performance can similarly be shaped to afford certain kinds of behaviour. Blesser and Salter (2007) analyse many of the musical and non-musical ways in which spaces, either through coincidence or design, contribute to our experience of the events within them and can even become as or more important than them. In particular, their discussion of the Grotto of Jeita (Blesser and Salter, 2007) illustrates how unusual spaces can transform performances and inspire unusual musical responses. The behavioural consequences of performing spaces are not as well explored (see Brereton, this volume), however, and the second case study provided in this chapter attempts to flesh out what such an analysis of space as behaviour setting can offer.

The first case study below addresses the local space of the performer and how instrumental design constrains and affords instrumental techniques. It also serves to illustrate how changes in instrumental layout co-evolve with instrumental techniques to offer new sonic possibilities.

### *The design of the modern Böhm flute: co-evolution of affordances and constraints*

The modern orchestral flute is a fairly recent innovation that has remained largely stable since the 1830s despite changes in material and some evolution in respect of the precise placement and mechanics of the keys and tone holes, and a gradual evolution in the shape of the head joint. The Böhm flute enables the player to play at least three octaves of chromatic pitch, with fairly good tuning and good volume, without having to resort to uncomfortable finger stretches or half-fingering of tone holes (see Dikicigiller, 2014). Böhm's book on the flute remains a useful resource today (Böhm, 1871/1908), signalling the extent to which, despite some changes in detail (see Toff, 1996), a design innovation has resulted in a stable instrument. One might expect, therefore, that such stability and clear design history would make it a rather dull subject for studying the relationship between body, space and sound. However, not all flutes are alike in detail, and this continued diversity illustrates the micro-ecology of music rather well (the second case study provides an analysis of a larger-scale ecosystem).

To illustrate the co-evolution of musical possibilities and instrument design, two aspects of variation on design will be considered. One appears trivial, yet turns out to be non-trivial. The other is apparently more fundamental, yet actually had little impact on the music that the flute's design has inspired. First, however a brief and incomplete explanation of the Böhm flute is necessary (for more detail see, e.g., Toff, 1996). The modern flute is constructed from three sections, two of which are cylindrical and punctuated with tone holes that serve to alter the length of a vibrating air column, while the third is tapered and generally follows a parabola. The mechanism of keys attached to the body of the flute allows the player to open and close all the tone holes without moving the hands. Crucially, the precise positioning of the tone holes in manufacture determines the pitch produced when each hole is opened and closed by a key and also the degree of comfort available to the player. The layout of the keys is therefore both determined by an accommodation to the shape of the body and a consideration of acoustic goals. To illustrate this interaction, consider the left hand of the player, which operates the keys closest to the head joint. The fourth finger of the left hand (inclusive of the thumb) is both shorter than the third finger of most players and, due also to the angle of the left hand as it holds the flute, has to stretch to the 'G' key of the Böhm flute. To overcome this stretch, the position of the tone-hole and key is, on some instruments, offset to reduce the stretch, bringing it closer to the hand, without changing its distance along the main axis of the flute. However, not all flutes have such a design solution and many manufacturers (such as Miyazawa) offer it as an option (Miyazawa, 2015). The offset G option is regarded by some as a less professional solution, despite having no impact on the acoustic result, and Miyazawa pragmatically suggest that rather than choosing based upon socio-cultural criteria, a player should simply consider which design best matches the size of their hand. Figure 7.1 illustrates how the rotation of the G key has no effect on tuning but has a significant impact on the degree to which the left hand needs to rotate to avoid an uncomfortable stretch of the fourth finger, especially for players with relatively small hands or a large difference in lengths between third and fourth finger. The author plays an in-line flute despite having relatively small hands, and as he has a very small difference in the length of these two fingers, this presents no bio-mechanical disadvantage. Hence, for keys that are operated directly by the fingers (and do not rely on the clever Böhm mechanism), there are some aspects of key positioning that are the result of matching body scale and instrument that may or may not be influenced by socio-cultural practices.

Instruments, voices, bodies and spaces 121

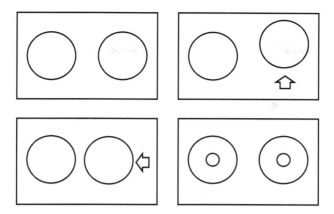

*Figure 7.1* 'In-line' (top left) and 'offset G' (top right) illustrate the relative position of the keys activated by the third (left key) and fourth (right key) fingers of the left hand (the hand closest to the head joint of the flute) in two alternative designs. Bottom left shows an offset along the tube which affects tuning, bottom right an open-hole design which affords glissando and other extended techniques not afforded by a closed-hole design.

The position of the tone holes, however, is, of course, non-arbitrary in terms of distance along the flute's main axis. This distance determines the length of the air column and the pitch that results. Many flute builders and designers (see Toff, 1996) have tinkered with these distances to best achieve 'good' relative tuning in relation to the well-tempered scale and to minimise the necessity for tuning adjustments made at the embouchure. The precise position of tone holes along this axis has little impact on the playability of the flute in terms of hand and finger position, occurring at a fine-grained scale (see Figure 7.1, bottom left). Moreover, many of the keys are not directly sitting under the player's fingers.

Although acoustically and bio-mechanically crucial to the tuning and operation of the flute, the placement of the keys has little impact on the music that is produced. Böhm flutes' keys differ in a seemingly less important detail with rather greater and unintended musical consequences. The keys which sit under the three main fingers of each hand are either 'closed' or 'open'. In the former case, the key is solid; in the latter, the key is a ring of metal which only becomes airtight if the finger sits on top of the central hole when the key is depressed. The illustration on the bottom left of Figure 7.1 represents the open-hole design which affords pitch-adjusting finger movements across the surface of the key. By dragging one can achieve glissandi, and by covering only a portion of the hole the player can adjust pitch microtonally without adjusting embouchure, and play a wider range of extended multiphonics.

Although flautists argue over which design is bio-mechanically, socio-culturally or acoustically preferable, the decision to choose one design over the other has some less obvious consequences. For standard (and especially tonal) repertoire, there is no music one cannot play on a closed-hole flute; it is capable of playing all chromatic notes necessary (after years of practice to accommodate the different finger patterns necessary for each scale or mode). However, composers, orchestrators and performers have explored the potential for the modern flute to produce a wider range of sounds. Glissandi and many other effects can be produced on a closed-hole flute, but the full range of effects considered by Bartolozzi (1982) or Dick (1975) assume an open-hole flute. Although still limited by the keys that cannot be half-holed (closed with the finger, leaving half of the central key opening uncovered), the open-hole flute allows for the easier control of glissandi, the production of quarter tones and even the production of a wider range of multiphonics (pseudo-chords). Here, what was once a matter of taste becomes a practical design choice with consequences for the player's repertoire and professional versatility. Although this may seem arbitrary, it illustrates neatly that the interaction of body and instrument is both limited by and stimulated by the design of the instrument that, without adaptation, turns out to be capable of producing a much wider range of sounds than it was designed for. The instrument has evolved through fairly arbitrary bifurcation into two versions, but only one is now fit for the wide range of modern music one might be called upon to perform.

### *The design of the Barbershop chorus: space, blend and expression*

If the consequences of open- versus closed-hole design of the flute are considered to be micro-structural, what about the macro-structure of musicians within a performing space? In this second example, I will explore the use of space in Barbershop choruses to achieve musical goals. The Barbershop style has evolved to include a particular focus on achieving blend between voices, resulting not only in close attention to tuning and balance, but also to the timbral quality of individual voices. This is partly due to the concept of ring, whereby, through singing chords with coincident harmonics, prominent harmonics above the fundamental tones become audible. The practice that has evolved to achieve this requires singers to focus their attention on micro-adjustments of pitch and vowel timbre and has led to a style where vibrato is used sparingly, if at all, and where musical devices such as 'posts' (where one voice holds a note and the others prolong and then resolve harmonic tension) play with the acoustic properties of mixed voices. Blend is explicitly referenced in the marking schemes used by judges at Barbershop singing competitions (see e.g., Gage, 2003; also see Garnett, 2005) and plays a role in the social cohesion within Barbershop ensembles: as Garnett (2005) notes, there is an conflation of the social and musical connotations of harmony in the narratives of Barbershop which sits at the heart of its collective identity.

In a standard expert quartet, the necessary matching between voices singing at different fundamentals can be achieved in a number of ways. Within a performance the singers can vary sound pressure, formant positioning during vowels (see Ringmasters, 2013b, for an example) and tuning. The prominence of higher harmonics between voices can also be varied, such that the lower or higher voices in a quartet have a brighter timbre for a given vowel, or a more even distribution is aimed for, as demonstrated by the Ringmasters (Ringmasters, 2013a). It is even the case that singers may be selected for the timbral quality of their voice and how it contributes to blend or that they may have to learn to adapt their natural formants to better blend with their colleagues.

Such adaptations in a quartet of different voice-parts require particular skills but are not beyond the capabilities of committed amateur musicians. Although such acoustic approaches to blend have not been extensively studied in vocal ensembles, there is evidence that singers do adjust their vocal sound when asked to blend (e.g., Goodwin, 1980; Rossing, Sundberg and Ternström, 1986) by, for example, reducing the prominence of higher harmonics. One might also apply work on blend from instrumental psychoacoustics (Kendall and Carterette, 1993) or indeed the broader field of auditory scene analysis (see e.g., Handel, 1989; Bregman, 1990).

Consider, however, how complex a performance problem blend becomes for the Barbershop chorus. Individual singers in the chorus come with different ranges and timbral qualities and may be less developed as singers than quartet performers. The perceptual challenges of hearing and adapting one's sound within a chorus are also non-trivial due to masking. The solution that choruses and their directors have developed to this problem is not just to ask singers directly to modify their voices (although such adaptation is encouraged to an extent); rather, it is to organise the different singers within a chorus in a 'stack' of voices on risers such that singers with similar steady-state vowel timbres stand near one another *regardless of part*. In a related practice, the numbers of singers to each part is controlled such that if a chorus director wishes to modify the overall timbral character they will reduce or increase the number of appropriate voices. Such stacking becomes particularly important in female Barbershop choruses where the 'basses' have to dominate in number in order to achieve the stylistically correct prominence of the lower part; conversely there may only be two or three female 'tenors' (the highest part). In summary, a chorus director moves singers around in space as an additional and crucial method of achieving blend and ring and to solve other balance issues (see for example Boutilier, 2009, p. 14):

> Often I'll put strong, experienced voices on row five, clear/clean voices on row two, and blend together the voices on rows three and four. Basses are in the middle mostly because this helps create a strong bass presence, the signature of our style of singing. Baritones that surround or are placed within the bass section enhance the depth of sound in

the bass clef. I sprinkle some independent, stronger voices within and around the basses so that the basses can hear all four parts, and so that the audience will, too. Voices on the ends of the rows must blend because they can be heard more easily.

Garnett (2009, p. 55) describes the way in which the classification of voices can help with this process:

> A common formulation is to classify voice timbres into types named after orchestral groups in order to aid choir stacking: 'flutes' and 'reeds' are particularly common, while some add strings to the taxonomy.

Garnett also here notes that more anatomical classification also may provide a conceptual background to such practice, and elsewhere in this book discusses the role of singers' disposition in space both in relation to musical and social blend. However, she does not discuss the practice that arises from this in relation to Barbershop here: her empirical analysis of a Barbershop chorus (Leeds' White Rosettes) focuses more on the overt movements during performance which support musical cohesion in the moment (see Garnett, 2009: Chapter 8). It is the movements that *precede* making music that I will turn to next, as they appear to have a significant and less well understood influence on the 'harmony' that Barbershop singers aspire to.

The clearest demonstration of the importance of stacking to Barbershop practice is found when a director either encounters a new chorus or has to add new members to an existing stack. The process of *restacking* is lengthy and can be based upon individual auditioning (which includes not just assignment of part but also voice quality) or upon wholesale re-organisation of the chorus. These processes are not well-documented in the literature but are demonstrated by Steve Tramack in a coaching session recorded for the British Association of Barbershop's Harmony College (Tramack, 2015). Tramack here demonstrates restacking to a chorus of student directors, bringing the entire baritone section out to stand in front of and facing the chorus. As they repeat a phrase from the piece they are working on he moves singers in the line around until the most similar singers are standing next to each other. At one point, Tramack asks a single singer to walk along the line until his voice is maximally blended. Interestingly, he suggests to the participants that part of this process is psychological in nature: standing next to a similar-sounding voice leads to a better feeling of blend, as well as directly to objective differences in timbre. Boutilier (2009, p. 14) claims that:

> At the end of the day, by the time we go on stage at regional contest, I bet I will be able to move anyone anywhere and the sound will stay intact and blended and exciting. But, I won't do that. I know that the psyche of being 'at home' in a chorus like ours is a very important one and I want your comfort level to be high whenever we perform!

The singers become used to the place they stand and the singers they stand near and perhaps this is a factor in the extraordinary sense of community that some choruses develop, such as Leeds' White Rosettes.

Although such live music spatial practice is, as far as I am aware, unique to Barbershop choruses (Gage does make reference to blend/ring in another choral tradition, but not stacking), it illustrates the way in which musicians manipulate musical parameters that are of aesthetic importance to their community of practice through an awareness of space that is far from metaphorical. This macrostructural manipulation of musicians' positions within a space creates an 'instrument' with flexible acoustic properties that would otherwise be extremely difficult to control. This musical community designs an instrument that mimics a quartet and redesigns it depending upon the acoustic and spatial constraints of each performance venue. Choruses may need to be restacked on the fly to accommodate a narrower or deeper stage or to offset a particularly dry or wet acoustic. Comparison with other vocal traditions, such as Anglican Church choirs, or indeed amateur festival choruses, where the polyphonic integrity of each voice is paramount, is far from trivial. The cohesive acoustic presentation of line in such music (and the possibility of counterpoint) is far removed from the desire for blended homophony in Barbershop practice and the layout into separate sections reflects this. It may be just as important *psychologically* that someone stands in between the same singers in each performance but it is at least as important that they are also basses. In Barbershop choruses with few tenors, one would not expect them to stand together – but they will stand next to leads, baritones or basses that blend well with them and derive comfort from the local experience of blend – replicating the quartet experience of ring at a local level within the chorus.

## Conclusions: listening to designed space in musical performance

Regardless of the level of interaction between body or bodies and spatial layouts, the sounds that we hear are related to these interactions in a lawful mapping. The shape, size, solidity and layout of the keys on a flute do not just afford comfort and tuning accuracy, they offer or deny musical possibilities: the difference between open and closed tone holes affords or denies finger movements that can produce microtones, quartertones and glissandi. This is not to deny the importance of tuning and bio-mechanical ease; not all instrumental design decisions have equal impact on the creative potential of an instrument. In the case of the Böhm flute, the difference between an offset or in-line G key has a significant bio-mechanical consequence but no obvious acoustic impact. On the contrary, small changes in position of the tone holes along the flutes length have almost no bio-mechanical impact yet change the flute's tuning perceptibly.

Unlike a flute maker, who can offer to the client a range of design choices, the chorus director cannot easily manipulate the vocal characteristics of each individual singer through physical means. Although the formants produced by a human head *can* be manipulated in real time or, longer-term through coaching, much more can be achieved quickly by simply accepting that 'the instrument' is a composite of the voices' positions in a stack; and there is a predictable acoustic consequence of their distribution. Redesigning a singer to better match another chorus member by changing their vocal apparatus might take years if it is possible at all; redesigning a chorus is a matter of minutes, with immediate and testable results.

Spatial manipulation is, of course, only one kind of musical design process. One might carry out a similar analysis of the relationship between material properties to discover which of these has any predictable acoustic consequence. The important consequence of considering space as a feature of design, especially in its interactions with body or bodies is that it helps relocate our discussion of space in music as a background for perception and action rather than as a metaphorical space in which metaphorical musical gestures are enacted. The attempts of Hanslick (e.g., 1974), Langer (e.g., 1953, 1957) and Scruton (1983), or indeed of von Helmholtz (1863/1954), to talk of space as a conceptual, rather than real aspect of musical language, have had a profound influence on the way in which we conceive of musical meaning. Such thinking underpins the representation of abstract musical structures in spatial terms in the work of Krumhansl (1990) or Lerdahl (2001). I would argue that paying attention to the ways in which bodies, instruments and spaces interact in the environment should do more than reveal psycho-sociological, acoustic or bio-mechanical issues of importance to musicology. Music is not an abstract art; it arises from our actions, and these actions are constrained and afforded by the spaces they are contained by and the layout of objects and events within them.

## Acknowledgements

This chapter would not have been possible without the thoughtful input of White Rosettes member Alison Crutchley, and a brief encounter with the late Albert Cooper, via Susan Milan and the late Jim Dower.

## References

Barker, R. G. (1978). *Habitats, environments, and human behaviour: Studies in ecological psychology and eco-behavioral science from the Midwest Psychological Field Station, 1947–1972*. San Francisco, CA: Jossey-Bass.

Bartolozzi, B. (1982). *New sounds for woodwind*. London: Oxford University Press.

Blesser, B., and Salter, L.-R. (2007). *Spaces speak, are you listening? Experiencing aural architecture*. Cambridge, MA: MIT Press.

Böhm, T. (1871/1908). *The flute and flute playing in acoustical, technical and artistic aspects* (Dayton C. Miller, Trans.). New York: Dover.

Boutilier, J. (2009). Let's talk about riser placement. *Pitchpipe, April*, 14.

Boyle, W. A., and Waterman, E. (2015). The ecology of musical performance. In: A. S. Allen and K. Dawe (Eds.), *Current directions in ecomusicology: Music, culture, nature* (pp. 25–39). New York: Routledge.
Bregman, A. S. (1990). *Auditory scene analysis: the perceptual organization of sound.* Cambridge, MA: MIT Press.
Burland, K., and Windsor, W. L. (2014). Moving the gong: Exploring the contexts of improvisation and composition. In S. Pitts and K. Burland (Eds.), *Coughing and clapping* (pp. 101–114). Farnham: Ashgate.
Clarke, E. (2005). *Ways of listening: An ecological approach to the perception of musical meaning.* Oxford: Oxford University Press.
Dick, R. (1975). *The other flute.* London: Oxford University Press.
Dikicigiller, B. B. (2014). Innovations of Theobald Boehm to the flute construction. *Journal of Arts and Humanities, 3*(11), 21–25.
Gage, A. (2003): *Four parts, no waiting: A social history of American barbershop harmony.* New York: Oxford University Press.
Garnett, L. (2005). *The British Barbershopper.* Farnham: Ashgate.
Garnett, L. (2009). *Choral conducting and the construction of meaning.* Farnham: Ashgate.
Gallagher, S. (2009). Philosophical antecedents to situated cognition. In P. Robbins and M. Aydede (Eds.), *The Cambridge handbook of situated cognition* (pp. 35–51). Cambridge: Cambridge University Press.
Gibson, J. J. (1966). *The senses considered as perceptual systems.* Boston: Houghton Mifflin.
Gibson, J. J. (1979). *The ecological approach to visual perception.* Boston: Houghton Mifflin.
Goodwin, A. W. (1980). An acoustical study of individual voices in choral blend. *Journal of Research in Music Education, 28*(2), 119–128.
Handel, S. (1989). *Listening: An introduction to the perception of auditory events.* Cambridge, MA: MIT Press.
Hanslick, E. (1974). *The beautiful in music: A contribution to the revisal of musical aesthetics* (G. Cohen, Trans.). New York: Da Capo Press.
Heft, H. (2001). *Ecological psychology in context: James Gibson, Roger Barker and the legacy of William James's radical empiricism.* Mahwah, NJ: Lawrence Erlbaum.
Juslin, P. N., and Madison, G. (1999). The role of timing patterns in recognition of emotional expression from musical performance. *Music Perception, 17*(2), 197–221.
Kendall, R. A., and Carterette, E. C. (1993). Identification and blend of timbres as a basis for orchestration. *Contemporary Music Review, 9*, 51–67.
Knakkergaard, M. (2013). The music that's not there. In M. Grimshaw (Ed.), *The Oxford handbook of virtuality* (pp. 392–403). New York: Oxford University Press.
Krumhansl, C. L. (1990). *Cognitive foundations of musical pitch.* New York: Oxford University Press.
Kugler, P. N., Shaw, R. E., Vincente, K. J., and Kinsella-Shaw, J. (1990). Inquiry into intentional systems I: Issues in ecological physics. *Psychological Research, 52*, 98–121.
Langer, S. K. (1953). *Feeling and form.* London: Routledge and Kegan Paul.
Langer, S. K. (1957). *Philosophy in a new key.* Cambridge, MA: Harvard University Press.
Lerdahl, F. (2001). *Tonal pitch space.* New York: Oxford University Press.

Miyazawa. (2015). *Options, features and enhancements: Inline G. vs. offset G.* Retrieved from http://www.miyazawa.com/media-library/educational-articles/options/inline-g-vs-offset-g/.

Mooney, J. (2011). Frameworks and affordances: Understanding the tools of music-making. *Journal of Music, Technology & Education, 3*, 141–154.

Norman, D. A. (2013). *The design of everyday things.* Basic Books.

Ringmasters. (2013a). *Ringmasters sound pyramid experiment.* Retrieved from https://youtu.be/cMm3XmqSPsE.

Ringmasters. (2013b). *16 resonance matching.* Retrieved from https://youtu.be/DYT2jB5o9fE.

Rossing, T. D., Sundberg, J., and Ternström, S. (1986). Acoustic comparison of voice use in solo and choir singing. *Journal of the Acoustical Society of America, 79*, 1975–1981.

Scruton, R. (1983). *The aesthetic understanding.* London: Methuen.

Small, C. (1988). *Musicking: The meanings of performing and listening.* Middletown, CT: Wesleyan University Press.

Sudnow, D. (1978). *Ways of the hand: The organization of improvised conduct.* Cambridge, MA: MIT Press.

Toff, N. (1996). *The flute book.* New York: Oxford University Press.

Tramack, S. (2015). *13 Directors Academy V – voice matching with Baris.* Retrieved from https://youtu.be/A4FS68BlwgU.

von Helmholtz, H. (1863/1954). *On the sensations of tone* (A. Ellis, Trans.). New York: Dover.

Windsor, W. L. (2000). Through and around the acousmatic: The interpretation of electroacoustic sounds. In Emmerson S. (Ed.), *Music, electronic media and culture* (pp. 7–35). London: Ashgate.

Windsor, W. L. (2004). An ecological approach to semiotics. *Journal for the Theory of Social Behaviour, 34*(2), 179–198.

Windsor, W. L., and de Bézenac, C. (2012). Music and affordances. *Musicae Scientiae, 16*, 102–120.

# 8 Sonic spaces in movies

## Audiovisual metaphors and embodied meanings in sound design

*Kathrin Fahlenbrach*

Sounds in music and sound design significantly contribute to the creation of filmic spaces. Sound enhances the reality effects of a filmic space (e.g., by atmospheric sounds) and contributes to how affective moods and emotions are displayed in a certain movie environment. Even more, sounds are relevant for formulating the higher narrative meanings of a filmic space.

This chapter presents an account of audiovisual metaphors in movies (cf. Fahlenbrach, 2010, 2016), which helps to explain how complex cultural and narrative meanings are associated with bodily based audiovisual Gestalts. Grounded on conceptual metaphor theory, it will be shown how sound design gives narrative meanings spatial Gestalts. After a theoretical introduction, four in-depth case studies will demonstrate the metaphorical creation of sonic spaces in film drama and their embodied dimension in narrative discourses.

## Embodied meanings in filmic spaces: some general principles in the interaction of moving pictures and sounds

In entertaining movies, cinematic spaces regularly follow the rules of transparency and of continuity. Moving pictures and sounds relate to bodily and cognitively rooted mechanisms of human perception (cf. also Anderson, 1996; Grodal, 1997, 2009). This allows filmmaking wherein the very act of creating filmic spaces is for the most part unnoticed by viewers. In the following section, I will focus on some general aspects of embodied meanings in filmic spaces that are generated in the interaction of moving pictures and sounds.

There has been significant research on general embodied aspects of audiovisual integration on the level of Gestalt perception (cf., e.g., Anderson, 1996; Smith, 1999; Cohen, 2013). This introduction will be rather selective and short, focusing on those embodied aspects in multimodal interaction of sounds and images that are especially relevant as metaphoric source domains in order to convey to narrative meanings an embodied Gestalt – an issue that will be treated specifically in the following.

Sound is significantly responsible for displaying the multi-sensory and kinaesthetic qualities of audiovisual spaces, which lay the ground for their embodied meanings. Because prototypical sounds can trigger reflexively sensorimotor and cross-modal associations in viewers (cf. Gallese and Keysers, 2001; Kohler et al., 2002), they significantly intensify the three-dimensional effect and physical presence of filmic spaces in the reception of a spectator. Especially the material characteristics of a place, its volume and its textures are considerably conceived by acoustic qualities of objects moving and interacting at a specific place in film (Flückiger, 2002). The cross-modal interaction of pictures and sound lets viewers integrate visual and acoustic information to coherent Gestalts and meanings, based on the processing of amodal qualities such as duration (long–short), intensity (strong–weak) and position (above–below, central–peripheral, close–distant). A few examples of the simultaneous appearance of cross-modal qualities in movies are:

- *Duration and tempo*: duration (long vs. short) and tempo (quick vs. slow) of shots and their temporal succession within the editing, the duration of the depicted movements in picture and of the camera movements might interact cross-modally with the acoustic duration and tempo of sounds and music.
- *Intensity*: visual and auditory elements in a cinematic sequence interrelate in their density of sensory stimuli, resulting in specific cross-modal intensities (strong vs. weak); on the visual scale the intensity of colours (e.g., intensity of colour saturation or intensity of colour contrasts) and of lightning (intensity of brightness vs. intensity of darkness) interacts on the auditory scale with the intensity of acoustic volume (loud vs. calm) and the pitch (intensity of high vs. low pitch) in music and sounds.
- *Position*: visual closeness or distance in camera shots and perspective, as well as spatial foreground and background in the picture interact with acoustic closeness or distance as well as acoustic foreground and background. These can be established, for example, by the acoustic perspective (point-of-audition; Chion, 1994) of characters in the fore- or background of a filmic space and by providing an acoustic perspective in the balancing of volume between loud (foreground) and low (background).
- In sound design, amodal qualities are important for conveying not only sensorial and material characteristics of a filmic space but also its embodied meaning structure (Sonnenschein, 2001; Holman, 2002). The material, bodily, emotional and cognitive attributes of objects and spaces may be altered by modulating significant acoustic characteristics, which were once established, such as pitch or timbre. By linking them cross-modally with corresponding visual features, different shades of meanings around a character, an object or place can be generated on the global scale of a movie, conceptually relating to its narrative discourse.

For the embodied meanings of filmic spaces, the audiovisual performance of movements is another basic element. Filmic spaces are generally structured by different actors: the characters moving and acting within a filmic space; the narrative actors (including all actors involved in the filmmaking), building a diegetic space by creating moving images (especially the camera) and sounds; and the viewers, generating mental spaces in their minds by activating sensorimotor schemata and associations. Following neurophysiological studies (Gallese, 2005), the mental simulation of movements is very close to active physical movements, since the same multi-sensorial mirror neurons in the sensorimotor area of our brain are activated. As a result, we not only recognise basic movements and the related action tendencies of persons and fictional characters in moving images, but we also experience them physically within our own body (see Wöllner and Hohagen, this volume). During the interaction we thereby perform with a person vis-à-vis a shared action space that Gallese (2005) calls a *peri-personal space*.[1] Spatial information is thus ultimately linked to physical movements in space, which refers not only to the characters in a film but also to the body of the viewer. Consequently the characters' movements – and thus the filmic space itself – are always experienced by the recipient as physical extensions of action tendencies and intentions (cf. Fahlenbrach, 2007, 2010; Gallese and Guerra, 2012). Cinematic atmospheres (Flückiger, 2002) densely composing prototypical acoustic elements of a certain space (e.g., traffic sounds of an urban space) offer viewers relevant cues for mentally simulating in their minds action tendencies of characters acting in these filmic spaces. Sound design regularly characterises a filmic action location by providing us with acoustic traces of movements and interactions of the characters moving there – acoustic traces that let us anticipate basic action tendencies and emotions of the depicted characters (cf. Kohler et al. 2002). Accordingly, cinematic spaces are highly structured by camera movements (cf. Coëgnarts and Kravanja 2012; Gallese and Guerra, 2014), by movements of the depicted actors (and objects) in a film and by the acoustic traces of their movements within a filmic space.

As I will outline more specifically in the following, the composition of filmic spaces also basically recurs on mental principles of spatial perception that imply innate, Gestalt-based meanings (cf. Anderson, 1996; Grodal, 1997, 2009). Pictures, sounds and movements that are performed by the camera and those that are depicted in a scene activate mental Gestalts such as the audiovisual manifestation of spatial size, brightness and multi-sensory image schemata (Johnson, 1987; Gallese and Guerra 2012, 2014) like the container-schema (in–out) and the path-schema (here–there) that already convey embodied meanings on a pre-conceptual level (cf. Grodal, 2009; Forceville, 2008).

## Audiovisual metaphors in movies: some basic premises and concepts

In cognitive research, metaphors have been shown to act as elementary structures of human thinking and mental imagination (Lakoff, 1987;

Johnson, 1987; Danesi, 1989; Boroditsky and Ramscar, 2002; Gallese and Lakoff, 2005): They help us to imagine complex, abstract or invisible ideas, concepts or emotions in terms of embodied schemata and Gestalts, such as exploding containers ('emotion is a container', e.g., 'bursting with joy'), paths ('life is a path', e.g., 'at the end of life'), or spatial hierarchies ('good is up and bad is down'). As 'intermediary structures' in our minds (Danesi, 1989), they integrate cultural knowledge with embodied meanings, based on Gestalt perception and image schemata.

Given the cognitive character of metaphorical understanding and imagination, films also refer to the metaphoric schemata and mechanisms that are anchored in our minds (Forceville and Urios-Aparisi, 2009; Fahlenbrach, 2007, 2010, 2016; Kappelhoff and Müller, 2011; Coëgnarts and Kravanja, 2012, 2014; Kappelhoff and Greifenstein, 2016). As Forceville (e.g., 2008, 2016) and Fahlenbrach (e.g., 2007, 2016) argue, this is especially evident in entertainment genres, which tend to strategically 'sell' their products by addressing their viewers' immediate, reflexive understanding and their affects multimodally through pictures, sounds and language. Drawing on conceptual metaphors allows filmmakers to communicate complex meanings in an embodied Gestalt that their audiences understand in a reflexive manner.

Based on these premises, it is evident that audiovisual media implicitly and explicitly draw on the mechanisms of conceptual mapping, thereby creating audiovisual metaphors. Audiovisual metaphors are understood as intentionally created symbolic forms and relevant elements in audiovisual media (Fahlenbrach, 2010, 2016). Audiovisual metaphors transfer cultural meanings in mentally based metaphoric Gestalts. Thereby they use salient Gestalt patterns in image, sound and movement that are closely related to embodied image schemata in our minds as metaphoric source domains (e.g., a container, or paths). Audiovisual metaphors thereby generate cross-modal mappings across different conceptual domains. They address multi-sensorial qualities of the related image schemata, which are manifested in the visual composition, sound design, music and movements. As I will outline later, this considerably implies the use of spatial Gestalts in pictures and sounds as metaphoric source domains. To give an example: with the container-schema as source domain, a spatial Gestalt can be conveyed to concepts such as identity (e.g., 'self is a closed space'), society ('society is a building'), or good vs. bad (e.g., 'good is top of a building', 'bad is the bottom of a building'), as well as complex and 'invisible' aspects of inner emotional states or moods of a character (e.g., 'anger is hot fluid in a container'; see Kövecses, 2003).

Audiovisual compositions in movies use such multi-sensorial Gestalts as source domains for specific concepts in order to give their audiences a sensorial impression of abstract or otherwise difficult-to-grasp target domains in the narrative, such as the emotions and moods of a character (cf. Fahlenbrach, 2010, in print; Bartsch, 2016). Thereby, they integrate different conceptual source and target domains into cross-modal Gestalts (Gallese and Guerra 2012, 2014). This is realised by synchronically relating, in one-shot, amodal qualities in picture, sound and movement such as rhythm, duration, intensity and direction of movement (change of position). As a result cross-modal intensity of picture and sound can, e.g., address the mental image schema of a 'natural force' as a source domain in order to give viewers a sensorially concrete notion of narrative target domains (e.g., 'emotion is a natural force').

## Audiovisual metaphors in the sound design of sonic spaces

### *Spatial sounds as metaphoric source domains in sound design*

Considering more specifically the interaction of visual and acoustic source and target domains in metaphoric mappings, I would argue that the abstract target domains of an audiovisual metaphor are rather established by language or in the visual motif of a sequence than in the sound, while sound rather provides metaphoric source domains. On a general scope, Grimshaw and Garner (2012) even argue that acoustic analogues to a visual representation of an idea always imply metaphorical concepts. As Chion (1994) and also Cohen (2013) state, visual elements (including not only pictures, but also written texts) tend to dominate in the semantic interplay of vision and sound in film. This results in what Chion (1994) calls the spatial magnetisation of sound by image: the broader polyvalent spectrum of sound tends to be reduced to a narrower meaning when being combined with visual elements. Even if, of course, sounds significantly influence the meanings of visuals in a movie (Smith, 1999; Chion, 1994; Cohen, 2013), it is mostly the image that establishes the more abstract semantic framework for interpreting and experiencing the meaning of an audiovisual scene. The depicted motifs and topoi (e.g., spatial topoi as big city, rural area, bazaar, castle) build on our cognitive and cultural knowledge. With their presentation films establish a narrative, historical and cultural framework that acts, at the same time, as conceptual framework for the creation of audiovisual metaphors. In other words, the visually represented motifs and topoi offer *conceptually* rich material for metaphoric target domains. At the same time, both the visual and acoustic mental Gestalts that are manifest in each audiovisual composition (e.g., spatial Gestalts such as as up–down, in–out, central–peripheral), offer rich sensory material for metaphoric source domains. This will be explained more specifically in the following by drawing on audiovisual space-metaphors.

Many sounds offer indexical information about a certain place in a movie. Noises, spatial key sounds (e.g., the tolling of church bells) and complex acoustic atmospheres (e.g., of an urban or a rural setting) indicate material, architectural, and sometimes also historical and cultural characteristics of a certain action place in a movie (Flückiger, 2002; Sonnenschein, 2001; Holman, 2002). Implying cultural knowledge, indexical sounds can, of course, also indicate a metaphoric target in a narrative. More importantly, however, such acoustic indices and their Gestalts act as metaphoric sources in an audiovisual composition: The size of a place, for example, which is being acoustically performed by sonic reverberation of objects and people moving and acting in it, can serve as a source domain for generating metaphors of social power in vision and sound and, often related, of the emotional distance between people acting at such places. A canonic example is a key sequence in *Citizen Kane* (Orson Welles, USA, 1941), a film that tells the story of a rich and successful publisher, whose increasing power distances him more and more from his social surroundings, including his wife. The sequence shows two similar meetings of the couple in the oversized hall of their huge castle, interrupted in the editing by an ellipsis that indicates a huge leap in time between the two situations. Both times when Kane enters the hall, his wife is sitting alone in front of the big fireplace, doing a puzzle and expressing her boredom. The emotional distance between them is acoustically transported not only by their dialogue, but also by the echo of their voices reflecting from the walls of the hall. In combination with the pictures of the oversized room, emphasised by the deep focus of the camera, in some moments highly contrasting the two characters in the fore- and the background in one-shot, 'big size' and spatial distance clearly act as multi-sensorial source domains for displaying metaphorically both Kane's power and his emotional isolation: 'social power is a big space' and 'emotional distance is spatial distance'. Focusing on the acoustic resonance as a metaphoric source, the mapping can be further specified: 'emotional distance is high acoustic reverberation'. Hence by hearing the echo of their voices and of Kane's steps in the hall, the spectator is invited to associate these not only with the size of his place but also his social power and his related emotional distance to his social environment.

### *Metaphoric atmospheres in sonic spaces of movies*

As psychological studies have shown, the sound quality of music as well as in acoustic atmospheres (the sounds displaying acoustically a certain place) are already reflexively associated by listeners with affective and emotional qualities (cf. studies on the expression and experience of emotions and of music, and their interactions, e.g., Juslin, 1997, 2003; Scherer, 1995). 'Warm' and 'soft' auditory Gestalt qualities typically trigger hedonic values such as 'harmonious', 'pleasant' and 'un-offensive' and are consequently related to positive emotions such as pleasure, love and affective closeness. In contrast, 'sharp' or 'rough' acoustic Gestalts allow us to experience rather stressful and negative affects and emotions, such as aggression, anger, or fear. As studies in the perception of pitch show (e.g., Eitan and Timmers, 2010; see also Eitan, this volume), such cross-modal attributions to sound imply a general metaphoric character. As these studies equally demonstrate, basic cross-modal metaphors of sound (e.g., 'high vs. low pitch') bear a salient psychological reality for listeners of sound and music when describing their experience of pitch in music. Following up on these studies, I would argue that cross-modal metaphors of auditory qualities constitute relevant mental elements in metaphorically mapping visual and acoustic features in a movie scene. In other words: primary cross-modal mappings of auditory qualities (e.g., 'high vs. low pitch') offer significant mentally and experientially based material for metaphoric source domains to give abstract narrative meanings in a film an acoustic Gestalt. Hence I would argue that automatically triggered affective associations can also act as Gestalt-based and embodied source domains in the audiovisual design of filmic spaces in order to create conceptually richer meanings. Framed by a filmic narrative and by semantic interaction of the sounds with the pictures, the sound quality of music, of noises and single sounds, as well as of complex acoustic atmospheres can generate an added value (Chion, 1994), implying differently layered metaphoric meanings. Accordingly the auditory quality being accompanied cross-modally by equivalent visual features (e.g., 'sharp' or 'soft' Gestalts) and being framed by indexical and symbolic information given in the visual and spatial motifs and topoi of the pictures (sometimes also in the sounds) that characterise a given filmic place often generate metaphoric meanings that go beyond a purely reflexive association of auditory qualities. Referring to the Congruence-Association-Model of Cohen (2013) it could be argued that the meaning structures of the visual and acoustic elements generate together a new metaphoric audiovisual meaning in the 'working narrative' (Cohen, 2013).

The metaphoric use of sound is often used in sound design to contrast the spatial atmospheres of different places in a movie. One prototypical example is the early sound film *Applause* by Rouben Mamoulian (USA, 1929), one of the first movies that significantly used atmospheric sounds (as spatial sounds) to characterise different action places. It introduces a young girl named April who has been sent as child to a convent by her mother so that she can grow up in a safe place, far away from her mother's own life as a burlesque vaudeville star. In a key scene the viewers accompany the adult girl leaving the convent to join her mother in the big city. The camera slowly follows her during 2:30 minutes walking in a thoughtful way for the last time through the corridors of the convent, led by a nun. Paralleled by the slow rhythm and the soft timbre of a female chorus singing Schubert's *Ave Maria* off-screen, the filmmaking shows her melancholically taking a last glance at different emotionally significant places in the convent and at the nuns, both portrayed as peaceful and friendly. The tender character of the chant is acoustically reinforced by the silence of the nuns and the lack of spatial sounds. Both the inner rooms of the convent and its garden are shown in bright pictures that create an atmosphere of a pleasant harmony between the nuns, the religious architecture and nature. In this sequence, not only the visual motif and topos of the convent but also the chant provide rich cultural and symbolic meanings, establishing a place reigned over by religion.

In the interaction of pictures and music, a rather general metaphor is being generated: 'a religious community is a harmonious space'. Considering more specifically the auditory quality, which is primarily characterised by cross-modal mapping of a 'soft sound' and its interaction with visual Gestalts of 'tenderness' in the atmosphere of the place, the audiovisual metaphor – 'a religious community is a tender and soft space' – is created. The multi-sensory metaphoric meaning structure of this sequence is made evident at its end by creating a strong dichotomy of spatial atmospheres: after April has said goodbye to the nun at the gate of the convent and has opened the door to walk out, the filmmaking transports the viewer with an abrupt match-cut to her arrival at Grand Central Station in New York by blending a close shot of her face at the gate with another close shot of her face when leaving the train. This abrupt ellipsis progresses with a strong change in the acoustic atmosphere: the music stops and the filmic space is now dominated by the simultaneity of many different loud and rough noises at the station, including the sharp noises of wheels on the rail tracks, acoustic alarms in high pitch, and loud metallic noises resonating in the huge hall of the station, paralleled by the camera showing April's gaze looking up at its ceiling. Structured by the multi-sensory container-schema, her exit from the 'religious space' through the gate into the 'mundane and urban space' is clearly marked metaphorically by creating a strong dichotomy between an 'in'-space (of the religious community) and an 'outside'-space ('world outside the community'). Thereby the sound design significantly contributes to the metaphorical display of the sequence in contrasting the atmospheres of these different places: as a movement from an enclosed, sheltered and 'soft' space, reigned over by religion, to a mundane and urban place with a loud, sharp and offensive atmosphere. Framed by the narrative we are invited to relate this atmosphere to a place, ruled by a 'capitalist society', a society from which April's mother wanted to protect her. Accordingly the staging of her arrival in New York creates the metaphor: 'a capitalist society is a huge and rough space' with the match-cut performing her movement from one place to the other as a movement from 'religion as a soft space' to a 'capitalist society as a huge and rough space'.

With regard to the reception of a film, metaphorical conceptualisation of filmic spaces provides two important advantages: when visual and auditory qualities of places are conceptualised with reference to specific metaphoric meanings, it is possible to anchor cognitive and emotional attributes in their very material and bodily Gestalt in both the short- and long-term memory of viewers. Accordingly, the spectator's associations can be structured in an embodied way while simultaneously providing the filmic spaces with a coherent and evident cross-modal Gestalt during a film (cf. Sonnenschein, 2001; Holman, 2002). At the same time, as is shown in the last example, specific meanings of different places can be conveyed and contrasted by the use of audiovisual metaphors. This is pivotal for the construction of embodied audiovisual Gestalts because in this way the places appear coherently in their acoustic and visual representation on the level of cross-modal associations both on the local and global scale of a movie.

In the final section, four detailed case studies in film drama will be presented that elaborate more precisely on how cross-modal Gestalts, the image schemata of moving pictures and sounds, can interact in movies as source domains in order to convey narrative meanings in an embodied way. By focusing on film drama, it will be argued that genre-typical topics are displayed by generating specific audiovisual metaphors. As a methodological remark: the studies do not present empirical research but film-analytical results, based on a systematic analysis of mapping structures in the audiovisual material of film scenes. Thereby they will draw on the most salient auditory and visual features in sound design, music and filmmaking that seem to evidently interrelate in a metaphoric way with the narrative discourse of a movie. The presented metaphors tend to be genre-typical; however, they are foremost specifically created by the given filmmaking. No conclusion will be presented about the empirical reception of such metaphors by viewers.

## Sonic spaces and audiovisual metaphors in film drama: four case studies

In entertainment movies, drama is one of the most pervasive genres, often closely related to more specific genres, such as melodrama, crime fiction, psycho-thriller, science fiction or horror. Hence genre-typical topics differ. While in sci-fi and horror, the dramatic story is related with fantastic and mysterious elements, the narratives of social drama, melodrama and psycho-thriller are more rooted in realistic scenarios. Accordingly, sounds and spaces are less artificially designed and the symbolic and metaphoric use of sounds and spaces is often less obvious for viewers than in the other genres. However the filmmakers make equally significant use of metaphoric meanings when combining pictures and sound in order to present the inner emotions of characters as well as higher narrative meanings in an embodied Gestalt.

Traditional topics in social film drama (including melodrama) concern at least one of three arenas: conflicts between individuals and society and the confrontation between moral values and norms of different social groups; the conflict between human civilisation and nature; or inner, psychological conflicts related to identity crisis or personal traumata. Hence, even if filmic spaces in social drama often correspond to a high degree to the paradigm of filmic realism, they imply at the same time both symbolic and metaphoric meanings. In this regard, music, acoustic spatial atmospheres, noises and other sounds performed in filmic spaces symbolise different kinds of conflicts that are rather 'invisible', abstract or complex to depict. In the following case studies of canonic examples in social film drama especially the metaphoric display of interior spaces will stand at the fore.

## Metaphoric embodiment of cultural norms and their critique in sonic spaces in early and recent film drama

The restriction of individual freedom and desires by social constraints has been the topic of many early film dramas. The adaption of women to traditional social norms has particularly been treated in several melodramas, both in an affirmative and a critical way.

Orson Welles' melodrama *The Magnificant Ambersons* (USA, 1942) tells the story of Isabel Amberson, who is the daughter of a traditional upper-class family. As a young girl she is not allowed to pursue her love, the young inventor Eugene, who does not meet the social requirements of her family. After having been steered to marry Wilbur, a rich man with whom she has a son, she meets Eugene again years later, after her husband has died. They still love each other and, for a moment, hope that they still might be able to come together. In a key scene, Isabel meets her grown-up son George to whom she has given a letter beforehand, in which Eugene had tried to prove his earnest and respectable love for Isabel. After George has read the letter, he walks towards Isabel's room in a huge and sombre corridor. His entrance into the corridor is acoustically marked as he slams the door, indicating his rather aggressive and decisive attitude at this moment. The darkness of the corridor he is walking down is accompanied in the filmmaking by a slow tempo and sombre sounds of instruments. It gives George's stride a severe and also a fateful touch. When he reaches his mother's room and knocks on her door, the music stops. After a cut the visual perspective changes and we anticipate his entrance from inside the room, with his mother sitting in the foreground of the picture, expecting him (see Figure 8.1). Accordingly, Isabel's room is emphasised in the filmmaking as an isolated and limited place in the house. As her private place, it displays a metaphor of her personal identity ('self is a closed space'), embracing her social self as well as her inner desires and feelings.

The abrupt change of perspective and sound supports the idea that George is an invader in his mother's private space. The following confrontation

*Figure 8.1* The Magnificant Ambersons (Orson Welles, USA, 1942) 'self is a closed space': confrontation of self and society.

results in a conflict between her romantic love for Eugene and her parental love for her son, including her social responsibility for him. Even though the spatial setting and the performance of the actors already gives viewers a reflexive idea of the inner feelings of both characters, the sound and music significantly convey a more specific understanding of them, also offering evaluating cues to affectively and cognitively appraise the situation: at the first moment, when they are talking about the letter, the silence in the room emphasises the emotional distance between the two, generating the specific audiovisual metaphor 'lack of empathy is silence'. Then George confronts his mother with sharp words with the potential social consequences of her romance. When Isabel stands up from her chair subsequently, admitting her love for Eugene with a direct and self-confident gaze, the music starts. Accompanying this rising movement of Isabel with the ascending melody of the strings, the audiovisual performance metaphorically evokes a cross-modal and affective experience in viewers that 'love is a rising force'. This audiovisual love-metaphor is put forward when, in his reaction to his mother's change of attitude, George drops his gaze, sits down and lowers his head, 'pushed down' by the force of her romantic feelings. This time, the music accompanies his movement by a descending melody. The next reaction shot shows Isabel, now affected by George's low spirits. As the melody of the music begins ascending again in an accelerating way, she quickly approaches her son, taking his head in her hands. After the music finds a balanced constant pitch, the mother decides to renounce, again, her beloved Eugene and to stay alone with her son – a decision that will later contribute to her early death. The emotional change in Isabel at this moment is indicated by her body language and the accompanying music, generating a shift in metaphoric meaning: framed by the depicted movements of the characters and their dialogues, the specific meaning of 'love is a rising force' changes from romantic to maternal love.

This example demonstrates the well-known potential of film music both to illustrate the inner feelings of characters by 'mickey mousing' their movements and mimicking their characters, and for affective congruence (cf. also Smith, 1999). Moreover, it illustrates that moving pictures and sound interact in their structure of meaning (Cohen, 2013) in that cross-modal Gestalts (rhythm, duration and patterns of movements) interact as metaphoric source domains, generating specific audiovisual space-metaphors within the narrative framework of the drama. These metaphors let viewers not only affectively and bodily but also cognitively and culturally interpret and evaluate the dramatic conflict: the suppression of romantic love by maternal love according to tradition. This can result in severe scepticism in many viewers about the cultural norms and values of the depicted era. Accordingly, audiovisual metaphors in social drama can serve to articulate social critique of the filmmakers in an embodied way. This embodiment of a cultural critique significantly builds on the use of spatial and affective sounds in music and sound design.

Inner conflicts in families, caused by strict and even inhuman values, norms and taboos are treated also in more recent social film dramas, such as Michael Hanekes *Das Weiße Band. Eine deutsche Kindergeschichte* [*The White Ribbon*] (Germany, Austria, France, Italy, 2009). The film presents the residents of a small village in Germany at the dawn of World War I – a community ruled by a strict authoritarian order. The story centres on the family of a pastor who tortures his children with cruel psychological and physical punishments every time they seem to dismiss his severe Protestant ethics. The interior rooms of this family house are shown to be dark and silent, indicating the emotional coldness reigning in this place, generating, as in the previous example, the metaphor 'lack of empathy is silence'. In a significant sequence, the pastor forces his little son Martin with perfidious psychological tricks to confess that he has secretly masturbated. The scene significantly expresses the film's critical deconstruction of the Protestant norms prevalent at the time, especially in rural areas of Germany. Accordingly, the spatial performance densely composes symbolic and metaphoric meanings that viewers might already grasp on an embodied level.

The father's room, where the interview is taking place, is shown as a rather narrow place, stuffed with many books and dark furniture. At the beginning the situation is predominantly presented from Martin's perspective, with the editing switching between his point-of-view looking at his father, and long reaction shots of his face with his father's voice talking off-screen. Behind Martin, we see a huge dark Christian Cross hanging on the wall. While Martin is standing motionless in front of the desk during the whole conversation, he follows the actions and movements of his father with his eyes. At the beginning of the scene, the symbolical dimension of the situation is put forward, when he silently observes his father feeding a canary in a cage. During the feeding, the pastor starts the interrogation by expressing the deep concern that he and his spouse have about the changes in Martin's appearance and attitudes that they have noticed lately. Furthermore, he underlines their worries by beginning with an anecdote about another boy who is at Martin's age and showed the same symptoms and, as we learn towards the end of the scene, died, because he 'touched himself at the most sensitive parts of his body'. The psychological cruelty of the father is saliently marked by paralleling the expression of his paternal concern with the act of feeding the bird, sitting in a small cage. This action is acoustically emphasised by the loud sound produced by the birdseed being put on the paper, which contrasts distinctively with the silent atmosphere in the room. Accordingly the filmmaking, combining dialogue and the father's action in vision and sound, generates the metaphor 'parental care is feeding an animal in a cage', which not only symbolically but also affectively and bodily leads us to grasp the ambiguous psychological cruelty of the pastor towards his son. Framed by the introductory metaphor 'lack of empathy is silence', the contrasting sounds of the father's feeding of the bird let spectators anticipate the dishonest bigotry of his moral attitude towards his son in an embodied way.

Even more, the cinematography offers only very limited views of this room – switching at the beginning of this sequence between the unchanging, quasi static, point-of-view of Martin and of his father – one of them being 'trapped' and the other, observing him and pretending to treat him with care. When the scene continues, the movements and actions of the father are again marked by significant sounds that contrast with the silence in the room: it is not only his voice that acoustically dominates the place, but also his steps on the wooden floor produce loud creaking noises as acoustic traces of the father's movements in the room. Framed by the psychological dimension of the conversation, these acoustic traces not only indicate his physical but also his psychological power, using the acoustic volume as a significant metaphoric source domain: 'power is a loud force'. The frightening presence of the father is reinforced during the scene when, in the narrow visual field of Martin, the father is constantly approaching him, while he is himself not allowed to move but is 'trapped' in front of the desk. When the father directly stands in front of him, the camera perspective switches: from an over-shoulder-view we now observe the reactions of Martin with the pastor's gaze, while the boy is being confronted with his father's insistent intimate questions that finally aim to make him confess his 'sin'. Also in this example, audiovisual metaphors are being generated as an 'interior space' that lets viewers experience affectively and bodily the social disciplining of an individual's intimate self and critically reflect upon the underlying social, in this case, religious order.

In both films, the Gestalt of a limited interior space is used as a metaphoric source domain for depicting the conflict of an individual with a social order. Thereby both films use comparable metaphors: 'lack of empathy is silence' and 'psychological power is a loud force'. However, while in the early drama by Welles, the film score significantly dominates the sonic space, the later example by Haneke completely excludes the use of music and creates a dense acoustic atmosphere by single spatial noises and dialogue. Both music and the atmospheric sounds in the two examples obviously offer rich embodied source domains. Accordingly, pictures, sounds and movements involved in these metaphors serve relevant narrative functions of the drama to represent and criticise the depicted order of norms and values. The narrative's cultural critique of these norms and values is displayed in the metaphoric shaping of sonic spaces allowing spectators to both experience and reflect on them in an embodied way.

### *Metaphoric embodiment of identity crisis in sonic spaces of social drama and psycho-drama*

Another relevant topic in social drama that is recurrently displayed by generating metaphoric audiovisual spaces refers to identity crisis, caused by biographical traumata and psychological crisis, displayed in social drama and in psycho-drama. This will be analysed in the following two case studies.

In its story about a Vietnam War veteran, the social drama *Taxi Driver* (Martin Scorsese, USA, 1976) deals with the psychological and social consequences of war on soldiers. Ex-soldier Travis Bickle is hired by a taxi company in New York. Traumatised by war and unable to sleep, he spends his days and nights driving a taxi and observing people on the street. As his mind fills with aggression against urban life, he develops a growing desire to 'clean up' the town. Travis' feelings of hate and disgust, combined with his loneliness and incapacity to get close to people, are conveyed to viewers during the movie by dense compositions, including audiovisual metaphors. As in the examples discussed earlier, canonic spatial motifs – most significantly the taxi and the big city – are used as metaphoric source domains and help to clearly display in vision and sound the ambivalent and traumatised personality of the protagonist.

The movie opens with a metaphorically shaped affective introspection of Travis Bickle, whom at first we come to know only by detail shots of his eyes. The opening shot is filled with white steam on a street and then Travis' taxi slowly passing through it, accompanied by a prominent saxophone sound, playing an ascending melody in a slow tempo and with a full jazz sound. Accompanied by this score, the low angle shot introduces the taxi as a heroic agent, passing through an environment full of obstacles. As his taxi subsequently circulates by night through rainy New York, the city is presented from Travis' point-of-view through the windshield of the car, and, intermittently, we see a close-up of his eyes, seemingly searching for something. Everything in the scene is displayed from his point-of-view and clearly marked by a melancholic and rather pessimistic mood, which is established in the film score by the calm jazz music (created by Bernard Hermann) and by the slow motion, showing social life on the streets in a delayed manner. The slow motion, cross-modally paralleled with the slow rhythm of the music, indicates the melancholic and distanced perspective of Travis of his surroundings. Generating the audiovisual emotion metaphor 'melancholy is delayed motion' (cf. Fahlenbrach, in print), the music and the pictures create a *synchresis* (Chion, 1994)[2] and provide viewers with an intense multi-sensory experience of Travis' inner feelings.

After we have learned more about his biographical background and his personal situation in the following sequence of the film, his nocturnal rides through New York generate a global metaphoric meaning of the narrative: 'coping with identity crisis is a ride'. This is made evident in a voice-over at the beginning, with Travis mentioning that he keeps on driving every day and every night because he cannot sleep – a statement that we are motivated to relate to his war experience. During his ride we get access to his inner thoughts and feelings both through the music and the voice-over of his monologue – which acoustically interact, again, in their slow tempo, and in their lack of variation in pitch and prosody, paralleled by slow camera movement. Constantly the metaphor 'melancholy is delayed motion' is put forward in a cross-modal way by music, voice and camera movement.

Together with the music the inner monologue in the voice-over during his trip offers viewers an affective introspection that informs us about his rejection of the people on the streets and the way he feels about his being in the world as an outsider. Both the music and his inner monologues fill the interior acoustic space of the taxi. The taxi is clearly presented as a significant personal space of Travis, providing us with a metaphorical and multi-sensory experience of his inner identity crisis. The filmmaking displays it as a limited space 'filled' by pictures and sounds of his inner thoughts, perceptions and feelings (Figure 8.2). Driving in this limited but mobile space through an environment experienced by him as 'hostile' and 'disgusting' not only marks a strong dichotomy between the interior and exterior space of the taxi but also gives Travis' trips a psychological dimension. Framed by the aforementioned biographical information, we are invited to experience both the taxi and Travis' trips in terms of the embodied metaphors 'self is a limited space' and 'coping with identity crisis is a ride'.

By the manifestation of the mental path-schema as embodied source domain for the ride metaphor, viewers are invited to anticipate the psychological dimension of his trips not only emotionally but also by activating sensory-motor associations of 'moving forward', 'moving along a path' – a path that is actually full of obstacles. This Gestalt element of 'moving forward' is simultaneously present in the music. This is realised both by the music's very nature of 'moving forward in time' and, more specifically, by accelerating single sounds, for example by the stretched and slow sounds of the saxophone that dominate the motif and the entry of some quick drumbeats. Taking sounds as the result of an action in time, the extension and action could be considered as part of moving forward in time. Hence in this case

*Figure 8.2* Taxi Driver (Martin Scorsese, USA 1976), 'coping with identity crisis is a ride'.

metonymic mappings are generated: 'accelerated sounds for movements forward'. As a metonymic pars-pro-toto for 'moving forward', the music offers a general embodied meaning structure to the sequence that conceptually contributes to the display of its overarching metaphorical meaning: 'coping with identity crisis is a ride (along a path)' and 'is movement forward'.

It is especially through these movement-based metaphors and metonymies in the audiovisual display of his taxi rides through New York that viewers can get an embodied understanding of the deep identity crisis Travis is suffering. As has been shown, the filmmaking saliently accentuates his movements and trips through the city and his emotional expressions, inviting viewers to generate peri-personal spaces (Gallese, 2005) with the protagonist, letting us mentally simulate his inner feelings. At the same time this mechanism of mental simulation is metaphorically performed when relating multi-sensory Gestalts to 'movement', as well as the container-schema (in–out) in pictures and sounds to the global narrative discourse on a Vietnam War soldier, being unable to re-integrate in society and experiencing a severe emotional alienation. Also in this film drama, the metaphorically shaped sonic spaces not only serve to embody but also critically reflect upon a certain social problem, in this case the effects of the Vietnam War on soldiers.

The most direct way to expose identity crisis, traumata and psychoses lies in the insertion of dream sequences, for example in psycho-dramas. Such sequences also use cross-modal spatial Gestalts as metaphoric source domains to give viewers both an embodied and a cognitive access to the inner horror a character is experiencing.

In *Lost Highway* (David Lynch, France, USA, 1997) we are confronted with the story of Fred, who suffers from a growing emotional alienation of his wife, which causes strong, even psychotic jealousy in him. Fred's story is intertwined with the story of another man, Pete, who falls in love with a woman (Alice) who looks exactly like Renée, Fred's wife, with the only difference being the colour of her hair. The non-linear and enigmatic dramaturgy of Lynch seems to suggest that both characters are two parts of one and the same person (cf. Buckland, 2009). While there are several possible explanations for how these two men and women and the events around them interrelate, Fred obviously suffers a severe psychotic crisis, progressing to the experience of a split identity. This is made explicit by a nightmarish sequence, in which it remains unresolved in the global narrative of the film whether the depicted events happened only in his dreams or actually took place in his life. This is further reinforced later in the film, when part of the sequence is repeated as if it had actually happened, adding cruel and shocking details to it. In line with the movie's global play with the reality status of the depicted actions and persons, the spectator's uncertainty about this scene significantly contributes to the representation of Fred's psychotic and maybe even schizophrenic crisis, initiated by his jealousy. By the use of audiovisual metaphors in this sequence, we selectively experience

*Sonic spaces in movies* 145

an embodied access to different shades of his inner state. These metaphors may even help us to understand the enigmatic dramaturgy of the sequence.

The sequence begins with a high-angle shot of Fred's wife Renée lying in bed. While she is lying there motionless and looking up beside the camera, in contrast, the shot is accompanied by a quiet but constantly high random noise indicating some motion at this place caused by a non-visible actor. The subsequent high-angle shot shows Fred lying in the same bed, his body turned towards the left side, before he slowly moves his body to lie on his back; he has a stressed expression on his face, breathes heavily and finally whispers, 'This dream last night ...' With the entry of Fred's heavy breath and whisper, the atmospheric noise slowly begins to rise in volume – as if it was an externalisation of his breathing, expressing his inner horror, acoustically filling the space. His fear being a possible agent of this noise, the audiovisual representation of his inner horror creates a metaphoric meaning: 'horror is a high random noise'.

After a cut we see Fred in single shots, moving very slowly in the apartment, while in the off-space he continues telling his wife of his dream by gasping in a stressed manner: 'You were inside the house' ... 'You were calling my name'. At this moment, we hear from a far distance off-screen the echo of Renée's voice, calling him. Now a considerable change of the hedonic value begins to take place: after Renée's call, Fred looks at a big fire in the fireplace. In a close shot the fire is displayed with a loud, even exaggerated sizzling noise, strongly dragging upwards into the fume hood, as if it were pulled up by a strong undertow. After a cut the camera gets back to Fred who now has changed his affective expression: his previously rather anxious-looking face has altered into a resolute expression, underlined by the slight high angle of the camera. It seems as if we are now confronting a second, 'angry' persona of Fred. In cross-cutting this reaction shot with the shot of the fire, it is suggested that Fred has been affected by the fire, metaphorically indicating the cause of his crisis. The insertion of the fire and its superimposed performance in the previous close shot give it the appearance of a strong 'natural force'. In interaction with the viewers' most salient hypothesis, taking his jealousy as the initiation of Fred's crisis, and the shots showing him now with an angry expression, the fire seems to act here as an audiovisual metaphor for his jealousy: 'jealousy is a strong natural force' or more specifically: 'jealousy is a strongly mounting fire'.

In the subsequent shots the hand-camera performs as an autonomously acting instance, guided by an invisible actor. Initially, the camera moves around Fred's head, accompanying him while slowly turning around him. However, the camera moves faster than he does. After his other (anxious) persona has whispered off-screen: 'I couldn't find you ...', a point-of-view shows us his still resolute look at a stairway, while an enigmatic white smoke is slowly appearing behind it and simultaneously the random noise is constantly growing into a loud drumming noise. In interaction with the previously established fire metaphor, this is another metaphoric manifestation of Fred's growing aggression, caused by his 'burning jealousy' – this time being audiovisually performed as: 'jealousy is an upwelling smoke'.

Subsequently the camera is detached in an even more obvious manner from Fred's movements, moving as an autonomous actor: while he still seems to be turning around in the very same place, shots of the camera running fast along a gangway and passing a red curtain give us the impression of another, third actor moving in the apartment, beside 'anxious' Fred talking off-screen of his dream and the aggressively looking Fred slowly turning around. This happens again in the foreground, when finally the invisibly hand-held camera very quickly reaches the bed where Renée is lying – the same way as she did at the beginning of the scene; with the camera above her head, Renée screams and holds her hand on her head as if protecting herself against an aggressive offender. This is accompanied by the ongoing random noise, initially introduced in the scene when Fred started to talk about his dream. Thus the filmmaking creates an ambiguous scenery by confronting us with three different agents in vision and sound – relating to the same character in the same interior place. Thereby his split identity and his emotional crisis are being conveyed in a multi-sensory way.

The last two examples demonstrate, again, that in social drama and in psycho-drama, interior spaces serve a key role to convey the identity crisis of their protagonists in narrative and bodily terms. In *Taxi Driver*, the car is displayed as an 'inner space' that spatially marks the difference between the individual and his social surroundings through the multi-sensory use of the container-schema and the path-schema. In this case the music dominates the sonic space in performing the inner moods and affects of the protagonist and contrasting them with the society around him. The identity crisis shown in *Lost Highway* has its roots rather in the inner psychology of the protagonist, combined by Lynch with a mysterious dimension. Also in this case the inner crisis is significantly performed in an interior place. Given the imaginative character of this mentally represented interior space, its rather non-realistic pictures and sounds create spatial metaphors for the protagonist's split identity. It is through the paradoxical experience of seeing and hearing a differently behaving persona of the same actor in the same place that we get an embodied idea of his schizophrenic crisis.

## Conclusions

As has been demonstrated in the four case studies, film drama significantly makes use of multi-sensory Gestalts and image schemata in pictures and sound in order to metaphorically provide abstract and complex narrative meanings and ideas with an embodied Gestalt. The cross-modal presentation of spatial image schemata (container, path, up/down etc.) particularly offers filmmaking rich sensory metaphoric source domains. Audiovisual metaphors invite viewers to affectively experience narrative topics in a bodily way, as well as cognitively reflect on them. In social film drama, audiovisual metaphors serve to initiate in spectators a critical consideration of social norms, values and behaviour in a society during a certain era. As has been shown, spatial Gestalts of sounds and pictures are cross-modally used for creating audiovisual metaphors of identity, society and moral orders, as well as of emotions and inner traumatic states. Most significantly, interior spaces seem to be genre-typical metaphors for depicting 'self' and inner crisis; this is paralleled with a salient metaphorical use of movements from inside to outside, making use of container- and path-schemata.

In the creation of sonic spaces in film drama, music, atmospheric sounds and noises offer rich sensory structures to provide spectators with an embodied understanding of the depicted narrative topics. The metaphorical interaction of vision and sound in the spatial design of films significantly contributes to creating a synchresis of audiovisual meaning structures that widely transcend the sum of visual and auditory meanings.

## Notes

1 Since the performance of a peri-personal space (Gallese, 2005) is a fundamental condition for emotional communication, it is, at the same time, important for the emotional and physical response to audiovisual media (cf. Fahlenbrach, 2007; Gallese and Guerra, 2012).
2 By *synchresis* Chion means a close combination of temporal synchronisation and semantic synchresis of pictures and sound in a film scene.

## References

Anderson, J. D. (1996). *The reality of illusion: An ecological approach to cognitive film theory*. Carbondale, IL: Southern Illinois University Press.
Bartsch, A. (2016). Embodied emotion metaphors in moving images. In K. Fahlenbrach (Ed.), *Embodied metaphors in film, television, and video games: Cognitive approaches* (pp. 222–217). London/New York: Routledge.
Boroditsky, L., and Ramscar, M. (2002). The roles of body and mind in abstract thought. *Psychological Science, 2*, 185–189.
Buckland, W. (2009). Making sense of Lost Highway. In W. Buckland (Ed.), *Puzzle films. Complex story telling in contemporary cinema* (pp. 42–61). Malden, Oxford: Wiley-Blackwell.
Chion, M. (1994). *Audio-vision: Sound on screen*. New York: Columbia University Press.
Coëgnarts, M., and Kravanja, P. (2012). Embodied visual meaning: Image schemas in film. *Projections: The Journal of Movies and Mind, 6*(2), 84–101.
Coëgnarts, M., and Kravanja, P. (Eds.) (2014). Image [&] narrative. Special Issue: *Metaphor, Bodily Meaning, and Cinema, 15*(1).
Cohen, A. J. (2013). Congruence-association model of music and multimedia: Origin and evolution. In S.-L. Tan, A. J. Cohen, S. D. Lipscomb and R. A. Kendall (Eds.), *The psychology of music in multimedia* (pp. 17–47). Oxford: Oxford University Press.
Danesi, M. (1989). The neurological coordinates of metaphor. *Communication & Cognition, 1*, 73–86.

Eitan, Z., and Timmers, R. (2010). Beethoven's last piano sonata and those who follow crocodiles: Cross-domain mappings of auditory pitch in a musical context. *Cognition, 114*, 405–422.

Fahlenbrach, K. (2007). Embodied spaces: Film spaces as leading audiovisual metaphors. In J. D. Anderson and B. Fisher Anderson (Eds.), *Narration and spectatorship in moving images* (pp. 105–124). Cambridge: Cambridge Scholar Press.

Fahlenbrach, K. (2010). *Audiovisuelle Metaphern. Zur Körper- und Affektästhetik in Film und Fernsehen*. Marburg: Schüren Verlag.

Fahlenbrach, K. (Ed.) (2016). *Embodied metaphors in film, television, and video games: Cognitive approaches*. New York: Routledge.

Fahlenbrach, K. (in print). Audiovisual metaphors and metonymies of emotions and depression in moving images. In E. G. Ervas and M. G. Rossi (Eds.), *Metaphor in communication, science and education*. Berlin: De Gruyter.

Flückiger, B. (2002). *Sound Design. Die virtuelle Klangwelt des Films*. Zürich: Schüren Verlag.

Forceville, C. (2008). Metaphor in pictures and multimodal representations. In R. Gibbs (Ed.), *Cambridge handbook of metaphor and thought* (pp. 462–482). Cambridge: Cambridge University Press.

Forceville, C. (2016). Visual and multimodal metaphor in film: Charting the field. In K. Fahlenbrach (Ed.), *Embodied metaphors in film, television, and video games: Cognitive approaches* (pp. 17–32). London: Routledge.

Forceville, C., and Urios-Aparisi, E. (Eds.) (2009). *Multimodal metaphor*. Berlin: Mouton de Gruyter.

Gallese, V. (2005). Embodied simulation: From neurons to phenomenal experience. *Phenomenology & Cognitive Science, 4*, 23–48.

Gallese, V., and Guerra, M. (2012). Embodying movies: Embodied simulation and the film studies. *Cinema: Journal of Philosophy and the Moving Image, 3*, 183–210.

Gallese, V., and Guerra, M. (2014). The feeling of motion: Camera movements and motor cognition. *Cinema & Cie. International Film Studies Journal, 14*, 22–23.

Gallese, V., and Keysers, C. (2001). Mirror neurons: A sensorimotor representation system. *Behavioral and Brain Sciences, 5*, 983–984.

Gallese, V., and Lakoff, G. (2005). The brain's concepts: The role of the sensory-motor system in conceptual knowledge. *Cognitive Neuropsychology, 22*, 455–479.

Grimshaw, M., and Garner, T. (2012). The use of sound to represent data and concepts as a means to engender creative thought: Some thoughts on implementation and a research agenda. In *Proceedings of the 7th Audio Mostly Conference: A Conference on Interaction with Sound* (pp. 9–15). New York: Association for Computing Machinery.

Grodal, T. (1997). *Moving pictures: A new theory of film genres, feelings, and cognition*. Oxford: Oxford University Press.

Grodal, T. (2009). *Embodied visions: Evolution, emotion, culture, and film*. Oxford: Oxford University Press.

Holman, T. (2002). *Sound for film and television* (2nd ed.). Burlington, MA: Focal Press.

Johnson, M. (1987). *The body in the mind. The bodily basis of meaning, imagination, and reason*. Chicago: Chicago University Press.

Juslin, P. N. (1997). Emotional communication in music performance: A functionalist perspective and some data. *Music Perception, 14*, 383–418.

Juslin, P. N. (2003). Five facets of musical expression: A psychologist's perspective on music performance. *Psychology of Music, 31*(3), 273–302.
Kappelhoff, H., and Greifenstein, S. (2016). Audiovisual metaphors: Embodied meaning and processes of fictionalization. In K. Fahlenbrach (Ed.), *Embodied metaphors in film, television, and video games: Cognitive approaches* (pp. 183–201). London: Routledge.
Kappelhoff, H., and Müller, C. (2011). Embodied meaning construction: Multimodal metaphor and expressive movement in speech, gesture, and feature film. *Metaphor and the Social World, 1*(2), 121–153.
Kohler, E., Keysers, C., Umiltà, M. A., Fogassi, L., Gallese, V., and Rizzolatti, G. (2002). Hearing sounds, understanding actions: Action representation in mirror neurons. *Science, 297*, 846–848.
Kövecses, Z. (2003). *Metaphor and emotion: Language, culture, and body in human feeling*. Cambridge: Cambridge University Press.
Lakoff, G. (1987). *Woman, fire, and dangerous things: What categories reveal about the mind*. Chicago: Chicago University Press.
Scherer, K. R. (1995). Expressions of emotion in voice and music. *Journal of Voice, 9*, 235–248.
Smith, J. (1999). Movie music as moving music: Emotion, cognition, and the film score. In C. Plantinga and G. M. Smith (Eds.), *Passionate views. Film, cognition and emotion* (pp. 146–168). Baltimore, MD: Johns Hopkins University Press.
Sonnenschein, D. (2001). *Sound design: The expressive power of music, voice, and sound effects in cinema*. Saline, MI: Michael Wiese Productions.

# 9 The colourful life of timbre spaces

## Timbre concepts from early ideas to meta-timbre space and beyond

*Christoph Reuter and Saleh Siddiq*

In orchestration treatises, musical features like pitch, instrument registers and timbre are often described with an idea of spatiality. They are perceived in spatial dimensions such as high versus low, thin versus wide, full versus empty (Francoeur, 1772/1972; Gevaert, 1887; Jadassohn, 1889; Widor, 1904; Berlioz and Strauss, 1844/1904; Forsyth, 1926; Kennan, 1962; Jacob, 1962; Rogers, 1970; see Eitan, this volume). Timbre similarity has also been mostly described with a near-versus-distance-paradigm (Mattheson, 1713; Schubart, 1806/1969; Hofmann, 1893, Vol. 4; Rimski-Korsakow, 1912). So it stands to reason that for musicians the idea of timbre is commonly located in an imaginary two- or three-dimensional space.

As early as the end of the 19th century, the multidimensional aspects of timbre came under the attention of psychologists and musicologists with the works of Carl Stumpf (1890). In 1939 a first three-dimensional attempt at timbre description was published by Gerhard Albersheim and the empirically ascertained, so-called 'timbre spaces' followed in the 1970s. Before dealing with the pro and cons of actual known timbre spaces it is helpful to take a look at the history of timbre concepts, starting with the well-known simple questions about timbre: What is timbre? How is it quantifiable? Where does the concept of musical timbre come from? 'Why is musical timbre so hard to understand?' (Krumhansl, 1989, p. 43); and which paradigms move(d) ideas in the discussion about the phenomenon of musical timbre?

### Early considerations of timbre

The nature of sound and its propagation without regard to timbre as the quality of sound has been a central topic of acoustical research for many centuries. While the German word 'Klangfarbe' makes its first appearance as late as the early 19th century in a publication by Gottfried Weber (1822, p. 53), the evolution of the word 'timbre' as a description of the 'quality of sound' can be traced back to the mid-18th century. An article in an encyclopaedia from 1765 describes timbre very tangibly as the rattles on a tabor and – in a more modern, intangible sense – moreover as the sound of a bell's resonance, the human voice and musical instruments made of ore or metal

(Jaucourt in Diderot and d'Alembert, 1765). Another article in the same encyclopaedia even delivers a metaphorical approach: 'tymbre' is the very property of a tone that makes it sweet or bitter, dull or bright, dry or soft (Rousseau in Diderot and d'Alembert, 1765). Interestingly, this latter take on timbre not only anticipates modern psychological approaches that seek to describe timbre through sensory adjectives borrowed from other modalities but also seems to find the same main axes (e.g., dull–bright), despite using a slightly different vocabulary. In the article 'son' in the same encyclopaedia, Rosseau, who almost rewrote the same articles for his 1768 published *Dictionnaire de musique* (Muzzulini, 2006, p. 248ff.), elaborated even further on the description of timbre: the distinction in the quality of two tones produced by different instruments is neither caused by the 'elevation' (i.e., pitch) nor the 'force' (i.e., intensity, ergo loudness) but by a further, yet unknown entity (Rousseau in Diderot and d'Alembert, 1765). For a more detailed review see Muzzulini (2006).

### *Timbre in a narrow and broad sense*

Almost a century after the *Encyclopédie* of Diderot and d'Alembert, Hermann von Helmholtz (1863) gave the first answer to the open question about the unknown entity which causes the impression of characteristic timbres of musical instruments: like his predecessors, he stated that timbre (or 'quality of tones' as in the translations by Ellis) is a characterising and distinguishing feature of musical instrument sounds (von Helmholtz, 1863; von Helmholtz and Ellis, 1885). Sounds, or 'musical tones', are themselves distinguished by three features: (1) their 'force', the impression of loudness, which is caused by the amplitude of the wave form; (2) their 'pitch' which is caused by the period or cycle duration of the wave form; and (3) their 'quality', the impression of timbre, which is caused by the shape of the wave form, i.e., the amplitudes and distribution of the partials (von Helmholtz and Ellis, 1885, pp. 10, 18–19 and 65; von Helmholtz, 1863, p. 19, pp. 31–32 and 113). Von Helmholtz concluded 'that differences in the quality of musical tones must depend on the form of the vibration of the air' (von Helmholtz and Ellis 1885, p. 65), i.e., solely the harmonic spectrum; he labelled this difference 'musikalische Klangfarbe' (von Helmholtz, 1863, p. 116; literally translated: 'musical timbre', translated by Ellis 1885 as: 'musical quality of tone', p. 67).

Based on his own findings, von Helmholtz provided the first verbal timbre classification system (von Helmholtz, 1863; von Helmholtz and Ellis, 1885), which was borrowed and extended by Carl Stumpf in the second volume of his work *Tonpsychologie* (Stumpf, 1890; for a synoptic table see Reuter, 2013). Stumpf drew a clear distinction between the associated semantic characteristics of timbre (labelled 'Manichfaltigkeit der Praedicate' (Stumpf, 1890, p. 514), 'variety of attributes') and the physical characteristics of the sounds themselves (the features discriminating between musical instruments as described above, 1890, p. 516). Furthermore, Stumpf labelled von Helmholtz's 'musikalische Klangfarbe' as 'Klangfarbe im engeren Sinn' ('timbre in a narrow sense', i.e., timbre as a result of the harmonic spectrum of the sound, Stumpf, 1890, pp. 516, 520–524 and 539) and supplemented it with 'Klangfarbe im weiteren Sinn' ('timbre in a broad sense', i.e., temporal features such as roughness, noise-components, transients, articulation and musical figures (Stumpf, 1890, pp. 516–518 and 548).

*Vowel-colour and interval-colour*

Robert Willis (1832, pp. 397–437), Franciscus Cornelius Donders (1858, pp. 157–162) and Hermann von Helmholtz (1863, p. 171) identified the vocal tract resonances that cause the perceptual impression (timbre) of the vowels produced by the human voice. These resonances, or the amplified partials respectively, were labelled 'Vocaltöne' (von Helmholtz, 1863, p. 179; 'vowel tones'). Ludimar Hermann (1894) was the first one to refer to these 'vowel tones' as 'formants'. Initially solely an outcome of voice-research, the evolving concept of formants was increasingly adopted by researchers investigating musical instrument timbre. Wolfgang Köhler – a student of Carl Stumpf – developed a 'Psychological theory of timbre' by proposing three key aspects to distinguish the timbre of vowels from the timbre of musical instruments (Köhler, 1909): (1) The same timbre impression is produced by the same intensity relations between partials. (2) Shifting these intensity relations along the frequency axis has no impact on the perceived timbre (theory of relative formants). This means that the timbre of musical instruments is caused by the interval of the two strongest partials, thus the labelling 'Intervallfarbe' ('interval-colour'). (3) The critical difference between these interval-colours and the 'Vokalklangfarbe' ('vowel-colour') is the fact that the latter stem from fixed and pitch-independent frequency ranges within the spectrum (theory of absolute formants).

With the work of Wolfgang Köhler, the formant paradigm changed from one single timbre-defining partial in the spectrum of vowels to a fixed, pitch-independent narrow frequency band in the spectrum. This change of perspective was pivotal for the further work of Carl Stumpf (1926), Karl Erich Schumann (1929) and Gerhard Albersheim (1939).

*Formant areas as timbre descriptors*

Carl Stumpf's deep impact on timbre research goes far beyond his intriguing multidimensional description of timbre in a narrow and broad sense. More than a century after Rosseau considered 'bright' as one of several tone qualities elicited by what timbre is, Carl Stumpf incorporated brightness as a basic feature of timbre. Furthermore, he was the first to apply the paradigm of fixed formant positions to the timbre of musical instruments in 1926. Before then, fixed formants were exclusively used to describe the timbre of vowels (therefore, Stumpf was careful to call the formants he discovered in the spectra of musical instruments 'side-formants'; Stumpf, 1926, p. 382: 'Nebenformanten').

Based on Stumpf's finding, Schumann tested the sounds of the most common wind instruments (played by professional musicians) at every obtainable pitch and most musical dynamics as well as through changes in dynamic level. Schumann found regularities in the behaviour of the spectral envelope as a function of pitch and dynamics which resulted in three fundamental principles of timbre (Schumann, 1929; Mertens, 1975; Reuter, 1995):

- *Principle of formant areas ('Formantstreckengesetz')*: formants of musical instruments are fixed and pitch-independent areas of the spectrum, wherein partials have exceptionally strong amplitudes, so that the timbre impression is influenced mainly by partials located in these areas.
- *Principle of formant shifting ('Formantverschiebungsgesetz')*: with increasing musical dynamics the strongest amplitude of the partial in the formant area is shifted to a partial of higher order in the same formant area.
- *Principle of spectral gap skipping ('Sprunggesetz')*: with very intense musical dynamics the highest amplitude of the first (or lowest) formant area is shifted to a partial in the second (higher) formant area, skipping over the partials between these areas.

Schumann also described an additional fourth principle of formant intervals ('Formantintervallgesetz'), where the strongest partial of the first (or lowest) formant area and the strongest partial of the second (or higher) formant area result in an interval which he considered typical for the respective instrument (Schumann, 1929). This last principle is more or less obsolete, since it contradicts the principle of formant shifting (see above). Furthermore, due to the comb filter effect, different formant intervals are obtained when placing the recording microphone in different positions. However, the first three principles had a major impact on German-speaking timbre researchers.

While in English-speaking countries the 'Spectral Centroid' (Sandell, 1995; Peeters, Giordano, Susini, Misdariis and McAdams, 2011) has acquired the leading position in the discussion of spectral features, in German language papers the concept of formant areas has been established as a robust paradigm for the description of the spectral characteristics of vowel and (wind) instrument sounds (Meyer, 2004, p. 33, 2008). The pulse-forming theory gave a physical explanation for the concept of formant areas (Fricke, 1975; Voigt, 1975; Auhagen, 1987), which led to predictable results in auditory streaming experiments (Reuter, 2000, 2003a) as well as in timbre blending experiments with a large amount of instrument combinations (Reuter, 1996a, 2002) and in the explanation of typical vibrato curves of musical instruments (Oehler, 2008) and much more. The concept of formant areas yields several advantages: (1) it supports recommendations for timbre blending and separation in orchestration treatises; (2) it supports the results of streaming experiments in the area of auditory scene analysis; (3) it works independently of pitch and dynamic level; (4) it is physically based on the pulse-forming principle and with the help of pulse-forming synthesis it is possible to generate authentic sounding instrument timbres; (5) measured formant areas are characteristic for different instrument types, robust and generalisable for wind instruments; (6) formant principles have been found with the help of authentic instrument sounds at all obtainable pitches and dynamic levels (instead of synthetic sounds). Of course, the formant concept also has some disadvantages: It is just a one-dimensional-concept which only works in the frequency domain, while fluctuations and modulations (like vibrato, tremolo etc.) are not explained (even if they are included in the pulse-forming principle).

## First three-dimensional attempts: cylinder of sound colours

For over a century it has been obvious that timbre is more than just the shape of a wave form or the distribution of partials in a sound. In 1890, Stumpf set the record straight by stating that timbre should be described in several dimensions. Unfortunately, Stumpf's two-volume *Tonpsychologie* was never translated into English. It was Joseph Carl Robnett Licklider, who reinvented the wheel more than 60 years later by – once again – characterising timbre as a 'multidimensional dimension' (Licklider, 1951). Therefore since 1890, or at least 1951 (for Anglo-American research), it has been a further aim for acousticians to find the individual dimensions of timbre. One of the very first steps in this direction can be found in the work of Gerhard Albersheim, who drew analogies between (1) the timbre of vowels (vowel quality or 'Vokalität', see above) and the hue of optical colours; as well as (2) the sharpness/brightness of sounds with optical brightness; and (3) the relationship between vowel quality and brightness and colour saturation (Albersheim, 1939). In other words: Albersheim developed a timbre paradigm on the basis of the hue–saturation–brightness concept. In this concept he assumed a so-called sound colour triangle with two axes: brightness or sharpness ('Helligkeit') and saturation ('Sättigung'). According to this sound colour triangle, vowel or instrument timbre is a result of the amount of brightness and saturation between brightness and a particular vowel quality ('bunt'= coloured). From an electroacoustic perspective, these two axes of the triangle can be interpreted as a description of a bandpass filter, where the brightness describes the centre frequency and the saturation the bandwidth: the smaller the bandwidth the more colourful (i.e., vowel-like) is the timbre impression (see Figure 9.1, top left).

As a next step, Albersheim put the German vowels (U – O – A – Ä – Ö – Ü – E – I) analogous to different colours along the circumference of a semicircle around one point of grey (see Figure 9.1, bottom left: semicircle of vowels). On this basis, he proposed that each of these vowels (or hues) can build up its own sound colour triangle, which he could combine (following the model of the two-component theory of pitch; Révész, 1913) to form a cylinder of sound colours ('Akustischer Farbenkörper') with the brightness axis in the middle, the saturation axis as the radius and a helical hue (or vowel) axis at the perimeter of the cylinder (see Figure 9.1, right).

Albersheim tried to reconcile the concept of brightness and vowel quality into one three-dimensional timbre model, but he could not establish his paradigm to a further extent for many understandable reasons (e.g., because of World War II, because it is difficult to compare timbre and colour perception in a non-metaphoric way, because he made no timbre perception experiments to prove his concept, to name a few).

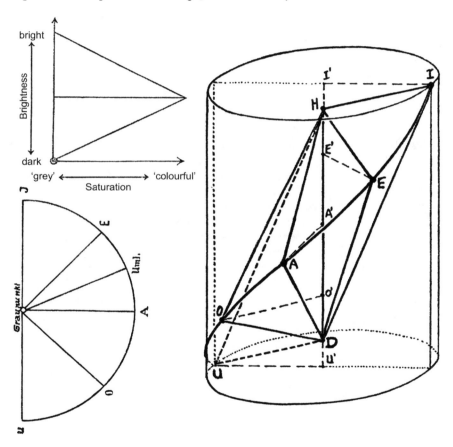

*Figure 9.1* Top left: sound colour triangle with the axes brightness ('Helligkeit') and saturation ('Sättigung') applied to one single vowel quality (coloured point at 'bunt') (Albersheim, 1939, p. 252). Bottom left: semicircle of vowels (Albersheim, 1939, p. 350). Right: cylinder of sound colours (Albersheim, 1939, p. 353).

### Sharpness and compactness

After World War II, timbre research shifted more and more into the Anglo-American realm and there the concept of timbre received its first standardisation by the American National Standards Institute (ANSI): 'Timbre is that attribute of auditory sensation in terms of which a listener can judge that two sounds similarly presented and having the same loudness and pitch are dissimilar' (ANSI, 1960, p. 45 §12.9). It is a definition in the (Helmholtzean) tradition of definition-by-negation, which are not definitions at all, or to put it into the words of Albert Bregman (1990, p. 93): 'We do not know how to define timbre, but it is not loudness and it is not pitch.' There are numerous objections against this definition. The main arguments are:

- It is a definition-by-negation: it describes only what timbre is not.
- Timbre is only defined as a result of a comparison between two sounds, it is not an independent feature.
- It is implicitly assumed that timbre is always combined with a certain pitch, which is not always the case in reality.

This official ANSI timbre definition had severe consequences for timbre research, because researchers examined instrument timbres in respect to a consistent pitch and not in respect to typical registers of an instrument (not to mention that in most timbre studies musical instruments are represented by only one single pitch; Reuter, 1995, 2003b). This specification of the comparison at the same pitch was really absurd in cases where (among others) the timbres of a flute and a double-bass were examined (e.g., Nitsche, 1978; other similar examples are listed in Reuter, 2005).

It was most notably Gottfried von Bismarck, in 1971, who established the concept of 'sharpness' and 'compactness' in German publications, while in Anglo-American literature John Grey (1975) established the first three-dimensional timbre space which had a lasting influence on timbre research (see below). Von Bismarck found 'sharpness' and 'compactness' (or 'density') as the main timbre dimensions by using 35 different synthetic sounds (at the same pitch), which had been described in terms of their timbre by 35 subjects via 30 pairs of adjectives in semantic differentials (von Bismarck, 1971, 1972; precursors of von Bismarck: Stumpf, 1890; Lichte, 1941; Solomon, 1959). 'Sharpness' (as opposed to 'dullness') meant that the higher the energy peak is located in the spectrum, the sharper the timbre impression. The concept of 'compactness' or 'density' (as opposed to 'diffuseness') describes whether the overall distribution of partials is more harmonic (compact) or whether it tends towards noise (diffuse). Beside its role as one of the most important timbre dimensions, 'sharpness' is also used as a parameter for the description of sensory pleasantness (reference point: 1 acum corresponds to the impression of a narrowband noise at 1 kHz with a bandwidth of 160 Hz and a sound pressure level of 60 dB SPL; Fastl and Zwicker, 2007, p. 239). With the concept of 'roughness' Wilhelm Aures (1984) added a further dimension to both paradigms (timbre description and sensory pleasantness), which describes the presence of fluctuations between 20 and 300 Hz in a sound.

## Dimensions of the timbre space

'Sharpness' was also identified as one of timbre's principal dimensions through a fundamental empirical study published by John Grey in his 'Exploration of Musical Timbre' (1975). Although the method of processing empirically derived data via multidimensional scaling (MDS) was initially introduced by Wedin and Goude (1972), it was heavily influenced and became popularly known as 'timbre space' through the study by Grey.

In a hearing experiment, 20 subjects had to rate the timbral (dis)similarities of 16 re-synthesised instrument sounds with equalised pitch (approx. 311 Hz, E≅4), loudness and duration (approx. 300 ms). Fifteen subjects took the test twice, giving Grey a total of 35 datasets to work with. The subjective ratings were stored in dissimilarity matrices. By means of an individual differences scaling (INDSCAL; see Carroll and Chang, 1970), a (metric) MDS technique that weights dimensions to account for individual differences (Grey, 1975; McAdams, 1999), a Euclidean space was calculated (Figure 9.2). The timbral dissimilarities of the sounds tested are translated into spatial distances along the axes of the virtual space. The closer together two sounds are located, the stronger their timbres resemble each other perceptually (Grey, 1975; Grey and Gordon, 1978; McAdams, 1999). Each axis of the space is interpretively assigned to a perceptual dimension of timbre (McAdams, 1999). Usually, particular features of the harmonic spectrum, but also the temporal envelope, are considered as the most salient cues for timbre discrimination/identification. Thus, unsurprisingly, the first and second axes of the virtual space (i.e., the first and second timbre dimensions) are commonly interpreted as some kind of a spectral-scale (i.e., sharpness/brightness, spectral centroid, etc.) or temporal-scale (i.e., rise-/attack-time, transients, onset-offset-patterns, etc.) respectively. The assignment of a specific feature to the third axis does not appear to be as commonly established. Mostly it is interpreted as a scale of certain (temporal) spectral parameters (e.g., spectral flux, fine structure, spread) (e.g., Caclin, McAdams, Smith and Winsberg, 2005). The method of conducting a hearing experiment, storing the subjective ratings in a dissimilarity matrix, processing a MDS and finally interpreting the results in an attempt to connect the physical input and the perceptual output is – if you will – the blueprint for deriving a timbre space (McAdams, 1999).

Based on Grey's timbre space study, a whole series of timbre space experiments followed, with stimuli-pairs with swapped spectral energy distributions (Grey and Gordon, 1978), with involvement of a pseudo-musical context (Grey, 1978) or with streaming experiments in the tradition of auditory scene analysis (Wessel, 1979) (the pros and cons of these studies have been discussed in Reuter, 1995). Other authors and research groups published

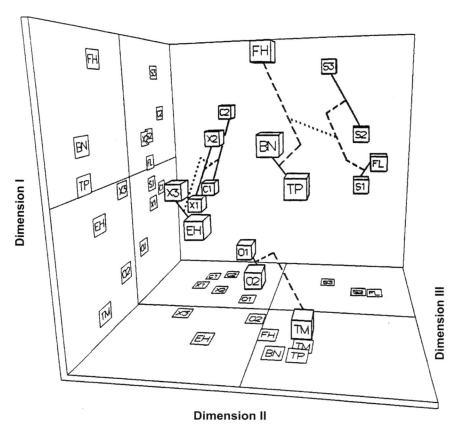

*Figure 9.2* Timbre space with axis I (sharpness), II (spectral fluctuations) and III (attack transients). O1 and O2 = oboes; C1 and C2 = clarinets; X1, X2 and X3 = saxophones; EH = English horn; BN = bassoon; FH = French horn; TP = trumpet; TM = trombone; FL = flute, S1, S2 and S3 = cellos (Grey 1975, p. 62).

further timbre spaces (e.g., Krumhansl, 1989; Iverson and Krumhansl, 1993; Cosi, Poli and Lauzzana, 1994; McAdams, Winsberg, Donnadieu, de Soete and Krimphoff, 1995; Lakatos, 2000). Some studies factored in the influence of pitch by testing a number of differently pitched tones per instrument (Marozeau, Cheveigne, McAdams and Winsberg, 2003; Handel and Erickson, 2004; Lembke, 2006).

Such timbre spaces are, in principle, an adequate tool to depict the perceptual similarities of instrument timbres, but, in practice, some fundamental weaknesses have to be taken into account: (1) instrument sounds were generally (re-)synthesised; (2) even though a few studies do indeed factor in the effect of pitch, it is fair to say that instruments were usually reduced to only a single tone; and thus (3) compared on the same pitch (Reuter, 1996b; Siddiq, Reuter, Czedik-Eysenberg and Knauf, 2015b). What are the implications of this finding? One single tone can never represent a whole musical instrument because it simply cannot account for the vast range of timbral varieties any given musical instrument can easily produce. First, the timbre of an instrument can differ significantly from one register to another (Reuter, 2002). Second, musical dynamics and articulations, both having a huge influence on timbre, are not taken into account. Third, the different natural pitch-ranges of musical instruments are not taken into account. Obviously, musical reality is not properly incorporated. Moreover, the reduction of a musical instrument to a single tone minimises the chance of significant data overlap between two studies, which, in turn, has a negative impact on the comparability and therefore the validity of the studies (Siddiq et al., 2015b).

All the above stated facts were subject of an empirical meta-study (Siddiq, Reuter, Czedik-Eysenberg and Knauf, 2015a). The original stimuli of the three most popular timbre spaces (Grey, 1975; Krumhansl, 1989; McAdams et al., 1995) were tested along with recorded instrument sounds from the Vienna Symphonic Library (VSL).

Seven instruments were tested in all three of the compared studies and thus included in the meta-study: bassoon, clarinet, cor anglais, French horn, strings (cellos), trombone and trumpet. The 24 stimuli of the meta-study consisted of the original sounds of these seven instruments from Grey's study (including two clarinets and three celli, making a total of ten), seven of the Krumhansl sounds (McAdams et al. reused the Krumhansl sounds for their study) and seven of the VSL sounds. A total of 35 participants (15 females, 20 males, aged 19–72, M = 30.9, SD =13.3) participated in the experiment. Of these, 24 considered themselves musicians (i.e., one of these conditions was met: playing an instrument, singing, conducting), eight were formerly active and three were nonmusicians (M = 19.6 years of experience, SD = 14.2). The task was to rate the subjective dissimilarities of the stimuli in a pairwise comparison. The ratings were stored in a dissimilarity matrix and processed by means of a non-metric MDS (MDSCAL in Matlab). A four-dimensional configuration (Kruskal's stress = 0.036) was calculated.

This empirical meta-timbre space yielded some unambiguous findings: sounds of the same synthesised stimuli-set showed a greater timbral resemblance than sounds of the same instrument. The sounds rather grouped in 'stimuli-set clusters' instead of instrument clusters. On the contrary, the recorded instrument sounds from the VSL spread over the whole space (Figure 9.3).

In other words, the stimuli-sets used by Grey and Krumhansl/McAdams et al. differ from one another so widely that these differences prevail as primary discrimination cues and render the timbral differences between different musical instruments practically irrelevant (Siddiq et al., 2015a, 2015b).

Hence, it is safe to assume that the major weakness of timbre spaces is the use of synthetic stimuli. Moreover, in the vast majority of the studies,

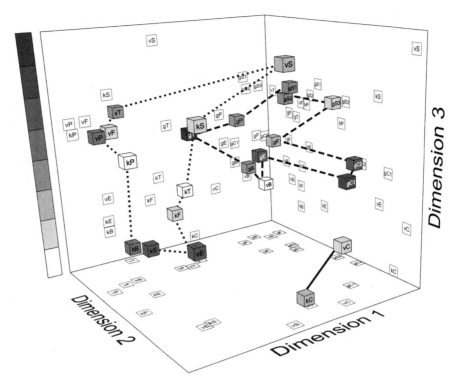

*Figure 9.3* Empirical meta-timbre space (EMTS): X-axis: Dimension 1, Y-axis: Dimension 2, Z-axis: Dimension 3, Colour bar: Dimension 4. Grey-sounds: gB (bassoon), gC2 (bass clarinet), gC1 (E♭-clarinet), gE (English horn), gF (French horn), gS1 (cello sul ponticello), gS2 (cello normal), gS3 (cello sul tasto (muted)), gT (trombone), gP (trumpet). Krumhansl/McAdams-sounds: kB (bassoon), kC (clarinet), kE (English horn), kF (French horn), kS (strings), kT (trombone), kP (trumpet). VSL sounds: vB (bassoon), vC (clarinet), vE (English horn), vF (French horn), vS (strings), vT (trombone), vP (trumpet).

the sound range of an entire instrument is reduced to only one tone. Thus the influence of pitch and musical dynamics is automatically taken out of the equation. On the other hand, the major advantage of the timbre space as such is its vividness. The complex multidimensional coherences are very intuitively visualised by translating the timbral dissimilarities into spatial distances. Unfortunately, Euclidean geometry limits the number of simultaneously displayable dimensions to just three. This may become a problematic constraint because timbre perception will most likely exceed the number of three independent dimensions, once factors like pitch, dynamics and articulation are taken into account.

## Conclusions or 'beyond timbre space'

In summary, there are on the one hand a few advantages of timbre spaces: they are very descriptive, comprehensible and intuitive, because we are used to moving and thinking in a three-dimensional world. Everyday spatial concepts like distance, altitude, movement and acceleration can easily be transferred to the concept of timbre space, and (to some extent) they are consistent with the results of the streaming experiments in the field of auditory scene analysis. On the other hand it could be shown that the concept of timbre space is afflicted with a lot of disadvantages. Timbre spaces are hardly generalisable or even comparable. They are more or less limited to three dimensions, usually based on only (re)synthesised sounds in only one pitch (which cannot be taken as a *pars pro toto* for a musical instrument) while dynamics, articulation and modulations are generally not taken into account.

The timbre space concept thus is a model primarily suited for intuitively visualising the complex multidimensional coherences of musical instrument timbre. But, combined with a more complete and adequate concept of musical timbre itself, as well as a more elaborate analysis of the physical correlates of timbre, its methodical layout could provide the basis for a (more) universal and thus very powerful model of timbre description: Some timbre spaces have already entered the realm of musical pitch (Marozeau et al., 2003; Handel and Erickson, 2004; Lembke, 2006). However, the timbre of musical instruments varies greatly not only with pitch but also with dynamics. Plucking a string or blowing into a wind instrument with greater force will always result in a brighter timbre. This shifting of spectral energy to higher partials as a function of increased excitation force is a universal phenomenon that applies to every musical instrument. It might be considered as a rough adaption of Wien's displacement law (Wien, 1896, pp. 666–668) to acoustics (Fricke, 2011). Hence, the next step is to expand the number of stimuli per instrument to not only cover a range of pitches but also different dynamics. For the sake of feasibility, both ranges have to be somewhat limited because the number of stimuli increases exponentially with each newly added step (pitch or dynamics). Such sets for every tested instrument would (1) vastly widen the overall and instrument-specific data; (2) take most of the evident timbral variances of musical instruments into account; and (3) make it possible to investigate instrument timbres per se (i.e., perceptual properties, identity); as well as (4) their relations to each other (discrimination) in an appropriate way. Such an arrangement will most probably contradict the currently established perceptual dimensions because 'sharpness' would obviously become a variable of every instrument's timbre and – despite it remaining the most salient perceptual dimension for single tone timbres – would therefore presumably be disqualified as a dimension on the level of instrument comparison.

Another important step is a substantial enhancement of the correlation of physical properties and perceptual dimensions. Currently, the interpretational connection between the physical input and the perceptual output is an empirical-loop-based educated guess at best (McAdams, 1999). The rapidly developing tools of music information retrieval (MIR) constantly facilitate the (real-time) in depth analysis of sounds. To put it simply, MIR makes it possible to generate physical timbre spaces (i.e., timbre spaces that are based not on perception but on the physical properties of compared sounds) consisting almost every conceivable combination of timbre descriptors. These 'physical timbre spaces' will substantially improve the matching of physical and perceptual dimensions of timbre (e.g., timbre spaces in the assessment of non-musical sounds such as audio logos: so it could be shown, for example, that by reference to the physical timbre properties 'spectral centroid', 'mean spectral flux' and 'roughness' one can separate the audio logos of two industrial branches (retail/laundry/home care vs. organisation/education) into two clearly divided parts of an calculated timbre space (Anzenbacher, Czedik-Eysenberg, Reuter and Oehler, 2015).

What this all amounts to is that the combination of MIR and music-psychological timbre research (which is also widely and enlighteningly discussed in Siedenburg, Fujinaga and McAdams, 2016) leads to promising implications inside and beyond the timbre space concept.

Inside timbre space: timbre descriptors like MFCC or spectral centroid, roughness and first attack-time enable us to derive reliable non-empirical timbre spaces, based solely on the acoustical properties of the sounds involved. This is particularly interesting for a rough depiction of musical instrument timbres (as in Loughran, Walker, O'Neill and O'Farrell, 2008) as well as the classification of everyday noises (like the annoyance of motorcycle sounds in Czedik-Eysenberg, Knauf and Reuter, 2015).

Beyond timbre space: to get a closer idea of the perception of musical timbres, the concept of timbre space is not enough, because differences in musical instruments' sound properties like pitch, dynamics and articulations have been neglected so far. Furthermore, it could be shown that the already known timbre spaces are not comparable or generalisable. So it is time to enlarge or even leave the timbre space concept towards a more complex construct. Siedenburg, Jones-Mollerup and McAdams were recently able to show that when speaking of timbre one has to differentiate between 'the sound' by itself and 'the idea of a musical instrument' (Siedenburg, Jones-Mollerup and McAdams, 2016, p. 15; the same idea was already mentioned in Stumpf, 1926, p. 393; Barthet, Depalle, Kronland-Martinet, Ystad, 2010, p. 136). So the opportunity arises to add not only the different aspects of pitch, dynamics and articulations (and all their timbral influences) to the multidimensionality of a sound but also the European timbre concept of formant areas, which was initially developed with the purpose of representing the idea of a whole musical instrument.

## Acknowledgements

Supported by funds of the Oesterreichische Nationalbank (OeNB, Anniversary Fund, project number: 16473). Special thanks to the Vienna Symphonic Library for supporting our work with two free 'Vienna Super Package' licenses.

# References

Albersheim, G. (1939). *Zur Psychologie der Toneigenschaften* [On the psychology of sound properties]. Strassburg: Heitz.

ANSI. (1960). *American standard acoustical terminology (including mechanical shock and vibration)*. New York: American Standard Association.

Anzenbacher, C., Czedik-Eysenberg, I., Reuter, C., and Oehler, M. (2015). Der Klang der Marken – Branchentypische psychoakustische Eigenschaften von Audiologos [The 'sound of brands' – sector-related typical psychoacoustical properties of audio logos]. *Fortschritte der Akustik, 41. DAGA 2015* (pp. 928–931), Nuremberg.

Auhagen, W. (1987). Dreiecksimpulsfolgen als Modell der Anregungsfunktion von Blasinstrumenten [The usability of triangle-shaped pulses in the synthesis of wind instruments]. In *Fortschritte der Akustik, 13. DAGA'87* (pp. 709–712), Aachen.

Aures, W. (1984). Der Wohlklang: eine Funktion der Schärfe, Rauhigkeit, Klanghaftigkeit und Lautheit [Euphony: A function of sharpness, brightness, tonality and loudness]. In *Fortschritte der Akustik, 10. DAGA'84* (pp. 735–738), Darmstadt.

Barthet, M., Depalle, P., Kronland-Martinet, R., and Ystad, S. (2010). Acoustical Correlates of Timbre and Expressivenes in Clarinet Performance. *Music Perception, 28*(2), 135–153.

Berlioz, H. (1844/1904). *Instrumentationslehre* (rev. and complemented by Richard Strauss) [Orchestration treatise]. Leipzig: C. F. Peters.

Bregman, A. S. (1990). *Auditory scene analysis: The perceptual organization of sound*. Cambridge, MA: MIT Press.

Caclin, A., McAdams, S., Smith, B. K., and Winsberg, S. (2005). Acoustic correlates of timbre space dimensions: A confirmatory study using synthetic tones. *Journal of the Acoustical Society of America, 118*(1), 471–482.

Carroll, J. D., and Chang, J. J. (1970). Analysis of individual differences in multidimensional scaling via an N-way generalization of Eckart-Young decomposition. *Psychometrika, 35*(3), 283–319.

Cosi, P., de Poli, G., and Lauzzana, G. (1994). Auditory modelling and self-organizing neural networks for timbre classification. *Journal of New Music Research, 23*(1), 71–98.

Czedik-Eysenberg, I., Knauf D., and Reuter C. (2015). Psychoakustische Aspekte der Lästigkeit von Motorradgeräuschen [Psychoacoustical aspects of the annoyance of motorcycle sounds]. *Proceedings of the 31st Annual Conference of the German Society for Music Psychology (DGM), 11–13 September* (pp. 43–44), Oldenburg.

Diderot, D., and d'Alembert, J. B. le Rond (1765). *Encyclopédie ou dictionnaire raisonné des sciences, des arts et des métiers* (Vol. 16). Paris: Briasson, David, le Breton, Durand.

Donders, F. C. (1858). Ueber die Natur der Vocale [On the nature of vowels]. In F. C. Donders, and W. Berlin (Eds.), *Archiv für die holländischen Beiträge zur Natur- und Heilkunde* (Vol. 1, pp. 157–162). Utrecht: Kemink & Zoon.

Fastl, H., and Zwicker, E. (2007). *Psychoacoustics: Facts and models*. Berlin: Springer.

Forsyth, C. (1926). *Orchestration*. London: Macmillan & Co.

Francoeur, L.-J. (1772/1972). *Diapason general de tous les instruments a vent* (reprint Geneva: Minkoff). Paris: Des Lauriers.

Fricke, J. P. (1975). Formantbildende Impulsfolgen bei Blasinstrumenten [Formant-shaping pulse chains in the excitation function of wind instruments]. In *Fortschritte der Akustik 4. DAGA'75* (pp. 407–411), Braunschweig.

Fricke, J. P. (2011). Klang und Klangfarbe – gestern, heute (und morgen) [Sound and timbre – yesterday, today and tomorrow]. In A. Schmidhofer and S. Jena (Eds.), *Klangfarbe. Vergleichend-systematische und musikhistorische Perspektiven* (pp. 9–42). Frankfurt/M.: Lang.

Gevaert, F.-A. (1887). *Neue Instrumenten-Lehre* [Orchestration treatise]. Leipzig: Otto Junne.

Grey, J. M. (1975). *An exploration of musical timbre using computer based techniques for analysis, synthesis and perceptual scaling*. PhD dissertation, University of Stanford.

Grey, J. M. (1978). Timbre discrimination in musical patterns. *Journal of the Acoustical Society of America, 64*, 467–472.

Grey, J. M., and Gordon, J. W. (1978). Perceptual effects of spectral modifications on musical timbres. *Journal of the Acoustical Society of America, 63*(5), 1493–1500.

Handel, S., and Erickson, M. L. (2004). Sound source identification: The possible role of timbre transformations. *Music Perception, 21*, 587–610.

Hermann, L. (1894). Phonophotographische Untersuchungen VI. Nachtrag zur Untersuchung der Vocalcurven [Supplement to the study of vowels and formants]. In E. F. W. Pflüger (Ed.), *Archiv für die gesammte Physiologie des Menschen und der Thiere* (Vol. 58, pp. 255–263). Bonn: Hager.

Hofmann, R. (1893). *Praktische Instrumentationslehre* [Orchestration treatise]. Leipzig: Dorfling & Franke.

Iverson, P., and Krumhansl, C. (1993). Isolating the dynamic attributes of musical timbre. *Journal of the Acoustical Society of America, 94*(5), 2595–2603.

Jacob, G. (1962). *The elements of orchestration*. New York: October House.

Jadasson, S. (1889). *Lehrbuch der Instrumentation*. Leipzig: Breitkopf & Härtel [Orchestration treatise].

Kennan, K. W. (1962). *The technique of orchestration*. New York: Prentice-Hall.

Köhler, W. (1909). *Akustische Untersuchungen I* [Acoustic oberservations]. Leipzig: Barth.

Krumhansl, C. (1989): Why is musical timbre so hard to understand? In S. Nielzen and O. Olsson (Eds.), *Structure and perception of electroacoustic sound and music* (pp. 43–53). Amsterdam: Elsevier.

Lakatos, S. (2000). A common perceptual space for harmonic and percussive timbres. *Perception & Psychophysics, 62*(7), 1426–1439.

Lembke, S. A. (2006). *Dimensionen der Klangfarbe: Skalierung von Instrumentalklängen unterschiedlicher Tonhöhe* [Timbre dimensions – Scaling of instrument timbres on different pitches]. Unpublished MA thesis, Technical University of Berlin.

Lichte, W.H. (1941). Attributes of complex tones. *Journal of Experimental Psychology, 28*, 455–480.

Licklider, J.C.R. (1951). Basic correlates of the auditory stimulus. In S. S. Stevens (Ed.), *Handbook of Experimental Psychology* (pp. 985–1039). New York: John Wiley and Sons.

Loughran, R., Walker, J., O'Neill, M., and O'Farrell, M. (2008). The use of mel-frequency Cepstral coefficients in musical instrument identification. In *Proceedings of the International Computer Music Conference, 24–29 August*, Belfast, Northern Ireland.

Marozeau, J., Cheveigne, A. D., McAdams, S., and Winsberg, S. (2003). The dependency of timbre on fundamental frequency. *Journal of the Acoustical Society of America, 114*, 2946–2957.

Mattheson, J. (1713). *Das Neu-Eröffnete Orchestre* [The re-opened orchestra]. Hamburg: B. Schiller.
McAdams, S. (1999). Perspectives on the contribution of timbre to musical structure. *Computer Music Journal, 23*(3), 85–102.
McAdams, S., Winsberg, S., Donnadieu, S., de Soete, G., and Krimphoff, J. (1995). Perceptual scaling of synthesized musical timbres: Common dimensions, specificities, and latent subject classes. *Psychological Research, 58*(3), 177–192.
Mertens, P.-H. (1975). *Die Schumannschen Klangfarbengesetze und ihre Bedeutung für die Übertragung von Sprache und Musik* [Schumanns principles of timbre (formants) and their relevance for transmission of speech and music]. Frankfurt: Bochinsky.
Meyer, J. (2004): *Akustik und musikalische Aufführungspraxis* [Acoustics and the performance of music]. Bergkirchen: PPVMedien.
Meyer, J. (2008). Musikalische Akustik [Musical acoustics]. In S.Weinzierl (Ed.), *Handbuch der Audiotechnik* (pp. 123–180). Berlin: Springer.
Muzzulini, D. (2006). *Genealogie der Klangfarbe* [Genealogy of timbre]. Bern: Lang.
Nitsche, P. (1978). *Klangfarbe und Schwingungsform* [Timbre and vibration shape]. Munich: Katzbichler.
Oehler, M. (2008): *Die digitale Impulsformung als Werkzeug für die Analyse und Synthese von Blasinstrumenten* [The digital pulse forming as an analysis and synthesis tool for wind instruments sounds]. Frankfurt: Lang.
Peeters, G., Giordano, B. L., Susini, P., Misdariis, N., and McAdams, S. (2011). The Timbre Toolbox extracting audio descriptors from musical timbre. *Journal of the Acoustical Society of America, 130*(5), 2902–2916.
Reuter, C. (1995). *Der Einschwingvorgang nichtperkussiver Musikinstrumente* [The starting transient of non-percussive musical instruments]. Frankfurt: Lang.
Reuter, C. (1996a). *Die auditive Diskrimination von Orchesterinstrumenten* [Timbre discrimination of simultaneously playing musical instruments]. Frankfurt: Lang.
Reuter, C. (1996b). Erich Schumann's laws of timbre as an alternative. *Systematische Musikwissenschaft, 4*(1–2), 185–200.
Reuter, C. (2000). Verschmelzung und partielle Verdeckung [Formant-based blending and partially masking of musical instruments]. In *Fortschritte der Akustik DAGA2000* (pp. 176–177), Oldenburg.
Reuter, C. (2002). *Klangfarbe und Instrumentation* [Formant-based orchestration treatise]. Frankfurt: Lang.
Reuter, C. (2003a). Stream segregation and formant areas. In *Proceedings of the 5th ESCOM Conference, September 8–13* (pp. 213–217), Hanover.
Reuter, C. (2003b). Wie und warum in der Geschichte der Klangfarbenforschung meistenteils am Klang vorbeigeforscht wurde [Milestones and fallacies in timbre research]. In W. Niemöller (Ed.), *Systemische Musikwissenschaft. Festschrift Jobst Peter Fricke zum 65. Geburtstag* (pp. 293–301). Frankfurt: Lang.
Reuter, C. (2005). Klangfarbe: Beziehungen zur Tonhöhe und Lautstärke [Timbre and its relation to pitch and loudness]. In H. de la Motte and G. Rötter (Eds.), *Musikpsychologie. Handbuch der Systematischen Musikwissenschaft* (Vol. 3, pp. 250–262). Laaber: Laaber.
Reuter, C. (2013). Von der 'Manichfaltigkeit der Praedicate' zum Timbre Space [Timbre models from the end of the 19th century to timbre spaces]. In C. Utz (Ed.), *Organized Sound: Klang und Wahrnehmung in der Musik des 20. und 21. Jahrhunderts* (pp. 97–112). Saarbrücken: Pfau-Verlag.

Révész, G. (1913). *Zur Grundlegung der Tonpsychologie* [On the basics of sound psychology]. Leipzig: Feit.
Rimski-Korssakow, N. (1912). *Principles of orchestration*. New York: Kalmus.
Rogers, B. (1970). *The art of orchestration. Principles of tone color in modern scoring*. Westport, CT: APP Greenwood Press.
Rousseau, J.-J. (1768). *Dictionnaire de musique*. Paris: Duchesne.
Sandell, G.J. (1995). Roles for spectral centroid and other factors in determining blended instrument pairings in orchestration. *Music Perception, 13*(2), 209–246.
Schubart, C.F.D. (1806/1969). *Ideen zu einer Ästhetik der Tonkunst* [Ideas about an aesthetics of music]. Darmstadt: Wissenschaftliche Buchgesellschaft.
Schumann, K.E. (1929). *Physik der Klangfarben* [Physics of timbres]. Berlin: University of Berlin.
Siddiq, S., Reuter, C., Czedik-Eysenberg, I., and Knauf, D. (2015a). Vergleichende Untersuchungen zu Timbre Space Studien [Comparative studies on different timbre spaces]. In *Fortschritte der Akustik, 41. DAGA2015* (pp. 811–813), Nuremberg.
Siddiq, S., Reuter, C., Czedik-Eysenberg, I., and Knauf, D. (2015b). Towards the comparability and generality of timbre space studies. In A. Mayer, V. Chatziioannou and W. Goebl (Eds.), *Proceedings of the 3rd Vienna talk on music acoustics* (pp. 232–235). Vienna: Institute of Musical Acoustics (Wiener Klangstil).
Siedenburg, K., Fujinaga, I., and McAdams, S. (2016). A comparison of approaches to timbre descriptors in music information retrieval and music psychology. *Journal of New Music Research, 45*, 27–42.
Siedenburg, K., Jones-Mollerup, K., and McAdams, S. (2016). Acoustic and categorical dissimilarity of musical timbre: Evidence from asymmetries between acoustic and chimeric sounds. *Frontiers in Psychology, 6*(1977). Retrieved from https://doi.org/10.3389/fpsyg.2015.01977.
Solomon, L. N. (1959). Search for physical correlates to psychological dimensions of sounds. *Journal of the Acoustical Society of America, 31*, 492–497.
Stumpf, C. (1890). *Tonpsychologie* [Psychology of sound perception] (Vol. 2). Leipzig: Hirzel.
Stumpf, C. (1926). *Die Sprachlaute* [Phonological investigations]. Berlin: Springer.
Voigt, W. (1975). *Untersuchungen zur Formantbildung in Klängen von Fagott und Dulzianen* [Studies about the origins of formants in the sounds of bassoons and dulcians]. Regensburg: Bosse.
von Bismarck, G. (1971). Psychometrische Untersuchungen der Klangfarbe stationärer Schalle [Psychometrical investigations into the perception of timbre]. In Verein Deutscher Ingenieure (Eds.), *Akustik und Schwingungstechnik* (pp. 371–375). Düsseldorf: VDI.
von Bismarck, G. (1972). *Extraktion und Messung von Merkmalen der Klangfarbenwahrnehmung stationärer Schalle* [Extraction and measurement of timbre features]. Munich: aku-Fotodruck.
von Helmholtz, H. (1863). *Die Lehre von den Tonempfindungen als physiologische Grundlage für die Theorie der Musik* [On the sensations of tone as a physiological basis for the theory of music]. Braunschweig: Vieweg.
von Helmholtz, H., and Ellis, A. J. (1885). *On the sensations of tone as a physiological basis for the theory of music*. London: Longmans, Green & Co.
Weber, G. (1822). *Allgemeine Musiklehre für Lehrer und Lernende* [Generic music treatise for teachers and pupils]. Darmstadt: Leske.

Wedin, L., and Goude, G. (1972). Dimension analysis of the perception of instrumental timbre. *Scandinavian Journal of Psychology, 13*(1), 228–240.
Wessel, D. (1979). Timbre space as a musical control structure. *Computer Music Journal, 3*(2), 42–52.
Widor, C.-M. (1904). *Die Technik des modernen Orchesters. Ein Supplement zu Berlioz' Instrumentationslehre* [Orchestration treatise]. Leipzig: Breitkopf & Härtel.
Wien, W. (1896). Ueber die Energievertheilung im Emissionsspectrum eines schwarzen Körpers [Towards the energy distribution in the radiation spectrum of a black body]. *Annalen der Physik, 294*(8), 662–669.
Willis, R. (1832). Ueber Vocaltöne und Zungenpfeifen [About vowel sounds and reed pipes]. In J. C. Poggendorff (Ed.), *Annalen der Physik und Chemie* (vol. 24, pp. 397–437). Halle: Rengersche Buchhandlung.

# 10 'Music as fluid architecture'
## Investigating core regions of the spatial brain

*Christiane Neuhaus*

People's quirks, tics and disorders are fruitful sources for understanding the functioning (and the mysteries) of the human brain. Oliver Sacks, the famous neurologist and bestselling author, gained this insight quite early in life and made a fortune from case studies he came across in his Manhattan medical practice. One of these clinical disorders, termed 'visuo-spatial neglect', is relevant in this context here. Patients suffering from neglect blend out the contralateral half of space. It makes them draw only half of an animal or flower, forget to read the left pages of journals or music scores, and shave or make up the right side of their face while omitting the left. The reason for this dysfunction of environmental and body awareness is a lesion in the posterior parts of the brain. Typically, the right inferior region is affected (e.g., Karnath, 1997). These examples illustrate that the posterior parietal cortex (PPC) is one of the core regions of the human brain for processing spatial information. It is activated during spatial perception as well as during action planning, movement control and visuo-motor transformation.

Anyone engaged in the performing arts, be it a conductor, a dancer or an instrumentalist, uses this cerebral region in a natural way for balancing body posture and for building a spatial framework to orientate in the space around him/her (Rizzolatti, Fadiga, Fogassi and Gallese, 1997). Strangely enough, many researchers are not fully aware of the multifarious roles of this region of the brain, some do not even know about its functioning at all. I suggest the following reasons: First, philosophers and scholars such as Locke, Hume, Herbart and Külpe share the view that spatiality can be experienced better through certain sensory modalities than through others, that is, best through vision and touch and far less through hearing. Révész (1937) even raised the question of whether auditory space exists as an autonomous concept, that is, independently from visual and tactile space. In addition, Fechner and other representatives of early psychoacoustics interpret pure tones as unidimensional sonic events; they refute the opinion that tones have spatial qualities at all (see Schneider, 1997). Second, invasive methods have a long tradition in research using monkeys but may have prevented further investigations of the human PPC: to precisely investigate how PPC neurons discharge microelectrodes are implanted into the brains of macaques and rhesus monkeys to record single-cell activity, for instance, when they plan to grasp a piece of food in near space (e.g., Fogassi et al., 2005).

Despite these limitations from the traditional and the methodological side, space, spatiality and movement are current issues in research. 'From time to space' is a shift in thinking, dubbed the 'spatial turn' that has been typical of modern philosophy since Foucault but also shapes the humanities and the social sciences as a paradigm (Quadflieg, 2012). The spatial turn manifests itself in (social) network constellations and virtual reality scenarios, emphasising parallel and simultaneous processes far more than the sequential and chronological ones.

This chapter describes the neural processes underlying spatial thought and spatial action. I will also touch upon insights from other disciplines, in particular from music psychology. Many aspects refer to the functioning of the brain at the micro and the macro levels, invisible to the naked eye. The reader might come to the conclusion that any generative process, be it a conducting gesture, a movement sequence for choreography, a new composition or even sight-reading contains spatial aspects independent from time and to a greater extent than expected. It might also be interesting to learn which functional roles the PPC plays to better understand the concept of embodiment or the theoretical background of dance performance and of playing a musical instrument. I will explain the PPC's anatomy and function in detail. However, the main focus of this chapter is on an active type of spatial imagery called mental rotation and its underlying neural substrate. I will also give a short overview of research findings on auditory and visuo-spatial imagery.

## Space: nomenclature and some philosophical ideas

'Space' in its general meaning includes connotations such as 'distance', 'expansion' and 'coordinate system', hence words typical of any shape beyond a dot, showing that space needs dimensionality for existence. But space is also a sort of precondition for locomotor activity that enables living beings to move and change their position. Stumpf (1873), however, maintains the opposite in that patterns of movement create spatiality and give rise to spatial imagination. So, 'space' and 'movement' are concepts inextricably linked with each other, although causality is not clear. Both, however, demand a well-functioning sense of direction (or orientation).

The human brain has two cortical regions that allow one to decide what type of spatial orientation is currently required to execute the respective action. The first region is the PPC. It is activated whenever we make hand, arm or head gestures within working space (as conductors do). The second is the hippocampal system as part of the limbic system: The one on the right side reacts to spatial tasks and requirements (whereas the one on the left side stores personal, episodic memories). So, right hippocampal structures are activated while remembering well-known landmarks or while navigating through the environment.

In order to systematise what functional roles the PPC and the hippocampal structures play, researchers use a special nomenclature to describe the inner and outer (action) circles within 3-D space. Often, the terms 'peripersonal space', 'locomotive extrapersonal space' and 'earth fixed space or geo-space' are used (Previc, 1998; but see, e.g., Leman and Naveda, 2010, for another type of nomenclature; see also Leman, this volume). The term 'peripersonal space' describes the reaching radius (0–2 m) centred to the body and with eyes, head, trunk and the limbs serving as flexibly changing coordinate axes. 'Extrapersonal space' refers to the walking radius outside the reaching distance of arms and legs (2–30 m), whereas the term 'earth fixed space' deals with fixation points and landmarks such as towers or market places. In other words, actions like touching, grasping or conducting take place within peripersonal space. They are 'ego-centred' and the source of activation can be found in the PPC. Actions like navigating by car through complex (virtual) reality environments take place within earth fixed space. They are 'allo- or geocentric' and, thus, hippocampal structures are activated.

Interestingly, this space naming convention corresponds closely with ideas about relative and absolute space as advocated by Leibniz, Newton, Kant and other philosophers (cf., Levinson, 2003; Quadflieg, 2012). Space as interpreted by Leibniz means relative space as determined by figures or geometric points located within a grasping and/or walking distance. His understanding of space results from certain patterns or immovable constellations, in short, from the arrangement itself that may change according to situational influences. Leibniz's idea of relative space is fundamental to any approach found in the social and cultural sciences to explain the behaviour of individuals, acting as social agents in certain places. Newton, by contrast, a contemporary of Leibniz, conceived space (and time) as absolute, that is, as an invariable entity, indivisible and infinite. Space as interpreted by Newton is often compared to a 'container', a 'vessel' or a 'three-dimensional box' (Levinson, 2003, p. 27). Newton's understanding of space is somehow a physical prerequisite for any sort of animated or unanimated material on earth. Thus, from a neurophilosophical perspective, PPC and hippocampus might be considered as the corporeal (neural) correlates of ideas about relative and absolute space as represented by Leibniz and Newton: Whenever body–object relations in near space are in the centre of attention, the PPC is activated (and this is what we will focus on), whereas for navigating through far space by car the right hippocampal structures are activated.

Our short excursion into philosophical views about space should not fail to include Immanuel Kant. His opinion on that matter is far more abstract, from an ontological point of view. He thinks of space as a pure category of mind, existing *a priori* and guiding all kinds of sensual experience (cf. Levinson, 2003; Quadflieg, 2012). Space according to Kant is an ontological precondition for any type of discovery within the external world.

## The 'where' and the auditory cortex

I will continue with the PPC as viewed by neuroscience and explain its multifunctional roles. Cortical regions, such as the PPC are capable of multitasking and need various inputs to perform tasks in an adequate manner. Since the PPC operates on a multimodal rather than on a domain-specific level (Gallese and Lakoff, 2005), we should first address the question of where and how sensory information exactly enters and converges.

There is general consensus among scientists about a certain information-distributing mechanism, named 'dual pathway' and also known as the 'what' and 'where' system (e.g. Rauschecker and Tian, 2000). The dual pathway originates in the primary cortices and then splits into a ventral and a dorsal fibre bundle, respectively. It was first discovered by Mishkin, Ungerleider and Macko (1983) for the visual domain, followed by Rauschecker and Tian (2000) for the auditory domain. The term 'what system' means that stimulus features, necessary to identify an object (or a sound), move along the ventral branch, probably terminating in the inferior frontal cortex. Spatial information, on the other hand, necessary to localise an object (or a sound; the 'where' information), moves along the dorsal branch, probably terminating in the PPC.

Let me take a closer look at what is known regarding the auditory cortex and explain some of the details. Interestingly, the primary auditory cortex (PAC) is the region where the splitting of sound information starts, but it is also that part of the brain where we consciously perceive 'high versus low', the essential piece of spatial information, for the first time. The PAC enables us to distinguish between high tones and low tones (see also Eitan, this volume) due to a tonotopic organisation of the primary auditory cortex that makes neurons respond to the fundamental frequency of sound in a strictly organised and histologically determined manner (Pantev, Hoke, Lütkenhöner and Lehnertz, 1989; Pantev et al., 1998). Using magnetoencephalography (MEG) and source analysis techniques, Pantev et al. (1998) could show that the medial-lateral axis of the PAC consists of different (tonotopically arranged) sections responding in a spotwise manner to pure tones and piano tones played in octave distance (C4, C5, C6, C7). Additionally, Rauschecker and Tian (2000) observed during single-cell recordings that PAC neurons located in the antero- and caudo-lateral belt regions of the monkey's auditory cortex do have specific properties: The antero-lateral type of neuron shows specificity to either tonal, harmonic or noisy monkey calls (the semantic cues), whereas the caudo-lateral type primarily responds to monkey vocalisations placed differently in the surroundings (the spatial cues). This line of research was pursued by Robert Zatorre, Bouffard, Ahad and Belin (2002). Using positron emission tomography, his team took a closer look at the spatial sensitivity of the human auditory cortex. By simulating a free-field spatial presentation through radiating sound from one to six headphone positions simultaneously, Zatorre and colleagues could distinguish between PAC activity on the one hand and PPC activity on the other while participants had to detect the sounds' spatial positions. The results suggest that PPC sensitivity depends on whether an active response is required or not. That is, whenever participants had to move a joystick to solve the localisation task the right inferior part of PPC was activated, whereas pure discrimination of sound positions without any motor response did not yield any PPC effects at all (Zatorre et al., 2002). This result leads to the conclusion that audio input followed by motor output triggers responses in the PPC (but not in the PAC). It should be noted that a temporary handling with spatial information on the domain-general level, known as *spatial working memory*, takes place in the superior frontal sulcus as part of the human frontal cortex (e.g. Courtney, Petit, Maisog, Ungerleider and Haxby, 1998). However, I am keeping to the main points in regard to the posterior parietal regions and will not explain the role of spatial working memory in detail.

## Anatomy and function of the posterior parietal cortex

Let me briefly describe some neuroanatomical facts to better understand how the PPC as a core region for processing near space information really works. The PPC covers a large part in the upper back of the head and belongs to the associative areas of the brain. These regions do not directly communicate (or interact) with the external world as primary areas do, but rather work on a higher, more abstract level. Across species – rats, rabbits, cats, monkeys and humans – and also in terms of human evolution – from the chimpanzee to Homo sapiens (and his hominid ancestors) – the associative areas have increased in size tremendously, and this especially holds true for the inferior part of the PPC. Thus, drawing parallels between the parietal structures of humans' and monkeys' brains is difficult, since anatomy differs substantially (cf. Jäncke, 2007).

In addition, Hyvärinen (1982) suggests a functional specialisation between the right and the left PPC in the human (but not the monkey) brain. According to Hyvärinen, the left PPC is involved in mechanisms related to linguistic processing, in particular reading and writing, whereas the right PPC is activated during spatial attention and the planning of constructive actions. However, results should be replicated to validate these assumptions.

Now let me describe the anatomical details. There is general agreement that the PPC consists of three parts: the superior parietal lobule (SPL), the inferior parietal lobule (IPL) and a special furrow, called intraparietal sulcus (IPS) that deserves special attention (e.g. Hyvärinen, 1982; Jäncke, 2007, see Figure 10.1). In terms of nomenclature, a certain map with numerals based on the cytoarchitectonic (histological) peculiarities of the cerebral cortex is widely in use (Brodmann, 1909). According to this cortical map, BA5 and BA7 are two subdivisions synonymous with SPL, whereas BA39 and BA40 are two subdivisions synonymous with IPL (Hyvärinen, 1982; Jäncke, 2007; BA stands for Brodmann area).

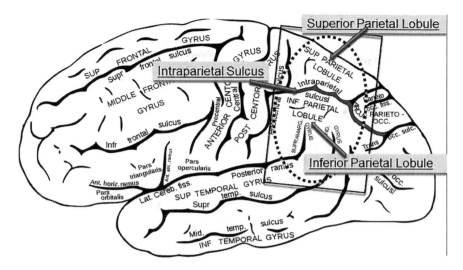

*Figure 10.1* The intraparietal sulcus divides the PPC into a superior and an inferior part (SPL and IPL).
Source: Wikimedia Commons.

### The superior parietal lobule

What is the specific role of the upper part of PPC abbreviated as SPL? The SPL creates spatial stability: despite eye and head movements due to changes in gaze direction it makes us perceive the environment as manageable, never changing within ultra-short time frames of several ms length. Thus, the SPL provides a constant background, a sort of prerequisite for any type of movement in peri- and extrapersonal space (Hyvärinen, 1982). In more detail, SPL creates a sort of *adaptable* spatial reference system in that information about body position in relation to space is continuously updated as we move along. This upgrade demands a sort of online computation, and the brain seems to continuously process incoming visual, auditory, vestibular and kinaesthetic signals from body movement to build this spatial, multimodal reference frame (cf. Jäncke, 2007; *Sinnesraum* [sensory space] Révész, 1937, p. 142).

A term frequently used in this context is 'proprioception'. Proprioception means to feel and balance posture, the body position. It also means to perceive the body self within space. Proprioception provides an artist with information about initial positions of arms, legs and feet in relation to room coordinates before the performance begins. Feelings of proprioception are especially developed in ballet dancers, acrobats and, to some extent, also in instrumentalists for the control of movements and limbs (cf. Figure 10.2). Thus, periods of deliberate practice (Ericsson, Krampe and Tesch-Römer, 1993) typical of any kind of professional artistic or musical training will

174  *Christiane Neuhaus*

*Figure 10.2* While dancing, proprioception provides the artist with information about body posture set in relation to room coordinates.
Source: Sanches 1980, Dreamstime.com.

certainly lead to either a structural enlargement or a functional enhancement of SPL, a process commonly known as brain plasticity (cf. Münte, Altenmüller and Jäncke, 2002). In summary, the superior parietal lobule serves as an integration centre where visual, auditory and other signals from different senses, carrying spatial information, converge. This process creates a stable but flexible reference system necessary for orientation and the guiding of movements in peri- and extrapersonal space. The SPL is activated in anybody walking, dancing, playing the violin or learning acrobatic tricks and feats.

### *The inferior parietal lobule*

The IPL is an area for generating motor plans. It is directly connected via fibre bundles with the ventral premotor cortex (BA 6), which is a region for further adjustment of movements by regulating their speed, force and direction. More interestingly, however, is the discovery of a special type of neuron, the 'parietal mirror neuron' found by Fogassi et al. (2005) during single-cell recordings. The majority of IPL mirror neurons discharge very specifically according to the subsequent motor act that follows. Neuron number 167, for instance, fires when a monkey has to grasp some food to raise it to the mouth, whereas neuron number 161 discharges when a monkey has to grasp a piece of food in order to place it into a container (Fogassi et al., 2005).

## The intraparietal sulcus

Anatomically speaking, the IPS divides the PPC into the superior and the inferior part (SPL and IPL). In the human brain, the sulcus itself is relatively long (~ 7 cm) and quite deep (~ 2 cm) (Jäncke, 2007). Monkey fMRI reveals that the walls of this sulcus consist of a mosaic of subareas, including an anterior, a medial and a caudal intraparietal part (AIP, MIP and CIP). Each is highly specialised in transforming sensory information into grasping movements or other motor responses (Grefkes and Fink, 2005). Obviously, this sulcus (and also the IPL) is responsible for a fundamental change regarding body frames and functions: from perception to action, from head-centred to body-centred coordinates, from sensory input to motor output.

The AIP, for instance, is activated when a monkey identifies the shape of 3-D objects by sight and transforms these signals into an adequate concept for grasping. Regarding function, the CIP comes before the AIP. This subarea receives input from the visual cortex to analyse the surface, shape and orientation of the respective 3-D object without any further 'programme' for transformation. Functionally speaking, the CIP remains in the visual mode. The MIP, by contrast, is a subarea involved in online-control and the correction of movement errors (see Grefkes and Fink, 2005).

Are there any implications for the music domain? The question can be answered in the affirmative: visuo-motor transformation, activating the IPL, IPS and partly SPL, seems central for learning to play any type of musical instrument. Motor plans can be built from sight-reading music or from learning hand actions as an imitating process. Buccino et al. (2004) showed with fMRI that while learning to play a novel chord, amateur musicians activated the left SPL as well as bilateral IPS and IPL when instructed to first observe the teacher showing them how to grasp the novel hand position on the guitar neck. This SPL activation still increased during a short pause in order to prepare the respective hand movement, indicating further transformation effort. During action execution, activity then shifted towards the right primary motor areas. Similarly, Schön, Anton, Roth, and Besson (2002) demonstrated by using fMRI that participants with experience in playing the piano strongly activated their right SPL and IPS during sight-reading melodies which had to be played on a small keyboard immediately afterwards. Regarding brain activation it made almost no difference whether

*Figure 10.3* Visuo-motor transformation is central while learning to play a musical instrument. During sight-reading, SPL and IPS are activated.
Source: Jason Hawkins, Dreamstime.com.

notes were transformed into movement patterns from music notation (the graphic symbols), from syllables (do, re, mi, etc.) or from numbers used for fingering. Again, visuo-motor transformation was the underlying principle (see Figure 10.3).

It should be noted that for any type of movement pattern to be played on a musical instrument a precise spatial alignment between hand, fingers and the sound-producing mechanism such as fingerboards, guitar frets or piano keys is an essential prerequisite. A manipulated piano with arbitrarily permuted keys (as used for experimental purposes in a DC-EEG study by Bangert and Altenmüller, 2003) may therefore lead to malactivations of the SPL and IPL, making the process of generating motor plans somehow unpredictable, thus, being an inhibiting factor in the process of skill improvement.

## Some reflections on the concept of 'embodiment'

Since the work of developmental psychologist Jean Piaget sensorimotor co-ordination or, generally speaking, body-centred experience in near space has been considered to be the first key stage characterising the cognitive development of humans in the first two years of life (see Montada, 2002). It may be suggested (and has to be proven by experiment) that the IPS seems to be among the first anatomical landmarks that newborns and toddlers instinctively train by learning to grasp a ball, a cube or a rattle. From an ontogenetic perspective this means that the concept of embodied cognition already begins to develop between birth and age two. Embodied cognition is a common position in philosophy and has also inspired music psychologists (see, e.g., Godøy, 2010; Leman, 2008; see Leman, this volume). The embodied theory posits that the capacity of the human mind is substantially anchored in the brain's sensorimotor systems, in other words, that conceptual knowledge is built through a body-based understanding of the world (Gallese and Lakoff, 2005). To illustrate this theory take the functioning of mirror neurons as an example. In principle, mirror neurons discharge when two scenarios are given: when a monkey performs a goal-directed action, or when it observes another individual doing a similar action. This mechanism works on a common neural representation that is activated whenever a goal-directed gesture is transformed into motor activity or vice versa. It makes us understand actions by intuition and also deduce the underlying purpose (Fogassi and Luppino, 2005). Thus, certain abstract concepts (but not all) seem to be embodied, that is, implemented in our sensorimotor systems (but see Chatterjee, 2010, for a critical assessment of an embodied approach to cognition).

In terms of abstract and embodied concepts, we may think of *human spatial abilities*. Abstract geometric reasoning as well as spatial imagery are processes that fall within the concept of embodiment (Corballis, 1997). Spatial imagery abilities are often quantified via psychometric tests, and Frances Rauscher's mental paper-folding and cutting test serves as a good example (Rauscher, Shaw and Ky, 1993). In her famous but controversial study, participants had to mentally fold two-dimensional patterns into three-dimensional cubes. They scored better after listening to a Mozart sonata (KV 488) compared to silence or to listening to a relaxation tape, a result commonly known as the 'Mozart effect'. Until now no causal relationship between spatial reasoning and music cognition has been established, and most researchers attribute the participants' high scores after listening to preferred sounds to a change in mood or an increase in arousal (Nantais and Schellenberg, 1999).

### *Spatial imagery abilities: mental rotation*

Mental rotation is another type of spatial imagination. It has long been recognised as an embodied spatial ability, and many empirical studies consistently confirm that mental rotation skills have their origin in the posterior parietal areas of the human brain. In an fMRI study Jäncke and his team (Jordan, Heinze, Lutz, Kanowski and Jäncke, 2001) could identify the centre of activation as bilaterally located in the IPS. The participants in this study were asked to judge pairs of letters as well as pairs of abstract figures as same or different by mentally rotating them into congruence. The strategy of rotation (turn the right figure clockwise to match the left, Jordan et al.,

2001) was given in advance to reduce inter-individual variance. However, the focus of activation within the PPC can differ according to task, instruction, methods and stimuli. Corballis (1997), for example, favours a shift in activation towards the right hemisphere, as for him mental rotation of simple shapes is a Gestalt-like but not a language-related process, making holistic but not analytical strategies plausible.

Note, it is interesting to observe that empirical studies about spatial imagination and their respective neural correlates as briefly discussed in this context here are the cause of a long-running dispute about the type of mental representation of thought. What is true and what is adequate in terms of mental imagery and mental representation? Is it a non-symbolic, pictorial and analogous type of representation or rather a symbolic and propositional one (e.g., Corballis, 1997; Glück and Vitouch, 2012; Rumelhart and Norman, 1988)? This discussion, also known as the 'imagery debate', is currently taking place between Stephen Kosslyn on the one side and Zenon Pylyshyn on the other: Kosslyn, Pinker, Smith, and Shwartz (1979) claim that knowledge underlying images is analogous, whereas Pylyshyn (2003) argues that this type of knowledge is propositional.

I have not yet dealt with the seminal work of psychologist Roger N. Shepard, who was the first to choose a behavioural approach to studying spatial imagery, in particular mental rotation. Shepard explored spatial imagination by measuring reaction time, which, at first glance, appears as a rather unconventional method. In Shepard's studies (see in particular Shepard and Metzler, 1971), subjects had to decide (by pulling a small lever) whether pairs of 3-D cube figures were same or different. Cube figures could vary in perspective view (in picture plane or in depth) as well as in angular size (from 0° to 180° by increments of 20°, see Figure 10.4). The data showed that reaction time increased linearly with angular size but independently of perspective view (picture plane vs. depth). The mean reaction time was 2.8 s to identify sameness, and 3.8 s to judge whether a cube-figure was the mirror image of the other. Introspective reports showed that subjects solved this mental task by imagining one cube as being rotated into congruence with the other, which is a strong argument for a non-symbolic, analogue type of mental representation (Kosslyn et al., 1979).

## *Mental rotation: gender-related differences*

Interestingly, the sexes differ in their mental rotation skills and in other types of spatial imagination. Men usually outperform women (Glück and Vitouch, 2012). This gender gap also becomes evident on the cortical level even in groups of men and women who scored equally well on the behavioural level. Men show activation in the left parietal cortex (left IPS, left SPL) as well as in the zone between the parietal and occipital cortex (right parieto-occipital sulcus). Women activate the IPS bilaterally with an additional activation of the inferior temporal lobule (Jordan, Wüstenberg, Heinze, Peters and Jäncke, 2002). Obviously, the strategies for solving these tasks differ according to sex. Men use types of movement-related visual strategies whereas women rely on the more analytical tactics, perhaps through verbalising geometric issues (Jordan et al., 2002). Other explanations are possible, ranging from different hormone concentrations, in particular testosterone (Moffat and Hampson, 1996), to gender socialisation as evident, for example, from buying dolls for girls and toy cars for boys. More speculative is an explanation from evolutionary biology that posits that prehistoric men moved through large territories to hunt mammoths, which requires the building of spatial field maps in mind, whereas prehistoric women trained their route memory through learning and remembering paths while picking fruits and plants (Glück and Vitouch, 2012).

In this context a study by Marianne Hassler is worth mentioning. Hassler (1985) tested the relationship between visuo-spatial intelligence and musical creativity in 60 boys and 60 girls at the beginning of puberty (between age nine and 14). In contrast to Rauscher et al.'s study (1993) where effects between visuo-spatial intelligence and pure listening were shown to be small and contestable, this study established a relationship between visuo-spatial abilities and the generative processes in music. The children had to prove their skills by composing a short piece of music. Those having invented an imaginative little piece as judged by an independent jury also did well at several tests for visuo-spatial intelligence, including spatial imagination and orientation. Talented boys outperformed talented girls in the number of successfully performed visuo-spatial subtests, suggesting that this gender-specific advantage in terms of visuo-spatial imagery might be one of several plausible reasons why musical composition has been a male-dominated field for centuries. The overall result of this study is that creative musical talent and spatial intelligence are significantly correlated with each other.

## *Mental rotation in the fine arts*

Let me take a closer look at the compositional practice itself. Does musical structure reflect processes of visuo-spatial imagery, in particular mental rotation, in a certain way? Think, for instance, of Johann Sebastian Bach or of Arnold Schönberg and his school. Music composed in a contrapuntal (or polyphonic) style, as typical of the baroque period or in dodecaphony, uses compositional techniques such as inversion (upside down transformation), retrograde (the backward form, that is, a musical permutation that requires reversal in time) and retrograde inversion (both types combined) that need vertical and/or horizontal axes for their constructions. It thus seems plausible that composers such as Bach or Schönberg mentally transformed their musical rows and motifs, for instance to juggle with musical ideas or combine melodic lines with each other (and while doing so their IPS probably showed activation). To justify this compositional practice Schönberg once said that he considered musical space as a unity. On this assumption it should be discussed (and proven by further experiments) whether transformations of the 12-tone row seem perceptually equivalent, and whether or not Schönberg's supplementary comments make his dodecaphonic work more comprehensible to the listener (Schönberg, 1950; see also Deutsch, 2013).

It does seem as if during certain creative stages, composers imagine their artwork as independent from time (e.g., the metrical units) but rather in terms of form, spatial dimensions and construction. Schelling's (1802/1803) characterisation of architecture as 'frozen music' (as cited in Schelling, 1859, p. 576) fits well into this context here. This idea can also be found in slightly modified form in the works of Schopenhauer (1819) and Goethe (1829) (as cited in Schopenhauer, 1859, p. 517 and in Eckermann, 1836, p. 88 respectively). Wellek, the music psychologist, uses the vice-versa form by speaking of 'music as fluid architecture' (1982, p. 324).

Furthermore, mental transformation can also be found in the fine arts, be it modern art or architecture. Consider, for instance, oil paintings in the style of analytic cubism such as Picasso's *Still Life with Compôte and Glass* (1914/15) or Braque's *Violin and Palette* (1909/10). Each time, all sides of the portrayed item are pictured simultaneously. Or think of architectural masterpieces, in particular buildings of twisted shape like the recently completed Cayan Tower in Dubai. Another example is the Philips Pavilion designed by the office of Le Corbusier for the Expo '58 in Brussels showing nine hyperbolic paraboloids bound together.

### *Experiments on auditory as compared to visuo-spatial imagery*

Let me continue with musical issues. Juggling with musical motifs in the mind's ear and eye has already been studied by experiment. Music psychologist W. Jay Dowling (1972) was among the first to raise the question of whether atonal melodies of the inverse, retrograde and retrograde inverse form were indeed perceptible or simply of mere constructive value. Dowling used five-tone-sequences of very small ambitus with intervals of less than a major third (and with tones built from sawtooth waves). Inverse and retrograde forms had to be compared against the standard forms, each comparison melody starting on a tone other than the standard. All transformed versions were identified by undergraduates above chance level, and the inversion (upside down) was more easily recognised than the retrograde (backward form). A different approach was taken by Krumhansl, Sandell, and Sergeant (1987). In four listening experiments on the perceptibility of 12-tone rows (two of them were preceded by training sessions), they tested participants with different musical backgrounds, using similarity judgements and the probe tone method for data acquisition. The participants had to evaluate pieces of chamber music by Schönberg – the complete excerpts on the one hand and the underlying tone rows on the other hand. Keypoints such as 'Do people learn to anticipate successive tones in the row?' or 'Is listening impartial or still preshaped by tonality and tradition?' could be explained through results from this extensive study. However, large individual differences were found, so further studies are needed. In addition, Shepard (see Dowling, 1972) suggested that the strategy for judging upside down (in that a melody going 'down–down–up–down' becomes 'up–up–down–up') is tone-by-tone with a focus on the beginning which does not work for the retrograde and retrograde inversions. These backward types take the entire melody as a basis that demands more mental effort than an element-wise comparison with the focus on the beginning.

A study by Cupchik, Phillips, and Hill (2001) directly compared the skills in mental cube rotation with those in musical permutation (inverse and retrograde), that is, the cognitive processes underlying visuo-spatial and auditory imagery types, respectively (see Figure 10.4). However, in comparison with Dowling's study (1972) musical sequence structure was different, this time consisting of easily perceptible intervals often larger than a third. In Cupchik's study, identification was better for the retrograde than for inverse forms, showing that the task-solving strategy depends for the most part on the musical structure itself. Furthermore, the accuracy of recognising the musical retrograde also predicted the accuracy of judging visuo-spatial rotations, suggesting that these tasks are solved on the basis of a Gestalt-like impression probably serving as a common underlying denominator. Moreover, a gender difference was found for Cupchik's visuo-spatial tasks but not for the auditory imagery tasks, showing that both sexes judged the correctness of musical inverse or retrograde figures equally well (serving as auditory counterparts of the Shepard figures). This result allows the modified conclusion that a male

*Figure 10.4* Testing visuo-spatial and auditory imagery: example items of mental cube rotation and music permutation (inverse and retrograde forms).
Source: Cupchik et al., *Brain & Cognition* 46, 2001; printed with permission from Elsevier.

advantage in most tests of visuo-spatial abilities alone (see above) is not sufficient evidence to explain why the field of musical composition has been dominated by men.

Zatorre, Halpern and Bouffard (2010) designed two further fMRI experiments on auditory mental rotation. They restricted themselves to the retrograde form, that is, to those types of musical permutation that require reversal in time. Musically trained participants had to decide whether an immediately played second section was the retrograde of the first. This study confirms that the PPC (especially left and right IPS) acts in a task-related manner on an abstract level by computing steps necessary for figure transformation (irrespective of mode or the eliciting type of stimulus). Zatorre further points out that transformation of musical figures in mind is an illustrative example of an active type of auditory spatial imagery, commonly known as 'audiation' (a term coined by Gordon in 1975; see Gordon, 2001).

## The spatial character of individual tones and musical intervals (one-tone and two-tone sonic objects)

I would like to close this chapter with some remarks on the spatial character of tones and intervals, that is, on single sonic events as extensively investigated by Carl Stumpf (see his two volumes of *Tonpsychologie*, 1883, 1890). As we have already seen, the conscious impression of high versus low has a neuroanatomical origin due to a tonotopic organisation of the PAC. Besides this, music psychologists often choose a phenomenological approach based on introspection to describe their perceptual impressions. This way Drobisch (1855), Révész (1937) and other researchers discovered that pitch itself consists of two, somehow spatial components: a circular one, named pitch chroma and a linear one, called pitch height (see Eitan, this volume). Both dimensions are intertwined with each other and can be made visible by a geometric shape, the pitch helix. Using fMRI as well as tones of all pitch classes (two thirds of them manipulated in pitch height by attenuating the odd harmonics), Warren, Uppenkamp, Patterson and Griffiths (2003) could demonstrate that Drobisch's subjective assessments of pitch do have neuroanatomical counterparts: single tones (manipulated in pitch height while pitch chroma was kept constant) activate two independent brain regions in the immediate vicinity of the PAC. The first, known as planum polare (PP), responds to pitch chroma whereas the second, known as planum temporale (PT), responds to pitch height. That is, whenever we listen to an individual tone either to identify its overall pitch (high–low) or to grasp its circular and linear spatial components, the brain reacts on its first processing level, the auditory cortex: PAC neurons respond in a tonotopic manner whereas the PP and PT (as parts of the secondary auditory cortex) react independently to pitch chroma and pitch height (Pantev et al., 1989; 1998; Warren et al., 2003; Zatorre et al., 2002).

Note that Stumpf (1883, 1890), and especially von Hornbostel (1926), extended these assessments by adding subjective impressions like weight and density to further characterise the spatial quality of pitch. Von Hornbostel considered these features as tone-inherent, whereas Stumpf obviously felt less sure of his judgements, partly considering these tone qualities as mere associations (Révész, 1937). To my knowledge, no fMRI study has yet been carried out to find a neural correlate for these additional subjective evaluations of the quality of pitch (*Gehörserscheinungen*; von Hornbostel, 1926, p. 315).

The spatial character of musical intervals is another point at issue. Do they simply activate the PAC at frequency-related positions? Or are there some abstract and Gestalt-like aspects processed beyond, in accordance with the concept of embodiment? Musical intervals as such illustrate tone distance, that is, the amount of space between two boundary marks labelled pitch 1 and pitch 2. Révész (1937; also Wellek, 1982) points out that the interval's spatial impression is stronger when both tones are presented in succession rather than played in a simultaneous manner, that is, when choosing a dynamic instead of a static approach. A successive presentation of tones, however, implies motion or movement. Having in mind that intervals do also appear in their inverse form (e.g., thirds become sixths, sixths become thirds) and that playing them on keyboards, guitar necks or fingerboards elicits additional visuo-tactile feelings, it seems likely that interval-related sensual information converges and will be transformed, showing activation in the PPC, in particular in the IPS. It might be interesting to see to what extent these interval-related spatial impressions do interact with the interval's dissonance level (for the latter, Blood, Zatorre, Bermudez and Evans, 1999 could demonstrate that the right parahippocampal gyrus is gradually activated with different signal intensity). At present, researchers know that the IPS bilaterally reacts to melody transposition (as an example of mental transformation), and that an increase in transposition difficulty (by shifting a melody to closely related or more remote keys) activates the IPS with different cortical strength (Foster, Halpern and Zatorre, 2013). Foster et al. therefore suggest that the IPS is the common neural substrate for processing three types of mental transformation: mental rotation (a visuo-spatial skill), shifts in pitch (melody transposition) as well as reversal in time (the retrograde forms).

## Conclusions

It is said about Mozart that he was able to see the complete musical architecture in his mind's eye (Konrad, 1992). The investigation of the PPC, in particular the IPS, shows that this report of one of Mozart's contemporaries now can be confirmed with fMRI. Obviously, mental rotation and its neuroanatomical correlate, the IPS, seem to play a specific role in musical composition in particular when the focus of imagination is on form, spatial dimensions and construction, that is, on aspects somehow independent from time. Interestingly, mental rotation and the IPS do also serve as good examples to validate the concept of embodiment as a common opinion in philosophy and relatively recent trend in cognitive (music) psychology.

In contrast, the SPL and IPL, that is the superior and inferior parts of the PPC, handle spatial issues in a less creative but far more pragmatic way by integrating real-world impressions of the auditory, visual, kinaesthetic, vestibular and tactile type to build a stable body-centred reference system for proprioception and movement planning, respectively. Révész' question of whether auditory space exists autonomously therefore has to be answered in the negative. Instead, multimodal sensual experiences, that is, vision, hearing and touch linked together, contribute to the impression of a stable spatial reference system (*Sinnesraum* [sensory space]; Révész, 1937).

In summary, the key points of this chapter are as follows. The PPC is one of the core regions of the spatial brain. It is activated whenever body–object relations such as touching, grasping or conducting are in the focus of attention. The upper part of the PPC (abbreviated as SPL) serves as an integration centre where visual, auditory, kinaesthetic, vestibular and tactile signals carrying spatial information converge. Due to this process an adaptable reference system (a multimodal *Sinnesraum* [sensory space]) is formed which is necessary for orientation in extrapersonal space. The term proprioception is connected with activity in the SPL. Proprioception means to feel and balance posture, also to perceive the body self within space. Feelings of proprioception are especially developed in ballet dancers, acrobats and instrumentalists for the control of movements and limbs. The IPL appears to be an area for generating motor plans. The majority of IPL mirror neurons discharge specifically according to the subsequent motor act that follows. Motor plans are built from sight-reading music or from learning hand actions as a pure imitative process, and visuo-motor transformation seems central for learning to play a musical instrument (activating the IPL, IPS and partly the SPL).

Furthermore, mental rotation skills seem to be substantially grounded in the PPC (which is in accordance with the concept of embodiment). These skills are bilaterally centred in the IPS and differ according to sex, showing an advantage for males. In addition, distinctive types of musical permutation skills are also anchored in the IPS, in particular melody transposition and reversal in time (the retrograde forms). Thus, mental rotation and its neuroanatomical correlate, the IPS, play a specific role in polyphonic music as well as in the fine arts, pointing out the relationship between mental transformation and creative processes from a neuroscience perspective.

## References

Bangert, M., and Altenmüller, E. O. (2003). Mapping perception to action in piano practice: A longitudinal DC-EEG study. *BMC Neuroscience, 4*(26). doi: 10.1186/1471-2202-4-26.

Blood, A., Zatorre, R. J., Bermudez, P., and Evans, A. C. (1999). Emotional responses to pleasant and unpleasant music correlate with activity in paralimbic brain regions. *Nature Neuroscience, 2*(4), 382–387.
Brodmann, K. (1909). *Vergleichende Lokalisationslehre der Grosshirnrinde: In ihren Prinzipien dargestellt auf Grund des Zellenbaues* [Comparative localisation studies in the brain cortex: Its fundamentals represented on the basis of cellular architecture]. Leipzig: Barth.
Buccino, G., Vogt, S., Ritzl, A., Fink, G. R., Zilles, K., Freund, H. J., and Rizzolatti, G. (2004). Neural circutis underlying imitation learning of hand actions – An event-related fMRI study. *Neuron, 42*(2), 323–334.
Chatterjee, A. (2010). Disembodying cognition. *Language & Cognition, 2*(1), 79–116.
Corballis, M. C. (1997). Mental rotation and the right hemisphere. *Brain & Language, 57*, 100–121.
Courtney, S. M., Petit, L., Maisog, J. M., Ungerleider, L. G., and Haxby, J. V. (1998). An area specialized for spatial working memory in human frontal cortex. *Science, 279*, 1347–1351.
Cupchik, G. C., Phillips, K., and Hill, D. S. (2001). Shared processes in spatial rotation and musical permutation. *Brain & Cognition, 46*, 373–382.
Deutsch, D. (2013). The processing of pitch combinations. In D. Deutsch (Ed.), *The psychology of music* (3rd ed.) (pp. 249–368). Amsterdam: Elsevier.
Dowling, W. J. (1972). Recognition of melodic transformations: Inversion, retrograde, and retrograde inversion. *Perception & Psychophysics, 12*(5), 417–421.
Drobisch, M. W. (1855). Über musikalische Tonbestimmung und Temperatur [On musical pitch estimation and temperature]. In *Abhandlungen der Königlich Sächsischen Gesellschaft der Wissenschaften*, 2 (pp. 1–120). Leipzig: Hirzel.
Eckermann, J. P. (1836). *Gespräche mit Goethe in den letzten Jahren seines Lebens: 1823–1832* Theil 2 [Conversations with Goethe in the last years of his life: 1823–1832 (Vol. 2)]. Leipzig: Brockhaus.
Ericsson, K. A., Krampe, R. T., and Tesch-Römer, C. (1993). The role of deliberate practice in the acquisition of expert performance. *Psychological Review, 100*, 363–406.
Fogassi, L., Ferrari, P. F., Gesierich, B., Rozzi, S., Chersi, F., and Rizzolatti, G. (2005). Parietal lobe: From action organization to intention understanding. *Science, 308*, 662–665.
Fogassi, L., and Luppino, G. (2005). Motor functions of the parietal lobe. *Current Opinion in Neurobiology, 15*, 626–631.
Foster, N. E. V., Halpern, A. R, and Zatorre, R. J. (2013). Common parietal activation in musical mental transformations across pitch and time. *NeuroImage, 75*, 27–35.
Gallese, V., and Lakoff, G. (2005). The brain's concepts: The role of the sensory-motor system in conceptual knowledge. *Cognitive Neuropsychology, 22*(3/4), 455–479.
Glück, J., and Vitouch, O. (2012). Psychologie [Psychology]. In S. Günzel (Ed.), *Raumwissenschaften* [Spatial sciences] (3rd ed.) (pp. 324–337). Frankfurt am Main: Suhrkamp.
Godøy, R.-I. (2010). *Musical gestures: Sound, movement, and meaning.* New York: Routledge.
Gordon, E. E. (2001). *Preparatory audiation, audiation and music learning theory: A handbook of a comprehensive music learning sequence.* Chicago, IL: GIA Publications.
Grefkes, C., and Fink, G. R. (2005). The functional organization of the intraparietal sulcus in humans and monkeys. *Journal of Anatomy, 207,* 3–17.

Hassler, M. (1985). Kompositionstalent bei Mädchen und räumliche Begabung [Compositional talent of girls and spatial ability]. In K.-E. Behne, G. Kleinen., and H. de la Motte-Haber (Eds.), *Jahrbuch der Deutschen Gesellschaft für Musikpsychologie, 2* (pp. 63–85). Wilhelmshaven: Heinrichshofen.

Hyvärinen, J. (1982). Posterior parietal lobe of the primate brain. *Physiological Reviews, 62*(3), 1060–1129.

Jäncke, L. (2007). Neuroanatomy of the parietal cortex. In F. W. Mast and L. Jäncke (Eds.), *Spatial processing in navigation, imagery and perception* (pp. 135–145). New York: Springer.

Jordan, K., Heinze, H. J., Lutz, K., Kanowski, M., and Jäncke, L. (2001). Cortical activations during the mental rotation of different visual objects. *NeuroImage, 13*, 143–152.

Jordan, K., Wüstenberg, T., Heinze, H. J., Peters, M., and Jäncke, L. (2002). Women and men exhibit different cortical activation patterns during mental rotation tasks. *Neuropsychologia, 40*(13), 2397–2408.

Karnath, H.-O. (1997). Spatial orientation and the representation of space with parietal lobe lesions. *Philosophical Transactions of the Royal Society B: Biological Sciences, 352*, 1411–1419.

Konrad, U. (1992). *Mozarts Schaffensweise – Studien zu den Werkautographen, Skizzen und Entwürfen* [Mozart's compositional method: Studies on autographs, drafts and sketches]. Göttingen: Vandenhoeck & Ruprecht.

Kosslyn, S. M., Pinker, S., Smith, G. E., and Shwartz, S. P. (1979). On the demystification of mental imagery. *Behavioral & Brain Sciences, 2*(4), 535–548.

Krumhansl, C. L., Sandell, G. J., and Sergeant, D. C. (1987). The perception of tone hierarchies and mirror forms in twelve-tone serial music. *Music Perception, 5*(1), 31–78.

Leman, M. (2008). *Embodied music cognition and mediation technology*. Cambridge, MA: MIT Press.

Leman, M., and Naveda, L. (2010). Basic gestures as spatiotemporal reference frames for repetitive dance/music patterns in Samba and Charleston. *Music Perception, 28*(1), 71–91.

Levinson, S. C. (2003). *Space in language and cognition: Explorations in cognitive diversity*. Cambridge: Cambridge University Press.

Mishkin, M., Ungerleider, L. G., and Macko, K. A. (1983). Object vision and spatial vision: Two cortical pathways. *Trends in Neurosciences, 6*, 414–417.

Montada, L. (2002). Die geistige Entwicklung aus der Sicht Jean Piagets [The cognitive development from a Piagetian perspective]. In R. Oerter and L. Montada (Eds.), *Entwicklungspsychologie* [Developmental psychology] (5th ed.) (pp. 418–442). Weinheim: Beltz.

Moffat, S. D., and Hampson, E. (1996). A curvilinear relationship between testosterone and spatial cognition in humans: Possible influence of hand preference. *Psychoneuroendocrinology, 21*(3), 323–337.

Münte, T. F., Altenmüller, E., and Jäncke, L. (2002). The musician's brain as a model of neuroplasticity. *Nature Reviews Neuroscience, 3*, 473–478.

Nantais, K. M., and Schellenberg, E. G. (1999). The Mozart effect: An artifact of preference. *Psychological Science, 10*(4), 370–373.

Pantev, C., Hoke, M., Lütkenhöner, B., and Lehnertz, K. (1989). Tonotopic organization of the auditory cortex: Pitch versus frequency representation. *Science, 246*, 486–488.

Pantev, C., Oostenveld, R., Engelien, A., Ross, B., Roberts, L. E., and Hoke, M. (1998). Increased auditory cortical representation in musicians. *Nature, 392*, 811–814.
Previc, F. H. (1998). The neuropsychology of 3-D space. *Psychological Bulletin, 124*(2), 123–164.
Pylyshyn, Z. (2003). Return of the mental image: Are there really pictures in the brain? *Trends in Cognitive Sciences, 7*(3), 113–118.
Quadflieg, D. (2012). Philosophie [Philosophy]. In S. Günzel (Ed.), *Raumwissenschaften* [Spatial sciences] (3rd ed.) (pp. 274–289). Frankfurt am Main: Suhrkamp.
Rauschecker, J. P., and Tian, B. (2000). Mechanisms and streams for processing of 'what' and 'where' in auditory cortex. *PNAS, 97*(22), 11800–11806.
Rauscher, F., Shaw, G. L., and Ky, C. N. (1993). Music and spatial task performance. *Nature, 365*, 611.
Révész, G. (1937). Gibt es einen Hörraum? Theoretisches und Experimentelles zur Frage eines autochtonen Schallraums nebst einer Theorie der Lokalisation [Does an auditory space exist? On the question of an autochthonous sound space together with a theory of localization]. *Acta Psychologica, 3*, 137–192.
Rizzolatti, G., Fadiga, L., Fogassi, L., Gallese, V. (1997). The space around us. *Science, 277*, 190–191.
Rumelhart, D. E., and Norman, D. A. (1988). Representation in memory. In R. C. Atkinson, R. J. Herrnstein and G. Lindzey (Eds.), *Stevens handbook of experimental psychology 2* (2nd ed.) (pp. 511–587). New York: Wiley.
Schelling, F. W. J. v. (1859). Philosophie der Kunst (Vorlesung) [Philosophy of art (lecture)]. In F. W. J. v. Schelling, *Sämtliche Werke I* [Complete works], vol. 5 (1st ed.). Stuttgart: Cotta.
Schneider, A. (1997). *Tonhöhe – Skala – Klang. Akustische, tonometrische und psychoakustische Studien auf vergleichender Grundlage* [Pitch – scale – sound. Acoustic, tonometric and psychoacoustic studies on a comparative basis]. Bonn: Verlag für Systematische Musikwissenschaft.
Schön, D., Anton, J. L., Roth, M., and Besson, M. (2002). An fMRI study of music sight-reading. *Neuroreport, 13*(17), 2285–2289.
Schönberg, A. (1976). *Stil und Gedanke – Aufsätze zur Musik* [Style and idea – Selected writings of Arnold Schönberg] (I. Vojtech, Ed.). Frankfurt am Main: Fischer.
Schopenhauer, A. (1859). *Die Welt als Wille und Vorstellung* [The world as will and representation] (3rd rev. ed.). Leipzig: Brockhaus.
Shepard, R. N., and Metzler, J. (1971). Mental rotation of three-dimensional objects. *Science, 171*, 701–703.
Stumpf, C. (1873). *Über den psychologischen Ursprung der Raumvorstellung* [On the psychological origin of spatial imagination]. Leipzig: Hirzel.
Stumpf, C. (1883, 1890). *Tonpsychologie* [Psychology of tone] (vol. 1 and 2). Leipzig: Hirzel.
von Hornbostel, E. M. (1926). Psychologie der Gehörserscheinungen [Psychology of the phenomena of hearing] (reprint 1986). In C. Kaden and E. Stockmann (Eds.), *Erich Moritz von Hornbostel. Tonart und Ethos: Aufsätze zur Musikethnologie und Musikpsychologie* [Erich Moritz von Hornbostel. Mode and ethos: Studies in ethnomusicology and the psychology of music] (pp. 315–366). Leipzig: Reclam.
Warren, J. D., Uppenkamp, S., Patterson, R. D, and Griffiths, T. D. (2003). Separating pitch chroma and pitch height in the human brain. *PNAS, 100*(3), 10038–10042.

Wellek, A. (1982). Der Raum in der Musik [The space in music]. In A. Wellek (Ed.), *Musikpsychologie und Musikästhetik* [Psychology and aesthetics of music] (3rd ed.) (pp. 295–334). Bonn: Bouvier.

Zatorre, R. J., Bouffard, M., Ahad, P., and Belin, P. (2002). Where is 'where' in the human auditory cortex? *Nature Neuroscience, 5*(9), 905–909.

Zatorre, R. J., Halpern, A. R., and Bouffard, M. (2010). Mental reversal of imagined melodies. A role for the posterior parietal cortex. *Journal of Cognitive Neuroscience, 22*(4), 775–789.

Part III
# Presence and immersion in networked and virtual spaces

# 11 Music as artificial environment
## Spatial, embodied multimodal experience

*Peter Lennox*

This chapter is a speculative exploration of the near-future possibilities of spatial music. Technologically, we can control many hundreds of loudspeakers and, conceivably, many thousands. What would we do with them? Here, music is considered as a particular example of artificial information environments, with consequences for the perception of space. Artificial information environments are those environments in which information transactions are governed by design. The distinction is clear in comparison with natural environments, but a finer distinction can be drawn between man-made environments (such as buildings), where some information transactions are haphazard, and information environments whose main purpose is to display information.

All organisms affect their environment, but only humans expend great ingenuity and effort to decorate theirs with elaborate symbolic representations that evoke affective responses. Such creative responses might have their roots in those real environment circumstances such as dangerous animals, hunting scenes, the sea, and so on, but their utilisation in artificial information environments rarely involves immediate survival needs, enabling us to use our evolved cognitive machinery to consider more abstract, non-real-time concepts.

We can even afford the luxury of concentrating on single-sense perception, which, in the wild, would be peculiar. One such example would be music, which is conveyed largely by the single sensory channel of audition (though vibrotactile stimuli may be relevant in some circumstances). Fine temporal perceptual discrimination is critical in music; spatial acuity less so. The purpose of this chapter is to discuss whether we could reintegrate some aspects of the embodied nature of place perception into music. A relevant distinction here is that between the space in the music and the music in the space (Malham, 2003). Music can metaphorically depict spatial matters such as object properties (ponderous and heavy, or quick and light) and trajectories, along with place characteristics such as open or enclosed, intimate or spacious. Music can also be designed for specific places. Ceremonial music tends to be heard in large places, finely detailed delicate music in more intimate places. It is reasonable to expect interactions between spatial metaphor and the physical circumstances of the listening space. Understanding and controlling those interactions for optimal perceptual effect are goals for spatial music design.

## Music: why?

Why do we expend extraordinary effort to make such complex patterns in sound, when the real world is at least equally complex and informative? Given that music is peculiar to humans, it is also peculiar in abstract. If one were to try to explain music to an objective observer with no prior experience of it, one would struggle to explain what it is or does, and why we expend so much effort on it. We could suppose that music is epiphenomenal, caused as a by-product of the evolution of complex perception, but in itself does no causing; system idle processes that stave off boredom. The epiphenomenal argument is summed up in Pinker's (1997) auditory cheesecake analogy. Pinker suggests that music exemplifies exaptation – the rededication of an evolved capacity to a new function (Gould 1996; Gould and Vrba, 1982) where cognitive capacities associated with language competence have subsequently come to also be used for the non-survival-related activity of music. The counter-argument runs along the line that music constitutes offline processing that enhances readiness for survival-related cognition when needed; it is related to survival but not in immediate, real-time ways (Levitin, 2006). Evidence for ontogenetic development exists; musical practice causes structural development in individuals' brains, bringing cognitive advantages in auditory processing (Kraus and Chandrasekaran, 2010) and offsets in age-related deficits (Sluming et al., 2002).

Theories of why music exists are extrinsic to musical theory, and are best contextualised in the wider arguments about why we physically construct so much of our environment. Marvin Minsky approached this problem from the perspectives of cognitive science and artificial intelligence in 'Music, Mind and Meaning' (1981); for him, music typifies human development of representation of knowledge.

An important perspective on music is that, as with all systems of ideas, it evolves. Mutations occur in the hands of individual composers, thereafter to become part of the common experience. Philosopher Karl Popper (1972) used the concept of 'World 3' to refer to the domain of ideas that have achieved independence of their originators. We might think of this as a musical ideasphere that we draw from and contribute to.

### *Defining and characterising music*

The difficulties in concisely defining music are well known (e.g., Kania, 2014; Levinson, 1990; Levitin, 2006). For the purposes of this chapter, 'artificial sonic pattern' might be a useful general characterisation; it implies human intentionality and stipulates non-randomness, though falls short of specifying precise structural constraints or usages.

These patterns yield musical diverse forms: massive, intricate polyphonic ensemble pieces, simple single-instrument pieces, improvisations, complex or simple rhythms, and so on. Each of these forms is associated with affective responses. Music can be solemn or carefree, ponderous or delicate, aggressive or poignant, serious or humorous, massive or just plain ambient. The range of possible affective responses is reflected in diverse usage of music; it can excite, calm, threaten, soothe, distract or simply mask unwanted sound. It can be used to amplify existing emotional states, enhance social cohesion or provide a comforting sonic backdrop to a solitary pursuit; it can alleviate sadness or avert boredom or stimulate wild dancing. Music can be an accompaniment to events, actions and occasions in ceremonies, films and computer games. For a comprehensive discussion on musical universality, diversity, evolution and the possible influence on human evolution, see Cross and Morley (2008). So, we have sonic patterns to move to, patterns that relax us, or excite us or encourage thoughtful contemplation. This sonic pattern-making appears to have some deep metaphorical connection with our cognitive states, which may go some way to explaining the ubiquity and pervasiveness of music.

## Music as an artificial environment

The term *environment* refers to the totality of circumstances surrounding a given entity, encompassing opportunities and threats such as food, water and predators. Organisms engage with and negotiate environments by means of perception. An environment is here defined as that which supports perception; and *artificial* is used in the sense of constructed by humans. An artificial information environment therefore refers to a human construct that facilitates interaction with codified information.

Broadly, we could think of music as one of a range of activities in which our species engages, allowing us to manifest ideas in some physical form and so we can share, modify and communicate them through putative conceptual sets, or 'artificial information environments'. Concepts in artificial environments can be quite literal – concrete concepts such as 'a dog' – but they can also utilise *counterfactuals*: we could discuss what could happen if the enemy attack us at night, and what we might do to gain advantage. Artificial environments could also represent that which is fanciful or cannot directly be observed, such as spirits, gods or the will of our ancestors.

Environment perception fundamentally entails embodiment; the organism exists in a surrounding physical context and perception is how it minimises risks and maximises opportunities; perception is not fundamentally abstract computation. This is in line with theories of embodied cognition (e.g., Clark, 1997). Real environments are intrinsically spatial. An ambulant organism uses considerable cognitive processing to navigate toward rewards, taking care to keep appropriate distances between it and threats. Perception is therefore egocentric, operates in real time (defined here as:

timeliness with respect to external events) and is spatial. 'Spatial' in this context means more than three-dimensional; it does feature direction and distance but also affordances (Gibson, 1977): obstacles, escape routes, objects and, of course, the presence or possible presence of other organisms. We might use the term 'place perception' to draw the distinction between abstract Euclidian space and the real places that are naturally spatially heterogeneous but are also suffused with life-or-death meaning.

Defining environment in terms of perception facilitates examination of the qualities of environments that are perceptible. Phylogenesis has been shaped by a material world of probabilistic causal regularities, opportunities, events and consequences. We have structural propensities toward intuitive physics (Cooper and Munger, 1993; Spelke and Van de Valle, 1993), discerning meaningful patterns, detecting agency and predicting intentionality. Real environments are interactively experienced and explorable through processes of interrogation by corporeal interaction – moving through and round, poking, prodding, lifting, testing – and so information is extracted by stimulating the environment and assessing the returning signals This is the real meaning of embodied perception; perception does not merely consist of the passive reception and processing of signals, behaviour is as much at the service of perception as vice versa. In this model of perception as active hypothesis testing (Gregory, 1974, 1980; Batteau, 1968), perception is not functionally discrete from behaviour, and experience is not a passive term. The tight coupling between perception and behaviour reflects the fundamental requirement that we need to harvest information, process it and behave appropriately in real time (i.e., driven by external events), and continuance of the organism constitutes the measure of success.

By comparison, our artificial environments, whilst safe, are causally truncated and can foster disembodiment: a framed picture shows a 'letterbox' section of an environment; a film must have a beginning, middle and end within a tightly constrained time-span, as must a piece of music. Computer environments are spatially unadventurous; even the best virtual reality technologies do not allow us to run, jump, hide, lift, navigate and manipulate as fully as in the real world. Most people's experience with a computer is sitting in front of a screen, with a QWERTY keyboard and mouse – a distinctly spatially impoverished activity. Overall, our artificial information environments do not utilise our full range of spatial perceptual abilities and there is scope for optimising them for greater information throughput.

In the 21st century, a significant proportion of our cognitive activity is taken up with engaging with artificial stimuli (see Brereton, this volume). Music is cast here as an example of what Andy Clark and David Chalmers (2010) call 'extended mind' that features 'active externalism' whereby items in our environment are coupled with our cognitive processes to the extent that they form parts of our cognition. So language, tools, software and art are so constructed as to facilitate kinds of cognition that would not be otherwise feasible. This, in turn, can be contextualised in terms of 'extended perception' (Lennox, 2015): evolution, where it has generated increasing morphological complexity, has also generated extended perceptual abilities. Humans have used intelligence to fashion tools that extend sensory range (telescopes, mobile telephones, Geiger counters) and can understand environmental circumstances at micro and macro scales beyond other species' capabilities. Artificial environments extend this principle by accommodating counterfactuals – things that are not so, but if they *were*, then such and such would follow. This kind of mental operation facilitates simulation of courses of action and possible consequences and so can furnish anticipation, extending perception temporally as well as spatially.

Music can be just one item in the overall auditory environment such as a radio in the room, a complete auditory environment such as listening over headphones with eyes closed or part of a multimodal environment such as when experiencing a film.

## *Space and music*

Why is music temporally sophisticated, but not spatially so? Sound is intrinsically spatial. Physically, it consists of spatially propagated disturbance of a medium (air) that carries information about initial conditions of source size, construction, types of excitation such as impact, rubbing, scraping, etc. (Warren and Verbrugge, 1984) along with the location of the initial disturbance, which is perceived as source direction and distance from the perceiver. Sound also carries information about movement, the physical characteristics of the moving items, the characteristics of the local environment (open/enclosed, large, etc.) and facilitates perception of causality (no sound occurs at random) and possible animate agency. The sound world is replete with potential meanings, and auditory perception engages in detecting possible threats and opportunities in terms of understanding what things are, where they are and, importantly, what might happen next. So hearing elicits the nature of items involved in sound events, their location (distance and direction from the perceiver) and their causal trajectories. The latter could be in the form of physical spatial trajectories and intentionality of agents (organisms).

Music, by contrast, does not necessarily convey all these attributes; it is simpler in some respects (the range of possible consequences is muted, without real time life-or-death considerations), yet more complex in the temporal intricacy of sonic patterns. Spatial matters are traditionally less prominent in music than in the world around us, but perhaps this is simply an evolutionary phase, determined in part by technological constraints.

## *Space and music: a brief historical perspective*

Space might have featured quite substantially in very early ceremonial music. Neolithic ceremonial structures were impressive and would have had quite particular sonic characteristics; they were often circular, partially enclosed and with many large stone surfaces featuring complex reverberations, producing psychologically impressive acoustic characteristics that accentuated the ceremonial other-worldliness.

A burgeoning field of archaeological study focuses on the properties of prehistoric sites: *archeacoustics* (sometimes: archaeological acoustics) uses modern measurement techniques to analyse and reconstruct what the auditory experience of such sites might have been. There is a conjecture that the acoustic properties of many ancient ceremonial sites were not entirely accidental, but were painstakingly tuned to resonate at the lower frequencies produced by male voices in drones or chants (Watson, 2006; Devereux, 2001), or the shells of marine creatures found at the ancient Chavín De Huántar site in Peru (Abel et al., 2008). For a discussion of a methodological framework for analysing the experienced soundscapes of ancient cultures, see (Blake and Cross, 2015). Certainly, the reverberant qualities of surviving sites have been found to produce distinctive and sometimes disturbing results, the soundscape rolling round the space, enveloping and transporting the listener (Reznikoff, 2006; Kolar, 2013). It appears that ceremonial music and ceremonial spaces could have co-evolved. This tradition of impressive sounding ceremonial spaces continued in the temples and cathedrals throughout documented history. Spatial inventiveness featured in some large-scale ceremonial works such as the eight-part *Vespers* by Adrian Willaert in 1550 and the 40-part motet 'Spem in alium' by Thomas Tallis in 1570.

In the 20th century, experimentalist composers such as Charles Ives and Luigi Russolo used spatial orchestration in large public works, and the advent of electroacoustics facilitated spatial compositions by artists such as Pierre Schaeffer, John Cage, Karlheinz Stockhausen, Edgard Varèse and Iannis Xenakis. For fuller historical discussions of spatial music, see Zvonar (2005). Nevertheless, spatial parameters have usually not been central or *primary* musical parameters in the popular conception of music and the music distribution industry could not be more than peripherally concerned with large-scale public works.

## *The constraints of 20th-century recording technologies*

Visual capture of facsimiles of events, objects and people has existed for millennia (from Neolithic cave paintings onwards). Sound scenes were more challenging, since capturing ephemeral temporal patterns of pressure fluctuation requires complex technological infrastructure. For most of human history, sound could only be stored in memory (notoriously fallible) or the analogue transcription of descriptive metadata, in the form of music notation: a recipe from which the piece of music could be reconstructed. This had the advantages of being highly portable and technologically feasible, but exact reproduction, including all the acoustic factors of the original performance, could not be guaranteed. In effect, a recipe is only as good as that which goes into it.

With the advent of recording and electronic transmission-and-replay technologies in the early 20th century, spatial matters actually became marginalised. The earliest recording technologies, based on Edison's 1890 dictation machine, were predicated on capturing the human voice for later replay, not on capturing complex scenes with many sources and spatial relationships. Hence the first recordings of sound entirely destroyed spatial aspects of the captured sound, homogenising direction and defeating localisation. Additionally, vocalists or musicians had to be very close to the pickup device to optimise signal-to-noise ratio, thus defeating distance perception.

These technologies coincided with developments in mass production and the rise of consumerism so that, gradually, music became popularly conceptualised as that which could be recorded and purchased, for listening to in the comfort of one's own home. Even large-scale popular musical events utilised technologies and formats similar to the domestic ones, so that a rock concert with thousands of attendees features spatially bland musical offerings.

The hegemony of the electronic capture, storage, manipulation and transmission of music gave rise to the recording studio and associated techniques. Chiefly, these included the non-simultaneity of musical recording so that separate components can be more finely treated and the *close mike* (Hodgson, 2010) approach to sound capture to remove unwanted ambient acoustic characteristics. Unintended consequences included the loss of the directional output characteristics of musical sources and the relationships between these and the environment. Real objects became two-dimensional images. Similarly, the spatial relationships between ensemble elements, including 'ensemble depth' (Neher, Brookes and Rumsey, 2003) were flattened into a left–right soundstage. Ironically, stereophonics, originally coined to mean 'firm or solid sound', intended to imply almost-tangible realistic sources, came to actually mean 'flat'.

Another consequence was the sacrifice of the relationship between performers and between performer and space; real-time improvisational musical conversations, the drawing of inspiration from each other and from the acoustic space, were inhibited (for relevant discussion, see Brereton, this volume). Whether the trade-off between enhanced manageability and depleted spatial subtlety was entirely necessary or momentarily expedient, the usual experience of music came to be of something that was mediated by the intervening technology, engendering a state of disembodiment.

Paradoxically, music is more widely accessible than ever in human history, yet much popular modern music is like fast food: inexpensive, consistent and predictable; music has become mundane, a ubiquitous soundtrack accompanying everyday activities. The unplanned soundscapes of the world around us, being carelessly noise-polluted, are masked by portable personal music players and ignored, as R. Murray Schafer (1977, 1993) warned. An unfortunate by-product of this process could be a general forgetting of the auditory acuity of which we are capable. Kurt Fristrup, a senior scientist at the US National Park Service says: 'This learned deafness is a real issue ... we are conditioning ourselves to ignore the information coming into our ears' (Fristrup, 2015).

## *Reintroducing spatiality*

The invention of stereophonic sound reintroduced a modest illusion of spatiality to artificial sound fields for cinema and music listening. At its best, stereo (from the Greek word *stereos* meaning solid) can present a compelling illusion of almost-tangible sources in apparently discriminable locations across a left–right sound stage. The system takes advantage of cognitive processing shortcuts in humans, whereby, if the ears receive precisely identical signals, audition concludes a source equidistant from both ears; this is the phantom image (Snow, 1953). However, many disparate factors can interfere with the proper experience of stereophonic presentation, and it is a rare privilege to actually hear stereo properly. In terms of information preservation through successive transductions in the capture (or synthesis), storage, transmission and display processes, there arise many opportunities for spatial distortions. Essentially there is only one set of circumstances where the signals produced at the loudspeakers precisely govern the signals received by the binaural hearing system. If the listener turns their head, moves around the room or sits nearer one speaker than the other, phantom imagery is degraded. Spatial audio information is subtle, delicate and easily homogenised during successive transductions. For a fuller discussion of basic stereophonic principles, see Snow (1953).

Nevertheless, stereo proved such a commercial success that it seemed obvious that reproducing the entirety of the captured environment would be the logical next step. However, early attempts to commercially exploit horizontal surround-sound quadraphonics, which offered the possibility of immersing listeners in a whole musical environment, met with failure. Technological inadequacies and lack of psychoacoustic theoretical underpinnings were blamed (Gerzon, 1974), but, equally, popular music had become resolutely non-spatial and so grafting on spatiality afterwards was doomed to failure.

There is an apocryphal story (source unknown) about a salesman demonstrating the latest expensive quadraphonic technology to a prospective customer when, to his dismay, a rather shabby old chap walked in to hear the demo. The salesman thought he might be an unwelcome distraction. But the old man was well-behaved, listened intently then declared 'it's just like listening from in the middle of the orchestra!' The salesman seized on this and enthusiastically agreed, hoping the sale was in the bag. But then the old man said '... but an orchestra sounds terrible from in the middle' and left the shop. The sale was lost and so was Quadraphonics. Without clear musical reasons for spatiality, surround sound is little more than a gimmick. Without buoyant consumer demand for some extra musical experience, expensive developments cannot be commercially justified. Without some means to convey to the domestic customer the results of spatial composition, composers could have no incentive to work in a medium that would receive no exposure. Consequently, the paradigm shift that had occurred in going from mono to stereo was not reprised in a move from stereo to surround.

**Intriguing new possibilities**

New surround sound technologies have emerged for conveying more enveloping, involving and complete auditory environments to accompany visual stimuli in film and computer games. Whilst the latter are predicated on domestic environments with one or two players, larger scale auditorium systems ought to provide spatially coherent results for many listeners. The increasing ubiquity of such systems potentially offers composers opportunities to explore spatial parameters in music, and we might expect burgeoning experimentation in this area.

Forthcoming new technologies offer even more relaxation of technological constraints. The BBC research department is part of a research consortium (S3A Future Spatial Audio, 2014) that is actively developing a loudspeaker-layout agnostic scene description approach that can convey a complex 3-D description of an audio scene to an arbitrarily large number of loudspeakers, depending on the decoding capabilities at the consumer side of the chain. Melchior and Spors (2010) describe the fundamental differences in concepts and production between the previous channel-based and this new object-based approach. The intermediate software environment can accommodate detailed parameters of many individual objects (sound sources) and their spatial relationships. An important caveat is that, as with previous scene description approaches (such as musical notation), if a perceptually relevant parameter is not captured in the recipe, that information is lost. The decoding system could utilise any or all of a range of spatial projection systems including mono, stereo, vector-based amplitude panning (VBAP), ambisonics and Wavefield Synthesis (WFS).

Interestingly, according to Frank Melchior, head of the audio research team at BBC Research and Development, one strand of thinking anticipates that this new approach will facilitate greater user interaction and exploration of programme material (Melchior 2015). This would mean that the traditional unidirectional flow of information from broadcaster to recipient will give way to a bidirectional paradigm placing choice in the hands of the end user; instead of music being conveyed to passive percipients, perceivers will actually assume some of the compositional responsibility for their experiences. This process has already begun: increasingly, instead of listening to broadcasts, people assemble their own listening experience from podcasts, downloaded selections and customised playlists.

As intermediate spatial software environments develop, control of increasing numbers of transducers is feasible; the engineering goal is finer control of the listeners' ear-signals. However, some issues of perceptual experience extend beyond sensory matters. Prior knowledge (memory and experience), anticipation and individual subjective biases may all putatively contribute substantially to perceptual experience in everyday perception, but are not in themselves amenable to an engineering approach to managing sensation. Given that various perceptual theorists, including Hermann von Helmholtz (1925) William James (1890, p. 102), Richard Gregory (1998) and Andy Clark (2015) aver that perception is not merely informed or contaminated by top-down cognitive components but is largely comprised of such components, the philosophy of perception underlying engineering approaches requires something more. Indeed, in real environments, ear-signals themselves fluctuate significantly according to environmental factors (complex reflections, scattering and occlusions) and are disambiguated only by prolonged or repeated exposure and ambulant exploration by the perceiver. Essentially, the momentary sensory qualities are not the primary objects of perceptual mechanisms. Whilst the relationships between sensory qualities and perceptions are undoubtedly powerful, the contributions of cognitive mechanisms are at least as important. The events, objects and relationships 'out there' are the targets, and sensory apparatus is deployed during the extraction of causal narratives from the surrounding environment.

From an engineering perspective, the next challenge consists of incorporating a fuller conceptualisation of perception, with tools that manage causal consistency. This means some evolutionary development of the physics engine used in computer games, which we could call a 'causality engine'. A physics engine simulates an environment by modelling object physics (mass, size, rigidity and orientation within an environment), substance physics (fluidity, hardness, temperature) and environment physics (gravity, ground surface texture, spatial parameters). A 'causality engine' would additionally model parameters for intentional agents (simulated organisms or machines) that would interact with the simulated physics, but would also be constrained to a range of behaviours governing inter-agent interactions. Agents are of an order of magnitude more complex than inert physical objects, but are not chaotic in their behaviours. Additionally, such an enhanced modelling system could operate on perceptual phenomena such as auditory looming (Seifritz et al., 2002) and other characteristics of objects' trajectories to enhance cognisance of key features of the simulated environment.

### *Composing for embodied cognition*

From a compositional perspective, a paradigm of composing *with* space rather than simply spatialising pre-existing musical materials, is indicated. Environments are not simply collections of objects and features that happen to be in close proximity, but comprise densely textured, complex, multimodal patterns (single-sense perception is exceedingly rare) that perceivers actively sample to grasp the ongoing causal context. Agents, objects, obstacles,

*Music as artificial environment* 201

passageways, spatial relationships, movements and opportunities for interaction are the affordances (Gibson, 1977) that comprise our perceived environment (see Windsor, this volume).

We are adept at discerning what things are, where they are and where they will be next. We predict the behaviour of animate agents and take cognisance of features of the landscape that might offer opportunities for advantage, hiding or escape and what obstacles exist. In hearing terms, we are skilled at identifying material properties and causes of sound, especially organic sounds such as vocalisations and locomotion, and physical interactions between objects and environmental features.

We utilise sophisticated cognitive mapping (Tolman, 1948; see also: O'Keefe, 1993) to keep track of the affordances in our environments, refocusing selective attention on items by cognitively and *pre-consciously* (Dixon, 1971, 1981) selecting for *inattention* currently non-urgent items. This 'perceptual significance grading' (Lennox, Myatt and Vaughan 2001, pp. 395–306) exemplifies cognitive causal mapping (Gopnik, Meltzoff and Kuhl, 1999) and the degree of cognitive spatial mapping varies; an item not perceived as potentially urgent might simply be mapped as 'over there, somewhere'.

We are inordinately attentive to approaching items, referred to as 'auditory looming' (Seifritz et al., 2002, pp. 2147–2151) and 'acoustic tau' (Shaw, McGowan and Turvey, 1991, pp. 253–261) and sensitive to the transition from approaching to departing via the Doppler effect (McBeath and Neuhoff, 2002). We use cognitive 'cocktail party effect' (Cherry, 1953, p. 976) mechanisms to suppress unwanted signals in favour of interesting ones. We are able to cognitively suppress background reverberant sounds in 'precedence effects' (Litovsky, Colburn, Yost and Guzman, 1999) without even noticing we are doing it. Most notably, we elicit information from real environments through interrogation via head movements, locomotion and physical interaction; we explore and extract what we need to know (Gibson, 1988).

## *Spatial perception as embodied place perception*

Although we often conceptualise spatial perception in metric three-dimensional terms, we do not actually perceive it in degrees, radians or metres. What we actually perceive are places consisting of affordances. More narrowly, we perceive the place we currently inhabit which we call *here,* and *here* contains what just has been, what is now and might be next; there is a temporal aspect to here-perception that can be overlooked if we conceptualise the problem in Euclidean terms. Clark (2015, p. 3) describes humans as 'proactive predictavores'; in other words, to perceive is to predict. So we do not simply experience a succession of here-and-nows, we use our sensory experiences to align and update predictions.

Notably, 'heres' are nested egocentrically. So I may be sitting here at a workstation, here in a room, which is here in this building and so on. Whilst the concept of *here* is intuitively obvious, it is a complex perceptual phenomenon whose boundaries are delineated by subjective elements such as comfort, safety, threat and accessibility (Lennox, 2005). Hence spatial judgements are not abstractly absolute but relative to opportunities for interaction. Unsurprisingly, our perception is most acute for the region nearest to us, the within-reach 'peripersonal space' (Lourenco, Longo and Pathman, 2011, pp. 448–453; Tajadura-Jiménez, Pantelidou, Rebacz, Västfjäll and Tsakiris, 2011) in which most opportunities and necessities for interaction are situated. Nevertheless, if I am too lazy to get up to adjust the television, it will seem too far; if a tiger were in exactly the same position as the television, it would be perceived as uncomfortably close.

Reflecting on the kinds of places humans seek out, we are somewhat 'bi-polar' in our cognitive preferences. Exciting places incite high cognitive load; the thrill of (simulated) danger in a theme park, the sensory overload of sound and light that constitute the environment in a dance club makes us feel alive, alert; literally: excited. By contrast, calm, safe places allow us to relax because we need not be hyper-alert. The kind of contemplative places where people can think long, slow, intricate thoughts or idle musings can evince concepts that would not occur in demanding, urgent places. An important observation is that we participate in places, and we utilise as many senses as are available and necessary. We may operate fully multimodally when circumstances demand, less so when urgency is low. Multimodality is often thought of as referring to reception of signals across two or more sense modes. We feel (for texture and weight), hear, smell and see a given object. The problem of how we coherently integrate data from multiple senses is conceptualised in the 'binding problem' (Smythies, 1994, p. 54).

But this view is unnecessarily narrow, predicated on a substantive distinction between perception and behaviour. There is no logical reason to reify such a distinction. The conceptual distinction between perception (as receipt and processing of signals) and behaviour (moving through and acting on the environment) can mask the observation that environments react to occupants, just as occupants react to the environment. Therefore, we can discuss multimodality in terms of perception and behaviour. The binding problem becomes a 'perception and action binding problem' – we behave multimodally in order to extract multimodal information from the world. We might scratch and sniff (disturbing the surface oxidised layer to release chemicals) or we might heft and drop to hear information about weight and material construction. This multimodal active interrogation is what is logically implicit in the term *embodied cognition*.

**New musical thinking**

Perhaps it is possible to compose music in an analogous manner. The number of different genres and usages of music could be cast in terms of the number of kinds of cognition we can deploy in sundry environments: narrow focus forefront or background perception, wide dynamic range of significance grading demanding choosing for attention, reflective meandering, physical or cerebral, facile or spiritual. We could even go further and conjecture that the reason for so many types of musical activity is precisely that they metaphorically reflect the wide range of cognitive structures we use in everyday environments.

Reflecting on the relationship between the space in the music and the space the music is in (Malham, 2003), music often features spatial metaphors depicting scenes, events, otherworldly landscapes, large or small objects, movement, clashes or call-and-response. Metaphorical spaciousness does not inevitably benefit from a literal mapping to 3-D space in the listening area. Space should be applied as carefully as any other musical parameter. In very large musical works, large spatial separations could benefit call-and-response, but interfere (due to the finite speed of sound) with rhythmic timing and harmonies. Far from simply positioning the sources around a listener for little discernible reason, spatial music should *want* to be spatial; spatialisation decisions would have to be taken parsimoniously, in line with some 'internal causal connectedness' (Campbell, 1993, pp. 76–82) of the musical environment, which makes sense to the listener.

### *Listening to the music, or immersed in it?*

Would one actually want a musical sound field to be isotropic (i.e., having no direction dependence or preference) and equally meaningful in every direction? I find with students' ambisonic[1] experiments that I can often detect when they have made a technical mistake in orienting the sound field and where the intended front is, even when the soundscape is entirely synthesised. This could be that they subconsciously have a front in mind and have built around that, or that I have an expectation that certain key elements belong in front of me.

However, there are musical forms that have no front preference, when audience are not seated, as in dance club music. This example is more akin to earlier musical forms where musicians and listeners intermingled, the listeners sometimes participating, rarely passively listening. Interestingly, cultures that have this kind of musical paradigm might not even have separate words for music and dance (for example, see Stone, 1982; Cross and Morley, 2008) indicating that music is participative and immersive, rather than simply listened to.

We should also avoid any assumption that full spatial sound naturally requires the listener to be surrounded by transducers. For an experience featuring depth of field and auditory parallax for mobile listeners and/or mobile images, surround sound is neither necessary nor sufficient.

### *Spatially scalable music*

I had some students explore the question of scaling; they wanted to produce an 'ambisonic mousetrap' (a famous board game that features marbles that run along troughs, drop a level, run some more, etc.). They wanted to scale this board game up to the size of a room. Initially, starting with a Soundfield™ microphone[2] in a real mousetrap game, the results were disappointing. So they recorded a selection of rolling balls and panned them in to our 24-speaker periphonic ambisonics lab at the University of Derby, manufacturing appropriate early reflections. The result was excellent and was recorded into a second-order ambisonics file. On transferring to a larger system in an auditorium, the plausibility disintegrated; instead of gently rolling down a shallow incline, the ball apparently moved at improbable speed and the angular displacement in the larger system did not match the sound of the speed of rolling. The space in the soundscape did not match the space the soundscape was in and the anomaly invoked a perception of artifice, like a clumsy magic trick. Remastering to correct the angular displacement restored plausibility. Scaling is possible, but plausible matching of cues is paramount.

### *Do we need the sweet spot?*

It is not logically necessary to assume that precisely the same balance of musical elements is required for all listening positions – we can understand it in the living room (though one could imagine doing it differently) but why in a large place?

In another soundscape example, some students reconstructed a large line source event in equivalent dimensions. Using multiple microphones, they recorded a bowling alley lane. They displayed this auditory scene using 16 reciprocally placed speakers in a corridor so that one could stand anywhere along the path and hear the ball pass and strike appropriately. Covert observation of visitors revealed that they tended to subconsciously move out of the way of the virtual ball as it passed, demonstrating successful manipulation of perception. The sound field available at any single listening position was never identical to any other, yet all listeners could agree on the commonality of the experience. Although this was a soundscape exercise rather than a musical one, there is no absolute constraint on music being conceptualised in this way. In theory, this approach could be applied to depict massive objects and events, from a marching band passing right through the audience, a jumbo jet landing in a stadium, to a spatially realistic depiction of a thunderstorm. Composing entirely artificial massive events, with no single ideal listening position, would be an exciting challenge.

### *Music in an environment, as an environment*

The experiencing of music might rest in travelling though and round it, rather like in a promenade theatre. We recorded a choir in Derby Cathedral using three Soundfield™ microphones: one in the stalls, one in the choir and one near the altar. The recording was reconstructed in a large volume via three rings of 12 speakers each. Visitors walked toward, through and past the choir. The direct-to-indirect ratio and direction of reflections were preserved, producing a realistic musical soundscape that had no favoured listening position. This cellular sound field principle could be up-scaled using more microphones and more cells of speakers, perhaps to the dimensions of a large village. A surrounding ring of speakers covering a large area could not generate the fine-grained local spatial detail that would be available to perception in real, large environments. Especially, the facility for listeners to move and explore to extract more information from the artificial auditory environment requires complex multi-scale spatial treatment.

A cellular approach was embodied in the sculpture *The Morning Line*, for which composers were commissioned to produce musical soundscapes featuring multiple zones that visitors could explore (Lennox and Myatt, 2011). The Ambisonix dance nights at University of York (Malham, 1996) featured concentric rings of speakers, one simple four-stack arrangement for the dance floor, and one 12-speaker ring around the outside of the room. The aim was to furnish all occupants of the room with interesting spatial sound woven into the music, such that no two positions supplied precisely the same sound field. The cellular and concentric approaches could be utilised to depict places within places, like Russian Dolls, here within here, within here.

### *Environments persist*

One could conceive a composition that does not have a sharply delineated beginning, middle and end. There is no logical reason why a piece of music should have to be finished, pristine and untouchable. Music could be ongoing, not a piece but a place. A piece of music could be like a public botanical garden, retaining its identity yet constantly changing in detail so that it could be often revisited to observe the seasonal changes and the latest work done by the composer(s). It could have exciting areas, detailed areas and relaxing areas, areas that are intimate featuring sounds within the peripersonal space and areas that are grandiose, dwarfing the individual. Music could actually be a form of metaphorical data display that can take in economic activity data, keyword data from social media, climate measurements and any other real-time streamed dataset and conflate these to produce unanticipated correlations (see Vickers et al., this volume).

### *Musical artificial intelligences*

A complex musical environment could utilise sophisticated sensors and processing so that it reacted to the presence and behaviour of occupants. It might even recognise particular regular visitors and adapt to their tastes or mood, or assign them a musical motif as a companion to travel with them; no two visitors would ever experience precisely the same environment, just as with real places, and no single visit could capture the entire environment.

A piece could even contain composed synthetic musical agents that swarm, flock, chase, communicate, harmonise, squabble and have personalities. One could feel kindly disposed toward certain musical characters and irritated by others. We could create these entities, give them different starting conditions, voices, attributes and relationships, then set them free to see what happens. Music could be set free from determinism to become probabilistic.

**Conclusions**

The speculations here concern what composers might do with the new tools of intermediate software environments, burgeoning understanding of the relationships between temporal and spatial perceptual factors and technological developments in controlling very large numbers of transducers. Aside from the capacity for realistic depiction of spatial environments, the exciting challenges are in developing new metaphorical spatial relationships. Designing spatial music and spatial music systems from a starting point of active, embodied multimodal perception, considering what perceptual impressions we might wish to evince, allows us to draw from the palette of spatial experiences that are available to us in real environments.

This conceptualisation of spatial music is of an evolution beyond representations of sound stage performances toward holistic enveloping and explorable musical environments. These incorporate some of the virtues of real environments, appealing to the evolved perceptual mechanisms with which we understand the world. Given that, in the last 60 years we have not exhausted the aesthetic and perceptual possibilities of stereo, this is likely to be a lengthy developmental process that takes us far from where we are now. Some of the developments may appear anarchic, unwelcome even, and it would be a pity if spatial complexity came at the price of temporal complexity. The hope is that we could retain both.

Spatial music cast as an environment that we can inhabit necessarily recontextualises how we would experience it, toward active, multimodal engagement rather than passive listening. Hence the embodied, multimodal perception of music could be richer than the experience of reception of patterned sound. We could have music as a spatial environment that we inhabit, stimulate, interrogate and explore.

**Notes**

1 Ambisonics: a technology invented by Michael Gerzon and Peter Craven, whereby three-dimensional sound scenes (including the up-down dimension) featuring many sources can be captured (or synthesised) stored, transmitted and displayed using a finite, manageable signal set. It is essentially a mathematical extension of the 'mid-and-side' stereo recording principle.
2 The Soundfield™ microphone, also invented by Gerzon and Craven, utilises a tetrahedral microphone capsule array to facilitate full-sphere ambisonics spatial sound recording.

# References

Abel, J. S., Rick, J. W., Huang, P., Kolar, M. A., Smith, J. O., and Chowning, J. M. (2008). On the acoustics of the underground galleries of ancient Chavín de Huántar, Peru. *The Journal of the Acoustical Society of America, 123*, 3605.

Batteau, D. W. (1968). World as source, world as sink. In S. Freedman (Ed.), *The neuropsychology of spatially oriented behavior* (pp. 197–203). Illinois: Dorsey Press.

Blake, E. C., and Cross, I. (2015). The Acoustic and Auditory Contexts of Human Behavior. *Current Anthropology, 56*(1), 81–103.

Campbell, J. (1993). The role of physical objects in spatial thinking. In N. Eilan, R. McCarthy and B. Brewer (Eds.), *Spatial representation* (pp. 65–95). Oxford: Oxford University Press.

Cherry, E. C. (1953). Some experiments on the recognition of speech, with one and with two ears. *The Journal of the Acoustical Society of America, 25*(5), 975–979.

Clark, A. (1997). *Being there: Putting brain, body and world together again.* Cambridge, MA: MIT Press.

Clark, A. (2015). Embodied prediction. In T. Metzinger and J. M. Windt (Eds), *Open MIND: 7(T)*. Frankfurt am Main: MIND Group.

Clark, A., and Chalmers, D. (2010). The extended mind. In R. Menary (Ed.), *The extended mind* (pp. 27–42). Cambridge, MA: MIT Press.

Cooper, L.A., and Munger, M.P. (1993). Extrapolating and remembering positions along cognitive trajectories: Uses and limitations of analogies to physical motion. In N. Eilan, W. Brewer and R. McCarthy (Eds.), *Spatial representation* (pp. 112–131). London: Blackwell.

Cross, I., and Morley, I. (2008). The evolution of music: Theories, definitions and the nature of the evidence. In S. Malloch and C. Trevarthen (Eds.), *Communicative musicality* (pp. 61–82). Oxford: Oxford University Press.

Devereux, P. (2001). *Stone age soundtracks: The acoustic archaeology of ancient sites.* London: Vega.

Dixon, N. F. (1971). *Subliminal perception: The nature of a controversy.* London: McGraw-Hill.

Dixon, N. F. (1981). *Preconscious processing.* Chichester: John Wiley & Sons.

Fristrup, K. (2015). Predicting sound and light levels at large spatial scales. Presented at the *Annual meeting of the American Association for the Advancement of Science*, February, San Jose, USA.

Gerzon, M. (1974). What's wrong with quadraphonics? *Studio Sound, 16*(5), 50–56.

Gibson, E. J. (1988). Exploratory behavior in the development of perceiving, acting, and the acquiring of knowledge. *Annual Review of Psychology, 39*, 1–41.

Gibson, J. J. (1977). The theory of affordances: Toward an ecological psychology. In R. Shaw and J. Bransford (Eds.), *Perceiving, acting, and knowing* (pp. 127–143). Hillsdale, NJ: Erlbaum.

Gopnik A., Meltzoff, A. N., and Kuhl, P. K. (1999). *The scientist in the crib: What early learning tells us about the mind.* New York: William Morrow.

Gould, S. J. (1996). The pattern of life's history. In J. Brockman (Ed.), *The third culture: Beyond the scientific revolution* (pp. 51–73). New York: Simon & Schuster.

Gould, S. J., and Vrba, S. (1982). Exaptation – a missing term in the science of form. *Paleobiology, 8*, 4–15.

Gregory, R. L. (1974). Perceptions as hypotheses. In S. C. Brown (Ed.), *Philosophy of psychology* (pp. 195–210). London: Macmillan.

Gregory, R. L. (1980). Perceptions as hypotheses. *Philosophical Transactions of the Royal Society of London, 290*, 181–197.
Gregory, R. L. (1998). Brainy mind. *British Medical Journal, 317*, 1693–1695.
Hodgson, J. (2010). *Understanding records: A field guide to recording practice.* London: Bloomsbury Publishing.
James, W. (1890). *The principles of psychology.* New York: Henry Holt.
Kania, A. (2014), The philosophy of music. In E. N. Zalta (Ed.), *The Stanford encyclopedia of philosophy.* Retrieved from http://plato.stanford.edu/archives/spr2014/entries/music/.
Kolar, M, (2013). Experimental archaeology at Chavín de Huántar, Perú: In-Situ Psychoacoustics. Presented at the *Institute of Andean Studies 53rd Annual Meeting*, 11 January, Berkeley, USA.
Kraus, N., and Chandrasekaran, B. (2010). Music training for the development of auditory skills. *Nature Reviews Neuroscience, 11*, 599–605.
Lennox, P. P. (2005). *The philosophy of perception in artificial auditory environments: Spatial sound and music.* PhD Thesis, University of York, UK.
Lennox, P. P. (2015). Extended perception; extended stupidity. Keynote presentation, *21st International Conference on Auditory Display (ICAD)*, 6–10 July, Graz, Austria.
Lennox, P. P., and Myatt, T. (2011). Perceptual cartoonification in multi-spatial sound systems. In *Proceedings of the 17th International Conference on Auditory Display*, Budapest, Hungary. Retrieved from http://hdl.handle.net/1853/51739.
Lennox, P. P., Myatt, A., and Vaughan, J. (2001). 3D audio as an information environment. In *Proceedings of Audio Engineering Society 19th International Conference on Surround Sound Techniques, Technology and Perception*, Schloss Elmau, Germany.
Levinson, J. (1990). *Music, art, and metaphysics: Essays in philosophical aesthetics.* Ithaca: Cornell University Press.
Levitin, D. J. (2006). *This is your brain on music: The science of a human obsession.* New York: Dutton.
Litovsky, R. Y., Colburn, H. S., Yost, W. A., and Guzman, S. J. (1999). The precedence effect. *Journal of The Acoustic Society of America, 106*(4), 1633–1654.
Lourenco, S. F., Longo, M. R., and Pathman, T. (2011). Near space and its relation to claustrophobic fear. *Cognition, 119*, 448–453.
Malham, D. G. (1996). *Dance music goes 3D: Experiments at the University of York, UK.* Retrieved from http://www.york.ac.uk/inst/mustech/3d_audio/ambix/ambisoni.htm.
Malham, D. G. (2003). *Space in music – music in space.* Unpublished master's dissertation, University of York, UK.
McBeath, M. K., and Neuhoff, J. G. (2002). The Doppler effect is not what you think it is: Dramatic pitch change due to dynamic intensity change. *Psychonomic Bulletin & Review, 9*(2), 306–313.
Melchior, F. (2015). Let the sound interact and not the user – responsive and immersive experiences for the next generation broadcasting. Keynote presentation, *The International Conference on Auditory Display (ICAD)*, 6–10 July, Graz, Austria.
Melchior, F., and Spors, S. (2010). Spatial audio reproduction: From theory to production. In *Proceedings of the 128th Convention of the Audio Engineering Society*, 22–25 May, London, UK. Retrieved from http://www.deutsche-telekom-laboratories.de/~sporssas/publications/talks/AES128_Tutorial_Spatial_Audio_Reproduction.pdf.

Minsky, M. (1981). Music, mind and meaning. *Computer Music Journal, 5(3),* 28–44.
Neher, T., Brookes, T., and Rumsey, F. (2003). Unidimensional simulation of the spatial attribute 'ensemble depth' for training purposes. Part 1: Pilot study into early reflection pattern characteristics. In *Proceedings of the AES 24th international conference* (pp. 123–137), 26–28 June, Banff, Canada.
O'Keefe, J. (1993). Kant and the sea-horse: An essay in the neurophilosophy of space. In N. Eilan, R. McCarthy and B. Brewer (Eds.), *Spatial representation* (pp. 43–64). Oxford: Oxford University Press.
Pinker, S. (1997). *How the mind works.* New York: Norton & Co.
Popper, K. R. (1972). Chapter three: Epistemology without a knowing subject. In K. R. Popper (Ed.), *Objective knowledge* (pp. 106–152). Oxford: Clarendon Press.
Reznikoff, I. (2006). The evidence of the use of sound resonance from Palaeolithic to Medieval times. In C. Scarre and G. Lawson (Eds.), *Archaeoacoustics* (pp. 74–84). Cambridge: McDonald Institute for Archaeological Research.
S3A Future Spatial Audio. (2014). Retrieved from http://www.s3a-spatialaudio.org/wordpress/.
Seifritz, E., Neuhoff, J. G., Bilecen, D., Scheffler, K., Mustovic, H., Schächinger, H., Elefante, R., and Di Salle, F. (2002). Neural processing of auditory looming in the human brain. *Current Biology, 23,* 2147–2151.
Schafer, R. M. (1977). *The tuning of the world.* New York: Random House.
Schafer, R. M. (1993). *The soundscape: Our sonic environment and the tuning of the world.* Rochester, Vermont. Inner Traditions / Bear & Co.
Shaw, B. K., McGowan, R. S., and Turvey, M. T. (1991). An acoustic variable specifying time-to-contact. *Ecological Psychology, 3,* 253–261.
Sluming, V., Barrick, T., Howard, M., Cezayirli, E., Mayes, A., and Roberts, N. (2002). Voxel-based morphometry reveals increased gray matter density in Broca's area in male symphony orchestra musicians. *NeuroImage, 17,* 1613–1622.
Smythies, J. R. (1994). *The walls of Plato's cave: the science and philosophy of brain, consciousness, and perception.* Aldershot: Avebury.
Snow, W. B. (1953). Basic principles of stereophonic sound. *Journal SMPTE, 61,* 567–587.
Spelke, E. S., and Van de Walle, G. A. (1993). Perceiving and reasoning about objects: Insights from infants. In N. Eilan, W. Brewer and R. McCarthy (Eds.), *Spatial representation* (pp. 132–161). Oxford: Basil Blackwell.
Stone, R. (1982). *Let the inside be sweet: The interpretation of music event among the kpelle of liberia.* Bloomington: Indiana University Press.
Tajadura-Jiménez, A., Pantelidou, G., Rebacz, P., Västfjäll, D., and Tsakiris, M. (2011). I-space: The effects of emotional valence and source of music on interpersonal distance. *PLoS ONE, 6*(10): e26083. DOI: 10.1371/journal.pone.0026083.
Tolman, E. C. (1948). Cognitive maps in rats and men. *The Psychological Review, 55*(4), 189–208.
von Helmholtz, H. (1925). *Treatise on physiological optics.* English translation produced by Optical Society of America. Electronic edition (2001), University of Pennsylvania. Retrieved from http://poseidon.sunyopt.edu/BackusLab/Helmholtz/.
Warren, W. H., and Verbrugge, R. R. (1984). Auditory perception of breaking and bouncing events: A case study in ecological acoustics. *Journal of Experimental Psychology: Human Perception and Performance, 10,* 704–712.

Watson, A. (2006). (Un)intentional sound? Acoustics and neolithic monuments. In C. Scarre and G. Lawson (Eds.), *Archaeoacoustics* (pp. 11–22). Cambridge: McDonald Institute for Archaeological Research.

Zvonar, R., 2005. A history of spatial music: Historical antecedents from renaissance antiphony to strings in the wings. *eContact!: The online journal of the Canadian Electroacoustic Community (CEC), 7*(4). Retrieved from http://econtact.ca/7_4/zvonar_spatialmusic.html.

# 12 Music perception and performance in virtual acoustic spaces

*Jude Brereton*

Music-making always happens in some sort of space; whether that be in the open air, the echoing spaces of a cathedral, the meticulously designed interiors of a modern concert hall, or just the intimate surroundings of one's own living room. Recent technological advances have allowed acoustic space for classical instrumental and vocal music to be simulated in the studio or audio laboratory, either through post-processing or in real-time. Indeed the most sophisticated systems let musicians perform in one room (e.g., an acoustically 'dry' studio) whilst hearing themselves as if in another space (e.g., a pleasingly reverberant concert hall).

This chapter outlines the role of acoustic environment in the perception of musical performance by first examining how the acoustic environment of a performance space affects a listener's perception of music. It goes on to investigate the ways in which sound is shaped by acoustic space, how this altered sound is in turn perceived by the performer and ultimately leads to the musician modifying his/her own performance in response. Questions around the presentation and coordination of musical performance in 'virtual acoustic spaces' are stimulating investigation and debate amongst those seeking to understand music perception, cognition and action. Some of the current virtual acoustic technology is then described, whilst considering whether it can plausibly re-create the experience of performing or listening to music in a real space. A richer understanding of the effect of acoustic space on the physical properties of sound, which plays an important role in the embodied cognition of music (Leman, 2008), will enhance current and future musical practice. Future developments are described which flag up many exciting applications for this technology; allowing time-travel through auditioning spaces which no longer exist, facilitating musical collaboration across dispersed locations and providing a new impetus to shape musical compositions.

### Listening to music in acoustic spaces

Throughout history music has been written and performed with a particular 'space' in mind; composers and musicians understand that the acoustic features of the performance venue play a vital role in shaping not just the listeners' perception of musical performance, but also the musical characteristics of the performance itself. Indeed, much of this knowledge became codified in rules of musical composition in the classical tradition through treatises by composers such as Zarlino, Quantz and Mozart (see Fischinger, Frieler and Louhivuori, 2015 for more on this historical view).

### Acoustics and musical style

Although it is difficult to pinpoint the causal relationship between physical architecture of performance venues and the development of musical style for that particular place, most would agree to accept the notion of a co-evolution of style and space, informed by listening to musical performance practice and the resulting soundscapes produced. Several examples are described by Lennox (see Lennox, this volume), which underline how distinct performance styles are influenced by room acoustic characteristics and in turn inform compositional style, reinforcing the symbiotic relationship between music-making and space. This relationship reinforces the influence of environmental aspects on music cognition such as architectural aesthetic and cultural context of performance spaces; activation of primed contexts no doubt affects our perception of different styles of music in certain spaces, for example, resonant church music in reverberant church buildings, or intimate jazz music in small and acoustically dryer spaces.

It is probably true that, in the western world, Christian buildings such as monasteries and cathedrals 'determined the nature of music for a thousand years' (Blesser and Salter, 2007, p. 92) and this music was stylised and constrained by the unique acoustics of the spaces for which it was conceived and in which it was performed. Large-scale religious buildings, built to show off the state-of-the-art building technologies of the day result in impressive open spaces, comprising robust, expensive and acoustically reflective surfaces – stone, marble, polished or painted wood. Highly contrapuntal music with many independently moving musical lines will be blurred and muddied in such a space whose long reverberation time suits better slow moving homophonic choral music or plainchant.

The acoustics of many of the Renaissance churches of Venice have been extensively studied and documented by Howard and Moretti (2009). With the Choir of St. John's College Cambridge (directed by David Hill), they undertook a series of experimental performances asking audiences to rate both the acoustics of the church and the performance of music within it, finding that the largest churches were rated as poor for the 'performance of complex choral music involving advanced polyphony and/or multiple choirs' (Howard and Moretti, 2009, p. 200). At first this seems perplexing since, in popular terms, Renaissance polyphony reached its zenith in Venetian churches, nurtured and developed by composers such as Orlande de Lassus, Palestrina and Victoria. Nevertheless, architectural and decorative fashions change over time; further investigations by Boren, Longair and Orlowski (2013) demonstrated that on important occasions, for which much of this repertoire was written, acoustic absorption would have been greater due to the presence of heavy wall tapestries, large congregations and extra seating. Computer acoustic models of two Venetian churches in this study showed reverberation times and clarity measures to be more suited to the complex polyphony performed in and composed for this space.

Similarly, changes in architectural fashions also played a vital role in the development of German church music during Bach's time, since the building of galleries and boxes in St Thomas' Leipzig not only reflected the importance of the church as a building but also 'created the acoustic conditions that made possible the seventeenth century development of Cantata and Passion' (Bagenal, 1930, p. 149). Today, audiences are well used to listening to music performed in a great variety of venues and, as such, an often overlooked factor is the high level of skill developed by modern musicians, which allows them to adapt their performance to the varied room acoustic characteristics in which they perform.

## *Measuring room acoustics*

Within a room, sound waves are transmitted through the air from sound source to listener, and the surrounding walls, ceiling, floor and other reflective surfaces within the room all play a part in transforming the sound that eventually reaches the listener's ears. Direct sound travels in a straight line from the sound source and arrives first at the listener's ears usually followed by a number of early reflections, which have reflected off two, three or more surfaces. Even within a large room early reflections typically arrive at the listener within about 50–80 ms of the direct sound; these are not perceived as separate 'echoes', but rather reinforce or colour the direct sound of the voice or instrument (Barron, 1993).

The next reflections to arrive at the listener decrease in sound intensity (at a rate of 6 dB for each doubling of distance travelled) but their timing and timbre differ according to size and position of the walls and ceiling and the reflective qualities of the materials from which they are made (Vorländer, 2007). In medium to large concert halls the first reflections to reach the audience position are from the nearest side walls (lateral reflections) or from the ceiling. After a certain time reflections arrive at the listener that are much lower in amplitude, temporally closely spaced and are perceived as reverberant sound (reverberation).

Room acoustic characteristics can be quantified through the measurement of a *Room Impulse Response* (RIR), which can be thought of as the 'acoustic signature' of a room. More precisely it is the acoustic response of a room to an excitation signal for a given source and receiver combination, captured across frequencies between 20 Hz to 20,000 Hz, the limits of the human hearing range.

The most well-known and widely quoted room acoustic parameter is *Reverberation Time* (RT60), which is indirectly proportional to the total level of sound absorption within a room; as such a room with a high proportion of sound absorbing material covering the walls will have a shorter RT60 than one with acoustically highly reflective surfaces. But of course RT60 alone cannot fully describe the complex room acoustic conditions of performance spaces such as concert halls or churches. Although room acoustic parameters quantify the acoustic properties relating to the physical nature of the performance venue, musical performance is perceived by human listeners whose subjective responses must be captured by another set of subjective measures.

A small number of room acoustic parameters is summarised in Table 12.1 with indications of their subjective correlates. Full descriptions of these parameters and how they are calculated are found in ISO3382 (International Organization for Standardization (IOS), 2009) unless otherwise stated. Subjective impressions do not correlate simply with objective room acoustic parameters; complex combinations of the measurable acoustic parameters influence the subjective impressions of a listener or performer within a venue.

### *Optimum acoustics for performance spaces*

It is generally agreed (e.g., Beranek, 2004; Gade, 1989; Dammerud, 2009; Marshall et al., 1978; Barron, 1993) that optimum room acoustic conditions for music performance (especially concert halls) have to strike a good balance between *clarity*, *loudness* (strength) and *reverberance*. All three factors depend on a critical relationship between *Reverberation Time* and the reverberant level of the sound within the venue.

Music performed in spaces with poor acoustics, where the desired balance between reverberance, clarity and loudness has not been sufficiently well met, can leave the listener disappointed and the performer frustrated, sharing a feeling that something was missing from the performance. An extreme example is performing music in anechoic conditions, in rooms that are specially designed to absorb all acoustic energy and hence produce no sound reflections at all. Whilst such conditions are useful for scientific research of sound quality, where only the direct sound of a voice or instrument is required, the unnatural acoustic surroundings disrupt musical performance, through the lack of auditory feedback available for the performer, and recordings captured here sound 'dead' or 'raw'. There is no acoustic to emphasise or dampen certain regions of the acoustic spectrum, to enhance and enrich the performer's sound. For the musician trying to make music in such a space the first noticeable difference is how quiet everything sounds, without reflections to reinforce the reverberant sound level. As a direct result of this lack of sound level a first unconscious response is to play/sing louder, illustrating the inherent reliance musicians place on an aural feedback loop.

*Table 12.1* Room acoustic parameters and subjective correlates

| Room acoustic parameter | Description | Influenced by ... | Subjective correlate |
|---|---|---|---|
| **Reverberation time (RT60)** | Time taken for the sound level in a room to decrease by 60 dB | Room volume, area and nature of sound absorbing surfaces within the room | *Reverberance fullness of tone warmth* related to long bass reverberation time (Barron, 1993) or strong low frequency levels and bass ratio (Bradley, Soulodre and Norcross, 1997; Beranek, 2004) |
| **Early Decay Time (EDT)** | Time taken for the sound level in a room to decrease by 60 dB – extrapolated from the initial measure of decay by 10 dB | Number, size and absorption characteristics of nearby surfaces | *Reverberance* Shorter EDT can lead to perception of overall shorter reverberation (Howard and Moretti, 2009) Perceptually important for the performing musician. |
| **Strength (G)** | Level of sound in room, compared to level measured in free-field (outside) at distance of 10 m | Inversely proportional to the total sound absorption in a room | *Loudness Intensity of sound Listener envelopment* related to levels of G at mid-frequencies |
| **Clarity (C80)** | Ratio between the early arriving (first 80 ms) and late arriving sound energy (reverberant sound) | Relative strength of the direct and early arriving sound and later reflections | *Clarity* or 'definition' of words in speech, or notes in phrases Low clarity values perceived as 'fullness of tone' but can lead to an impression of 'muddiness' (Howard and Moretti, 2009) |
| **Initial Time Delay Gap (ITDG)** | The time delay between the direct sound and the first reflection arriving at the listeners' ears | Direction and strength of early reflections arriving from sides of concert hall (Marshall, Gottlob and Alrutz, 1978) | *Intimacy* When ITDG is less than 20 ms hall is judged as intimate (Beranek, 2004) |

The reader is invited to explore such extreme acoustic conditions by listening to Stephen Fry popping a balloon in two very different acoustic spaces (Fry, n.d.). This happens first in a reverberation chamber where the balloon pop sounds very impressive indeed (note also the way Fry's speech is slow and deliberate to counter the lack of clarity in the long reverberation time). Towards the end of the same audio clip another balloon is popped in (hemi-)anechoic conditions and the effect is startling.

The effect of adding room acoustic reverberation to pre-recorded sounds can be investigated via the OpenAir.lib website (OpenAir, 2015). The site includes a database of anechoic recordings of musical instruments that can be auralised in acoustic spaces, through a process of digital 'convolution' via the website portal. Although this allows one to listen to anechoic recordings mixed with the acoustics of real space, to illustrate how that instrument might sound if it were played in that space, there is one key element missing from this digital magic: when performing in real (or virtual) acoustic spaces musicians adjust their musical performance to fit the surroundings.

## Performing music in acoustic spaces

Many of the studies referred to above have quantified concert hall acoustics from an audience member's point of view, but if we want to appreciate how performances are altered according to different room acoustic conditions we need first to understand musicians' perception from their usual position on the stage. When describing conditions for the performer, the additional aspect of capturing the room acoustic characteristics from the 'point of view' (point of listening) has only really been considered since the late 1970s (for example Marshall et al., 1978; Gade, 1989; Ueno and Tachibana, 2003; Dammerud, 2009). This section outlines several aspects of stage acoustic conditions, which are of importance to the performing musician both for the perception of his/her own sound and also to convey musical meaning to an audience.

### *Performers' perception of stage acoustics*

Although musicians' preferences in terms of stage acoustics are varied, influenced by the repertoire and by the performing forces employed (Gade, 1989; Jeon and Barron 2005), most musicians agree that there is benefit from having access to different types of aural feedback from the performance venue. Harpsichordist Tom Beghin who took part in recordings made in a virtual acoustic space summarises:

> Musicians prefer smaller, narrower spaces where much of the emitted sound returns to them relatively early, but they also like rooms of larger cubic capacity where ambient sound does not become excessively loud or reverberant.
>
> (Woszczyk and Martens, 2008, p. 1042)

Gade's (1989) seminal work on musicians' perception of concert hall stages involved *in situ* measurements and experiments on concert hall stages as well as laboratory experiments with simulated acoustic reflections. He was the first to demonstrate performers placed prime importance on the relative levels of early and late energy of sound on the stage (captured by measures of Early and Late Support), which effect the perceived level of support for a musician's own sound, the ease of hearing others on stage and enabling the performer to form an impression of how the performance is heard in the auditorium. Table 12.2 summarises some of the relationships between objective stage acoustic measures and performers' subjective impressions which have been more recently investigated (e.g., Beranek, 2004; Jeon and Barron, 2005; Dammerud, 2009).

For singers, the link between performance and room acoustic is even more entwined, not just because of the role that the room plays in shaping

*Table 12.2* Overview of stage acoustic parameters and correlations with subjective impressions

| Stage acoustic parameter | Description | Subjective impression |
| --- | --- | --- |
| Early Support | Energy ratio between direct sound and early reflected sound from the hall/stage area | *Hearing oneself* How well the performer can hear his/her own sound |
| Late Support | Energy ratio between direct sound and late reflected sound from the hall/stage area | *Hearing others* How well musicians on stage can hear each other |
| Strength (G) | Level of sound in room, compared to level measured in free-field (outside) at distance of 10 m | *Hearing the hall* Correlates to performers' subjective impression of support from the hall (Dammerud, 2009) |
| Running Reverberation | Ratio between sound energy in first 160 ms of the RIR and the total response (Griesinger, 1995) | *Perception of reverberance* Relates to performer's perception of reverberation as they are producing sound at the same time as listening |
| Voice support ($ST_v$) | Amplification by the room of the vocal sound measured at the singer's ears; includes airborne sound, but discounts bone-conducted sound (Brunskog, Gade, Bellester and Calbo, 2009) | *Voice comfort* Singers report higher levels of comfort when voice feels supported by the room/stage |

aural feedback, but also since the instrument (the voice) is an integral part of the singer. Blesser and Salter refer to singers as 'aural detectives', who adapt their singing performance, both consciously and subconsciously, according to the instantaneous auditory feedback they receive by 'investigat(ing) the acoustics of a room the way a child investigates a toy' (2007, p. 63).

*Conceptual models of performance (room and instrument)*

Musicians alter their performance according to the auditory feedback they receive, which in effect has been 'coloured', 'filtered' or 'processed' by the size, shape and fabric of the performance space giving the performer clues about the impression gained by those in the audience. Ueno, Kato and Kawai describe the musician's experience of playing in a concert hall – a process of action, feedback and reaction – using the theory of 'tacit knowing', suggesting a 'circulative system of feedback between performer and room acoustic conditions' which consists of two distinct feedback loops (Ueno, Kato and Kawai, 2010, p. 513). The first feedback loop is the 'automatic response system' common to all human perception and action. The second feedback loop is an 'acquired feedback system' which is learnt through musical training, relating directly to the musician's skill, background and experience. This learnt feedback system illustrates embodied cognition (Leman, 2008) for the performer: the concert hall acoustic environment (space) together with aural feedback (sound) on the performed musical expression, combine to form a mental representation of how the performance will be perceived by the listener in the audience area, which is then subsequently used to control his/her performing actions (body).

A similar 'triangle of listening' is described by harpsichordist Tom Beghin who recorded solo keyboard pieces for the Virtual Haydn project (see Woszczyk and Martens, 2008, p. 1043). He identifies three aspects of listening whilst performing:

- listening to the sound of the instrument (direct sound) to judge the articulation of notes/phrases;
- listening to the early reflected sound to judge the effect of the room;
- listening to the later reverberation to judge what the audience will hear.

For this musician, recording solo pieces for harpsichord or pianoforte in the simulated acoustic recreations of some of the music rooms known by Haydn, 'the instrument, performer and room become triune entity (*sic*)' (Beghin, 2009), and this is true whether in real or virtual acoustic spaces.

Often, it is the absence of auditory feedback that alerts the musician to its very existence. For example, trombonist Will Kimball, recorded in an anechoic chamber for a study of instrument directivity noticed that

> when there is nothing for the sound to bounce off of, ..., it is challenging to hear what you are doing! ... The tendency is to play louder and louder

in order to hear yourself and try to create some kind or resonance. Dynamic shadings are difficult because of the lack of aural feedback, and you end up going as much by the feel of your embouchure as by sound.

(Kimball, 2010)

The development of virtual (acoustic) systems means that music can be performed, recorded and analysed under conditions more natural than the anechoic chamber, and the relationship between music performance and acoustic space can be investigated.

## Virtual acoustic technology for music performance

Evaluating concert halls *in situ* provides the most realistic and reliable listening experience, of course, but there are a number of drawbacks, including the time and costs involved in visiting the real venues and in ensuring a controlled comparison. Lokki (2014) has developed a lab-based method of assessing concert hall acoustics using anechoic orchestral recordings and auralisation techniques. Auralisation is analogous to visualisation, in that it allows listeners to hear the acoustic information intrinsic to a room, by mixing (via digital convolution) the room acoustics of the concert hall with a pre-recorded sound source. In some ways auralisation can be viewed as a remedy to the 'pernicious effects on space of 20th recording technology' (see Lennox, this volume). Nevertheless, in the recording studio or anechoic chamber, any musical performance is, in effect, spatially sampled. This means that the sound captured by the microphone is a facsimile of the sound at that particular spatial location. Although music-making always happens in space, studio spaces are specially designed to avoid extraneous acoustic reflections (anechoic chambers even more so), allowing only the direct sound of the voice or instrument to be captured and recorded and avoiding 'unwanted' room acoustic ambience.

If, as many musicians would agree, the performer, the sound of the instrument and the sound of the room are actually three symbiotic aspects of one whole, then recording inherently captures only one small part of the musical performance. Also, listening to very close-recorded, dry instrument or vocal sounds becomes eventually annoying; the lack of room ambience, reflections or reverberation subconsciously remind the listener of sounds produced very close to the ears, giving the impression of standing close, maybe too close, to the person performing, adding to the listener's sense of discomfort.

Digital convolution techniques allow the audio engineer to 'mix back in' some of the spatial qualities lost in the recording process, adding some kind of room ambience or reverberation to colour and augment the raw recorded sound. But since musicians are constantly, consciously and subconsciously, altering their performance to fit the space (Ueno and Hideki, 2005), the success of these techniques can only be limited; auralisation can only ever add some 'room acoustic gloss' to a recording, it can never fully re-create a performance as it would actually have been performed in that space.

Similarly, although recent advances in some home entertainment systems make it possible to listen to music in a simulation of an acoustic venue, these are usually generic stereotypical versions of particularly attractive venues, such as a 'concert hall in Vienna' or a 'jazz club in New York'. Nevertheless, such experiences of music listening in virtual acoustic spaces cannot successfully approach the experience of the real event. Apart from the fact that the recording has been made in studio surroundings and hence the link between performance, sound and space has been lost, one can presume that at least the visual mismatch between one's physical surroundings (living room) and the simulated acoustic (concert hall in Vienna) influences the listener's acceptance of this mediated listening experience.

Applying room acoustic convolution in the post-processing stages of a recording has been possible for a number of years, since any processing delays can be compensated by time-shifting in the mixing and editing stages. It is only with the relatively recent increased availability and falling cost of fast computer chips that applying these complex signal processing techniques across multiple channels has been possible in real-time. This offers up huge potential for 'including the room' back in during the recording process, and several research teams have implemented augmented reality techniques, to complement or enhance existing acoustic spaces or virtual reality technology to fully simulate an acoustic environment for performing musicians. A number of current systems are outlined in briefly in the following sections.

## *Augmented reality for improved room acoustics*

Active acoustic systems, sometimes also known as Reverberation Enhancement Systems, are in use in a number of concert halls and studios around the world; these include the LARES system (LARES Lexicon Inc., n.d.), SIAP (SIAP, n.d.), the Constellation Acoustic System (Meyer Sound, 2015) and Yamaha Active Field Control (Yamaha Ltd, 2015).Working in tandem with the architectural and existing acoustic properties of the venue, the sound in the auditorium is captured by multiple microphones, processed to add in reflections and delays over a number of channels, which lengthens the overall reverberation time (Poletti, 2010). In the best systems the resulting augmented acoustics enhance the original, since digital filters are used to avoid unwanted colouration of the sound or acoustic feedback.

John Crooks has made excellent use of a newly designed regenerative system in the studio of film music composer John Powell (Crooks, 2015), which enhances the room ambience by feeding processed live sound back into the studio space in real-time and can be used during rehearsal and recording. An array of 16 microphone and loudspeaker pairs is mounted in the double height studio ceiling high above the performers (Figure 12.1). Digital audio processing controls the room ambience in real-time, adding as much or as little extra reverberation as desired by the musicians, composer or studio engineer.

*Music perception and performance* 221

*Figure 12.1* John Crook's live array installation for studio, which transforms the room sound in real-time. The system comprises loudspeakers and microphones located unobtrusively high above the musicians (out of this shot).
Source: Tom Hall used with permission.

Active acoustic systems are currently marketed as solutions for individual music practice rooms. According to their website, the Wenger V-Room® virtual rehearsal room 'frees you from the acoustical confines of small sterile practice rooms, allowing you to experience the warmth and support that good musical acoustics provide' (LARES Lexicon Inc., n.d.). It also lets the user change the acoustics of the space at the switch of a button, choosing between different room acoustic environments so that they can 'immediately sense how to adapt (their) playing for differing environments'. Pätynen (2007) has also developed a virtual acoustic technology system for small practice rooms, which incorporates a number of loudspeakers, fed by microphones positioned close to the performer, to enhance the reverberation characteristics of the room. Since 2005 McGill University have been pioneers of virtual acoustic technology, developing hardware and software for high-resolution audio convolution over 24 channels (Woszczyk, Ko and Leonard, 2012). The present Space Builder engine incorporated into the McGill Virtual Acoustic Technology (VAT) system includes a 'live' configuration which can be used to augment stage acoustics for music performance and recording.

Augmented acoustic reality systems build on the natural acoustics of the performance space, studio or practice room, allowing the audience to share in the simulated acoustics implemented for the artist. Such systems, where the stage acoustics (early reflections) stem from the physical room and the later reverberation is enhanced electronically, can be thought of as a partial step towards a full *virtual acoustic environment* (VAE).

### Virtual acoustic environments

A number of full VAE systems for performing musicians have been developed, mostly by university research teams; they are often implemented to exploit multi-channel audio reproduction and include elements of user interaction. A VAE requires an acoustically treated listening space to avoid any colouration of the sound from the room in which the system is housed. In practice this is difficult to achieve and involves the use of complex real-time audio filters, or setting up the system in an anechoic chamber.

I developed the *Virtual Singing Studio* (VSS) in the AudioLab at the University of York, a real-time room acoustics simulation system, over an array of 16 loudspeakers, which is based on an interesting acoustic venue, a medieval church refurbished to provide a flexible concert and conference space. The venue incorporates adjustable acoustics (acoustic panels and drapes in the ceiling) allowing the room to be used for a variety of purposes with appropriate acoustics, for example a dry (RT60 of 1 s) setting for speech and a more reverberant setting (RT60 of 2.3 s) for larger choral music. Having a flexible, controllable VAE to simulate a performance venue in real-time means that changes in musical performance under different acoustic conditions can be studied in some depth.

Other researchers have implemented similar systems, for example recreating different concert halls and churches using multiple loudspeakers in a six-sided anechoic room (Ueno and Tachibana, 2003, Ueno, Kato and Kawai, 2010) or simulating stage acoustics for a solo cellist over headphones (Schärer, Kalkandjiev and Wienzierl, 2013). The Virtual Haydn project (Beghin 2009; Martens and Woszczyk, 2004; Woszczyk et al., 2012) undertaken by an inter-disciplinary team at McGill University re-created nine original rooms known to Haydn. The sound radiation pattern of a pianoforte was measured and simulated using a group of omnidirectional loudspeakers for RIR measurements undertaken in surviving music rooms, known to be performance venues of Haydn's keyboard pieces. In the performance situation the sound of the pianoforte is captured using a spaced microphone array, this is then convolved in real-time with the measured RIR and reproduced over 24 loudspeakers which surround the keyboard player. The VAE built at McGill University for the Virtual Haydn project led to the development of their Space Builder system, which allows the user to 'build' their own RIRs from early, mid and late sections drawn from a library of RIRs recorded at various venues such as stages, concert halls, churches and recording studios around the world (Woszczyk et al., 2012).

The Constellation Centre (n.d.) currently being built in Cambridge, Massachusetts, incorporates five different concert halls in one building. Each one has carefully curated acoustics, informed by years of extensive research lead by Arup Acoustics, who have captured impulse responses at over 800 historically important concert halls and performance venues around the world, including the London Wigmore Hall, the Amsterdam Concertgebouw and the Vienna Konzerthaus to name but a very small selection. During the design phase, Arup's SoundLab enabled the project team to present acoustically three-dimensional simulations of concert halls in the lab in order to understand the connections between performer, listener, architecture and the built space.

## Performing music in virtual acoustic spaces

As we have seen, three main aspects of the acoustic conditions on stage are important for musicians: Hearing oneself, Hearing others and Hearing the hall. In any VAE, all three aspects, the 'triangle of listening' (see Figure 12.2), and the balance between them, must be achieved convincingly in order to provide a natural experience for musicians in which they can achieve high levels of musical expression and performance. Musicians' acceptance of virtual stage acoustics must first be assessed, for example via interviews and questionnaires. If the acoustic simulation does prove to be convincing, then it can be presumed that musicians will adapt their performance to virtual acoustic space in the same way as in response to real acoustic conditions. Then, through analysing and comparing musical performances in various VAEs, much more will be revealed about the connections between space and performance.

### *Musicians' subjective impressions of virtual acoustic space*

My research in the VSS showed that singers using the system found that the perception of clarity and quality of reverberation was differed between the simulation and the real space, but that overall singers were happy that the VSS was plausible and enjoyed singing in the simulation, with one singer commenting 'it was much more realistic than I thought it would be' (Brereton, Murphy and Howard, 2014, p. 266).

Ueno et al. (2010) also found that there was some tonal colouration in the higher frequencies in their system, musicians were nevertheless happy that the system presented a natural impression of playing on a stage in a concert hall. Pätynen's (2007) VAE for use in practice rooms was well liked by teachers and students alike. The enhanced reverberation proved satisfying for rehearsal purposes, together with the ability to switch the system off when needing to listen carefully to the precise sound of the instrument/voice.

In a recent experiment with the Virtual Concert Hall (Brereton, Southern and Kearney, 2015) we included the option of presenting a panoramic picture of

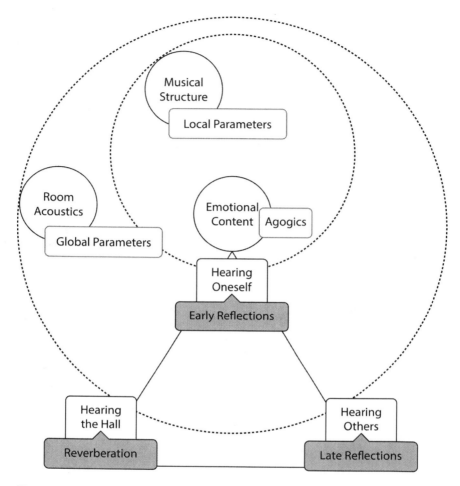

*Figure 12.2* Representation of the relationship between performance context features which influence changes in musical performance parameters.

the performance space via an Oculus Rift virtual reality headset to the performing musician. After performing in the simulated sound field with and without the picture, musicians perceived the reverberation time of the venue to be shorter when presented with the visual stimulus. Since listeners' and performers' perception of a space can be influenced by other properties of the environment, such as the visual modality, and musicians seem to accept that certain aspects will always differ between real and virtual acoustic spaces, it does seem plausible that virtual simulations of acoustic spaces may not need to reconstruct all the physical attributes of the space, for example by replicating exactly every objective acoustic parameter outlined above (p. 217). Instead, it might be sufficient to simulate the perceptual aspects of a space, since, if the perceptual correlates are similar, a virtual environment is successfully reproduced and realistic enough to support natural musical performance.

*Performing in virtual acoustic environments*

If musicians adjust their performance to fit acoustic conditions, and virtual acoustic spaces offer sufficient realism, it should be possible to quantify music performance parameters in a virtual simulation, taking into consideration the performer's perception of their own performances together with listeners' evaluation, to gain a true picture of the relationship between musical performance and acoustic space.

Although quantitative analysis of music performance is now a rich research endeavour, the performance itself is only one link in the chain between the composer's or performer's intentions and listeners' perception.

> measurements of performance should, as much as possible, be conducted and considered in relation to the composer's and/or the performer's intentions and the listener's experience ... After all, music is a means for communication and expression, and the characteristics of different performances may be easier to understand given this self-evident frame of reference.
>
> (Gabrielsson, 1999, p. 550)

Meyer Sound report that after the addition of their augmented acoustics system in the Clinton Frame Mennonite Church, Goshen, Indiana, USA, the congregational singing was 'energized' and 'more engaging', even suggesting that the addition of early reflections through the system improves the musical performance of the worship band, meaning that visiting choirs want to return because 'the singing sounds so amazing' (Meyer Sound, 2015). The reader may be reluctant to believe the hype around such systems, but empirical research in musical performance under different (virtual) room acoustic conditions has been quantified and demonstrated the intriguing and multifaceted ways that musicians adapt to the acoustics of their surroundings (Bolzinger and Risset, 1992; Brereton et al., 2014; Martens and Woszczyk, 2004; Ueno and Tachibana, 2003; Ueno et al., 2010; Schärer et al., 2013). Objective music performance parameters can be categorised broadly into four main groups and those which have been found to alter under different room conditions are listed in Table 12.3. (Comprehensive reviews of objective performance parameters and digital signal processing techniques used to extract them from audio signals are provided by Gabrielsson, 1999, and Lerch, 2012).

Ueno and her team (Ueno and Tachibana, 2003; Ueno and Hideki, 2005; Ueno et al., 2010) have undertaken a large number of in-depth studies with

*Table 12.3* Musical performance attribute groupings, musical performance attributes and objective (measurable) parameters which change according to the room acoustic conditions of the performance venue

| Performance attribute group | Performance attributes | Objective parameters |
| --- | --- | --- |
| Tempo and timing | Variation in global or local tempo<br>Rubato (expressive timing)<br>Variation of note lengths in phrases<br>Articulation of tones | Note-on-ratio<br>Tempo<br>Synchronicity (temporal alignment in ensemble playing) |
| Loudness/intensity | Musical dynamics<br>Crescendo and diminuendo<br>Accents<br>Tremolo | Sound pressure level<br>Intensity (breath pressure) vibrato rate and extent<br>Long-term and short-term dynamics<br>Loudness<br>Hammer velocity and sustain pedal (keyboard instruments)<br>Dynamic bandwidth |
| Pitch | Temperament,<br>Expressive intonation,<br>Vibrato<br>Glissando<br>Portamento | Fundamental frequency (pitch) vibrato rate<br>Fundamental frequency (pitch) vibrato extent<br>Intonation accuracy and precision |
| Timbre | Variation of sound quality resulting from instrumentation<br>Instrument-specific properties such as bow positioning, speed, articulation of tones, key press | Relative strengths of spectral regions<br>Relative strengths of harmonics<br>Timbral bandwidth (extent of changes in spectral characteristics)<br>Perceived timbre (e.g., soft–hard, dark–bright, lean–full) |

a variety of musical soloists (flute, oboe, bassoon, tenor singer) analysing performance parameters of musicians playing in real-time room acoustic simulations. They have correlated these objective analyses with feedback from the musicians about how their playing varied according to acoustics of the simulated performance venue and through listening tests and statistical analysis have concluded that the differences in performances in the various simulated room acoustic conditions were significant and perceivable.

However, research in real and virtual acoustic spaces has shown that all of the performance parameters listed in Table 12.3 can also be altered according to other aspects of performance and not just room acoustic conditions. The performance environment exerts an overall bearing on the choices, conscious and unconscious, made by musicians which alter in terms of tempo, timbre, loudness and pitch with other aspects influencing performance within the limits bounded by the acoustic conditions. For instance, musical phrasing (agogics) can be portrayed by combinations of changes in the above attributes such as shortening the length of notes, or modifying the use of vibrato on certain notes and can be used to both to signal musical structure and hierarchy (Repp, 1992), as well as emotional content and expression (Timmers, 2005). Figure 12.2 tries to capture the complex relationships between different features of the performance context, including room acoustic conditions, musical structure, emotional content and the 'triangle of listening', which all play a role in shaping the perception and performance of music.

Leman's (2008) model of embodied music cognition describes the intrinsic relationship between the human performer and his/her environment. Through bodily actions in performance (whether playing an instrument or singing), the musician translates mental representations of musical meaning into physical sound energy. The sonic form of this physical energy is transformed, not only by the acoustic environment in which it is produced but also by the performer's own subjective involvement, influencing his/her own perception of the musical meaning being conveyed.

For example, the acoustics of a reverberant space may lead a musician to play at a slower tempo, but within that global tempo choice the musical structure is revealed through local tempo changes, for instance at the ends of musical sections. Musical meaning is further still communicated by much shorter term changes in note lengths and timings. Similarly, there is also an interplay between short-term changes and longer-term settings. For example, it has been shown that short-term dynamics are not influenced by high levels of stage support, but the bandwidth of long-term dynamics is reduced under these conditions (Schärer et al., 2013), again suggesting that the acoustic conditions of the room have a greater impact on longer-term performance.

Any VAE that simulates a performance space must achieve the correct balance of all aspects, which make up the 'triangle of listening': early and late reflections from the stage and later reverberation in the hall. These fundamental acoustic conditions are required by the musician in order to make subtle changes to aspects of performance, to communicate musical structure and emotional meaning.

First, 'hearing oneself' is achieved through a suitable balance of direct sound and early reflections and relates to the performer's perception of support. A good balance allows the performer to hear the intricate details in the sound of the instrument, focusing on the technique of sound production. However, early reflections also produce, in effect, a time delay in auditory feedback that can lead to problems in timing and maintaining steady tempo.

Lower levels of early reflections can lead to increases in performance tempo (Schärer et al., 2013; Woszczyk et al., 2012).

Second, 'hearing others' requires a good balance between the direct sound and later arriving reflections, which allows the performer to hear the performance as a whole, as well as hearing his/her own instrument as part of the ensemble, and to synchronise with other players. The presence of later reflections improves synchronicity and helps maintain good intonation between players (Woszczyk et al., 2012; Ueno and Tachibana, 2003) and allows the player to play more softly, perhaps because good early and late support leads to a perception of increased reverberation (Schärer et al., 2013). Whilst it makes sense that a soloist can play more quietly when the stage support is optimal, they also found that increased reverberation time resulted in the musician playing at a significantly higher loudness level (Schärer et al., 2013). This supports the model of performance, which suggests that some aspects of responding to different acoustics may be a learnt technique that varies between individual musicians.

Finally, 'hearing the hall' is related to the loudness level in the performance venue, or the reverberant tail. Acoustical information here allows the performer to imagine the performance as heard by an audience member. Reverberant conditions can lead to wind instrument players suppressing the higher harmonics of instrument tones, decreasing the length of notes and increasing the silence between notes by playing more staccato (Uneo et al., 2010). Pianists play softer (lower hammer velocity), more staccato (lower note-on ratio) and more slowly in reverberant acoustics, with less use of the sustain pedal.

Playing more slowly in a reverberant space is a recognised strategy for many musicians, so that notes are not 'blurred together' by the long reverberation time. On the other hand, when the reverberation time of the venue is short, a musician may attempt to lengthen notes since the tones are not 'carried' to the listener by the reverberation characteristics of the room. However, this correlation between long reverberation time and slow tempo is not always clear-cut. A dry acoustic (short reverberation time) can also lead to a slower performance tempo (Schärer et al., 2013), a situation that is heightened in anechoic conditions, where the additional lack of early reflections might mean that the musician has to play more 'carefully' and precisely leading to a slower tempo.

There are differences also in fundamental frequency vibrato extent (the amount of pitch variation around the note) between reverberant and dry spaces (Ueno et al., 2010) with deeper vibrato often used by singers in dry venues, maybe to make up for the 'lack' of reverberation. In the VSS (Brereton et al., 2014), I found that vibrato extent differed between the real performance venue and the simulation, perhaps because of the singers' perception of the quality of reverberation in the VAE.

VAT is increasing our understanding of the links between context and performance, but a full picture of the complex relationship between the perception of acoustic space and the bodily action of performance has yet to be revealed and may emerge through continued development of technology for performance that incorporates interaction and collaboration.

## Future directions

### *Personalised performance*

Digital VAT offers the consumer (whether listeners or performers) the chance to tailor-make a musical event to suit their own taste. For example, researchers in the AudioLab, University of York have recently been working in partnership with York Theatre Royal to record and preserve for posterity the acoustics of the historic theatre before its recent refurbishment and re-development. Having captured the RIR of the auditorium from a number of different seats in the stalls, circle, upper circle and dress circle, a web-based tool has been developed which, at the click of a mouse, allows a potential theatre-goer to listen to a preview of the upcoming performance from various seats in the house, before choosing which ticket to buy. Future plans for such technology include the opportunity for broadcasters to deliver the sound source (orchestra, choir) separately from the room acoustic aspects, so that the viewer at home can pick their own position in the concert hall to listen to the show.

Indeed the Virtual Haydn project (Martens and Woszczyk, 2004) already offers the listener the opportunity to choose their own performance of a short piece by selecting the instrument and the room. It is a short leap of the imagination to think that this could be extended, through incorporating the VSS concept, to allow the viewer at home to experience a concert or show from a stage position and even sing or play along with the performers on stage.

### *Musician – hear thyself!*

Current developments in VAEs include the opportunity for the performer to hear their own performance from listener position, or indeed a variety of positions in the auditorium or on stage. Such functionality added to virtual acoustic systems would allow musicians to monitor their performance and provide a very useful tool for training and rehearsal purposes.

### *Relationship between performers*

Most existing room acoustic simulation systems can accommodate only one performer, whereas music-making is a collaborative activity. In the near future it should be possible for two physically separate musicians to choose and share a virtual rehearsal or performance space, with future developments possibly allowing multiple musicians and audience members to participate in the same musical performance from the comfort of their own homes. Current research at the University of York is already linking two performers in different buildings over an internet connection. Delays and latency in the system are of course a concern, since long delays in auditory feedback between the performer and other players has been shown to disturb synchrony and result in deceleration of tempo, as each performer waits to hear the sound of the other (Chafe, Gurevich, Leslie and Tyan, 2004). Since recent research on synchronisation of piano–piano and piano–violin duets has shown that synchronisation is still successful even when only audio information is available (Bishop and Goebl, 2015), it will be interesting to see how musicians interact and synchronise performance in a shared acoustic space, even without the presence of visual link up.

## *Composing for space*

Nevertheless, with modern digital audio technology it is now possible to identify and specify spatial properties during the musical compositional or performance process. York composer Ambrose Field has recently pioneered a compositional technique which takes into account the acoustics of the space for which the piece is composed. Two recent specially commissioned choral pieces by Field explore the intimate relationship between the spatial properties of the performance venue and singers' performance and exploits the 'precise and intricate connections between the musical material and the architecture of the venue' (Field, 2015). *Architexture 1* was composed specifically for York's medieval Guildhall (the RIR is available on Openairlib.net) and Field analysed the acoustics of the space, both in terms of temporal and spectral characteristics, to inform the melodic trajectories and overlapping rhythmic polyphony.

*Architexture 2* expanded on this idea but was written for the reconstructed acoustic of the ruined St Mary's Abbey, York. Impulse responses, with a reverberation time of nearly 11 s in certain regions of the sound spectrum, were based on an acoustic model produced by Oxnard and Murphy (2012), building on archaeological and historical research. In the recent outdoor performance the modelled acoustics were reproduced both for the singers on stage and for the over 800 audience members, accompanied by a specially commissioned light show projected onto the remaining walls of the ruins (Figure 12.3). Singers who took part in the performance commented that the piece 'made sense' once they could hear the virtual acoustic and indeed that performing without the acoustic simulation was much more difficult, as the phrases, melodic lines and interesting aural effects caused by the combination of direct and reverberated vocal sounds.

*Music perception and performance* 231

*Figure 12.3 Architexture 2* for unaccompanied voices, composed by Ambrose Field, performed in the ruins of St. Mary's Abbey, York. VAT provided a reconstruction of the original acoustics of the Abbey.
Source: Ian Martindale.

## Conclusions

The links between body, sound and space in musical performance are intimately intertwined. Music-making takes place in space and that space in itself influences the sounds produced, which the performer then interprets and adjusts, constantly and both consciously and subconsciously.

Virtual reality systems incorporating auralisation techniques now provide room acoustics in real-time to allow plausible performance spaces to be simulated under controlled laboratory-like conditions. The ability to simulate convincing room acoustic characteristics of concert halls, cathedrals, churches or other spaces in which musicians perform, means that researchers can undertake systematic analyses of musicians' perception and performance in acoustic spaces. Such room acoustic simulations need to be implemented with 'proper realism' (Gade, 1989, p. 195), although it may not be necessary to faithfully re-create all physical properties of the sound field in order to deliver a space which musicians deem sufficiently plausible for musical performance. With plausible virtual acoustic spaces in the recording studio or performance venue, it is possible to remain faithful to the inherent spatiality of music, which may have been lost with modern recording techniques.

Future developments of VAT will open up new fields of research into the presentation and coordination of musical performance and will ultimately lead to a deeper understanding of music perception, cognition and action. Nevertheless, it is not just acoustic research that will benefit from these developments in technology – ultimately, all musical performance, composition and collaboration will be transformed through advances in mediated shared environments.

## References

Bagenal, H. (1930). Bach's music and church acoustics. *Music and Letters, 11*(2), 146–155.
Barron, M. (1993). *Auditorium acoustics and architectural design.* London: E & FN Spon.
Beghin, T. (2009). *The virtual Haydn. Paradox of a twenty-first-century keyboardist.* Retrieved from http://www.music.mcgill.ca/thevirtualhaydn/.
Beranek, L. (2004). *Concert halls and opera houses: Music, acoustics, and architecture* (2nd ed.). New York: Springer.
Bishop, L., and Goebl, W. (2015). When they listen and when they watch: Pianists' use of nonverbal audio and visual cues during duet performance. *Musicae Scientiae, 19*(1), 84–110.
Blesser, B. and Salter, L. R. (2007). *Spaces speak, are you listening?* Cambridge, MA: MIT Press.
Bolzinger, S. and Risset, J. C. (1992). A preliminary study on the influence of room acoustics on piano performance. *Le Journal de Physique IV, 2*(C1), 93–96.
Boren, B., Longair, M., and Orlowski, R. (2013). Acoustic simulation of Renaissance Venetian Churches. *Acoustics in Practice,* 1(2), 17–28.
Bradley, J., Soulodre, G., and Norcross, S. (1997). Factors influencing the perception of bass. *Journal of the Acoustical Society of America, 101*(5), 3135.
Brereton, J. S., Murphy, D. T., and Howard, D. M. (2014). *Singing in space(s): Singing performance in real and virtual acoustic environments. Singers' evaluation, performance analysis and listeners' perception.* Retrieved from http://etheses.whiterose.ac.uk/7877/1/JSBRERETON_PHD.pdf.
Brereton, J. S., Southern, A. S., and Kearney, G. (2015). Multi-modal experience of a virtual concert hall: A tool for exploring the influence of the visual modality in interactive real-time room acoustic simulations. Presented at the *International Conference on the Multimodal Experience of Music (ICMEM)*, Sheffield, UK, 23–25 March.
Brunskog, J., Gade, A. C., Bellester, G. P., and Calbo, L. R. (2009). Increase in voice level and speaker comfort in lecture rooms. *The Journal of the Acoustical Society of America, 125*(4), 2072–2082.
Chafe, C., Gurevich, M., Leslie, G., and Tyan, S. (2004). Effect of time delay on ensemble accuracy. Presented at *International Symposium on Musical Acoustics (ISMA)*, Nara, Japan, 31 March–3 April 2014.
Constellation Centre. (n.d.) Introduction to the project. Retrieved from http://www.constellationcenter.org/intro/intro_inspirations.htm.
Crooks, J. (2015, November 30). Transforming room sound with a max patch. Retrieved from https://cycling74.com/2015/02/04/transforming-room-sound-with-a-max-patch.

Dammerud, J. J. (2009). *Stage acoustics for symphony orchestras in concert halls.* Unpublished PhD thesis, University of Bath, UK.
Field, A.E. (2015, 30 November). *Architexture 2: St Mary's reconstructed.* Retrieved from https://ambrosefield.wordpress.com.
Fischinger, T., Frieler, K., and Louhivuori, J. (2015). Influence of virtual room acoustics on choir singing. *Psychomusicology: Music, Mind, and Brain, 25*, 208–218.
Fry, S. (n.d.). Audioboom blog. Retrieved from https://audioboom.com/boos/54262-npl-boo#t=0m0s.
Gabrielsson, A. (1999). The performance of music. In D. Deutsch (Ed.), *The psychology of music* (2nd ed.) (pp. 501–602). New York: Academic Press.
Gade, A. C. (1989). Investigations of musicians' room acoustics conditions in concert halls. Part I: Methods and laboratory experiments. *Acustica, 69,* 193–203.
Griesinger, D. (1995). Further investigation into the loudness of running reverberation. *Proceedings of the Institute of Acoustics, 17,* 35–37.
Howard, D., and Moretti, L. (2009). *Sound and space in Renaissance Venice: Architecture, music, acoustics.* New Haven, CT: Yale University Press.
International Organization for Standardization. (2009). *ISO 3382–1:2009 Acoustics – measurement of room acoustic parameters – Part 1: Performance spaces.* Retrieved from https://www.iso.org/obp/ui/#iso:std:iso:3382:-1:ed-1:v1:en.
Jeon, J. Y., and Barron, M. (2005). Evaluation of stage acoustics in Seoul arts center concert hall by measuring stage support. *Journal of the Acoustical Society of America, 117,* 232.
Kimball, W. (2010, November 30). Anechoic recordings: A different kind of chamber music. Retrieved from http://kimballtrombone.com/2010/06/09/anechoic-recordings-a-different-kind-of-chamber-music/.
LARES Lexicon Inc. (n.d.). *Wenger V-Room®.* Retrieved from http://www.lareslexicon.com/musicrehearsal.html.
Leman, M. (2008). *Embodied music cognition and mediation technology.* Cambridge, MA: MIT Press.
Lerch, A. (2012). *An introduction to audio content analysis: Applications in signal processing.* New York: Wiley.
Lokki, T. (2014). Tasting music like wine: Sensory evaluation of concert halls. *Physics Today, 67*(1), 27–32.
Marshall, A.H., Gottlob, D., and Alrutz, H. (1978). The acoustical conditions preferred for ensemble. *Journal of the Acoustical Society of America, 63*(1), 35–36.
Martens, W. L., and Woszczyk, W. (2004). Virtual acoustic reproduction of historical spaces for interactive music performance and recording. *The Journal of the Acoustical Society of America, 116,* 2484.
Meyer Sound. (2015, 30 November). Meyer sound constellation revives congregational singing at Clinton Frame Mennonite Church. Retrieved from http://www.meyersound.com/news/2015/clinton_frame.
OpenAir. (2015, 30 November). Demo, download and share acoustic impulse responses for auralisation. Retrieved from http://www.openairlib.net.
Oxnard, S., and Murphy D.T. (2012). Achieving convolution-based reverberation through use of geometric acoustic modeling techniques. Presented at *15th International Conference on Digital Audio Effects (DAFX),* York, Ireland, 17–21 September.
Pätynen, J. (2007). *Virtual acoustics in practice rooms.* Master's thesis, Helsinki University of Technology.

Poletti, M. A. (2010). Active acoustic systems for the control of room acoustics. In *International Symposium on Room Acoustics* (pp. 1–10), 29–31 August, Melbourne, Australia.

Repp, B. (1992). Diversity and commonality in music performance: An analysis of timing microstructure in Schumann's Träumerei. *Journal of the Acoustical Society of America, 92*, 2546–2546.

Schärer, Z., Kalkandjiev, Z., and Weinzierl, S. (2013). The influence of room acoustics on solo music performance: An empirical case study. *Acta Acustica united with Acustica, 99*, 433–441.

SIAP. (n.d.) SIAP Systems for improved acoustic performance B.V. Retrieved from http://www.siap.nl/en.

Timmers, R. (2005). Predicting the similarity between expressive performances of music from measurements of tempo and dynamics. *The Journal of the Acoustical Society of America, 117*(1), 391.

Ueno, K., and Hideki, T. (2005). Cognitive modeling of musician's perception in concert halls. *Acoustics Science & Technology, 26*, 156–161.

Ueno, K., Kato, K., and Kawai, K. (2010). Effect of room acoustics on musicians' performance, Part i: Experimental investigation with a conceptual model. *Acta Acustica united with Acustica, 96*(3), 505–515.

Ueno, K., and Tachibana, K. (2003). Analysis of musicians' evaluation of Acoustics in Concert Halls based on the individual-scale method. *Journal of the Acoustical Society of Japan, 59*, 591–602.

Vorländer, M. (2007). *Auralization*. Berlin: Springer.

Woszczyk, W., Ko, D., and Leonard, B. (2012). Virtual acoustics at the service of music performance and recording. *Archives of Acoustics, 37*(1). 109–113.

Woszczyk, W., and Martens, W. L. (2008). Evaluation of virtual acoustic stage support for musical performance. *Journal of the Acoustical Society of America, 123*(5), 3089.

Yamaha Ltd. (2015, 30 November). *Active Field Control*. Retrieved from http://www.yamaha-afc.com.

# 13 Space and body in sound art
## Artistic explorations in binaural audio augmented environments

*Martin Rumori*

'Sound art' is the main topic of this chapter, so the reader may have an immediate idea of what that involves: certainly the chapter is not about 'music', rather something that is connected to an 'arts' context, probably received in an exhibition instead of a concert, something that appears to be an object rather than a composed piece unfolding in time. Yet something that 'sounds' – unlike a painting or a classic sculpture.

In this chapter, I will investigate aspects of body and space using a sound installation of mine as a concrete example. The installation *Parisflâneur* is conceived in the principal medium of virtual auditory space and therefore poses an example of a navigable audio augmented environment. Using a pair of headphones, listeners are invited to explore a virtual scene of seven mostly unmodified, narrative field recordings from Paris and around. By freely moving in the installation space, solely guided by spatial listening, the recordings may be identified, accessed and abandoned individually. Further bodily interaction allows for rearranging the recordings in the virtual scene. No intentional montage of the recordings was done that would, for instance, support a certain linear dramaturgy. Instead, listeners are invited to construct their personal story, introducing their own memories and experiences. I chose a particular example not only because a general examination of body and space in 'sound art' would be simply too manifold and extensive but also because the term does not denote a well-defined research area or an art form, as the initial paragraph of this chapter illustrates. Nevertheless, I will refer to the current discourse on sound art as a consequent motivation for investigating an actual work rather than a more generic field.

The technical framework of *Parisflâneur* and its aesthetic references serve as a platform for arts-based research on spatial listening, interaction modes, notions of immersion, narratives in music and reflections on medial conditions of perception and cognition. My aim is to provide insights into the close relation of technical building blocks and their aesthetic role in the artwork, in particular virtual audio technology using headphones along with psychoacoustic mechanisms and cultural implications of listening for personal, synthesised or recorded auditory spaces. This requires taking a more integral perspective on the components of the installation rather than approaching separate, isolated parameters as is usually pursued in scholarly research.

*Parisflâneur* investigates two closely related technologies, so-called binaural recording and synthesis, for presenting both navigable and static auditory environments in order to provoke different immersive listening modes. Not only shall these technologies transport the artistic narration of individually accessible sound situations within a composed immersive scene, but they should also expose the perceptual conditions of differently mediated acoustics. Binaural technology seeks to reproduce acoustic stimuli in the listeners' ears identical to those in a real-world situation. The basic assumption is that such stimuli evoke the same auditory events as in the real situation, that is, listeners will hear the same in both (Blauert, 1997). Most research efforts approach perceptual flaws of binaural systems as to minimise the difference between the reproduced and the original ear signals. Nevertheless, 'authentic reproduction is rarely required. ... [S]ound material on the radio and on disk is processed in such a way as to achieve the optimal auditory effect, for instance, from an artistic point of view' (Blauert, 1997, p. 374). While Blauert implicitly locates artistic questions outside the scope of scholarly research on binaural technology, my aim is precisely to investigate the boundary of scientific and aesthetic motivations of engineering. I do not regard the objectives of an authentic reproduction and an optimal auditory effect as a dichotomy of verified methods (i.e., 'scientific') and verified aesthetic results (i.e., 'artistic'). Rather, both scholarly and artistic processes underlie systematic decisions that are largely determined by aesthetic measures, which shall become visible by a detailed examination of the engineering undertaken for *Parisflâneur*.

In the first part of this chapter, I will provide some technological foundations on binaural technology and engineering issues that are also relevant for *Parisflâneur*. Subsequently, I will approach the abovementioned question of sound art in order to locate the following discussion in the relevant discourse. The last part will be dedicated to the *Parisflâneur* framework. I will describe its appearance to the listener and its realisation, followed by aesthetic and cultural references as well as implications of the installation and the technologies involved. Finally, I will report on approaches to a holistic evaluation of the work.

## Technological and perceptual foundations

### Binaural recording

Human spatial hearing is enabled by three major cues: inter-aural time differences, inter-aural level differences and directional spectral cues (Blauert, 1997). The basic idea of binaural stereophony is to preserve the spatial cues caused by the layout of the hearing apparatus in a recording, in order to maintain information on the spatial configuration of a certain auditory scene (Møller, 1992; see Lennox, this volume). This is usually achieved by using a so-called dummy head microphone, a schematic replication of a human head and especially the pinnae with microphones at the place of the eardrums or at the outer end of the ear canals (cf. Paul, 2009). The resulting signals are called binaural, head-related or ear signals to mark the difference from loudspeaker stereophony (for discussions on terminology see Sunier, 1960; Wade and Deutsch, 2008; Alexander 1999).

When played back, the recording should provide the same stimuli to the listener's ears as the original auditory scene, especially with respect to the spatial cues. This is only possible when the signals recorded for the left and right side are exclusively presented to the respective ear, and when they reach the eardrums without any subsequent manipulation. Thus, binaural recordings generally have to be listened to with headphones, although methods exist for presenting binaural signals via loudspeakers (Masiero, Fels and Vorländer, 2011; Choueri, n. d.; Xie, 2013).

Instead of a dummy head microphone, binaural recordings may also be carried out using the recordist's own head by placing miniature microphones at the outer end of the ear canal, sometimes called original head microphones. Such microphones were used for the recordings in *Parisflâneur*. As a consequence, the recordings contain individual spatial cues determined by the head and ears of the recordist as opposed to the experimentally found and improved generic properties of a dummy head. This means that other listeners might find the result less convincing, spectrally or spatially distorted, depending on their individual deviation from the recordist's hearing apparatus. Of course, this is also true for the generic dummy head, but probably to a smaller extent on average (Møller, Sørensen, Jensen and Hammershøi, 1996).

## *Binaural synthesis*

Binaural synthesis denotes methods of generating head-related signals without recording an entire auditory scene by means of binaural microphones. Instead, spatial cues are applied to one or more separate, usually monaural source signals in order to place them at certain positions in the binaural spatial field (Blauert, 1997; Vorländer, 2008; Blauert, 2013; Xie, 2013). Different approaches exist for realising binaural synthesis systems. Along with some fundamentals, two implementations used in *Parisflâneur* will be presented as examples for artistically motivated realisations.

Most binaural synthesis techniques are based on so-called head-related impulse responses (HRIR). They represent the transfer functions of a dummy or a human head for a certain source position to each of the ears. Thus they contain all the spatial cues for a particular source direction and distance. When applied to a monaural, dry signal by means of convolution, the resulting binaural signal represents a sound field with the source material encoded at the respective position. HRIRs are usually generated by measurements. A dummy head or, for individual HRIRs, microphones in a subject's ears are used to record a measurement signal that is played back at the desired location. Such measurements are typically carried out for multiple source positions that are organised in a grid with a certain horizontal and vertical resolution in order to synthesise virtual sources at different locations around the listener's head (Gardner and Martin, 1995).

HRIRs measured in an anechoic chamber, so-called free-field impulse responses, do not contain any spatial information other than the relative location of the direct source signal. In ordinary spaces, walls and other objects produce reflections of sound waves, whose amplitudes, spectra and temporal relations contain cues of the room's properties and the locations of sound sources (Blauert, 1997). In particular, the distance of a source is reflected in the energy ratio of its direct signal and the late reverb (Blauert, 1997; Xie, 2013). In binaural synthesis systems using free-field HRIRs, virtual auditory space is created by encoding simulated directional reverb signals into the soundfield according to a simplified room model, as in common reverb algorithms (Blauert, 1997; Vorländer, 2008; Xie, 2013). In contrast, binaural room impulse responses (BRIRs) are measured in reverberant spaces and hence already include all spatial information for a specific constellation of a sound source and the listener. The rendering, a binaural form of convolution reverb, results in a highly convincing spatial image as the complex acoustic properties of a real room are captured rather than synthesised. For this reason, *Parisflâneur* uses primarily BRIRs. A major disadvantage is their static nature. Subsequent or even dynamic changes to the contained spatial information are only possible to a limited extent, unlike the parameters of a model-based simulation. This restriction may be compensated for by a large number of measurements at a high spatial resolution, that is, for many source directions and distances, the so-called binaural room scanning (Horbach, Karamustafaoglu, Pellegrini, Mackensen and Theile, 1999).

In later implementations of *Parisflâneur*, a combination of binaural room and free-field impulse responses was applied. The latter were used without a room model to synthesise sources closer to the listener (that is, the direct signal portion dominates), while gradually cross-fading to the BRIRs for increasingly distant sources (that is, increasing reverb portion). This way, the rendering system provides a certain dynamic functionality with respect to the virtual source distance, while maintaining relatively low computational demands.

Changing the location of a virtual source relative to the listener's head, either due to moving sources or the moving listener, involves switching to a different impulse response representing the new source direction. Additionally, any synthesised distance cues or spatial simulation have to be dynamically adapted, too. In most cases, the directional granularity of measured impulse response sets is much lower than the sought synthesis granularity, which ideally reaches that of perception (see Blauert, 1997). Source directions in between measurements may be rendered by interpolation, for which different approaches exist. One is to understand the entire set of impulse responses as a virtual multichannel loudspeaker set-up around the listener's head, with the number and positions of speakers determined by those of the measured directions. For synthesising virtual sources at arbitrary positions, multichannel spatialisation techniques are applied to the virtual speaker set-up, for example Ambisonics (Noisternig, Musil, Sontacchi and Höldrich, 2003; see also Lennox, this volume). A different approach for HRIR interpolation works at the level of impulse response properties based on a principal component analysis (Martens, 1987; Kistler and Wightman, 1992; Larcher, Jot, Guyard and Warusfel, 2000).

*Parisflâneur* originally used the virtual Ambisonics approach using static BRIRs of a measured three-dimensional 24-channel hemispherical loudspeaker set-up. Later versions implemented only two-dimensional rendering using 12 BRIRs in a circular configuration, complemented by abovementioned free-field HRIRs especially for close sources. When combined with a tracking system for adjusting the source positions upon head movements, the spatial constellation of the listener and the virtual speaker system formed by the BRIRs cannot be changed retroactively and thus remains fixed, be it two- or three-dimensional. Therefore, the direct source signals and the modelled distance cues are updated correctly but the room acoustics, that is, the directional early reflections and late reverb, move and turn along with the listener, potentially causing misleading spatial cues. Nevertheless, this 'incorrect' implementation combines a convincing spatial impression due to the use of BRIRs with relatively low resource demands, while still allowing for a dynamic scene rendering.

## *Binaural sound projection using headphones*

Choosing appropriate headphones for use in binaural audio augmented environments requires the consideration of a number of relevant factors, among them the headphones' converter principle (closed-loop or open-loop), their shape (circum-aural, supra-aural or intra-aural), their reproduction quality and their mechanical properties. Mounting a tracking target of a certain weight or dimension requires a stable enough headphone bow and a sufficiently tight fit on the listener's head, especially if quick or upside-down movements are expected.

The closed-loop principle establishes an airtight sound transmission from the membranes to the eardrums, while open-loop headphones implement a non-isolated coupling with permeable foam layers or ventilation slits. Hence, closed-loop headphones usually have a tighter fit and provide a higher isolation against the environment. This is not always desired, for instance in augmented environments that are intended to acoustically blend into the existing surrounding.

Depending on their shape, headphones may completely enclose the listener's ears (circum-aural) or rest on the outer surface of the pinnae (supra-aural). Earbuds fit in the outer part of the ear canal and are called intra-aural. The headphones' shape influences binaural reproduction. More advanced binaural auditory displays seek to compensate for transmission distortions introduced by the headphones and their coupling to the ears. Such compensation is more stable for circum-aural headphones, as they suffer less from varying transfer functions when put on and taken off repeatedly (Paquier and Koehl, 2015). The transfer functions of some headphone models are generally more suitable for compensation in binaural systems than others (Møller, Hammershøi, Jensen and Sørensen, 1995). Flat-response intra-aural earphones may not need any compensation due to their direct coupling to the ear canal.

For freely moving in navigable audio augmented environments, wireless operation of headphones is desirable. Yet in today's technology there exists always a trade-off between transmission quality, interference-free operation and low latency. Digital transmission introduces a certain latency, which in the majority of cases is too high for real-time interactive operation. Most professional solutions still use analogue radio, which potentially suffers from interference noise. Both digital and analogue systems limit the signal's dynamic range, which may degrade binaural reproduction quality. The current situation regarding widespread low-latency, robust and high-quality stereo wireless audio transmission for interactive binaural applications is still unsatisfying and open for further exploration.

## Sound art?

A discussion of space and body in a sound installation cannot ignore the current discourse on the genre of sound art: whether it is a genre of its own at all, whether it should be subsumed in music or visual arts and how it should be distinguished from other art forms. Some positions suggest that sound art indeed forms a new independent genre (de la Motte-Haber, 1996), while some others claim that different art forms also dealing with sound would be excluded by an installation-centric notion (Fiebig, 2013, 2015). A progressive perspective in musicology identifies academic and political implications of the discourse on sound art and predicts its general disappearance (Straebel, 2010), as will be discussed below.

The title of this section, 'Sound art?', quotes a short text by pioneering artist Max Neuhaus in which he generally rejects the term (Neuhaus, 2000). In his view, it only serves as an arbitrary category for everything that involves sound in any form, in order to declare it to be appropriate for a presentation in visual art contexts, that is, in museums and galleries:

> These exhibitions often include ... the following: music, kinetic sculpture, instruments activated by the wind or played by the public, conceptual art, sound effects, recorded readings of prose or poetry, visual artworks which also make sound, paintings of musical instruments,

musical automatons, film, video, technological demonstrations, acoustic reenactments, interactive computer programs which produce sound, etc. (Neuhaus, 2000)

He claims that the criterion for inventing new terms should be the creation of new forms of art 'beyond the limits of music', which shall be enabled by 'our now unbounded means to shape sound'. But is it true that everything called sound art is 'essentially new music' (Neuhaus, 2000)?

In fact, the term 'sound art' is problematic as it 'has been used inconsistently throughout the years' (Landy, 2007, p. 11). An early example of the use of the term in a related context is an exhibition named 'sound art' in 1984 at the Sculpture Center in New York, dedicated mainly to visual arts (Straebel, 2010). To date, a notion of such kind is still widely accepted: 'sound art belongs in an exhibition situation rather than a performance situation' (Licht, 2007, p. 14), or 'sound art self-evidently is an area of visual arts, *too*' (Kiefer, 2010, p. 11, author's translation and emphasis). The term sound art 'currently ... is typically used to designate sound installations (associated with art galleries, museums, and public spaces)' (Landy, 2007, p. 11). In the case of *Parisflâneur*, which actually is a sound installation, this definition applies. Yet, according to Neuhaus (2000), it is still not clear which qualities distinguish an installation like *Parisflâneur* from music, given that it even refers to anecdotal *music*.

When noise became eligible as a musical object, musicology appears to have struggled to define its actual subject (Thom, 2007). Studies of electroacoustic as well as popular music introduced 'sound' as an object of research equal to musical notation that was initially refused especially by historical musicology (Thom, 2007). As a reaction, a separate discourse on sound art as a new genre has been established (Thom, 2007; Straebel, 2010). The genre of sound art has been located in between visual arts and music, as many works require a multimodal perception (de la Motte-Haber, 1990, 1996, 1999). Yet, the strong connection to installation art neglects other forms dealing with sound, such as radio art, which refers to radio plays and usually does not incorporate visual components (Fiebig, 2013). On the other hand, the designation 'sound installation' often overemphasises the auditive component of actual intermedia installations to the disadvantage of visual aspects (Straebel, 2010).

The general emancipation of sound in musicology is reflected in the term 'sound-based music' for an 'art form in which the sound, that is, not the musical note, is its basic unit' (Landy, 2007, p. 17). 'A liberal view of sound-based artworks would indicate it to be a subset of music' (Landy, 2007, p. 17). Similarly and more widespread, 'sonic art' has been coined as 'merely a convenient fiction for those who cannot bear to see the use of the word "music" extended' (Wishart, 1996, p. 4). Although both authors acknowledge sound as an integral part of music, they only reluctantly claim that their subject indeed belongs to music, apparently as a concession to dismissive tendencies in musicology. The proclamation of separate art forms and discourses will involuntarily approve and thus foster an outdated understanding of music instead of widening it, as in Wishart's ambitions (1996).

An alternative understanding considers the kind of sounds involved as a distinguishing feature of sound art from music:

> Those who claim that sound art is music seem to imply that none of the works created under the label of sound art over the last decades have succeeded in creating any sound that marks a specific difference from music.
>
> (Fiebig, 2015, p. 201)

But what would be a non-musical sound, after Luigi Russolo's *Intonarumori*, after Varèse, who 'broaden[ed] the definition of music to include all organized sound', after Cage, who 'went further and included silence' (Neuhaus, 2000)? 'There is no such thing as an *unmusical* sound-object', as Wishart (1996, p. 8) states.

The discourse as to whether sound-based art forms are music may overlook the fact that musicology's appropriation of sound art can be understood as a political programme in which sound art becomes a 'theoretical construct of the history of scholarship' (Straebel, 2010, p. 53). Nevertheless, Straebel ascribes certain merits to this 'project of musicology ... providing a theoretical foundation and political support for an art form of intermedia not only situated between genres but also between corresponding mechanisms of reception and market' (p. 59). Since this project's 'successful completion is foreseeable', 'sound art as an autonomous discourse ... will disappear' (p. 59). It is time 'to be concerned again with actual works in the discourse of sound art and to individually examine their historic and systematic references' (p. 57).

As a consequence of Straebel's analysis, my exploration of the *Parisflâneur* installation in this chapter is not regarded as a prototypal investigation of sound art, nor does it advocate the proclamation of a new genre. Rather, the discussion shall provide an instance for examination along the lines of Straebel's argument, that is, considering the references of an actual intermedia work, perhaps with the side effect of contributing to approaches and methods for dealing with such works in musicology.

## *Parisflâneur* – installation and framework

*Parisflâneur* emerged from several case studies of virtual acoustics (Rocchesso, 2011). It developed into a series of sound installations to serve as a framework for arts-based investigations of movement and interaction in audio augmented environments (Holl and Rumori, 2009; Rumori, 2012). *Parisflâneur* takes place in a navigable virtual auditory space that is presented via headphones. The installation invites listeners to explore and rearrange field recordings captured by the artist in and around Paris. The orientation and interaction in the installation is based exclusively on spatial listening and bodily movement, no intentional visual or other cues are involved.

What follows is the description of a typical set-up and its realisation. Subsequently, some relevant aesthetic and cultural references are discussed, namely field recordings and anecdotal music, virtual reality and audio augmented environment, and the implications of headphone listening and personal auditory spaces. Finally, pointing to the feedback received from installation visitors, this chapter endeavours towards an evaluation of the listeners' experience and interaction mechanisms in *Parisflâneur*.

## Showcase installation – laboratory set-up

The basic laboratory set-up consists of an empty area of about 5 m in diameter and a pair of headphones presented to the listener, who is invited to move freely in space. Once the listener has put on the headphones, a mixture of urban and rural audio recordings is heard, whose location of origin, supported by the title of the installation, is easily identified as the city of Paris and its surrounding. When listening more closely while moving around in the installation space, it turns out that the sound field consists of several strands. Each of them seems to have a certain individual position in space, as the audible direction of their origin remains fixed when turning and moving and, when getting closer, the respective sounds become more intense. In fact, the listener is part of a virtual auditory space comprising seven sound sources. While exploring the space and recognising the different recordings by their sonic qualities and their auditive narratives, the listener may develop a map of the seven auditory events including both their positions and their anecdotal references. Nevertheless, the auditive space within each of the recordings is collapsed into a single point and is thus transported by its anecdotic narrative only, in contrast to spatial or technical mediation such as stereophony.

Listeners 'enter' one of the sound situations by way of interaction. Performing a ducking gesture, that is, moving the head below a certain level and raising it again exactly at the position of the selected situation, will fade out all other recordings. The entered recording undergoes an audible transition towards a spatial opening. Narrative strands within the sound situation unfold in space and surround the listener. However, the entered recording is not navigable and remains static upon movement, thus the recording appears to be 'attached' to the listener's head.

Ducking again causes the selected recording to be 'left' and dropped at the listener's current position. The scene composed of all sound situations is then entered again with the dropped recording appearing at the new location. Thus, by moving around with a recording accessed, the composed scene may become spatially rearranged by each listener, but the result is only audible when the recording is abandoned again. The ducking gesture for entering and leaving singular sound situations is introduced to the listeners by the metaphor of putting on and taking off 'sound hats'.

## Technical realisation

*Parisflâneur* uses binaural synthesis combining free-field and room impulse responses as described above. The installation incorporates multi-camera infrared optical tracking so as to navigate in and interact with *Parisflâneur*'s audio augmented environment. The tracking uses configurations of four or five small reflective markers as tracking targets, arranged to form so-called rigid bodies mounted on top of the headphones.

Entering and leaving singular recordings is realised by gradual cross-fades between the synthesised binaural scenery and the original binaural recording. As mentioned before, the synthesised virtual scenery compensates for the listener's movements, while the original recordings remain static, that is, they move and turn along with the listener. Thus, the transition between the two auditory environments may be understood as a shift from a global spatial reference (i.e., the virtual scenery attached to the surrounding space) to a personal reference (i.e., the entered recording attached to the listener's head).

As mentioned above, the underlying field recordings were carried out using original head binaural microphones. With very few exceptions, they were taken from a static position without consciously moving or turning the head. The recordings themselves represent spatial auditory scenes similar to those created by binaural synthesis. However, in the virtual, navigable scene described above they appear in a reduced, monaural form as part of a 'meta space'.

## Artistic aims – research questions?

*Parisflâneur* involves a number of technologies. The artistic perspective informed the use of technology for an introspective reflection on the experience process. How do artistic aims account for the technologies they approach? Which factors determine research efforts in the respective domains of art and research? Is the artistic contribution merely the 'content' for a technical platform, resulting in an 'artistic application'?

From an artistic perspective, perception processes on different levels are regarded as parts of an integral aesthetic experience. In scientific research, complex integral experience is usually segmented so as to investigate singular processes without influence from others, for example by blindfolding participants or inhibiting their movements. By doing so, the relation of each segment to the integral experience may become questionable, distorted or even meaningless. Findings on aesthetical experience of artworks may very well be generalisable and systematically examined, while their individual mechanisms and cognitive interpretational strands are not (cf. Marentakis,

Pirrò and Kapeller, 2014). As a consequence, artistically relevant research efforts towards, for example, spatial sound projection technology can never approach the spatial dimension independently from the musical.

Artistic explorations in the framework of *Parisflâneur* target a kind of synoptical reflection on the two closely related technologies of binaural recording and binaural synthesis. The combination of both supports the presentation of the metaphorical narrative as described above, but to the same extent the narrative points back to phenomenological differences of the technologies involved and thus also instantiates medial properties for aesthetic experiences.

### *Field recordings and 'musique anecdotique'*

*Parisflâneur* incorporates recordings of and around Paris, so-called *field recordings*. Although their character is mostly static and, with very few exceptions, the microphone did not move during recording, they represent everyday sound situations and contain well-recognisable narrations. Listeners are explicitly invited to connect their own associations to these recordings – an invitation in the vein of anecdotal music (*musique anecdotique*) of the French composer Luc Ferrari (1929–2005). In the 1960s, Ferrari worked with Pierre Schaeffer, whose notion of reduced listening (*écoute réduite*) required listeners to hear a sound and its qualities as such, instead of identifying its source by immediate association. Ferrari's anecdotal music was conceived as a response to Schaeffer by favouring compositions incorporating narratives by everyday sonic photographs. Ferrari coined the term '*diapositive sonore*' to claim that everybody is capable of taking such a photograph – an indication of his egalitarian understanding of music creation (Pauli, 1971) – and not because 'acoustic reality shall be reproduced as objective as a photograph' (cf. de la Motte-Haber, 1999, p. 40).

In *Parisflâneur*, there is no intentional montage of fixed-media field recordings. Instead, the widely unprocessed recordings occur in simultaneous playback, 'in stretto', by a variable spatial arrangement which, along with the listener's perspective, determines their joint or separate reception. The temporal coincidence of independent narratives is further dispersed by loops of different lengths. The parallel presentation of several coincident micro-narratives for non-linear exploration and recombination refers to Ferrari's ambition of not presenting a linear story to the listener but rather letting the listener's own imagination construct the story: 'My anecdotal music brings the audience the pictures of its own reality and its own imagination' (Pauli, 1971, p. 47).

Providing an interface for auditory exploration by bodily movement in virtual space is a fragmentary anecdotal narrative itself. It incorporates the metaphor of an urban map, but is not meant as a sound map navigation interface such as the sonic cartographies of the London Sound Survey, the British Library UK Soundmap or the Radio Aporee global soundmap. The map metaphor is broken once the spatial arrangement of the recordings is changed by the listener.

The static binaural recordings that are heard after having 'entered' a virtual source hint at an ecological experience of field recordings, as argued from a more soundscape oriented perspective. It is possible to perform the listening act as an imaginary reconstruction of the recorded venues. Yet this notion is confronted with the alternative occurrence of the same recordings as virtual sources. Thus, the recordings always appear with an inherent reflection of their media conditions insofar as they represent 'framed art' (cf. de la Motte-Haber, 2010, p. 50).

## *Virtual reality and audio augmented environment*

*Parisflâneur* takes place in virtual auditory space and therefore relates to discourses and projects of virtual and augmented reality (VR/AR). Having been quite widespread during the mid- to late 1990s, VR and AR research has recently regained greater attention on account of the advent of affordable consumer-grade hardware such as the Oculus Rift (see also Brereton, this volume).

*Parisflâneur* replaces the acoustic surrounding with a binaural signal presented via headphones. In practice, it may also blend with the sonic contribution of the natural environment, depending on the kind of headphones used and the adjustment of the installation to augment rather than replace the surroundings. Although this mode occurred at some venues, it is not primarily intended nor conceptually accounted for. *Parisflâneur* could rather be regarded as an instance of virtual reality, since all the stimuli for one of the human senses – hearing – are provided through technical mediation.

Alternatively, the installation could be considered as an example of augmented reality, since it provides an overlay only of the sense of hearing and not of sight. There remain open questions, however, as to which factors qualify a system as 'fully virtual' rather than 'augmented'. How many and which senses would need to be supplied to retain technical or perceptual fidelity? Which factors should be assessed by scientific measures and which by the subjective experience of 'immersion' – through a 'suspension of disbelief'? In this context, there seems to be a fruitful conceptual distinction between intentionally overlaying, on the one hand, and the intentional replacement of stimuli, on the other.

Following the definition of Xie (2013), *Parisflâneur* may be partially regarded as a virtual auditory display (VAD) for the rendered sound scenery, but not for the mere playback of binaural recordings in which no binaural synthesis is involved. Even the virtual scene rendering involves techniques that are not entirely 'binaural' in a strict sense. One major inspiration for *Parisflâneur* was the LISTEN project, carried out between 2000 and 2003 at Fraunhofer Institute of Media Communication (Warusfel and Eckel, 2004). For its case studies, the project used the term 'audio augmented environment', which also refers to the history of installation art by describing one's everyday surroundings as an 'environment'. In the absence of well-defined terminology, and as a reference to the LISTEN project, the designation 'audio augmented environment' is adopted also to *Parisflâneur*.

## Headphone listening and personal auditory space

Headphone listening marks a cultural technique. Its origins are driven by the technical necessity to bring early sound converters as close as possible to the human ears, as the deliverable electromechanical energy was very small. Perhaps unintentionally, this technology introduces the notion of a private auditory space. Easily recognised from outside, the listener is often detached from her or his acoustic surrounding, though this is not compulsory (see below). Wearing headphones is also a strong social symbol for the resulting isolation. The social interpretation might be fostered by the intended technical isolation when using headphones in telecommunication, sound engineering and recording. In everyday life, wearing headphones symbolises an augmented environment entered into by the listener, insofar that the ears' acoustic supply has been replaced. These are the circumstances hinted at when the listener puts on headphones to enter *Parisflâneur*.

The aforementioned in-head localisation to be avoided in binaural reproduction is explicitly exploited in *Parisflâneur* for the inverse effect of surprise. It indicates that a virtual source has been reached, that is, that the listener is at the same position and therefore the auditory event is localised 'inside' his or her head, before the transition to the static binaural recording is triggered. Both concepts, that of sound inside the listener's head and its display via in-head localisation, have only one equivalent in non-mediated listening: sound produced by the listener's own body in or close to the head, such as the voice or chewing noises, which usually depend on conscious bodily action and whose major part is presented via bone conduction (cf. Blauert, 1997). Nevertheless, the prospect of recorded environmental sounds in the listener's head is surprisingly intuitive when supported by the narration of the sound scenery in *Parisflâneur*. The notions of in-head sound and in-head auditory localisation are not necessarily interdependent, despite their phenomenological relationship: The predominant narration of headphone listening to loudspeaker stereophonic signals suggests that auditory events of musical (e.g., orchestral) recordings are never meant to be in the listener's head, although they are localised there in terms of perception. To date, this narration is an intrinsic part of the established cultural technique of headphone listening. It can therefore only be broken explicitly, as Bernhard Leitner did in conceiving his 'Kopfräume' [head spaces] to be experienced inside the recipient's head (Leitner, 2003). For the same reason, binaural reproduction breaks with expectations when perceptive localisation suddenly approaches congruence with a cognitive spatial image, that is, when auditory events are actually localised outside the head where one would cognitively expect them to occur.

### Ways to evaluate a sound installation

*Parisflâneur* has been part of a research project that focused on evaluation methods in the realm of sonic interaction design (SID). The project called Klangräume – Situated Usability Evaluation of 3D Audio Interactive Sound Environments was carried out at the Institute of Electronic Music and Acoustics (IEM) of the University of Music and Performing Arts Graz between 2013 and 2015. The aim was to develop holistic approaches for the evaluation of human–computer interaction mechanisms in such environments and to directly involve a typical audience in test sessions and extended forms of practical examination (Marentakis, 2015; Marentakis et al., 2014). Figure 13.1 shows a freely inspired drawing by graphic artist Ksenia Nesterenko, which was created as a response to *Parisflâneur* during the *Klangräume* project.

*Parisflâneur* has been approached during two differently designed evaluation phases in two different incarnations of the installation. The first is the basic laboratory set-up as described above; the second has to some extent been conceived as a reaction to the first evaluation. In Klangräume, the evaluation did not target the artistic level, which is hardly possible at all, but the interaction methods involved and their relation to the intentions of the artist. Therefore, in the second installation, a special focus was laid

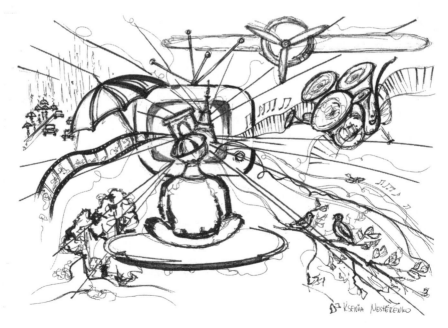

*Figure 13.1* Graphic interpretation of field recordings forming the virtual sound scenery in *Parisflâneur*.
Source: Reproduced with kind permission of Ksenia Nesterenko.

on audience experience with respect to spatial listening and bodily motion while exploring and interacting with the installation. Established quantitative evaluation methods of functional auditory environments do not apply in this context, as artworks rarely aim at achieving a certain well-defined user experience but may rather open spaces for a multitude of perceptual and interpretational strands (Marentakis et al., 2014). As a final publication of all project results is still pending, only a few major observations are presented here with reference to the internal project report (Marentakis, 2015).

The first evaluation session was carried out with 11 participants. They were generally interested in technology and media but not especially familiar with sound installations or related art forms. The aspects on which the evaluation focused were derived from an extensive questionnaire and additional material provided by the artist on the aesthetical aims of the installation, including technology and expectations towards the listeners. The evaluation procedure was based on an extension of the video-cued recall technique. Participants were filmed during their exploration of the installation. Subsequently, video playback helped them to recall several aspects of subjective experience that were recorded with a questionnaire and a structured interview. Findings referring to two main areas of investigations are presented here, namely the sensorial experience and the interaction with the installation.

In most cases, descriptions of the experience in the installation referred to its virtual objects and not so much to the listener's physical relationship with the installation. Most participants enjoyed the narrative framing of witnessing recorded sound situations from the city of Paris, which was also a rich source for various immediate associations. The feeling of immersion was more attributed to listening to the singular, static binaural recordings than to the rendered scene composed of all recordings. Although this observation may perhaps question the overall quality of binaural synthesis in *Parisflâneur*, it also supports the hypothesis that a graspable narration and a familiar spatial image are more important for the plausibility of auditory environments than the fulfilment of as many as possible parameters of a 'natural' listening situation, such as adaptive rendering according to the listener's head movements.

Another, initially surprising finding is the fact that the seven field recordings comprising the virtual scene were not necessarily perceived as separate entities, although they were assigned to different spatial locations. Instead, some narrative elements from several recordings were sometimes perceived as forming a unified, single recorded scene. This illustrates how much the artist's own perception was dominated by knowledge of the technical realisation of the scene, so that cognitive mechanisms of constructing plausible narratives dominate as soon as that knowledge is not present.

Some participants had difficulties appreciating the binaural sound reproduction in general in one or both cases of the virtual rendered scenery and the plain recordings. From a scientific perspective, reasons may be identified in obvious shortcomings of the reproduction technology such as the generic, that is, non-individualised binaural rendering, and the artist's individual binaural cues in the recordings, which may be inappropriate for other listeners. Beyond technical issues, an integral view as attempted in this chapter would need to question whether immersion can be appropriately evaluated as a mere spatial phenomenon, or whether cognitive aspects in close relation to anecdotal and narrative qualities of the presented auditory scene have to be taken into account as well. Another possible effect is the general confusion caused by unexpected binaural cues when wearing headphones, that is, disengaging from the familiar cultural technique of non-binaural headphone listening may be more difficult for some listeners than for others.

Regarding interaction, the evaluation showed that the task of the ducking gesture in order to enter a located sound situation could not be successfully performed by all candidates, as it was apparently too difficult to learn on the spot. Additionally, the gesture itself was not acknowledged to be intuitive with respect to the resulting effect. These observations address also concerns of the artist when developing *Parisflâneur*, such that mainly technical rather than narrative reasons were considered when implementing the gesture in the vertical direction, simply because this dimension was less 'occupied' for orienting bodily movements. Partially as a reaction to these findings, the second evaluation session was carried out based on a version of *Parisflâneur* that implemented a newly conceived interaction scheme.

The revised version of *Parisflâneur* used a different approach for the binaural synthesis and other refinements such as a more precise pre-processing of the underlying sound files. Most importantly, the interaction scheme was changed. The ducking gesture was dropped in favour of a simpler mechanism. When the listener moves into the middle of a virtual source, after a short time the binaural recording is entered without any further interaction. Additionally, a second mechanism is in effect: If the listener moves very slowly or not at all for a longer time, their inactivity would attract the closest virtual source which would start moving towards the listener until their position is reached and the recording is entered. Subsequent slow movements cause the recording to 'stick' to the listener's head and to rearrange the virtual scene just as in the first implementation. Only when the listener moves faster again, the recording is finally left and dropped in the virtual scene at the position of detachment.

The Klangräume project sought not only to evaluate the interaction mechanisms of participating works, but also to explore and to adjust alternative ways of evaluation, and a completely different procedure was conceived for the second evaluation session. For example, the given areas of investigation in the first session such as immersion or plausibility of interaction did not enable the participants to decide for themselves which aspects of the artwork they considered to be most significant for an integral understanding of their experience (Marentakis, 2015). Therefore, in the second session, five participants were selected depending on their field of expertise, one for each of the categories design, dance, instrumental performance, music aesthetics and computer music composition. They were asked for a threefold reaction to the artwork: first, to conceive a short performance in which participants enact their experience by interacting with the artwork; second, to introduce this experience into an independent work in the respective medium in which the participants were trained; third, a concluding interview for commenting on the process and their choices. On a meta-level, the participants were observed by a graphic artist who also listened to the audio output of the installation with a second pair of headphones. As mentioned before, she was asked to reflect her associations on the process in freely inspired drawings (see Figure 13.1). One participant remarked the following:

> As one attempts to capture a soundscape, it escapes; yet, if you try to run away from any given place, the soundscape magically reappears. ... [*Parisflâneur*] sneaks up on you when you' re least expecting it, and it abandons you when you need it the most.
>
> (Sofer, 2015, para. 3)

The quoted passage of the participant's textual contribution arguably refers to the newly conceived interaction scheme of the installation. While her description may sound contradictory to the actual implementation, it shows that the interactive behaviour seems to be considered as an intrinsic narrative component rather than an isolated control mechanism.

In all cases, participants of the second evaluation session spent significantly more time with the installation than participants of the first phase. The intensified exploration of the virtual space and of interaction mechanisms by bodily motion apparently yielded a closer connection to the installation and a deeper understanding of its aesthetic references. This was strongly illustrated by the abovementioned artistic responses to *Parisflâneur* that picked up certain aspects of the installation. For example, the computer music composer requested the seven recordings in order to conceive a corresponding game performance. He used a Nintendo Wii controller for switching the recordings upon hand rotation and for changing their playback speed with the joystick. The sound output of his interface was played back on loudspeakers to the audience. His performance consisted in entering *Parisflâneur*, selecting a recording and – using his interface – trying to replicate for the audience what he hears on headphones, that is, to switch to the currently entered recording and to synchronise their playback positions by means of the variable speed control. His artistic intervention provided a conceptual translation between two auditory spaces that were both structured by composition and accessed by bodily motion.

The described approach chosen for the second evaluation phase does not allow for a comparative assessment of both versions of *Parisflâneur*, for example, with respect to the binaural synthesis. As several factors were changed, the significance of the findings for each single parameter would be questionable anyway from a strictly scientific point of view. On the other hand, valuable insights on the experience and interpretation of *Parisflâneur* have been gained, which, due to their irreducible nature, are transported mainly on an aesthetic level in the respective artistic realm, naturally being subject to appropriate interpretations themselves.

## Conclusions

The currently dominating dichotomy of sound art and music may not be an adequate categorisation for investigating the role of space and body in actual works. The main reason is that sound art is neither concisely defined as a genre or an art form nor is it autonomous from music as it is universally accepted. In both domains, artworks may have similar qualities in dealing with spatial dimensions and human interactions by bodily motion, such as in live electronics or in installations. More generic terms such as 'sonic arts' or 'sound-based music' may not be a solution either since they are unspecific with respect to the actual artworks' properties. They may even widen the gap between notation-based and sound-based approaches in musicology, while an integrative approach would be needed in order to investigate present symbolic and medial representations of artworks in their meaning for the audience.

In a similar vein, the relationship between data-driven 'objective' approaches and human experiences need to be reconsidered. For instance, scientific research on binaural synthesis seeks to improve the listener's experience, especially with respect to localisation accuracy and unaltered reproduction quality. The reference is usually human spatial hearing in non-mediated contexts, that is, in real rooms, halls or outdoor surroundings. Evaluation of results mostly takes place by carrying out acoustical measurements and listening tests, which validate isolated properties of research implementations in comparison to such reference situations. To date, most of this research is driven by the assumption that reproducing acoustical signals in listeners' ears – equal to those occurring in the reference ('natural') situation – would cause the same auditory events to take place, that is, the listener would hear the same (Blauert, 1997). Yet Blauert admits that 'this basic assumption ... is obviously not true', since 'cross-modal or cognitive effects are negated by this assumption' (Blauert, 1997, p. 374). Effects of cross-modal perception and cognition in conjunction with auditory space have been investigated for as long as spatial hearing itself (e.g., Blauert, 1997; Bregman, 1990; Blesser and Salter, 2007; see also Brereton, this volume). Only recently, more integral listening tests incorporating narrative elements seem to become eligible in the realm of scientific binaural research (e.g., Geronazzo, Avanzini and Fontana, 2015).

The use of headphones in *Parisflâneur* is a technical condition for a successful binaural sound projection in a navigable, interactive environment. At the same time, the act of wearing headphones has several aesthetical side effects. Unlike listening to speaker-based stereophony on headphones, the reception of binaural signals is not a widespread established cultural technique to date. The sensation of externalisation during headphone listening, that is, the perception of auditory events outside the listener's head, does not seamlessly pick up on natural spatial hearing in the first place. Instead, it appears to be an unexpected, often exciting effect to the non-expert listener – in contrast to the usual in-head localisation of loudspeaker signals. With increasingly widespread applications of binaural audio and its possible introduction into ubiquitous everyday media, this boundary might shift in the future.

## Acknowledgements

*Parisflâneur* was initially conceived at Institute of Electronic Music and Acoustics Graz during two short-term scientific missions funded by the Sonic Interaction Design European COST action (COST IC0601, Rocchesso, 2011). The Klangräume project has been supported as part of the programme Exciting Science and Social Innovations of Zukunftsfonds Steiermark (funds for the future development of the region of Styria, Austria). I am very grateful to Danielle Sofer for helpful comments on a previous version of this chapter.

## References

Alexander, R. (1999). *The inventor of stereo: The life and works of Alan Dower Blumlein.* Waltham, MA: Focal Press.
Blauert, J. (1997). *Spatial hearing. The psychophysics of human sound localization.* Cambridge, MA: MIT Press.
Blauert, J. (Ed.) (2013). *The technology of binaural listening.* Berlin: Springer.
Blesser, B., and Salter, L. R. (2007). *Spaces speak, are you listening? Experiencing aural architecture.* Cambridge, MA: MIT Press.
Bregman, A. S. (1990). *Auditory scene analysis. The perceptual organization of sound.* Cambridge, MA: MIT Press.
Choueri, E. Y. (n. d.). *Optimal crosstalk cancellation for binaural audio with two loudspeakers.* Retrieved from https://www.princeton.edu/3D3A/Publications/BACCHPaperV4d.pdf.
de la Motte-Haber, H. (1990). *Musik und Bildende Kunst. Von der Tonmalerei zur Klangskulptur* [Music and visual arts. From sound painting to sound sculpture]. Laaber: Laaber.
de la Motte-Haber, H. (1996). Klangkunst – eine neue Gattung? [Sound art – a new genre?]. In Akademie der Künste Berlin (Ed.), *Klangkunst* [Sound art] (pp. 12–17). Munich: Sonambiente Exhibition Catalogue.
de la Motte-Haber, H. (1999). Klangkunst: Die gedanklichen und geschichtlichen Voraussetzungen [Sound art: Theoretical and historical preconditions]. In de la Motte-Haber, H. (Ed.), *Klangkunst. Tönende Objekte und klingende Räume* [Sound Art. Sonorous objects and sound spaces] (pp. 11–65). Laaber: Laaber.

de la Motte-Haber, H. (2010). Wahrnehmung – Im Rahmen der Kunst [Perception – in the frame of arts]. In P. Kiefer (Ed.), *Klangräume der Kunst* [Sounding spaces in the arts] (pp. 41–52). Heidelberg: Kehrer.

Fiebig, G. (2013). Wer nur hören kann, muss fühlen. Versuche, Klangkunst als Medien- und Konzeptkunst zu denken [Who only can listen, has to feel. Attempts of understanding sound art as media and conceptual art]. In A. Emde and R. Krolczyk (Eds.), *Ästhetik ohne Widerstand. Texte zu reaktionären Tendenzen in der Kunst* [Aesthetics without resistance. Readings in reactionary tendencies in arts] (pp. 115–132). Mainz: Ventil.

Fiebig, G. (2015). Acoustic art forms in the age of recordability. *Organised Sound, 20*, 200–206.

Gardner, W. G., and Martin, K. D. (1995). HRTF measurements of a KEMAR. *Journal of the Acoustical Society of America, 97*(6), 3907–3908.

Geronazzo, M., Avanzini, F., and Fontana, F. (2015). Use of personalized binaural audio and interactive distance cues in an auditory goal-reaching task. In *Proceedings of the International Conference on Auditory Display* (pp. 73–80), Graz, Austria.

Holl, U., and Rumori, M. (2009). Parisflâneur. Spaziergänge in binauralen Hörräumen. Martin Rumori im Gespräch mit Ute Holl [Parisflâneur. Walks in binaural listening spaces. Martin Rumori interviewed by Ute Holl]. *Zeitschrift für Medienwissenschaft, 1*, 115–122.

Horbach, U., Karamustafaoglu, A., Pellegrini, R., Mackensen, P., and Theile, G. (1999). Design and applications of a data-based auralization system for surround sound. In *Proceedings of the 106th Audio Engineering Society Convention*, Munich. Retrieved from http://www.aes.org/e-lib/browse.cfm?elib=8204.

Kiefer, P. (Ed.) (2010). *Klangräume der Kunst* [Sounding spaces in the arts]. Heidelberg: Kehrer.

Kistler, D. J., and Wightman, F. L. (1992). A model of head-related transfer functions based on principal components analysis and minimum-phase reconstruction. *Journal of the Acoustical Society of America, 91*(3), 1637–1647.

Landy, L. (2007). *Understanding the art of sound organization*. Cambridge, MA: MIT Press.

Larcher, V., Jot, J.-M., Guyard, J., and Warusfel, O. (2000). Study and comparison of efficient methods for 3-D audio spatialization based on linear decomposition of HRTF data. In *Proceedings of the 108th Audio Engineering Society Convention*, Paris. Retrieved from http://www.aes.org/e-lib/browse.cfm?elib=9241.

Leitner, B. (2003). Kopfräume [Headscapes] [CD booklet]. Berlin: Hatje Cantz.

Licht, A. (2007). *Sound art: Beyond music, between categories*. New York: Rizzoli.

Marentakis, G. (2015). *Final report on the Klangräume project*. Unpublished internal documentation, University of Music and Performing Arts, Graz.

Marentakis, G., Pirrò, D., and Kapeller, R. (2014). Zwischenräume – A case study in the evaluation of interactive sound installations. In *Proceedings of the Joint International Computer Music Conference/Sound and Music Computing Conference* (pp. 277–284), Athens, Greece.

Martens, W. L. (1987). Principal components analysis and resynthesis of spectral cues to perceived direction. In *Proceedings of the International Computer Music Conference* (pp. 274–281), Champaign, Urbana.

Masiero, B., Fels, J., and Vorländer, M. (2011). *Review of the crosstalk cancellation filter technique*. Retrieved from https://www2.ak.tu-berlin.de/~akgroup/ak_pub/

seacen/2011/Masiero_2011_P2_Review_of_the_crosstalk_cancellation_filter_technique.pdf.
Møller, H. (1992). Fundamentals of binaural technology. *Applied Acoustics, 36*(3/4), 171–218.
Møller, H., Hammershøi, D., Jensen, C. B., and Sørensen, M. F. (1995). Transfer characteristics of headphones measured on human ears. *Journal of the Audio Engineering Society, 43*(4), 203–217.
Møller, H., Sørensen, M. F., Jensen, C. B., and Hammershøi, D. (1996). Binaural technique: Do we need individual recordings? *Journal of the Audio Engineering Society, 44*(6), 451–469.
Neuhaus, M. (2000). Sound Art? Liner notes for volume: Bed of sound. P.S. 1 [audio CD]. New York: Contemporary Art Center.
Noisternig, M., Musil, T., Sontacchi, A., and Höldrich, R. (2003). 3D binaural sound reproduction using a virtual ambisonics approach. Presented at the *IEEE International Symposium on Virtual Environments, Human-Computer-Interfaces, and Measurement Systems (VECIMS)*, Lugano, Switzerland.
Paquier, M., and Koehl, V. (2015). Discriminability of the placement of supra-aural and circumaural headphones. *Applied Acoustics, 93*, 130–139.
Paul, S. (2009). Binaural recording technology: A historical review and possible future developments. *Acta Acustica united with Acustica, 95*, 767–788.
Pauli, H. (1971). *Für wen komponieren Sie eigentlich?* [For whom do you actually compose?]. Frankfurt: Fischer.
Rocchesso, D. (2011). *Explorations in sonic interaction design*. Berlin: Logos.
Rumori, M. (2009). Advanced binaural synthesis for interactive audio augmented environments. *Final report on a short term scientific mission (STSM call 3) in EU action COST-IC 0601, Sonic Interaction Design*. Graz: University of Music and Performing Arts.
Rumori, M. (2012). Figuration 'Flaneur' [Figuration 'Flaneur']. In Netzwerk Körper (Ed.), *What can a body do? – Praktiken und Figurationen des Körpers in den Kulturwissenschaften* [Practices and figurations of the body in cultural studies] (pp. 67–73). Frankfurt a. M.: Campus.
Sofer, D. (2015). *Response to the Klangräume Installation by Martin Rumori, 'Paris Flâneur'*. Unpublished Klangräume project material.
Straebel, V. (2010). Vom Verschwinden der Klangkunst. Der Begriff der Klangkunst als wissenschaftsgeschichtliches Konstrukt [On the disappearance of sound art. The term sound art as a theoretical construct of the history of scholarship]. In P. Kiefer (Ed.), *Klangräume der Kunst* [Sounding spaces in the arts] (pp. 53–60). Heidelberg: Kehrer.
Sunier, J. (1960). *The story of stereo: 1881–*. New York: Gernsback.
Thom, N. (2007). *Klang vs. Musik, Allgemeine Klangforschung vs. Musikbezogene Klangforschung, Sprachliche Beschreibung vs. Technische Vermessung – Überlegungen zur Gefahr einer einseitigen Theorie des Sonischen* [Sound vs. music, general sound studies vs. musical sound studies, verbal description vs. technical measuring]. In J. G. Papenburg (Ed.), *popscriptum 10, Das Sonische – Sounds zwischen Akustik und Ästhetik* [The sonic – sounds between acoustics and aesthetics]. Berlin: Humboldt University. Retrieved from https://www2.hu-berlin.de/fpm/popscrip/themen/pst10/pst10_thom.pdf.
Vorländer, M. (2008). *Auralization. Fundamentals on acoustics, modelling, simulation, algorithms and acoustic virtual reality*. Berlin: Springer.

Wade, N., and Deutsch, D. (2008). Binaural hearing. Before and after the stethophone. *Acoustics Today, 4*, 16–27.

Warusfel, O., and Eckel, G. (2004). *LISTEN. Augmenting everyday environments through interactive soundscapes*. Workshop at IEEE VR 04. Retrieved from http://resumbrae.com/vr04/warusfel.pdf.

Wishart, T. (1996). *On sonic art*. Amsterdam: Harwood.

Xie, B. (2013). *Head-related transfer function and virtual auditory display*. Plantation: J. Ross.

# 14 Embodiment and disembodiment in networked music performance

*Georg Hajdu*

In this chapter the physical, sonic and spatial aspects of networked music performance (NMP) or networked multimedia performance (with an added autonomous visual layer, which for simplicity's sake we will also refer to as NMP) will be explored from a particular perspective – that of remoteness or spatial distance. In NMP the performers (agents) are typically separated by distances, which in extreme cases add up to tens of thousands of kilometres. This implies that the interactions between the agents as well as the sounds they perceive are offset by latencies that can exceed the tolerable threshold for on-the-beat performance and may require the establishment of new musical genres.

There are two concepts in NMP, one in which high-quality, multi-channel sound is streamed across the globe, and another in which the sounds are created locally, albeit shaped remotely via control messages. The first – the method of choice for musicians on acoustic instruments – requires high-bandwidth, low-latency network connections, while the other – the preferred method of digital performers – brings sound generation processes to the foreground. As the players are separated by (large) geographical spaces, the relationships between them need to be represented virtually. The performances can take place in virtual space alone or in hybrid spaces where local audiences intersect with virtual ones. The interplay of the physical, sonic and spatial dimensions, taken for granted in most traditional forms of music performance, becomes all the more crucial when spectators create mental maps of the interactions they observe, which greatly influence the extent of their appreciation. The working hypothesis is that this appreciation relies on the plausibility between physical action and sonic result. Because of the remoteness of the participants, these actions may not always be perceived directly or immediately. Hence, they have to be embodied by adequate representations to overcome the disconnect, whereby a mutual bond between performers and the spectators, perceiving this interaction, is being negotiated.

In order to fully realise the implications of NMP, I will present in this chapter a short historical overview before turning the attention to concepts underlying the nature of distributed performances. Next, with those concepts in mind, I will zoom into and critique current practices by acknowledging that NMP is particularly susceptible to various types of disembodiment, namely spatial separation, microtemporal fluctuations and poverty of sound production and transmission. I will conclude this chapter by extrapolating the present state of affairs to predict what the future might hold in stock.

## Brief and personal history of networked music performance

NMP has a long history that started in the late 19th century fuelled by advances in telegraphic, radiophonic and early recording technologies. The first system is this area was the Telharmonium (Weidenaar, 1995), which consisted of a gargantuan additive synthesis engine delivering live music performances on an organ-like instrument to households via telephone wires. As with the radio, which had its first public performance only three years after the Telharmonium's opening season (1907 vs. 1910), both media delivered content without the performers having 'to be there'. This physical *disconnect* between a musician creating a sound and a loudspeaker reproducing it must have been a bewildering experience for people at the time, whether they were playing music into or listening to music from the machine. Hungarian composer and ethnomusicologist Béla Bartók, who had made most of his phonograph recordings and transcriptions between 1907 and 1918, visited Turkey in 1936 for a further field study and reported this amusing anecdote about a folk singer:

> Bekir oğlu Mustafa was the first singer to sing into the phonograph in his tribal settlement, and he could only be persuaded with great difficulty to do so; he was afraid he would 'lose his voice' permanently if the machine should 'take it'.
>
> (Bartók, 1976, p. 58)

As curious as this account may sound, it touches on some fundamental issues relating to embodiment and disembodiment of recorded and electronically generated sounds, which are an essential part of NMPs.

### *Electronic music*

After the short-lived attempts of the Telharmonium and the Pianola to bring music to households without musicians needing to be there, the radio (along with the turntable) established itself as a mass medium of the 1930s, transmitting music and speech to an ever-growing number of receivers. It comes as no surprise that John Cage, an early adopter of any technological progress, turned his attention to the radio as a musical instrument. His *Imaginary Landscape No. 4* from 1951 was conceived for 12 radios, whereas the first piece from this series was written for piano, cymbal and two variable-speed turntables with frequency recordings. While these pieces actually required performers acting in front of an audience, electronic music since the late 1940s was mostly listened to via radio loudspeakers or in front of empty stages. See the section 'Cause and effect' (below) for a more in-depth discussion.

*Network performance*

The advent of affordable digital computers, customised controllers and MIDI (as a standard to connect music devices) introduced new opportunities for experimental developers. In 1975, Kraftwerk started using custom-built electronic controllers on stage and, in 1978, the League of Automatic Music Composers began performing with networked microcomputers such as the Commodore KIM-1 (Brown and Bischoff, 2002). The effect on the audience was entirely different: While in case of Kraftwerk the audience could appreciate the connection between physical actions and the sounds produced, this aspect was partially hidden in the performance of the League and The Hub. In a memorable performance at the 1992 International Computer Music Conference in San José, California, the six male members of The Hub sat around tables mounted with computers, a MIDI hub (hence the name of the band) as well as various controllers and sound-producing devices. Although the performers did not face the audience directly, the audience could observe intense concentration and physical involvement during the show. After the last piece, the band radiated a sense of relief and satisfaction upon the successful ending of the concert, which the spectators appreciated even though it was difficult to connect the gestures made by the band members to the sonic outcome.

The 1980s also saw further development of a different kind of network music in which recorded sounds were sent over large distances via satellites or landlines and remixed in radio studios in real-time. People such as Max Neuhaus (Public Supply) and Bill Fontana (Soundbridge Cologne/San Francisco) fostered this approach between the 1960s and the 1980s. These distinct practices of local network performances mediated via control messages, on the one hand, and long-distance audio streams, on the other, started to merge in the mid to late 1990s when technologies became available to musicians to send data regardless of their type around the globe; yet a conceptual distinction between those approaches (audiovisual (AV) streaming vs. exchange of control messages) is still observable today. Improvising musicians such as Pauline Oliveros and Chris Chafe motivated the development of *telematic* performances, which essentially consist of musicians playing together over low-latency audio and video links – a practice that existed even before the popularisation of the internet. However, the exchange of control messages (discreet and continuous) takes advantage of the peculiarities of digital media and therefore is to be regarded as the actual innovation in NMP.

In the early years, though, internet music performances were hampered by severe issues as stated by Brown and Bischoff (2002):

> As such [musicians first and technologists second], we were the first (as far as we know) to make interactive, live electronic music in a computer network, and despite the primitive nature of that network (compared to those available at present) we were the first to experience its potentials and its problems. One of those problems has to do with distance. As instruments, and ensembles, get more complex, the direct interaction of people with sound becomes difficult to maintain. Computer music instruments are best when they take on a life of their own, surprising their creator/performers with a liveliness and character that could not be predicted; but there remains a need to guide them directly, to nudge their behaviour in this direction and the next by physical gestures, and to hear the results of those gestures begin to emerge immediately. When the network mediates those gestures further, a disconnect can take place that alienates the player from interaction with the music.

According to Brown and Bischoff this alienation could only be overcome by maintaining a balance between the behaviour and responsiveness in the design of electronic instruments and networks – an issue which has since been addressed by some developers and practitioners such as the people affiliated with SLork and PLork (the Stanford and Princeton laptop orchestras). Table 14.1 presents a comparison of the technical conditions surrounding early and late internet music performance in respect to local scenarios.

### *Quintet.net*

Unaffected by (or unaware of) the sobering experiences reported by The Hub, the newly available technologies attracted a significant number of computer musicians and multimedia specialists such as Pauline Oliveros, Atau Tanaka and Chris Chafe at the turn of the millennium to embark on a new journey on the internet. I described my own approach to NMP in an article I presented at the 1999 SoundArt Festival in Osnabrück, Germany (Hajdu, 2003). It contained the layout of a system which has been in constant development ever since and was the basis for countless multimedia projects ranging from an internet opera project at the Munich Biennale to local network performances with the European Bridges Ensemble or students of the Hamburg University of Music and Theatre.

Quintet.net (Hajdu, 2005) is a multi-user, real-time, server–client-based digital multimedia performance environment consisting of different types of nodes (up to five players, an unlimited number of listeners and viewers, one conductor) assuming different roles and communicating via network protocols by exchanging discrete and continuous control messages of different types. As the early years of internet performance were an uphill battle

Table 14.1 Comparison of different network scenarios

|  | Early internet music (discrete control data and low-quality streaming) | Late internet music (continuous control data and high-quality streaming) | Local performance (electronic/ acoustic) |
|---|---|---|---|
| AV cues (musicians/ audience) | No | Via streaming | Immediate |
| Other cues | Avatars | Avatars | Immediate |
| 3D visual perception | No | Technically possible | Yes |
| Spherical 360 degree visual perception | No | Technically possible | Yes |
| Sound localisation | Vector-based amplitude panning (VBAP) | Ambisonics, wave-field synthesis (WFS) | Immediate |
| Sound quality | mp3, aiff (16 bit, 44.1 kHz) | Any file type | Immediate |
| Network bandwidth | Dial-up modem, ISDN, low-bandwidth DSL | Internet2, GÉANT | Local |
| Network quality | Low throughput, Dropped packets, Errors, latency, jitter, out-of-order delivery | Quality of Service (QoS) | Local |
| Music styles | Collaborative soundscapes, control of generative music, loops, time brackets, free improvisation | Latency < 50 ms: beat-based/ metered music<br><br>Latency > 50 ms: Collaborative soundscapes, control of generative music, loops, time brackets, free improvisation | Any style |
| Music notation | Simple | Complex | Any means |

against technological shortcomings, the challenges that internet performance had been posing in the early days, and the solutions to be found to compensate for them, had to be addressed.

Music performance on the Internet also leads to socio-psychological questions as to the identity of the performer playing on the Net and how his or her presence is felt by the other musicians and their audiences, as well as where 'adequate' performances are supposed to take place and how they should be presented – questions that touch on the fundamental roles that musicians and their audiences have taken for granted for centuries.

(Hajdu, 2005, p. 24)

In the performance of my piece *MindTrip* at the 2000 Mystik und Maschine Festival in Münster, Germany, on 28 October 2000 (the very first performance of a Quintet.net composition), the five performers were located in different cities across the globe. They were linked by the Quintet.net server running locally in Münster, connected via a 128 kbit dial-in ISDN connection to the internet. Münster performer Erhard Hirt, who played a Roland MIDI guitar, reported that it was difficult for him to localise and identify his partners, as their sonic identities were masked by sounds assigned to each performer via the Quintet.net sampler. As a seasoned improviser who had been used to read subtle visual and acoustic clues from fellow musicians, Hirt felt insecure about his hybrid role and double presence in two distinct spaces with a real audience and remote, virtual partners. In an email to me after the performance he commented on the deadpan quality of the exchanged sounds:

> Isn't the problem most likely that the complexity of a musical action by a [remote] partner is not being communicated via Internet, but instead just its reduction via pitch-to-midi conversion?

Hirt as well as the audience, the latter largely not used to computer-generated music, let alone to sounds produced by musicians who weren't there, had to rely on the spatial arrangement of the five loudspeakers on which name tags of the remote musicians had been placed – in addition to the display of 'real-time event notation' projected onto a large screen in back of the stage. Although participating Hub member Chris Brown pointed out that using shared notation was 'breaking new ground', many people in the audience felt that the approach held promise but was not yet living up to its potential. This was partially due to the lack of real physical interaction between the performers, but also because of the blandness of the sampled sounds. Because of technological limitations, we had to take special care to keep the memory footprint of the audio samples small enough and just use a limited number of voices in the polyphonic sampler. Using reverb or other digital audio effects to smooth and enliven the sounds was absolutely out of the question, as this would have exceeded the computational power of our machines. Consequently, the sonic results sounded artificial, machine-like and disembodied, but we also had to deal with the hitherto unresolved psychological issues of remote performance.

In 2002, Dutch-American composer and flutist Anne La Berge devised a piece called *Vamp.net* in which the performers received textual instructions via the Quintet.net interface while improvising on their computer keyboards to a video. In the rehearsals the musicians, who all played from their private residencies, generally produced too many events, indicative of a communication problem. It was as if their solitary situation, the lack of secondary clues that musicians are sensitive to and the use of an on–off general-purpose controller had created a fear-of-void situation, for which they compensated by hyperactivity. This ultimately led to a breakdown of the type of interaction free improvisation ordinarily relies upon.

Therefore, under these circumstances, free improvisation was not the way to go. Instead, the participants had to be involved in scenarios in which clear instructions as to how to fill time had to be given. John Cage's number pieces, of which I transcribed *Five* (written in 1988), held promise in that they feature scores in which musical events are supposed to be performed within *time brackets* allowing a certain amount of indeterminacy as to their onsets. This also allowed us to regard network latency as an integral part of the performance rather than something that needed to be avoided or compensated for.

In the early days of Quintet.net, musical events were generated either by typing on the computer keyboard, playing on a MIDI instrument or using a pitch tracker to track the actions of acoustic instruments, with the former being our favourite playing mode, as it represented an aesthetical purity, particularly in local performances where laptops would be mounted on stable music stands arranged in semicircles (reminiscent of Kraftwerk's minimalistic stage set-up). The downside was its on–off paradigm allowing little expressive control over the sounds as they developed, further contributing to the sense of disembodiment.

Curiously, though, this was a welcome ingredient in the Munich Biennale opera *Orpheus Kristall* – an opera whose creation was instigated by musicologist Golo Föllmer and cultural manager Jens Cording of the Siemens Arts Program, touted as the first internet opera. In this opera, the stage of the Gasteig Carl-Orff-Saal was connected to four other locations in Amsterdam and the USA (New York and California). The sounds were converted into numeric data via pitch tracker. While the remote players spent the entire duration of the opera improvising, the result of that was to be heard in the concert hall only during certain predefined moments ('windows') which composer Manfred Stahnke had indicated in his score. During one of these moments, the digital multiplication of the notes produced by the performers was filtered through the spectrum of the baritone's speaking voice, analysed in real-time by the pitch tracker. The result eerily merged the qualities of the voice with the ongoing network improvisation. It meant to metaphorically *embody* the chaos of the outside world infringing on the life of Orpheus: by giving the chaos a voice as well as shaping and absorbing it, Orpheus thus reveals his quality as a true divine creator.

Again, for the audience, the role of the network was difficult to decode, as the remoteness of the participants prevented the establishment of a causal relationship between their actions and the sonic outcome audible through loudspeakers. Conceptually, the integration of the NMP posed serious challenges to the director, who in the end decided to hide the projection of the Quintet.net interface during the opera performance (only the Bayerischer Rundfunk production blended the imagery of the stage with the video of the computer screen). Although technically we succeeded to play through three performances and the dress rehearsal without crashes or other major accidents, a shift of paradigm for NMP was mandated. It can be summarised as follows:

- The current praxis of NMP needs to be put under scrutiny and its constituents extensively studied.
- NMP should not just mimic traditional forms of performance.
- A plausible relationship between the remote actions and their sonic and visual results ought to be established for performers and audiences alike.
- Expressiveness is to be achieved via continuous tracking of physical activity.
- Along the lines of Marshall McLuhan ('the medium is the message'), the narrative of network compositions needs to have a reference to its very technical nature.

With this aim in mind, I co-founded, in 2005, the European Bridges Ensemble (EBE) consisting of five electronic performers, a video artist and a 'conductor'. Two large grants allowed us to finance a number of activities, the first Music in the Global Village conference at the Budapest Kunsthalle among them. The first period from 2005 to 2007, in which we transitioned to using computers equipped with the powerful line of Intel Core processors, focused on the improvement of the audio system, allowing higher degrees of polyphony as well as other types of sound generation (besides simple sample playback), sound spatialisation and a more versatile video generation and processing component. A successful piece from this period was Sascha Lino Lemke's *Netze spinnen # Spinnennetze*, which premiered at the Akademie der Künste in October 2007 on the occasion of the György Ligeti composers' contest. Its two parts, inspired by the musical and nonmusical ideas of the great Hungarian composer, featured sophisticated user interfaces and sound generation modules as well as a rich textual score with instructions as to how and when to operate these interfaces via the computer keyboard. It also included a social, game-like component allowing the participants to interfere with each other, for instance by stopping the sounds of the other performers.

## Performativity in musical networks

### Cause and effect

The members of the EBE often found themselves in the position of having to explain the nature of their interactions to their audiences, which were to a great extent attracted by the novelty of their project. But does novelty itself suffice? Does an artwork or a performance need a lengthy explanation before it can be appreciated by the audience or would there have been ways of establishing a more intimate sense of causality (or, more accurately, plausibility, as we will see later on) between actions and the sonic and visual results? Would the disconnect between performers and audience thus be overcome by appealing to the knowledge embodied in the spectators?

The relationship of cause and effect is perhaps the most fundamental principle in music. In the acoustic environment before the advent of loudspeakers, a sound could only be produced by a physical effort causing a resonating body to vibrate. This relationship was so intimate that even in the absence of a perceivable cause, a trigger for a sonic event could safely be inferred. It is obvious that from an evolutionary standpoint such a close association between cause and effect makes sense when it comes to quickly deciding whether to fight or flight in front of imminent threats (Wallin, Merker and Brown, 2000). Experiments of audiovisual phenomenal causality (Guski and Troje, 2003) have shown that for the perception of audiovisual synchrony (i.e., synchrony between visual and auditory triggers), 'a sound may be judged to be synchronous with a visual event even when the sound occurs after a short delay. In contrast, a preceding sound is less likely to be judged as synchronous' (p. 790). In a similar vein, Chafe, Cáceres and Gurevich (2010) conducted tapping experiments with artificial latencies between two visually and sonically separated musicians and have shown that our nervous system is best attuned to naturally occurring latencies such as those happening on concert stages.

In music, the bond between cause and effect is so intimate that in musical semiotics the index ('a sign that is linked to its object by an actual connection or real relation') can be regarded as the most prevailing sign. In his book *Grundriss der musikalischen Semantik* [Fundamentals of musical semantics] Czech musicologist Vladimír Karbusický – basing his theory on the writing of Charles Sanders Peirce – elaborates on this intimacy:

> Its first ontologically significant factor is the immediate bond: something indicates ... the state ... of an object. ... The psychosomatic relevance of indices makes its application to music – an art form that touches the soul and moves the body ... The second factor is the energetic nature of this bond. Peirce spoke of the 'reactions of Secondness between the ego and the non-ego' and related this to 'Aristotle's use of energeia, action'.
> (Karbusický, 1986, p. 59, translated by the author)

The development of recorded media since the 1930s has fundamentally challenged this bond: By decontextualising (like in the early pieces of the *musique concrète* era), composers and sound artists were encouraging the listeners to experience sounds as such and not within the context of their production; and by processing, which allowed sounds to be 'denatured' to borrow a term from biochemistry, that is, change their properties until they become unrecognisable. Tape recorders permitted composers and sound artists to play a sound backwards metaphorically, reversing cause and effect. Extreme transpositions and time stretching also made sounds nearly unrecognisable. The 1950s added electronically generated sounds to the equation, and composers and their audiences experienced, for the first time in history, sounds devoid of the physical act of creation. Acousmatic music was the genre that logically grew out of this scenario and turned the non-physicality of an empty stage filled with nothing but loudspeakers into a virtue. Paradoxically, the most approachable pieces of this genre, often still maintain causality on higher semantic and syntactic levels, which can be exemplified by comparing 'intentional' music by Smalley and Gobeil to the non-intentional and non-causal pieces by John Cage (such as *Williams Mix*).

## Gestures, performativity and agency

In the same context Karbusický (1986) also indentified music as being permeated by gestures. He differentiated between three types: (a) real-life gestures (e.g., the motion of a conductor) represented as the energetic substance, constituting (b) the mimetic basis for music as well as (c) codified gestures in ballet. While Karbusický fails to make an explicit reference to the then budding genre of interactive music (his book was published in 1986), gestural control (sometimes referred to as *technical gestures*) has become an indispensable ingredient in the interactivity between man and machine. Kim and Seifert (2007) have extensively studied the nature of interactive music systems and discussed them in the context of recent theories of agency, situatedness and embodiment. Establishing the term performativity as the 'capacity to achieving efficiency which the moment of performance gives rise to', they posit that 'the framework of performativity offers an alternative perspective on music performance, which serves as the 'stage' integrating the processes of music production and perception' (p. 234):

> Francisco J. Varela [the Chilean biologist, philosopher and neuroscientist], who understands cognition as embodied action, places an emphasis on cognitive processes which depend on 'the kinds of experience that come from having a body with various sensorimotor capabilities' that are embedded in an environmental context, whether biological or cultural. In other words ... cognitive processes are considered as emerging from the 'continuous reciprocal causation' between mind/brain, body, and environment. According to this embodied approach in cognitive science, not only physical instantiation, but also an agent's situatedness in its environment is of importance to cognition.
>
> (Kim and Seifert, 2007, p. 234)

Kim and Seifert also discuss the distinction between embodied and disembodied music systems. According to them, closed as well as knowledge-based interactive systems (e.g., those which rely on score following to elicit a musical response), are disembodied whereas coupled interaction of one or several agents with the environment, guided by action-perception loops is a necessary condition for embodied systems.

## *Embodiment*

As the term embodiment (and its antonym disembodiment) has several meanings and connotations we should stop for a moment and carefully define them so as to not confound them later on (see also Leman et al., this volume). We encounter the term in the context of embodied cognition, referring to the unity of perception and action manifest in the mirror system (see below). Embodied agents are intelligent agents, which communicate with their environment via a physical or virtual body (Cassell, 2001). A branch of artificial intelligence focuses on empowering such agents to interact autonomously with humans. The most common use, though, refers to the materialisation of abstract concepts. In that sense, the semantic field of embodiment overlaps with those of the terms metaphor and allegory. Brandon LaBelle (2015) in his book *Background Noise – Perspectives on Sound Art* analyses Atau Tanaka's early network piece *Global String*, a multi-site network music installation, connected via the internet, consisting of a musical instrument in which the network forms the resonating body, by use of a real-time sound synthesis server. La Belle writes:

> Tanaka's own virtual creature, as embodiment of global bodies, inputs and connections, thrives on the hybridity of information/digital code/data files/etc., giving voice to the terrors and pleasures wearing a new skin presents. (p. 277)

In this context he also makes a reference to McLuhan's concept of the 'extended nervous system'. For McLuhan the physicality of electronic media (or lack thereof) is central to his media theory. In *The Global Village: Transformations in World Life and Media in the 21st Century* (McLuhan and Powers, 1989), McLuhan became increasingly concerned about the cultural and ethical effects of what he termed *discarnetism*, that is about the disembodiment implied and realised by much of our communication via electronic media. According to McLuhan, we assume a robotic state when we become unreflective extensions of our own technologies. But, when we are 'on the phone', we are disembodied or discarnate. Angelism, is what McLuhan called this state. According to McLuhan, angelism was actually fairly dangerous for humans, especially their social life:

> If he [the caller] is not identified or chooses not to identify himself, he loses touch with a geographic location and a social function. He

becomes truly discarnate and, in that psychic sense, uncontrollable – a phone poltergeist ... .

(McLuhan and Powers, 1989, p. 124)

For the audience, the success of a NMP (or of a staged performance in general) depends to a great extent on whether they can understand and anticipate the actions of the performers. Two mechanisms, the *mirror system* and the *theory of mind* have been implicated in how the human brain might accomplish these tasks (Gazzaniga, Ivry and Mangun, 2014). The mirror system consists of mirror neurons in premotor cortex and other areas that respond to an action both when the action is produced by a subject or observed when produced by another subject. The mirror system has been assumed to be an essential part of comprehending the actions of other subjects. It provides an intimate link between perception and action with the consequence that the brain does not form abstract representations of visual patterns that conform to various actions, but rather our comprehension of such actions depends on our own ability to perform those deeds. The fact that our conceptual knowledge is grounded in our body knowledge has also been referred to as embodied cognition. Remarkably, the extent and intensity of activation patterns reflect a subject's repertoire of particular motor patterns. It was suggested (Aglioti, Cesari, Romani and Urgesi, 2008) that a well-practised motor system is anticipatory in nature, giving it the ability to predict others' actions in the arena of their expertise. Mirror systems are also thought to play an important role in imitation and learning new skills and for the understanding of other subjects' intentions. A similar capacity of humans to infer mental states of other people has been coined theory of mind by Premack and Woodruff (1978).

### Causality, plausibility and illusion

While Kim and Seifert (2007) present their ideas from the perspective of agents involved in a particular performative situation, there is no mention of the role of the audience in observing the outcome of such performances. Taking the role of the neural mirror system and theory of mind into account it is safe to assume that the audience is either empathic or non-empathic to the outcome of a performance, depending on its effectiveness. As the audience in most cases does not participate in the performance, it cannot verify whether an action is causal or only pretends to be – nor does it really matter dramaturgically. Mark Applebaum has demonstrated this paradox convincingly in his piece *Aphasia* (Figure 14.1). The performer seems to trigger sounds with gestures typical for interactive music performances, yet the sounds are played back by a sound system. In his score, Applebaum (2010) writes that 'the hand gestures must be precisely synchronised with the sound, the illusion being that the gestures cause the sound or vice versa' (p. 2). He also points out that 'the flow will be most persuasive when memorised

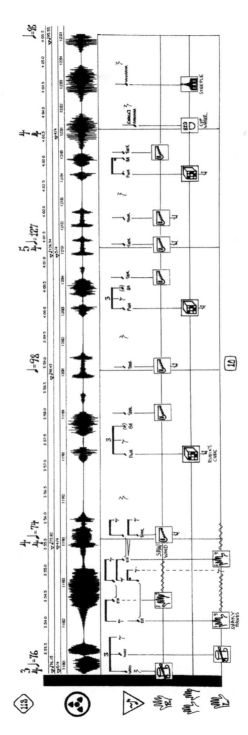

*Figure 14.1* Excerpt from *Aphasia* by Mark Applebaum. The performer synchronises his/her gestures to the playback and thus creates the illusion of causality.

and also allow the performer's eyes to remain fixed on the audience; furthermore the very presence of a score creates a barrier – both psychological and one of sight lines – between the performer and the audience' (2010, p. 2).

We are therefore encountering a contradiction between the definition of performative music systems as embodied – and closed, non-interactive systems (such as the one used in *Aphasia*) as disembodied. The performance may be disembodied from the strict definition given by Kim and Seifert, but it certainly does not appear that way. We have to therefore abandon causality as necessary condition for perceived reality and replace it with the concept of plausibility, which also encompasses the theatrical phenomenon of illusion.

Another issue with Kim and Seifert's definition of interactive performativity lies in their rejection of the intending artist as an agent wilfully acting in a closed artwork in favour of embodied aesthetic experience that emerges during an interactive performance. This may hold true for the types of interactive installations that audiences encounter in museums or other public spaces but falls short in describing the experience of musicians that practice and rehearse for any extended time to achieve expertise and fine control in their interaction with human–computer interfaces. It seems, therefore, that their definition of performativity calls for an extension in which hybrid, that is score-, memory- or knowledge-based scenarios can be integrated without contradiction.

In contrast, Gurevich and Fyans (2011) also studied digital musical interactions (DMI) as relationships between performers and digital music interfaces as well as their perception by spectators. Referring to an analysis of interactions with 'virtual musical instruments' (Johnston, Candy and Edmonds, 2008, pp. 208–209), the authors differentiate between three different modes of interaction – instrumental, ornamental and conversational – of which only the first corresponds to the traditional mode of continuous expressive control of an acoustic musical instrument – citing Cadoz (2009, pp. 207) that 'in the case where the gesture is performed on a physical device like a key or a joystick' the 'transduced signals have no physical (ergotic) meaning'. Non-instrumental modes, common in DMIs, are typically differentiated from the instrumental mode in that they rely on cognitive rather than perceptual-motor skills, as they control out-of-time or temporarily remote events (as opposed to continuous in-time events). It appears that instrumental modes facilitate the construction of mental model of the interaction, which is a key ingredient of the spectators' appreciation of the DMI–performer interaction. Without it 'some participants' perception seemed primarily informed by bodily cues – facial expressions or physical "confidence"'. This fact leads Gurevich and Fyans to stipulate that DMIs engage spectators in 'different modes of interaction, sometimes simultaneously'. Therefore, 'successful DMIs are more likely to be those that ... capitalise on this flexibility that digital devices afford' (p. 174).

One of these modes of engagement can also be found in the game-like nature of many network music projects,[1] which was studied in detail by Golo Föllmer (2005). He based his investigations on the social theories of Dutch philosopher Johan Huizinga, whose seminal work *Homo Ludens* provides an analysis of the play element of culture. This also explains why participatory concepts, in which the boundaries between performers and spectators disappear (Freeman, 2008), have become a popular ingredient in network music performances.

### *Virtual reality and telepresence*

Illusion is a key component of both magic and games, particularly on the internet, where people often mask their true identities and take on virtual ones. It has been shown that subjects are willing to accept low-dimensional virtual representations of themselves called avatars as long as the movements of such avatars are plausible. This is further supported by Wöllner (2012) who reports that conductors are capable of recognising their own gestures just from simple point-light displays.

In an article in the *Scientific American* Jaron Lanier wrote about avatars:

> Although the computer power of the day limited our early avatars to extremely simple, cartoonish computer graphics that only roughly approximated the faces of users, they nonetheless transmitted the motions of their hosts faithfully and thereby conveyed a sense of presence, emotion and locus of interest.
>
> (Lanier, 2001, p. 69)

In the same article, he also described a tele-immersion system that may eventually bring the world to one's desk. His system, designed for users to share virtual spaces involves streaming video from a battery of cameras creating a disparity map reflecting the degree of variation among the images from all aspects to create a single viewpoint-independent sculptural model of the scene. Experimenting with the system, Lanier noted that 'some critical aspects of a virtual world's responsiveness should not be subject to more than 30 to 50 milliseconds of delay. Longer delays result in user fatigue and disorientation, a degradation of the illusion and, in the worst case, nausea' (2001, p. 74). This is on a par with the observations of Chafe, Cáceres and Gurevich (2010), who reported that for remote musicians locking into each other's performances 35 milliseconds represent an optimal value within the acceptable range of latency.

There has been some hope that machines capable of predicting users' intent will be able to compensate for latency (Chafe, 2009; Alexandraki and Bader, 2014) and allow performances synchronised to a beat in which the combined latencies of round trip times (RTT) and audio buffering noticeably exceed the optimal range. (It is said that Internet2-type networks allow transmission speeds of up to half the speed of light. Under these conditions, tight beat-based performances may not work for distances larger than 5000 km, roughly the distance between the two North-American coastlines.)

Yet, is doubtful whether such prediction mechanisms hold the key to overcoming lag, as they also have to take discrepancies between intent and prediction into account, which may be perceived as mistakes. We would therefore trade a lack of temporal accuracy for a more pronounced likelihood of syntactic errors. The performance would also suffer from a decrease of expressiveness, as it would start to increasingly resemble a stream of algorithmically generated events controlled by what Johnston et al. (2008) call non-instrumental modes of interaction.

*Dramaturgy of networked music performance*

The beginning of the millenium was the time when the first telematic performances took place – their organisers seeking to employ telepresence technologies for remote interactions. The frequency of network music performances rose considerably over the following years and gave researchers an incentive to study the network topologies and social nature of such interactions, providing opportunities for distributed creativity. Rebelo, Schroeder and Renard (2008) came up with the notion of network dramaturgies encompassing aspects of authorship, collaboration, structure, content and as general term for a number of aspects that characterise performance practice. They posit that 'authorship and collaboration in particular are problematised in the context of network performance through questions of involvement of multiple sites/nodes and the relation between multiple kinds of artistic input' (p. 1). Therefore, notions of presence and environment become crucial to performance which is characterised by its multi-nodal nature.

Analysing the degree of independence the individual nodes may assume in a network, they distinguish between the following three approaches:

- projected dramaturgy (one node acts as author and the others as contributors);
- directed dramaturgy (authorship remains with an individual or group who take on the role of director);
- distributed dramaturgy (each node retains authorship).

These categories also apply to the nearly 30 compositions that have been written for Quintet.net and the EBE since 2000 (see https://en.wikipedia.org/wiki/European_Bridges_Ensemble for a selection thereof).

## Praxis of networked music performance

In 2007, two EBE members became partners in the European Culture 2007 project Cooperation and Mediation in Digital Arts (CO-ME-DI-A) with the aim of exploring the potential of NMP (http://e-b-e.eu). The opening three-way concert between Belfast, Graz and Hamburg was called *Disparate Bodies 2.0*, named after the eponymous piece by Pedro Rebelo of Queens University's Sonic Arts Research Centre in Belfast (Hajdu, 2008).

Cage's *Five* was also included in the programme, except this time Quintet.net was solely used to display the score in real-time, while the five performers played the music on acoustic instruments. This performance thus added a significant new component to our praxis of NMP: multi-channel, high-fidelity, low-latency audio streaming via JackTrip – with all participating partners being connected to the GÉANT backbone (the European equivalent of Internet2). This software relying on the Jack Audio Kit (http://www.jackaudio.org) is based on streaming technologies in development since 2000 and is maintained by Stanford University's SoundWire Group (Cáceres and Chafe, 2010).

Adding low-latency, high-fidelity audio and video streaming to the equation increased the sense of presence for all participants. However, the EBE was actually pursuing a different route – a route that was to embrace a virtual presence of the performers. Miller Puckette (2008) in his article 'Not Being There' also argues in favour of systems that, instead of (or in addition to) increasing the sense of presence by ever-refined streaming technologies, are based on the transmission of control messages, stressing the potential of game-like interactions by the participating parties:

> We quickly decided that instead of doing telepresence, ... we would try to do something that better responded to the idea of the physical distance between the sites. Instead of sending sounds and images across the network, we opted to send real-time audio analyses of the instruments. ... it was possible to associate any of the four instruments with a 'ghost' in the remote location, possibly very similar, but possibly quite different.
>
> (Puckette, 2008, p. 409)

In *Radio Music* (yet another adaptation of a piece by Cage), I devised for the five performers of Quintet.net an interface representing the physical actions of turning a USB rotary controller and acting as a dial for the virtual radio (Figure 14.2), for which I coined the term *radio avatar*. The audience experienced these actions in form of the combined movements of five cursors running along the display of virtual radio stations. At a performance at SIGGRAPH Asia with performers playing from Yokohama, Budapest and Belgrade the animation generated much interest among the audience. Despite the fact that three of the performers were in remote locations, there was no doubt that these actions were authentic.

EBE gave their last concert in November 2014 featuring Ádám Siska's piece *2_45* in which Wii Remote Controllers were used to simulate the actions of a ping-pong game. The piece was originally composed for a networked performance between the neighbouring capitals of Vienna and

*Figure 14.2* Georg Hajdu's adaptation of *Radio Music* uses a *radio avatar* to represent the actions of the (remote) musicians.

Bratislava, featuring a variety of sounds that were supposed to be 'tossed' to and fro via Wii Remote Controller strikes.

Thanks to wireless technology employed to send continuous control data to the individual computers, the players, exaggerating their movements according to Siska's choreography, were able to move about freely while observing a computer screen. On the screen, they were following a slider indicating the arrival of an object to strike. A successful strike was translated into a sonic representation, either iconic sound samples of crashes or spoken words. This piece had all the key ingredients of a successful (network) performance: Unbound by cables or idiosyncratic controllers the players were free to explore their perceptual-motor skills while feeling situated in a sonic environment that paid attention to small details of their interaction with the machine (such as simulating the sound of the approaching object). As a result of the game/sports metaphor, the spectators were able to quickly construct a mental image of the digital musical interaction and were able to identify the meaning of the sonic events generated by the remote participants. This piece was both engaging and entertaining, and thus did not require AV streams or an accompanying video playback to maintaining interest. After nearly ten years of exploratory work, the ensemble had set standards for NMPs in terms of aesthetic experience and performativity.

## The dialectical strive towards hyper-realism

The CO-ME-DI-A project was concluded in 2010 with a series of showcase events. A three-way, three-day network festival between Belfast, Graz and Hamburg epitomised the technical and aesthetical progress achieved throughout the first decade of the millennium: 45 uncompressed audio streams and five video streams ran with surprisingly few dropouts, delivering realistic multi-channel sound and video projections of the partner stages and audiences in addition to the video artwork on the screen in the centre. One of the highlights on the second day was the performance of Luigi Nono's composition *A Pierre. Dell'Azzurro Silenzio, Inquietum* for contrabass flute, contrabass clarinet and live electronics by Carin Levine (playing from Belfast) and Carola Schaal (playing from Hamburg). The quality of the audio and video streams as well as the unnoticeable latency created a deep sense of presence, which, for the performers and spectators alike, overrode the perception of medium's technicality and allowed an immersive experience, that is the audience was allowed to focus on the aesthetical experience rather than the technical means facilitating this experience.

In December 2010, another showcase event took place in Pécs, Hungary, featuring the third Music in the Global Village conference/symposium. The symposium invited select participants of the CO-ME-DI-A project and attempted to draw conclusions on NMP in light of the experiences gained throughout the project. There was a consensus that low-latency video streaming had not reached the same potential as audio streaming: in her demonstration during the lecture session 'Strategies for Finding Artistically Meaningful Applications of Internet Technology', Andrea Szigetvári of the Hungarian Computer Music Foundation harshly criticised *tunnel* vision and lack of true immersion caused by cameras and video streams at the time, the small resolutions either offering too small a viewing area or too little detail, and thus seriously limiting the amount of visual information available to performers and audience alike.

Another issue was the lack of standardisation. While the CO-ME-DI-A project had originally set out to develop a *CO-ME-DI-A bus*, into which different media streams were to conveniently be plugged in and received at each receiving end, this was abandoned, as the technical requirements were just too different for each scenario. Instead, each performance had to be configured by hand, which required lengthy preparation and rehearsals.

Nonetheless, the CO-ME-DI-A project hinted convincingly that technologies might eventually mature enough to gradually overcome most if not all of these hurdles. Currently, Ambisonics and wave-field synthesis spatialisation technologies offer a high degree of immersive realism in the audio domain, while 360-degree spherical video streams viewable with head-mounted displays have just become a reality. Therefore, in combination, holographic and 'holophonic' projection techniques (with the possible inclusion of haptic, temperature, olfactory and balance cues) will eventually offer unprecedented realism, which will come as close to *teleporting* people as one can imagine. Using 3D CGI-technologies, it is already possible to create realistic animated models of people (absent or deceased) and to place them in the midst of real-musicians on stage such as with the holographic projection of John Coltrane in the 2002 movie *Vanilla Sky*.

However, I called this section 'dialectical strive towards virtual hyperrealism', as art and design do not always follow the same paths as technological advances and might even occasionally oppose them. This opposition is often fuelled by power and economic structures in which elite technology is only available to a select few. But sometimes it is just about aesthetics: an example is Apple's move away from skeuomorphs, that is realistic user interface (UI) elements in their iOS operating system. Ableton has always favoured simple and abstract UI designs in the software Live while Reason, another digital audio workstation, which realistically mimics a studio rack. In the same vein, we will see continued interest in low-tech network music performances such as with Live Coding, both in local and remote networked scenarios. A memorable project in this area is the Powerbooks Unplugged laptop ensemble (http://pbup.net/s/), who promote themselves mockingly as the 'first acoustic computer music folk band: the laptop is their only instrument'.

## Conclusions

In this chapter I have shown that NMP represent a special case of digital musical interaction in which participating musicians may be hidden from sight or their presence only be experienced through the use of streaming technologies. Cognitive science provides the notions (such as embodiment/disembodiment) to identify the nature of man–machine interaction in networked performances and thus contributes to the improvement of the physical, sonic and spatial aspects – themes that are key to this book. The first decade of the first millennium saw a rapid co-evolution of technological and artistic solutions specific to this new genre, with the objective to create an ever more palpable musical experience for audiences and performers alike – the software Quintet.net and the pieces created and/or performed by the EBE being exemplary for this co-evolution.

Many properties of NMP have been aestheticised by the artists, for instance by using network delays as structural elements, motivating the metaphorical use of the term embodiment such as in the case of Tanaka's Global String project. While multimedia technologies continue to be developed, eventually offering unprecedented realism and immersion, the aim of NMP remains to create an audience involvement fundamentally different from classical music performances. These performances take machine–performer–spectator interactions into consideration, which, to a great deal, rely on embodied cognition and the sense of causality. From the audience's perspective, digital music interaction, particularly in NMP, poses a challenge as it builds its effect on illusion. Hence, classical cause-and-effect relationships (which also permeate the 'genuine' musical sign of the index) are replaced by plausibility, that is the amount to which performers and spectators are capable of 'buying' the outcome of a performance by building mental maps of the interaction. In NMP, this can be facilitated by the use of avatars, projected visually, and carefully orchestrated dramaturgies, involving participants in game-like scenarios.

## Note

1 In this context one should also mention the participatory piece *isms* by my former student Jacob Sello written for the European Bridges Ensemble (Lee and Freeman, 2013).

## References

Aglioti, S. M., Cesari, P., Romani, M., and Urgesi C. (2008). Action anticipation and motor resonance in elite basketball players. *Nature Neuroscience, 11*(9), 1109–1116.

Alexandraki, C., and Bader, R. (2014). Using computer accompaniment to assist networked music performance. In *Proceedings of the AES 53rd International Conference* (pp. 27–29), London, UK.

Applebaum, M. (2010). *Aphasia* [score]. Retrieved from http://londontreatise.blogs.wesleyan.edu/files/2011/06/APPLEBAUM-Aphasia1.pdf.

Bartók, B. (1976). *Turkish folk music from asia minor.* Princeton: Princeton University Press.

Brown, C., and Bischoff J. (2002). Indigenous to the net: Early network music bands in the San Francisco bay area. Retrieved from http://crossfade.walkerart.org/brownbischoff/hub_texts/points_of_presence_f.html.

Cáceres, J.-P., and Chafe, C. (2010). JackTrip: Under the hood of an engine for network audio. *Journal of New Music Research, 39*(3), 183–187.

Cadoz, C. (2009). Supra-instrumental interactions and gestures. *Journal of New Music Research, 38*(3), 215–230.

Cassell, J. (2001). Embodied conversational agents: Representation and intelligence in user interfaces. *AI Magazine, 22*(4), 67–84.

Chafe, C. (2009). Tapping into the internet as a musical/acoustical medium. *Contemporary Music Review, 28*(4/5), 413–420.

Chafe, C., Cáceres, J.-P., and Gurevich, M. (2010). Effect of temporal separation on synchronization in rhythmic performance. *Perception, 39*(7), 982–992.

Föllmer, G. (2005). *Netzmusik. Elektronische, ästhetische und soziale Strukturen einer partizipativen Musik* [Net music]. Hofheim: Wolke-Verlag.

Freeman, J. (2008). Extreme sight-reading, mediated expression, and audience participation: Real-time music notation in live performance. *Computer Music Journal, 32*(3), 25–41.

Gazzaniga, M. S., Ivry, R., and Mangun, G. R. (2014). *Cognitive neuroscience: The biology of the mind.* New York: W.W. Norton.

Gurevich, M., and Fyans, A.C. (2011). Digital musical interactions: Performer–system relationships and their perception by spectators. *Organised Sound, 16*(2), 166–175.

Guski, R., and Troje, N. F. (2003). Audiovisual phenomenal causality. *Perception & Psychophysics, 65*(5), 789–800.

Hajdu, G. (2003). Quintet.net – Präliminarien zur Entwicklung einer vernetzten, interaktiven Echtzeitkompositionsumgebung. In B. Enders and J. Stange-Elbe (Eds.), *Global village – global brain – global music* (pp. 298–303), Osnabrück: Rasch.

Hajdu, G. (2005). Quintet.net: An environment for composing and performing music on the internet. *LEONARDO, 38*(1), 23–30.

Hajdu, G. (2008). Getrennte Körper – Musiker im Netz [Separated bodies – musicians in the web]. *Positionen 74 – Dispositive,* 29–31.

Johnston, A., Candy, L., and Edmonds, E. A. (2009). Designing for conversational interaction. In *Proceedings of the International Conference on New Interfaces for Musical Expression* (pp. 207–212), 4–6 June, Pittsburgh, USA.

Karbusický, V. (1986). *Grundriss der musikalischen Semantik* [Foundations of musical semantics]. Darmstadt: Wissenschaftliche Buchgesellschaft.

Kim, J. H., and Seifert, U. (2007). Embodiment and agency: Towards an aesthetics of interactive performativity. In *Proceedings of 4th Sound and Music Computing Conference* (pp. 230–237), 11–13 July, Lefkada, Greece.

LaBelle, B. (2015). *Background noise – perspectives on sound art*. London: Bloomsbury.

Lanier, J. (2001). Virtually there: Three-dimensional tele-immersion may eventually bring the world to your desk. *Scientific American, 284*, 66–75.

Lee, S. W., and Freeman, J. (2013). Echobo: A mobile music instrument designed for audience to play. In *Proceedings of the International Conference on New Interfaces for Musical Expression* (pp. 450–455), 27–30 May, Daejeon, South Korea.

McLuhan, M., and Powers, B. R. (1989). *The global village: Transformations in world life and media in the 21st century*. New York: Oxford University Press.

Premack, D., and Woodruff, G. (1978). Does the chimpanzee have a theory of mind? *Behavioral and Brain Sciences, 1*(4), 515–526.

Puckette, M. (2008). Not being there. *Contemporary Music Review, 28*(4/5), 409–412.

Rebelo, P., Schroeder F., and Renard, A. B. (2008). Network dramaturgy: Being on the node. In *Proceedings of the International Computer Music Conference* (pp. 551–552), Belfast, UK.

Wallin, N. L., Merker, B., and Brown, S. (Eds.) (2000). *The origins of music*. Cambridge, MA: MIT Press.

Weidenaar, R. (1995). *Magic music from the telharmonium*. Metuchen, NJ: The Scarecrow Press.

Wöllner, C. (2012). Self-recognition of highly skilled actions: A study of orchestral conductors. *Consciousness and Cognition, 21*, 1311–1321.

# 15 Presence through sound

*Mark Grimshaw*

In 2015, with co-author Tom Garner, I published the book *Sonic Virtuality: Sound as Emergent Perception* (Grimshaw and Garner, 2015) that argued for a new definition and concept of sound as an emergent perception in an embodied system. There were several philosophical and practical reasons for doing this. One was a longstanding dissatisfaction with the standard Western definition, found in a variety of wordings in dictionaries and acoustics publications, that sound is a pressure wave in a medium that can be sensed via the auditory system; simply put, that sound is a sound wave. This dissatisfaction had a number of root causes not least of which is the number of inconsistencies in the use of the term to be found in acoustics textbooks and other physics-based documentation. These were discussed in the book and I have since expanded upon this problem elsewhere (e.g., Grimshaw, 2015), so below I limit myself to just a few examples of such inconsistencies to illustrate this issue.

A second reason for the necessity, it seemed to us, of a new concept of sound derived from the work that Tom Garner and I had long conducted on computer game sound, in particular work on biofeedback systems (e.g., Garner and Grimshaw, 2013a, 2013b) that led to the realisation that we needed a new concept of sound in order to make use of new technological possibilities. For example, work has been proceeding in recent years on the decoding of neural signals pertaining to visual perception, speech perception and music perception in order to then digitally synthesise images, speech and music from such brain activity (e.g., Nishimoto et al., 2011; Pasley et al., 2012; Thompson, Casey and Torresani, 2013). This raises the intriguing possibility of similar neural decoding for sound (that is neither speech nor music, as these involve other areas of the brain in addition to the auditory cortex). If one can decode and then re-synthesise activity in the brain triggered by the perception of sound waves or generated by the imagining of sound then a number of scenarios come to mind including direct 'thinking of sound' into a digital audio workstation (DAW). It follows that one could also de-synthesise audio into appropriate brain stimulation in order to trigger the perception of sound. To do this, one needs a conception of sound, and therefore a new definition of sound, in order to convert audio to the appropriate perception, a perception that, in this case, is triggered by something other than a sound wave. If one defines this perception as sound then it also follows that the imagining of sound, or the near synonyms auditory imagery and aural imagery, is itself sound (that is, sound is a perception whether arising as a result of imagination or through the stimulus of a sound wave) and thus the perception itself can be extracted into a DAW or, indeed, directly 'injected' into another person's brain by means of various brain stimulation methods (discussed further in *Sonic Virtuality*).

A third reason for the urge to rethink sound arose from a survey of auditory neurological or audiological evidence from the fields of psychoacoustics and cognitive science concerning the localisation of sound. Again, these were dealt with at length in the book but, below, I provide a summary of the main evidence we looked at because it has import for any discussion of the relationship between sound and presence.

As referenced above, in our experimental work, Tom Garner and I have for several years now investigated the use of biofeedback in the context of computer game sound. Our goal has been to devise a system that allows a far closer emotional integration between player and the game's virtual acoustic ecology such that the game engine, using data received from psycho-physiological devices such as EEG and EMG, can, in real-time, assess the player's emotional state and process the game's audio samples or synthesise audio signals for particular emotional purposes if the data indicate there should be a different or enhanced/reduced emotional state at that point in the gameplay. We are some way off this goal, primarily because the data from consumer psycho-physiological devices – those devices that are currently available to game players and are less cumbersome to use than clinical devices – are difficult to interpret as to the emotions they may or may not represent. For basic valence and arousal indicators, the data are perfectly serviceable and so we have been able to devise real-time game audio processing systems that, to a great extent, are responsive to player arousal states and are capable of inducing the desired level of arousal.

Work proceeds on this but one of the questions fundamental to this research is that of presence in virtual environments. (With the term 'presence' I follow Slater (2002, 2003), whom I discuss further below, in distinguishing between that and the term 'immersion'. Presence is the feeling of being within a space in which there is potential to act. It is subjective whereas immersion is objective and relates to the potential of the sensory technologies of the virtual environment to facilitate presence.) As regards my specific interests, if the audio system of a game's virtual environment can more closely track and respond to player arousal states, if not their emotional states, through the correct assessment of incoming psycho-physiological data and the appropriate processing of audio, then does this enhance the player's potential to feel present in the game world? It is precisely the relationship between sound and presence that I explore in this chapter by proposing the idea that presence derives mainly from the perception of sound in the context of a space whether that space is actual or virtual.

## The theoretical grounding

### *The standard definition(s) of sound and its inconsistencies*

In the 19th-century textbook *On Sound* (Tyndall, 1867), a work heavily indebted to von Helmoltz's *Die Lehre von den Tonempfindungen* published four years earlier and a justly celebrated part of the canon of modern acoustics, are found the following statements in close succession in the opening pages: 'It is the motion imparted to this, the *auditory nerve*, which, in the brain, is translated into sound'; (providing an analogy of balls in a row knocking into each other as a result of energy imparted from the first) 'thus is sound conveyed from particle to particle through the air'; and (describing how this motion causes the tympanic membrane to vibrate, such vibration being transmitted along the auditory nerve to the brain) 'the vibrations are translated into sound' (pp. 2–4).

Although Tyndall was an eminent physicist, renowned among other achievements for his work on infrared radiation, the greenhouse effect of the earth's atmosphere and the scattering of light by impurities in gases and liquids (an effect that bears his name), one could forgive such obvious imprecision and inconsistency by arguing that he was writing a popularised account of sound for a broad audience and that this was an early work in the field of modern acoustics.

Perhaps less forgivable are the incoherence and outright incomprehensibility of the definition of sound to be found in the *Acoustical Terminology* section of the American National Standard (ANSI/ASA) 2013 update. Here, sound is either: '(a) Oscillation in pressure, stress, particle displacement, particle velocity etc., propagated in a medium with internal forces (e.g., elastic or viscous) or the superposition of such propagated oscillation' or '(b) Auditory sensation evoked by the oscillation described in (a)' (American National Standard, 2013). Additionally, the following footnote to the definition is given: 'Not all sounds evoke an auditory sensation, e.g., ultrasound or infrasound. Not all auditory sensations are evoked by sound, e.g., tinnitus.' What is interesting about the definition is that there are two definitions provided (with in-built vagueness furnished through the use of 'etc.'). More interesting, though, is the footnote when viewed through the lens of the definition(s). With some substitution of terminology from the definition, the footnote can be restated as: 'Not all sounds evoke a sound ... Not all sounds are evoked by sound' and this can be further reduced and rephrased as: 'Some sounds evoke sounds.' While I am always delighted to find evidence of creative and pataphysical thinking within physics and the natural sciences more generally, there are so many more examples of the incoherence provided here (see, for instance, others provided by Pasnau (1999) and in the book *Sonic Virtuality*), that it could lead one to doubt the soundness of the foundations of acoustics.[1]

I leave the final word to an acoustician colleague who, when asked to clarify the wording of the ANSA/ASA definition provided above, gave the following response: '[the] definition [is] out of scope for most of the purposes I know [the definition] is only operational for some purposes ... It is therefore necessary to use domain-specific definitions.'[2] The conclusion to be drawn from this is that the standard definition(s) of sound is unsound. Thus, if one really wishes to get to grips with the study, design and use of sound, one must provide an alternative and more sound definition. More specific definitions of sound qualities, for instance those of timbre, also lack consistency (see Reuter and Siddiq, this volume).

## *Sonic virtuality*

The definition of sound we give in *Sonic Virtuality* is: 'Sound is an emergent perception that arises primarily in the auditory cortex and that is formed through spatio-temporal processes in an embodied system.' To expand upon this briefly, and stressing the main points that will be of interest to this chapter, sound in our conception is a perception dependent entirely or partly on cognition (therefore, it does not necessarily require sensation) and this perception is an enactive process centred on the auditory cortex (the cross-modal focus of sound-centred cognitive and (optionally) sensory activity). As an emergent process, sound unfolds over time, involving a spatiality that may derive from external stimuli but also a spatiality forming part of the sound itself and thus sound as a perception is indivisible from a system comprising brain, body and environment.

From this, a number of assertions arise of which the most pertinent to the chapter are: (a) the act of perceiving sound does not necessarily require sound waves; (b) imagined sound (auditory or aural imagery) is sound; (c) sound as a perception emerges and is actualised from the *sonic aggregate*, the virtual cloud of potential (to use Deleuzian terminology) comprising sensory stimuli (optional), moods, memories and experience, knowledge and reason, and elements of sensory and perceptual processes that are not sonic; and (d) we cognitively offload the location of sound onto the wider environment that is part of our embodied mind and this active location of sound is a significant part of the process of locating our selves in space and, indeed, might be the main route to accomplishing this. Of these assertions, the last I expand upon further below because of its relevance to presence.

There are clearly some significant differences between the concept of sonic virtuality and the standard view(s) of sound. In the first instance, and this is perhaps the most striking difference, in sonic virtuality sound is a perception as opposed to being a sound wave. We are not the first, even in modern times, to suggest that sound is something other than a sound wave. The Ancient Greek philosopher Democritus proposed that sound was a stream of particles (an idea that has gained a new lease of life in the quantum physics concept of the phonon) and various modern theorists have proposed other ideas such as sound as event and sound as property of an object (see various writings in the anthology *Sounds and Perception*, Nudds and O'Callaghan, 2009). In our view, sound as a perception does not require a sound wave and, therefore, regarding the concept of imagined sound, such perception is actually sound. In sonic virtuality, sound emerges as a perception from the sonic aggregate whereas, in the standard view of sound, sound exists either in the medium or as a sensation in the auditory system; this sonic aggregate consists of a number of elements of cognition and cross-modal perception and may optionally include sensations such as those produced by sound waves. Importantly for the idea presented in this chapter concerning the relationship between sound and presence, another significant difference revolves around the localisation of sound. In the standard view, the localisation of sound is the localisation of the sound wave source; that is, the locating of, in the sense of finding, the origin of the sound wave (the vibrating object) in external-to-self space. In sonic virtuality, that locating is not a finding but an active placing of internally perceived sound at a certain location within space (whether actual or virtual). This is the cognitive offloading of sound onto the environment that plays an important role in our locating our self within and, ultimately, the incorporation of our self into that environment. This location might be the vibrating source of any sound waves forming part of the sonic aggregate but it could equally be a different location as can be observed in the cross-modal effect of synchresis (Chion, 1994) in the cinema – wherever it cognitively makes sense to locate (place) that sound in the environment in relation to self (see Fahlenbrach, this volume).

## *Localising sound*

In *Sonic Virtuality*, Garner and I made the claim that the localisation of sound, far from being the process of the location of a sound wave source in space through the sensation and perception of the sound wave, is in fact the act of locating, that is, placing, sound within that space. This is a subtle distinction that, nevertheless, has importance to my idea concerning sound's relationship to presence. I therefore devote this section of the chapter to a short discussion of localisation and begin by briefly reviewing some of the answers provided in the literature to the question 'where is sound?' I then equally briefly survey some audiology localisation experiments before moving onto the concept of the localisation of sound encapsulated within the theory of sonic virtuality. Throughout, it is necessary to keep a close grip on precisely what meanings and concepts (and, therefore, perceptual worldview) lie behind the word 'sound'.

Casati and Dokic (2005) usefully provide a substantial discussion of a range of thinking concerning the location of sound and suggest that a number of theories of sound *per se* can be grouped according to where that theory claims the location of sound is. Thus, there are spatial theories of sound and there are aspatial theories. The latter, aspatial theories are more uncommon but, among their proponents is Strawson (1959) who argues that spatial concepts of direction (e.g., to the right of, below, behind) and magnitude (e.g., further, closer) 'have no intrinsically auditory significance ... A purely auditory concept of space ... is an impossibility' (pp. 65–66). According to Strawson, who rejects phenomenological evidence to the contrary as being caused by non-auditory sensory experience, sounds are therefore located nowhere in space.

Spatial theories, according to Casati and Dokic (2005), can be grouped into three categories: proximal, medial and distal. Proximal theories of sound suggest that sound itself is located as a sensation within the listener's auditory system or is located where the listener is (that is, it is not necessarily defined as a sensation). Such views account for a number of phenomena such as some forms of tinnitus and the experience of changes in the heard sound (not solely changes in intensity) as the listener's distance to the sound wave source varies. Medial theories concerning the location of sound are strongly linked to the definition of sound as a sound wave, a definition that is one of the acoustical definitions of sound (American National Standard, 2013). Such views of the location of sound maintain that sound exists in the medium between the sounding object and the listener.

Distal theories on the location of sound are typically argued for on the basis of our experience of the world around us. They are usually, then, phenomenological accounts suggesting that sound is located where the sound source is because that is where we experience sound to be. In other words, I hear birdsong outside my window, I can pan sound from one loudspeaker to the other. Our experience of sounds is that they are external to us and at a distance and they are not in themselves moving (thus sound, in these theories, is normally described as a form of event or property of the sounding object that then gives rise to the sound wave). However, in our everyday language, we appear quite content to use phrases such as 'the sounds passing under my window'. While, on the face of it, this appears to imply that we have a conception of sound as mobile and travelling in some direction relative to us, this is actually an example of conflation of sound wave with sound source. This confusion is also something that is found within the field of acoustics. Pasnau (1999) provides an example drawn from a textbook on the physiology and psychology of hearing:

> your auditory system ... in many everyday situations, is presented with an acoustic waveform made up from a mixture of sounds originating from a variety of sources. In the space of a few seconds these sounds might include a number of different people speaking, a car passing, music from next door's radio, a door slamming, and the wind whistling through a crack in the window. (Darwin and Carlyon, cited in Pasnau, 1999, pp. 318–319)

A number of audiological experiments have investigated sound localisation. In these studies, sound localisation refers to the subjects' abilities to locate the sound source, that is, the object from where the sound wave originates. The subjects of these experiments are often human (e.g., Hofman, Van Riswick and Van Opstal, 1998) but some test other species such as ferrets (e.g., Kacelnik, Nodal, Parsons and King, 2006) or owls (e.g., Knudsen and Knudsen, 1989) and so one must be careful of inferring too much about human sound localisation from the latter experiments. Due to the assumption that the subjects' binaural hearing underlies the ability to correctly localise sound, such experiments typically involve altering this hearing such that it becomes monaural. I have discussed the results elsewhere (e.g., Grimshaw and Garner, 2015) but the conclusion to be drawn from this is that the brain is able to adapt to the monaural condition after a short period of time and so re-learn the localisation of sound. Furthermore, when binaural hearing is re-established, the localisation of sound under this normal condition is not impaired. The overriding conclusion, though, is that these experiments concern the localisation of the sound wave and the direction from source to listener that the sound wave travels in; the 'correct' localisation of sound that the experiments are designed to test against is the locating of the sound wave source and the function of binaural hearing, according to the design of these experiments, is precisely that mode of localisation of sound.

There are, however, many instances in the human hearing experience, particularly in the modern world, where we have adapted to technical artefacts by 'incorrectly' localising the sound source (that is, according to the audiological definition, incorrectly localising the sound wave source) while 'correctly' (in perceptual terms) localising the sound as an event or an object. Indeed, one could argue that it was the advent of mechanical and electrical means of audio recording and reproduction at the close of the 19th century, a separation of source and listener over time and space that Schafer (1994) terms 'schizophonia', that led to the regular occurrence of this mode of localisation such that it has almost become the norm in many societies and groups of listeners. Such experiences typically include those involving cross-modality especially those forms of cross-modal perception concerning vision and hearing, experiences such as those found in the cinema, a cross-modality of vision and hearing that Chion (1994) terms 'synchresis'. Synchresis also takes place in other media, such as computer games, and the effect can be observed in other situations such as ventriloquism (thus, in psychoacoustics, it is known as the 'ventriloquism effect' (e.g., Warren, Welch and McCarthy, 1981)). In these cases, sound waves do not originate from where the sound is perceived to be. That is, audio technology (or, more rarely, oral dexterity) allows for Schafer's schizophonic split between sound wave source and perceived sound source; watching a film, sound is located with vision as a single perceptual event on the screen despite the fact that the loudspeakers are positioned away from the locus of the film's visual narrative.

In the theory of sonic virtuality, the assertion is made that the localisation of sound is an active localisation in which the listener places sound within the environment. Conceptually, this is accounted for by the view that sound is not a sound wave but an emergent perception arising within the brain, where the brain is part of a larger system comprising brain, body and environment (for a brief and critical introduction to such thinking as found within the concept of embodied cognition, see Wilson, 2002). There are a number of reasons for making this assertion, several of which are drawn from the summaries given above.

First, it is an idea that somewhat follows distal theories of sound in that it locates sound where we perceive the sound to be in the environment. This follows the everyday phenomenology of sound in that we regularly use terms such as 'the sound is coming from over there' or 'the sound outside my window is the trilling of cicadas'. Where it differs significantly from distal theories of sound is that it does not suggest that the sound source is the source of any sound waves (because sound arises in the brain) and it requires the active agency of the listener to locate (place) the sound. This agency may be conscious or subconscious as when we either cast around for the source of a sound wave on which to locate the sound or when we automatically make assumptions about the environment in which we are situated based on the sounds we perceive (and this includes visually hidden parts of that environment).

Second, the audiological evidence and the evidence of our synchretic experiences in cinemas suggests that we are able to shift the position of the sound source away from the location of the sound wave source to where it makes sense for the sound to be located.

### *Presence and immersion*

As with definitions of sound, there is some debate over the definition of presence and, in particular, there is disagreement over the terminological relationship between presence and immersion. This occasionally leads to conflicting and confusing use of the two terms in the literature. Equally as with sound, I do not have the space here to debate all possible definitions of presence and immersion and the terms' usages in the literature and so I limit myself to a brief discussion of those definitions that are useful to my idea and where I feel there is broad agreement.

Concerning presence, this broad agreement revolves around the feeling of being in some world or environment. 'Presence is the *feeling* of being in an external world' according to Waterworth and Waterworth (2014); 'Presence arises from active awareness of our embodiment in a present world around us' and this feeling of being present 'distinguishes the self from the nonself' (pp. 589–590). Furthermore, these authors state that mediated presence, as in the case of virtual environments, is 'fundamentally the same as natural presence' (p. 589). The frustratingly vague terms 'feeling' and 'sense' (a mood, a sensation, a perception, an illusion, a hallucination?) are common to many definitions and descriptions of presence. IJsselsteijn, Freeman and de Ridder (2001) quote a 1980 Marvin Minsky paper describing telepresence as the 'sense of being there' and define presence as the 'feeling of "being there", in the world' (p. 180). Slater (2002) uses the same definition for presence in virtual environments and later expands upon this by stating that presence is 'the extent to which the unification of simulated sensory data and perceptual processing produces a coherent 'place' that you are 'in' and in which there may be the potential for you to act' (Slater, 2003, p. 2).

Slater, in particular, is keen to distinguish between immersion and presence; the degree of immersiveness of a virtual environment can be objectively measured according to the degree of 'fidelity [of sensory stimuli] in relation to their real-world sensory modalities' while presence is subjective and 'a human reaction to immersion' (2003, pp. 1–2). For Slater, then, there is a direct equivalence between degree of immersiveness of a virtual environment and level of presence attained in that environment; to increase presence, improve the simulation of real-world stimuli and this is something IJsselsteijn et al. (2001) also claim when they state that the illusion of 'being there' in a virtual environment is enhanced by 'more accurate reproductions and/or simulations of reality' (p. 180). Contrasting this distinction between the terms presence and immersion is the use of immersion as a synonym for presence. This is particularly prevalent in the literature on computer games. As an example, Brown and Cairns (2004) provide three levels of immersion from engagement to engrossment to total immersion; regarding the latter, they unequivocally state: 'Total immersion is presence' and it is an 'experience' (pp. 2–3). Similarly, Ermi and Mäyrä (2005) state that immersion is part of the gameplay experience and it 'means becoming physically or virtually a part of the experience itself' (p. 3).

I myself have in the past used the term immersion as a synonym for presence when writing about computer game sound (e.g., Grimshaw, 2008; 2012), but, for the purposes of this chapter, I prefer to keep Slater's distinction between the two terms, although I do not agree with the direct equation made between degree of immersiveness/realism and degree of presence attained. First, the sliding scale of levels of presence implied by the equation does not appear to agree with the definitions of presence provided above. One is either embodied or 'in' a place or not; one is either here or there and cannot be in two worlds at once (see, however, Waterworth and Waterworth, 2014, for a discussion of *blended realities* mixing physical and virtual worlds, although, for me, this is still being wholly, or not, present in another environment). Second, presence and immersion (as a synonym for presence) are reported even in the most unrealistic virtual environments (something Slater (2002) himself acknowledges when he suggests the mind is capable of filling in the gaps in a poor simulation and hence users reporting that they feel present even in such environments). Some evidence for this may be found in audiological experiments (e.g., Hoshiyama, Gunji and Kakigi,

2001; Hughes et al., 2001; Kraemer, Macrae, Green and Kelley, 2005; King, 2006) where auditory imagery in the brain can be induced in the expectation of audio stimuli, when there are in fact none (such as watching the 'silent' image of a hammer falling onto an anvil). This is one of the reasons why, in sonic virtuality terms, we treat such imagination as sound no less than that sound perceived in the presence of sound waves.

Such technological determinism is likewise dismissed by Calleja (2014) who argues that, 'while high-fidelity systems are an important part of enhancing the intensity of an experience, they do not in themselves create a sense of presence' (p. 225). In favouring the term 'incorporation' in preference to either presence or immersion when discussing virtual environments such as computer games, Calleja suggests that 'incorporation occurs when the game world is present to the player while simultaneously the player is present ... to the virtual environment' (p. 232). This idea has some parallels to the sentiment expressed by Waterworth and Waterworth (2014) that we are on the cusp of a new way of being conscious as a 'virtual other body is incorporated (literally) into our sense of self' (p. 390). Calleja also argues for the role of player interpretation and agency in the incorporation of the player into the virtual environment (p. 225) and this, I think, bears similarity to the sonic virtuality assertion expressed above that the agency of the listener is required to locate (place) sound.

Slater (2002) introduces the idea that presence may (also?) be thought of 'as a perceptual mechanism for selection between alternate hypotheses' as an analogue to the idea (found in some areas of perceptual theory) that perception is the act of selecting between (visual) hypotheses (p. 435). Underlying the idea I present is the reversal of that notion – that presence arises out of the selection of one hypothesis from competing hypotheses and that presence is the end result of (in the main) sonic perception – but I need to provide one more section on perceptual hypotheses before I can proceed to setting out and arguing for that idea.

## *Reaching out to the world*

In a 2013 article, Andy Clark argues for a model of perception in which perception 'is the successful prediction of the current sensory signal using stored knowledge of the world' (pp. 1–2). This active self-prediction model, according to Clark, works through expectation (the prediction via stored knowledge) and the formation of hypotheses that are models of 'the distal elements and their typical modes of interaction' (p. 9) and that attempt to explain the current sensory input. This rolling generation of hypotheses about the external world proceeds from coarse hypotheses to fine hypotheses until that hypothesis is selected that best fits the current sensory situation. Such a perceptual process involves the 'Bayesian estimation of distal properties and features [and] explains why perception, although carried out by the brain, cannot help but reach out to a distal world' (p. 1).

## Presence through sound

The active self-prediction model of the generation of best-fit hypotheses has been gaining ground in the cognitive sciences as a means to explain perception and Clark cites a similar model applied to speech processing suggested in 2011 by Poeppel and Monahan. This model may be roughly paraphrased as: extract acoustic features of speech, elicit hypotheses about the classes of sound, synthesise potential sound class sequences from these hypotheses, test these sequences against the audio stimulus and re-hypothesise and re-synthesise if necessary, then extract and activate best hypothesis.

Clark's work is to do with the question of how we gain knowledge about the world and is not specifically directed towards presence. The generation and selection of hypotheses, though, has been suggested as being of relevance to presence by others (although there is clearly a link between knowledge of a world and presence in that world). I have mentioned one instance above where Slater (2002) suggests that the feeling of presence is itself the mechanism for selecting between visual hypotheses. Similarly, Brenton, Gillies, Ballin and Chatting (2005), building upon Slater's ideas, argue that the phenomenon of the 'Uncanny Valley'[3] results from a superimposition of hypotheses where doubt about the humanness of the character in the virtual environment precludes the selection of the hypothesis: 'The Uncanny Valley response correlates to a mismatch or break in presence: cues indicating believability and realism clash with cues indicating falsehood' (p. 6).

Interestingly, Brenton and colleagues go on to hypothesise that the sensitivity to falsehood cues is increased when the realism of the virtual character is increased. This appears to contradict Slater's and others' argument (given above) that the degree of presence attained in a virtual environment is directly proportional to the level of the realism of the output of the immersive technologies used to create that environment. Here, the suggestion is that the feeling of presence in the environment (the mechanism leading to the selection of the appropriate hypothesis) cannot be achieved under conditions of increased realism. A 2011 publication I co-authored suggested that the notion of the Uncanny Valley was better replaced with the concept of an 'Uncanny Wall' (Tinwell, Grimshaw and Williams, 2011). Here, it was argued 'that increased habituation with the technology used in the attempt to create realistic, human-like characters only serves to draw a viewer's attention to differences from the human norm' (p. 328). Although here is not the place, it would be interesting in future to attempt to draw a parallel between presence and the Uncanny Valley/Wall that looks at our attitudes towards increasing sophistication of simulations of reality; it may be that we find ourselves confronted by a 'presence wall' in virtual environments.

## Sound and presence

I am now in the position of being able to present and argue for the idea at the heart of this chapter: that presence derives mainly from the perception of sound. This is sound as an emergent perception and the presence that derives from it is not only presence in virtual environments but also presence in real-world, everyday environments. (While I accept the role of vision and other modalities, among my reasons for emphasising the primacy of hearing particularly over vision in the attainment of presence is the fact that hearing is an omnidirectional modality and thus, in terms of Cartesian or analytic geometry, hearing is more closely mapped to space than vision is. For thoughts on the relationship between hearing and smell in the context of presence, see Grimshaw and Walther-Hansen (2015), and there are a number of papers dealing with presence and haptics including Reiner and Hecht (2009).) I begin by summarising as a list the main building blocks, as presented above, that comprise the framework underlying this idea.

- Sound is a perception in an embodied system comprising brain, body and environment. Sound perception is part of the process of 'reaching out to the world' and is rooted in the generation of multiple stimulus hypotheses concerning the relationship between incoming sensory stimuli. Such generation is an attempt to make sense of these stimuli; perception is achieved upon selection of a best-fit hypothesis.
- This sound perception emerges and is actualised from a sonic aggregate, a virtual cloud of potential, consisting of elements of knowledge and reason, memory and experience, mood and emotion, non-sound-based cognition and perception and, optionally, sensory stimuli from sound and/or non-sound modalities.
- We consciously or subconsciously localise sound by placing it into the environment, ascribing to objects and events distally located in that environment the property of sound source. Thus, the location of sound in the environment is not necessarily the same location as that where the sound wave originates from even if that sound wave forms part of the sonic aggregate.
- The localisation of sound requires agency and is part of the process of actualisation of sound from the sonic aggregate which makes use of knowledge and experience of the current or similar environments.
- Sound is placed in the environment where it makes cognitive sense to locate it; this is a form of cognitive offloading and creates, or designs in the Normanesque sense, an environmental affordance (see Windsor, this volume).
- Presence is a feeling that 'distinguishes self from nonself' and it thus creates a space in which to be that is also a space for action.
- Within a virtual environment such as a computer game, presence may be seen as an incorporation of the player within that environment.

How, then, do I make use of this framework to argue for the idea that presence derives mainly from the perception of sound? To illustrate how this works, I take an example from a typical first-person shooter computer game. The computer game is taken as an illustrative example because it is a very widespread form of media and, in first-person games, it is a form of media using immersive technologies to facilitate presence in the games' worlds. First-person shooter games present me with a first-person perspective onto the game world where I sit in front of a screen in which my character's arms, clutching a weapon, recede into the game's visual environment. This environment is dynamically generated by the game engine and uses artistic perspective and parallax to create the illusion of a visual three-dimensionality in which I can navigate my character. In conjunction with this, using headphones or loudspeakers, I am at the centre of a soundscape comprising sound waves typically generated from the game engine's audio samples and that are, in modern first-person shooter game engines, processed in real-time with filtering, reverberation and three-dimensional positioning to match the objects, events, physical spaces and materials in the game. All this processing adapts according to my character's position in relation to these elements; I am not only a first-person spectator but also a first-person auditor.

Now begins a process of synchresis as the game starts. Assuming I am wearing headphones, the sound waves generated by the game engine have their origin directly to the sides of my ears. I am therefore, cognitively speaking, presented with two fundamental hypotheses as to where the sound sources should be: are they located at my ears or located somewhere else such as on the screen in front of me? As I am a thoroughly mediatised individual, I use my experience of media such as films and computer games to locate sounds on activity I see taking place on the screen and that relate to events within the game world (cf. Chion, 1994). This locating of sound on the screen is part of the actualisation of sound as it emerges from the sonic aggregate. This actualisation involves other hypotheses put forward to make sense of the auditory and visual (and possibly tactile) sensory stimuli I am receiving (cf. Clark. 2013). Could that particular sound wave I sense right now be connected to what looks like an explosion to my right in the game world and in the distance, or is it connected to my recent action (as a player rather than the character) that has initiated the visual sequence unfolding in front of me that indicates that my mouse click has fired the rifle that my character's arms are gripping? I have a hypothesis in the latter possibility that can make use of the convergence of auditory, visual and tactile stimuli and I have experience of such convergence from both this game and elsewhere; this hypothesis, therefore, is the best-fit hypothesis and so the sound is located at my character's rifle rather than to some other event or a vibrating object close to my ear.

The scenario presented above is a simplified example of the process of locating, that is, placing sound on various elements of an environment. In order to explain sound's role in the attainment of presence in such environments, I need to take it a little further. In the three-dimensional virtual environments of first-person perspective computer games, while sounds can be located on events taking place in the game world that are visually presented on the screen, I can also locate them on other events that are not thus visually represented and therefore take place in parts of the world beyond the limiting frame of the screen. If there are no events to see on which it makes sense to locate sounds – my knowledge of typical environments allows for the rejection of hypotheses suggesting that sound must be located within my visual field because there are potential sound sources visible – then I can locate sound outside my visual field. Thus, I hypothesise that sounds are located on a source within the game world that cannot be seen and so must be, as this is the likely situation in such games, either to one or the other side or behind my character. If I perceive the sound of footsteps then I can locate them behind and to the left of my character in the game world with the additional aid of a sound wave intensity differential at my ears (Interaural Intensity Differences – see, for example, Howard and Angus (1996)). Such intensity cues (alternatively, delay cues depending on the spatial audio system used by the game engine) are less reliable for locating sound when delivered through headphones than through surround sound loudspeakers, but are still useful as approximating components of the sonic aggregate, allowing for the generation of initial and coarse hypotheses.

In addition, therefore, to 'reaching out to the world' visually displayed in front of me, the hypothesising of potential stimulus models is also a way of reaching out to, of probing and testing, the world I cannot (yet) see. By this method, I situate my game character and, by extension, my self, within the virtual world of the game. By locating sounds distally in all directions within that environment, I distinguish between my self at the centre of the environment and what is not my self elsewhere in the environment. The agency I employ in locating sound by reaching out to the world allows for my incorporation in that world and thus I feel present in the space of the virtual environment.

The idea presented in this chapter begs a number of questions, two of which I will deal with here. First, as an explanation of presence in virtual environments such as computer games, can it also explain presence in real-world environments such as the room I sit in right now? The short answer is yes. As with a three-dimensional computer game world, I have a limited field of vision but an omnidirectional field of audition. Not only, then, can I locate sound on objects and events I can see using knowledge gained from past experience, I can also reach out to the invisible world behind me and the part of my environment that is occluded from my sight by structures such as doors and walls. In this way, I locate my self in the physical world by distally locating sound, sketching a three-dimensional space in which I have the potential to act and from which I can paint a fuller picture should I choose to turn around or to explore.

Second, I must ask: if, as I argue, sound is the main contributing factor to the feeling of presence, is it possible to be present using only vision? To this, too, I would answer yes but it is a limited presence, limited to that part of the environment that can be seen. I would speculate that, in the same way our brains adapt in localising sound waves under experimental conditions of monaural hearing, non-hearing humans likewise adapt and make use of strategies different from hearing humans in order to attain the feeling of presence. As I note below, there is an evolutionary and survival imperative to feel present in an environment and, as the theorists surveyed above inform us, it is presence that produces the place in which there is potential to act (e.g., Slater, 2003).

Before I conclude, there is one more issue I wish to deal with and this is the question of precisely when a hypothesis is selected and how this leads to the emergence of sound from the sonic aggregate. In an essay on visual perception, Brian Massumi (2014) uses Deleuze's concept of the virtual cloud of potential to explain how it is that we see the white triangle in the 'Kanizsa triangle' illusion (Figure 15.1).

He explains the 'popping-out' of the triangle as the result of tension being released from within the cloud: 'The pressure is unsustainable. Something has to give' (p. 62). Massumi gives as the cause of the release of this tension 'a force field of emergence' (p. 62) but does not take this any further. Tom Garner and I were influenced by Massumi's example when writing *Sonic Virtuality*; the sonic aggregate is the virtual cloud from which sound 'pops out'. Sound emerges when a best-fit hypothesis is selected but this selection occurs after a process of refinement of hypotheses and this takes time – theoretically, the process could comprise infinite refinements aiming for that hypothetical model that precisely matches the 'modes of interaction' between distal elements that Clark (2013) describes. Organisms do not, however, possess infinite time. Such hypothetical processes are therefore

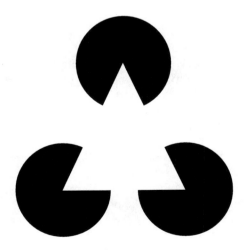

*Figure 15.1* A Kanizsa triangle.

time-pressured processes. One of the principles of embodied cognition informs us that cognition is time-pressured (e.g., Wilson, 2002) while Waterworth and Waterworth (2014) suggest that presence is driven by survival (more time-pressure) and is developed through evolution. Thus, I would speculate that the need to perceive sound in order to attain presence in the present surroundings is time-pressured and that it is this time-pressure that is the 'force of emergence' that drives the emergence of sound and so this time-pressure leads to the selection of a best-I-can-do-under-the-constraints hypothetical model despite the fact that, with a more leisurely time span, the perfect hypothesis might be available.

Such a time-pressured model might account for various observed anomalous phenomena such as the McGurk Effect. In a version of this well-known effect (another reason to discard the standard definition of sound as a sound wave), a video is recorded of someone pronouncing the syllable 'baa' and then pronouncing the syllable 'faa'. When the audio recording of 'baa' is superimposed on the video recording of 'faa', listeners always perceive 'faa' despite the use of the audio clip 'baa'. One could argue that time-pressure is *not* then an issue in the perception of sound as listeners have all the time in the world to listen carefully and then to re-listen. However, I would argue that we are evolutionarily attuned to 'pop out' sound in as short a time as possible (because sound is the main factor in the attainment of presence), and so make use of all components of the sonic aggregate including the visual cue of the person enunciating 'faa'. The time-pressure is thus inescapable and we cannot help but get it wrong, particularly where the scenario does not require sonic attendance to the surrounding environment but rather a visual mode of attending where we can, and are invited to, focus on the articulation of the mouth.

## Conclusions

In this chapter I have presented and argued for the idea that presence derives mainly from the perception of sound. This is presence in both virtual environments such as computer games and in real-world environments. I used a conceptual framework derived from the theory of sonic virtuality — that sound is an emergent perception — and expanded it to include the notion that presence is the feeling of being in a space in which there is potential to act and that we create this space through the locating of sound, that is, the placing of sound, out into the environment. At the same time, I explained the emergence of sound as a perception through the theory that perception is a matter of modelling incoming sensory input (both sound wave-based and otherwise) and then selecting the best-fit hypothesis. The generation of these sonic hypotheses is driven by the evolutionary requirement to attain presence and thus our locating of sound into the environment is a means of 'reaching out into the world', distinguishing self from nonself and thus achieving presence and the ability to act in that space.

## Notes

1 This is perhaps harsh. But I do think that acousticians are mistaken in believing they are studying sounds; they are in fact studying sound waves (which are different phenomena).
2 Personal email communication, 1 September 2015.
3 Briefly, an idea proposed in 1970 that there comes a point in the pursuit of human-like appearance for robots, near where the robot is almost indistinguishable from humans, at which the human observer experiences negative, uncomfortable feelings.

## References

American National Standard. (2013). *Acoustical terminology*. ANSI/ASA, S1.1–2013.
Brenton, H., Gillies, M., Ballin, D., and Chatting, D. (2005). The Uncanny Valley: Does it exist and is it related to presence? In *Proceedings of Human–Animated Characters Interaction*, 5 September, Edinburgh. Retrieved from http://bespokevr.com/pdfs/brenton_UncannyValley_2005.pdf.
Brown, E., and Cairns, P. (2004, 24–29 April). A grounded investigation of game immersion. Presented at *Human Factors in Computing Systems*, Vienna.
Calleja, G. (2014). Immersion in virtual worlds. In M. Grimshaw (Ed.), *The Oxford handbook of virtuality* (pp. 222–236). New York: Oxford University Press.
Casati, R., and Dokic, J. (2005). Sounds. In *Stanford Encyclopedia of Philosophy*. Retrieved from http://plato.stanford.edu/entries/sounds.
Chion, M. (1994). *Audio-vision: Sound on screen* (C. Gorbman, Trans). New York: Columbia University Press.
Clark, A. (2013). Expecting the world: Perception, prediction, and the origins of human knowledge. *Journal of Philosophy, CX*(9), 469–496.
Ermi, L., and Mäyrä, F. (2005). Fundamental components of the gameplay experience: Analysing immersion. Presented at *Changing Views: Worlds in Play*, 16–20 June, Toronto.
Garner, T. A., and Grimshaw, M. (2013a). The physiology of fear and sound: Working with biometrics toward automated emotion recognition in adaptive gaming systems. *IADIS International Journal on WWW/Internet, 11*(2).
Garner, T. A., and Grimshaw, M. (2013b). Psychophysiological assessment of fear experience in response to sound during computer video gameplay. *Proceedings of IADIS International Conference Interfaces and Human Computer Interaction, July 22–26* (pp. 45–53). Prague: IADIS.
Grimshaw, M. (2008). Sound and immersion in the first-person shooter. *International Journal of Intelligent Games & Simulation, 5*(1), 119–124.
Grimshaw, M. (2012). Sound and player immersion in digital games. In T. Pinch and K. Bijsterveld (Eds.), *The Oxford handbook of sound studies* (pp. 347–366). New York: Oxford University Press.
Grimshaw, M. (2015). A brief argument for, and summary of, the concept of Sonic Virtuality. *Danish Musicology Online, 2015 Special Edition*. Retrieved from http://www.danishmusicologyonline.dk/arkiv/arkiv_dmo/dmo_saernummer_2015/dmo_saernummer_2015_lyd_musikproduktion_05.pdf.
Grimshaw, M., and Garner, T.A. (2015). *Sonic virtuality: Sound as emergent perception*. New York: Oxford University Press.

Grimshaw, M., and Walther-Hansen, M. (2015). The sound of the smell of my *shoes*. Presented at the *10th Audio Mostly Conference*, 7–9 October, Thessaloniki.

Hofman, P. M., Van Riswick, J. G. A., and Van Opstal, A. J. (1998). Relearning sound localization with new ears. *Nature Neuroscience, 1*(5), 417–421.

Hoshiyama, M., Gunji, A., and Kakigi, R. (2001). Hearing the sound of silence: A magnetoencephalographic study. *NeuroReport, 12*(6), 1097–1102.

Howard, D. M., and Angus, J. (1996). *Acoustics and psychoacoustics*. Oxford: Focal Press.

Hughes, H. C., Darcey, T. M., Barkan, H. I., Williamson, P. D., Roberts, D. W., and Aslin, C. H. (2001). Responses of human auditory association cortex to the omission of an expected acoustic event. *NeuroImage, 13*, 1073–1089.

IJsselsteijn, W. A., Freeman, J., and de Ridder, H. (2001). Presence: Where are we? *Cyberpsychology & Behavior, 4*(2), 179–182.

Kacelnik, O., Nodal, F. R., Parsons, K. H., and King, A. J. (2006). Training-induced plasticity of auditory localization in adult mammals. *PLoS Biology, 4*(4), 0627–0638.

King, A. J. (2006). Auditory neuroscience: Activating the cortex without sound. *Current Biology, 16*(11), 410–411.

Knudsen, E. I., and Knudsen, P. F. (1989). Vision calibrates sound localization in developing barn owl. *Journal of Neuroscience, 9*, 3306–3313.

Kraemer, D. J. M., Macrae, C. N., Green, A. E., and Kelley, W. M. (2005). Musical imagery: Sound of silence activates auditory cortex. *Nature, 434*(158), 158.

Massumi, B. (2014). Envisioning the virtual. In M. Grimshaw (Ed.), *The Oxford handbook of virtuality* (pp. 55–70). New York: Oxford University Press.

Nishimoto, S., Vu, A. T., Naselaris, T., Benjamini, Y., Yu, B., and Gallant, J. L. (2011). Reconstructing visual experiences from brain activity evoked by natural movies. *Current Biology, 21*, 1641–1646.

Nudds, M., and O'Callaghan, C. (Eds) (2009). *Sounds & perception*. Oxford: Oxford University Press.

Pasley, B. N., David, S. V., Mesgarani, N., Flinker, A., Shamma, S. A., and Crone, N. E., et al. (2012). Reconstructing speech from human auditory cortex. *PLoS Biology, 10*(1). Retrieved from http://journals.plos.org/plosbiology/article?id=10.1371/journal.pbio.1001251.

Pasnau, R. (1999). What is sound? *The Philosophical Quarterly, 49*(196), 309–324.

Reiner, M., and Hecht, D. (2009). Behavioral indications of object-presence in haptic virtual environments. *Cyberpsychology & Behavior, 12*(2), 183–186.

Schafer, R.M. (1994). *The soundscape: Our sonic environment and the tuning of the world*. Rochester, VT: Destiny Books.

Slater, M. (2002). Presence and the sixth sense. *Presence, 11*(4), 435–439.

Slater, M. (2003). A note on presence terminology. *Presence Connect, 3*(3). Retrieved from http://publicationslist.org/data/melslater/ref-201/a%20note%20on%20presence%20terminology.pdf.

Strawson, P.F. (1959). *Individuals: An essay in descriptive metaphysics*. London: Methuen.

Thompson, J., Casey, M., and Torresani, L. (2013). Audio stimulus reconstruction using multi-source semantic embedding. Presented at *Neural Information Processing Systems workshop on Machine Learning and Interpretation in Neuroimaging*, 9–10 December, Lake Tahoe, USA.

Tinwell, A., Grimshaw, M., and Williams, A. (2011). The uncanny wall. *International Journal of Arts and Technology, 4*(3), 326–341.

Tyndall, J. (1867). *On sound*. London: Longmans, Green & Co.

Warren, D. H., Welch, R. B., and McCarthy, T. J. (1981). The role of visual-auditory 'compellingness' in the ventriloquism effect: Implications for transitivity among the spatial senses. *Perception & Psychophysics, 30*(6), 557–564.

Waterworth, J.A., and Waterworth, E.L. (2014). Distributed embodiment: Real presence in virtual bodies. In M. Grimshaw (Ed.), *The Oxford handbook of virtuality* (pp. 589–601). New York: Oxford University Press.

Wilson, M. (2002). Six views of embodied cognition. *Psychonomic Bulletin & Review, 9*(4), 625–636.

# Index

3D CGI-technologies 275

abstractive listening 98
acoustic spaces 211–219
acoustic tau 201
acoustics 213–222
active accoustic systems 220–222
active externalism 194
aesthetic computing 103
aesthetics: sonification 90–95, 104–106; subject-position in sonification 100–104
affordances 6, 114–115; Böhm flute 119–122; embodied music cognition 15–16
Ahad, P. 171
AIP (anterior intraparietal part) 175
air piano 78
Albersheim, G. 150, 154–155
ambiguous perception 90
ambisonic mousetrap 203–204
Ambisonix dance nights (University of York) 205
angelism 267
*Aphasia* 268–269
Appel, M. 75
*Applause* 135–136
Applebaum, M. 268
archeoacoustics 196
architecture, accoustics 212–213
Architexture 2 230–231
arms, micromotion 37
artificial environments, music as 193–199
artificial information environments 191
artificial intelligences, music 205–206
artificial sonic pattern 192
Arup Acoustics 223
aspatial theories of sound 284
atonal melodies 180

audiation 182
audio augmented environments, *Parisflâneur* 246–247
AudioLab 229
audiovisual metaphors 131–133, 146–147; sound design of sonic spaces 133–137
audiovisual phenomenal causality 265
auditory cortex, human brain 171–172
auditory looming 201
auditory perception 91
auditory versus visuo-spatial imagery, experiments 180–182
aural detectives 218
auralisation 219
Aures, W. 157
autonomous music 93
avatars 271

Baily, J. 77
Ballin, D. 289
Barbershop chorus 122–125
Barker, R. 116
Bartók, B. 258
beat synchronisation 15
Beghin, T. 216, 218
Belin, P. 171
binaural recording 236–237
binaural room impulse responses (BRIRs) 238–239
binaural synthesis 236–239
biofeedback 280
Bischoff, J. 260
Bjerkestrand, K. A. V. 32
Blauert, J. 236, 252
blend, Barbershop chorus 122–125
blended realities 287
Blesser, B. 119, 218
bodily responses: *Elisabeth's Prayer* 80; musical gestures 76–82;

## Index

self-recognition 80–82; sonification of gestures 80–82; Truslit, A. 78–80
body 2; abstractive listening 98; arms, micromotion 37; auditory cortex, human brain 171–172; brain *see* human brain; cadence, tempo 18–20; dancing 20–23, 74; deafness 198; ear-signals 199–200; embodied music cognition 13–16; everyday listening 92; exercise, empowerment 23–24; expressivity of movement 20–23; extended mind 194; eyes, micromotion 32, 37; feet, micromotion 37; foot tapping 14; head movements 76; hippocampal system 169; knees, micromotion 37; microexpressions 31; microinteraction 44; micro-level 41–42; micromotion 4, 29; microsaccades 32; microsound 42–43; singing, Barbershop chorus 122–125; synchronisation 13; voices, classification of 123–124; walking 20–23
Böhm flute, affordances and constraints 119–122
Boren, B. 213
Bouffard, M. 171, 182
bowling alley lane experiment 204
brain *see* human brain
Bregman, A. 72, 91, 156
Brenton, H. 289
Brereton, J. xiii, 7, 211–234
BRIRs (binaural room impulse responses) 238–239
Brown, C. 260, 262, 287
Buhmann, J. xiii, 13–28
Burger, B. 77
Burtt, H. E. 72

cadence, tempo 18–20
Cadoz, C. 270
Cage, J. 31, 104, 242, 258–259
Cairns, P. 287
Calleja, G. 288
de Campo, A. 98–99
Casati, R. 283–284
causality, NMP (networked music performance) 265, 268–271
causality engine 200
cause and effect, NMP (networked music performance) 264–266
ceremonial music 196
Chafe, C. 260
Chalmers, D. 194

Chatting, D. 289
Chion, M. 133, 285
Choir of St. John's College Cambridge 212
choruses, Barbershop chorus 122–125
CIP (caudal intraparietal part) 175
*Citizen Kane* 134
Clarity 215
Clark, A. 194, 201, 288–289
Clarke, E. F. 76, 90–91, 94
classification of voices 123–124
climatological features 116
Clinton Frame Mennonite Church 225
closed groove 98
closed-loop principle, headphones 239
CMC (cross-modal correspondences) 49; dynamic pitch 59–62; pitch 49–50, 56; pitch, tonality 58; pitch with space and motion 51–55; static pitch 59–62
cocktail party effect mechanisms 201
Cody, F. W. 77
cognition, embodied music cognition 13–16
cognitive casual mapping 201
cognitive mapping 201
cognitive spatial mapping 201
Cohen, S. D. 133
*CO-ME-DI-A* project 274–275
compactness, timbre 156–157
composing: for embodied cognition 200–201; for space 230–231
conceptual models of performance 218–219
Congruence-Association-Model of Cohen 135
consequential sound 100
Constellation Centre 223
constraints: of Böhm flute 119–122; of Twentieth-century recording technologies 196–198
Corballis, M. C. 178
Cording, J. 263
Crooks, J. 220–221
cross-modal correspondences *see* CMC
cross-modal qualities in movies 130
cultural norms, film drama 138–141
Cupchik, G. C. 181
cylinder of sound colours 154–160

dancing 20–23, 74
*Das Weiße Band. Eine deutsche Kindergeschichte* (*The White Ribbon*) 140–141
Davidson, J. W. 76

DAW (digital audio workstation) 279–280
deafness 198
degraded perception 90
Democritus 282
Derkse, W. 101
design: Barbershop chorus 122–125; Böhm flute 119–122; sonic spaces, audiovisual metaphors 133–137; space 125–126
Deutsch, D. 72, 92
digital music interactions (DMIs) 270
digital audio workstation (DAW) 279–280
digital convolution 219
digital VAT 229
dimensions of timbre space 157–160
directional asymmetry 61
discarnetism 267
*Disparate Bodies 2.0* 273
distal theories, sound 284
distance, pitch 53–54
distributed creativity 272
D-Jogger 19
DMIs (digital music interactions) 270
Dokic, J. 283–284
Donders, F. C. 152
Doppler Effect 53
Dowling, W. J. 180
dramas 137
dramaturgy of networked performances 272
dry acoustics 228
dual pathway 171
dummy head microphones 237
dynamic pitch 59–62

earbuds 240
Early Decay Time (EDT) 215
ear-signals 199–200
earth fixed space 170
EBE (European Bridges Ensemble) 264, 273
eco-behavioral science 116–117
ecological psychology 114–118
ecology of a performance 117–118
EDT (Early Decay Time) 215
Eiko and Koma 31
Eitan, Z. xiii–xiv, 49–68
electronic music 258–259
*Elisabeth's Prayer* 79–80
embodied agents 267
embodied cognition 13, 56, 74, 177, 193, 202, 211, 218, 267, 268, 276, 286, 294; composing for 200–201
embodied meanings, filmic spaces 129–131

embodied music cognition 13–16
embodied perception 194
embodiment: human brain 176–182; NMP (networked music performance) 267–268
emotion: natural forces 133; pitch 55–57
empathic listening 98
empowerment 23–24
emulation, embodied music cognition 14–15
entrainment 16–20
environments: artificial environments 193–199; music as 204–205; sensorimotor control 14
Epstein, D. 2, 73
Ermi, L. 287
European Bridges Ensemble (EBE) 264
evaluating sound installation, *Parisflâneur* 248–252
everyday listening 92
exercise, empowerment 23–24
expressivity of movement 20–23
extended mind 194
extended perception 194–195
extrapersonal space 170
eyes, micromotion 32, 37

Fahlenbrach, K. xiv, 6, 129–149
feedback loops 218–219
feet, micromotion 37
Ferrari, L. 245
Field, A. 230
field recordings, *Parisflâneur* 245–246
film drama 137–146
filmic spaces, embodied meanings 129–131
fine arts, mental rotation 179–180
Fishwick, P. A. 100
*Five* 263, 273
Föllmer, G. 263, 270
Fontana, B. 259
foot tapping 14
force of emergence 294
formant areas, timbre 152–154
Foster, N. E. V. 183
frequency change 52
Friberg, A. 76
Fristrup, K. 197–198
Frith, S. 83
Fry, S. 216
Fyans, A.C. 270

Gade, A. C. 217
Gallese, V. 131
Garner, T. 133, 279–280

Garnett, L. 124
Gaver, W. W. 92
gender-related differences, mental rotation 178–179
Gestalt principles 72, 134; audiovisual metaphors 131–133
gestures 70–71; bodily responses 76–82; kinaesthetic imagery 74–76; NMP (networked music performance) 266–267; overview 82–84; spatiality of pitch 71–72; temporal dimensions 73–75
Gibson, J. 114, 118
Gillies, M. 289
Global Village conference 275
Godoy, R. I. 78
Grey, J. 157, 159
Grimshaw, M. xiv, 8, 9, 133, 279–297
Grond, F. 98
Grotto of Jeita 119
Gurevich, M. 270

Haga, E. 78
Hajdu, G. xiv–xv, 8, 257–278
Halpern, A. R. 182
Hanekes, M. 140
Hanslick, E. 70–71
Hassler, M. 179
head movements 76
headphones 252; binaural sound projection 239–240; *Parisflâneur* 247
head-related impulse responses (HRIR) 237–239
hearing oneself 227, 229
hearing others 228
hearing say 99
hearing the hall 228
hearing-as 96–97
hearing-in 96–97
Heft, H. 116
here-perception 201
Hermann, T. 98
high-groove music 22
Hill, D. S. 181
hippocampal system 169
Hirt, E. 262
history of NMP (networked music performance) 258–264
Hogg, B. xv, xvii, 5, 89–109
Hohagen, J. xv, 5, 69–88
*Homo Ludens* 271
*House of Cards* 95
Howard, M. 212
HRIR (head-related impulse responses) 237–239

The Hub 260
Huizinga, J. 271
human brain 168; auditory cortex 171–172; embodiment 176–182; intervals and tones 182–183; overview 183–184; PPC (posterior parietal cortex) 172–176; space 169–170; where system 171–172
human pendulum 32–33
human spatial abilities 177
human spatial hearing 236–237
Huron, D. 58
Hyvarinen, J. 172

identity crisis, film drama 141–146
Idhe, D. 93
illusion, NMP (networked music performance) 268–271
imagery, kinaesthetic imagery 74–76
imagery debate 178
*Imaginary Landscape No. 4* 258–259
immersed in music 203
immersion 286–288
impressions of virtual acoustic space 223–225
improvising musicians 259
incorporation 288
inferior parietal lobule (IPL) 172, 174–175
Initial Time Delay Gap (ITDG) 215
instruments, Böhm flute 119–122
integral time 73
interaction, embodied music cognition 14
intermediate spatial software environments 199–200
internet music performances 260
interval-colour timbre 152
intervals 182–183
inversion 179
IPL (inferior parietal lobule) 172, 174–175
IPS (intraparietal sulcus) 175–176, 183
ITDG (Initial Time Delay Gap) 215

Jackson, M., Super Bowl half-time show 31
Jäncke, L. 177
Japanese Butoh 31
Jensenius, A. R. xv, 29–48, 78
Johnson, V. 36

Kangräume – Situated Usability Evaluation of 3D Audio Interactive Sound Environments, *Parisflâneur* 248–252
Kanizsa triangle 293
Kant, I. 170

Karbusický, V. 265–266
Kato, K. 218
Kawai, K. 218
Keller, P. E. 75
Kim, K. 266–270
Kimball, W. 218–219
kinaesthetic imagery 74–76
Klangfarbe 150
knees, micromotion 37
knowledge, representing 95
Kohler, W. 152
Kosslyn, S. 178
Kraftwerk 259
Kramer, G. 92–93
Krumhansl, C. L. 58–59, 180
Krumhansl sounds 159
Küssner, M. B. 61

La Berge, A. 262
*Laban Movement Analysis* 74–75
LaBelle, B. 267
laboratory set-up, *Parisflâneur* 243–244
Lanier, J. 271
latency 271
lateral position, pitch 53
League and The Hub 259
League of Automatic Music Composers 259
lectio divina (spiritual reading) 101
Leitner, B. 247
Leman, M. xv–xvi, 4, 13–28, 104, 227
Lemke, S. L. 264
Lennox, P. xvi, 7, 8, 191–210, 212
Leow, L. 22
Levine, C. 275
*Licht* 73
LISTEN project 246–247
listening 90, 93, 102–103; abstractive listening 98; empathic listening 98; everyday listening 92; to music 203; musical listening attitudes 97–100; while performing 218
localising sound 283–286
locked into the beat of music *see* synchronisation
Lokki, T. 219
Longair, M. 213
*Lost Highway* 144–146
low-groove music 22
Lynch, D. 144

Macko, K. A. 171
Maconie, R. 104
macro-level perspectives 41–42

Maes, P. J. 78
*The Magnificent Ambersons* 139
Mamoulian, R. 135
Massumi, B. 293
Mäyrä, F. 287
McGill Virtual Acoustic Technology (VAT) 221
McGurk Effect 294
McLuhan, M. 267
MDS (multidimensional scaling) 157
measuring room acoustics 213–215
medial theories, sound 284
Melchior, F. 199
men 182; mental rotation 178–179
mental rotation 177–180
meso-level 29, 41–42
metaphoric atmospheres in sonic spaces of movies 134–137
metaphoric embodiment of cultural norms in film drama 138–141
metaphoric embodiment of identity crisis in sonic spaces of social dram and psycho-drama 141–146
metaphorical conceptualisation 136
metaphors for music 70–71; audiovisual metaphors 131–133
Meyer Sound 225
microexpressions 31
microinteraction 44
micro-level 41–42
micromotion 4, 29; effect of music on 38–41; overview 45–46; performances 44–45; physical and spatial factors influencing micromotion 37–38; standstill *see* standstill
microsaccades 32
microsound 42–43
*MindTrip* 262
Minsky, Marvin 192, 287
MIP (medial intraparietal part) 175
MIR (music information retrieval) 162
mirror system 268
Mishkin, M. 171
model-based sonification 101
*Mondnacht* 79
Mooney, J. 116
Moretti, L. 212
*The Morning Line* 205
motion 2, 73; pitch 55–59
motional character 2
motivation, embodied music cognition 15
movement response, entrainment 18–20
movies *see also* filmic spaces: audiovisual metaphors 131–133; cross-modal

qualities 130; dramas *see* film drama; metaphoric atmosphere in sonic spaces 134–137; metaphoric embodiment 138–146
Mozart effect 177
multidimensional scaling (MDS) 157
multimodal perceptions 2
multimodality 202
Murphy, D.T. 230
music: as an artificial environment 193–199; ceremonial music 196; effect on micromotion 38–41; as an environment 204–205; new technologies 199–200; reasons for existence of 192–193; space and 195–196; spatiality 198; spatially scalable music 203–204
Music in the Global Village conference 264
music information retrieval (MIR) 162
musical artificial intelligences 205–206
musical gestures 69–71; bodily responses 76–82; kinaesthetic imagery 74–76; NMP (networked music performance) 266–267; overview 82–84; spatiality of pitch 71–72; temporal dimensions 73–75
musical listening attitudes 92, 97–100
musical styles, acoustics and 212–213
musical timbre 151
musicians, kinaesthetic imagery 74
music-related body motion 29
Musikpsychologie 70
Mustafa, B. 258

Nancy, J. 99
natural forces 133
network dramaturgies 272
network performances 259–260
*Netze spinnen # Spinnennetze* 264
Neuhaus, C. xvi, 7, 168–188
Neuhaus, M. 240–241, 259
Newton, Sir Isaac 170
NMP (networked music performance) 257, 272–274; CO-ME-DI-A project 274; history of 258–264; performativity 264–272
Nono, L. 275
Norman, D. A. 115
Norwegian Standstill Championship 38–41

Oliveros, P. 260
*On Sound* 281
OpenAir.lib 216

Orlowski, R. 213
*Orpheus Kristall* 263
Oxnard, S. 230

PAC (primary auditory cortex) 171
parameter-mapping sonification 100–101
*Parisflâneur* 235–239, 242–252
Pasnau, R. 284
Pätynen, J. 221, 223
Peirce, C. S. 265
perception 90–91, 288–289; composing for embodied cognition 200–201; multimodal perceptions 2; sound 289–294; spatial perception as embodied place perception 201–202
perception-action theories 74
perceptual significance grading 201
performance ecology 117–118
performance spaces, optimum acoustics for performance spaces 214–216
performances: listening while performing 218; virtual acoustic technology 219–223
performativity, NMP (networked music performance) 264–272
performers, relationships between 229–230
performers' perception: impressions of virtual acoustic space 223–225; of stage acoustics 216–218
performing music in acoustic spaces 216–219
performing in virtual acoustic spaces 223–229
period-synchronisation 16
peripersonal space 131, 170
personal auditory space, *Parisflâneur* 247
personalised performance 229
Peters, D. 98
phase-error correction 17
phase-synchronisation 16
Phillips, K. 181
physical size, pitch 54–55
Piaget, J. 176
pianists, kinaesthetic imagery 75–76
pianos 115
Pinker, S. 192
pitch 49–50; distance and speed 53–54; dynamic pitch 59–62; lateral position 53; motion 57–59; motion and emotion 55–57; physical size 54–55; shape 55; space 57–59; spatiality of pitch 71–72; static pitch 59–62; tonality 57–59; vertical spatial plane 51–52
pitch chroma 182

pitch contour 55
pitch direction 55
pitch height 182
pitch register 55, 60
pitch rise 61
pitch-emotion 56
pitch-laterality mapping 53
pitch-space 56
place perception 194
plausibility, NMP (networked music performance) 268–271
play element of culture 271
Popper, K. 192
Powell, J. 220
PP (planum polare) 182
PPC (posterior parietal cortex) 168–170, 172–176
Pratt, C. C. 2
precedence effects 201
prediction mechanisms 23–24, 271–272
Premack, D. 268
presence 280–281, 286–289; sound and 289–294
primary auditory cortex (PAC) 171
principle of formant areas 153
principle of formant shifting 153
principle of spectral gap skipping 153
principles of timbre 153
proactive predicavores 201
proprioception 173
prototypical sounds 130
PT (planum temporale) 182
Puckette, M. 273
Pylyshyn, Z. 178

QoM (quality of motion) stillness 36–37, 39
quiet standing 30
Quintet.net 260–264

radio 258–259
radio avatars 273
*Radio Music* 273
Rauschecker, J. P. 171
Rauscher, F. 177
Rebelo, P. 272
relationships between performers 229–230
religious buildings, accoustics 212–213
Renaissance churches 212–213
Renaissance polyphony 212
Renard, A. B. 272
Repp, B. H. 77
representations 103; sonification 95–97

resonance 16–17
retrograde 179
retrograde inversion 179
Reuter, C. xvi–xvii, 6, 150–167
reverberant conditions 228
Reverberation Enhancement Systems 220
Reverberation Time (RT60) 214–215
Révész, G. 168, 183
reward 15
rhythmic motion 72
Ringmasters 123
RIR (Room Impulse Response) 213
room acoustic convolution 220
room acoustics, measuring 213–215
round trip times (RTT) 271
RT60 (Reverberation Time) 214–215
RTT (round trip times) 271
Rumori, M. xvii, 8, 235–256
Russolo, L. 242

Sacks, O. 168
Salter, L.-R. 119, 218
Sandell, G. J. 180
scaling music 203–204
scene analysis 72
Schaal, C. 275
Schaeffer, P. 98–99, 245
Schafer, M. 99
Schafer, R. M. 197, 285
Schelling, F. W. J. 180
schizophonia 285
Schönberg, A. 179
Schopenhauer, A. 180
Schroeder, F. 272
Schumann, K.E. 153
Scorsese, M. 142
Scruton, R. 70–71
seeing-as 96–97, 99
seeing-in 99
seeing-that 96–97
Seifert, U. 266–270
self-recognition, bodily responses 80–82
SEMPRE (Society for Education, Music and Psychology Research) xi–xii
sensorimotor control, environment 14
Sergeant, D. C. 180
shape, pitch 55
shape of headphones 239–240
sharpness, timbre 156–157
Shepard, R. N. 178
Shove, P. 77
SID (sonic interaction design) 248
Siddiq, S. xvii, 6, 150–167
side-formants 153

sillon fermé 98
singing, Barbershop chorus 122–125
Siska, Á. 273–274
Slater, M. 287, 288
Sloboda, J. 3
Small, C. 116
Smalley, D. 93
socio-cultural practices 116
sonic aggregate 282, 293
sonic interaction design (SID) 248
sonic interactions 44
sonic spaces: audio visual metaphors in sound design 133–137; metaphoric atmospheres in sonic spaces of movies 134–137; metaphoric embodiment of cultural norms in film drama 138–141; metaphoric embodiment of identity crisis in sonic spaces of social dram and psycho-drama 141–146
sonic virtuality 282–283
sonification 89–91; aesthetics 91–95; aesthetics, overview 104–106; of gestures 80–82; model-based sonification 101; musical listening attitudes 97–100; parameter-mapping sonification 100–101; as representation 95–97; subject-position 100–104
sound 117; acoustic tau 201; acoustics 213–222; archeoacoustics 196; Arup Acoustics 223; aspatial theories of sound 284; atonal melodies 180; audiation 182; bodily responses 78–80; CMC see CMC; consequential sound 100; cylinder of sound colours 154–160; definition of 281–283; distal theories, sound 284; filmic spaces 130; localising sound 283–286; microsound 42–43; pitch 49–62; pitch chroma 182; pitch contour 55; pitch direction 55; pitch height 182; pitch register 55, 60; pitch rise 61; pitch-emotion 56; pitch-laterality mapping 53; pitch-space 56; presence 280–281, 289–294; prototypical sounds 130; spatiality of pitch 71–72; speed, pitch 53–54; static pitch 59–62; tonality 50; tones 182–183
sound art 235, 240–242, 252
sound colour triangle 155
sound events 99
sound installation, *Parisflâneur* 248–252
sound objects 99
SoundLab (Arup) 223

soundscapes, bowling alley lane experiment 204
Sowa, J. F. 95
space 2, 119, 203; acoustic spaces 211–219; Barbershop chorus 122–125; composing for 230–231; extrapersonal space 170; filmic spaces, embodied meanings 129–131; human brain 169–170; impressions of virtual acoustic space 223–225; intermediate spatial software environments 199–200; music and 195–196; overview of designed space in musical performance 125–126; performance spaces, optimum acoustics for performance spaces 214–216; performing music in acoustic spaces 216–219; performing in virtual acoustic spaces 223–229; peripersonal space 131, 170; personal auditory space, *Parisflâneur* 247; pitch 57–59; principle of formant areas 153; religious buildings, accoustics 212–213; room acoustic convolution 220; room acoustics, measuring 213–215; sonic spaces see sonic spaces; vertical spatial plane, pitch 51–52; virtual acoustic environment (VAE) 222–223; performing in 225–229; virtual acoustic spaces, performing in 223–229
Space Builder engine 221
space-emotion 56
spatial distribution, standstill 32–33
spatial imagery abilities 177–178
spatial magnetisation of sound by image 133
spatial music 206
spatial orchestration 196
spatial perception, as embodied place perception 201–202
spatial sounds, as metaphor source domains in sound design 133–134
spatial theories of sound 284
spatial turn 169
spatial working memory 171
spatiality 198
spatiality of pitch 71–72
spatially scalable music 203–204
spatio-kinetic domains 58
spatiotemporal categories 41–42
speech-to-song illusion 92
speed, pitch 53–54

spiritual reading (lectio divina) 101
SPL (superior parietal lobule) 172–174
Spors, S. 199
stage acoustics, performers' perception 216–218
Stahnke, M. 263
standstill 4, 30–38
static pitch 59–62
step length 22
stereo 198
stillness 30; effect of music on micromotion 38–41; quantity of motion 36–37
Straebel, V. 242
Strawson, P.F. 284
Strength (G) 215
stroboscopic motion 72
Stroop paradigm 54
Stumpf, C. 150–153, 182
subject-position 91; sonification 100–104
Sundberg, J. 76
superior parietel lobule (SPL) 172–174
Supper, A. 92–93, 94, 101
surround sound 198–199
Sverm 2 36
Sverm 3 41–45
Sverm project 29–30; performances 44–45
synchresis 6, 285
synchronisation 13, 16–23
Szigetvári, A. 275

Tallis, T. 196
Tanaka, A. 260, 267
*Tannhäuser* 79
*Taxi Driver* 142–144
technology 196–200
telematic performances 259
telepresence, NMP (networked music performance) 271–272
Telharmonium 258
tempo: cadence 18–20; synchronisation 15–16
temporal dimensions 73–75
temporal levels, standstill 33–35
theories, embodied music cognition 13–16
theory of mind 268
Tian, B. 171
timbre 151–160
timbre spaces 6, 150; dimensions of 157–160
time brackets 263
time-pressure 294

timing 71, 73
timing of movement response, entrainment 18–20
Todd, N. P. M. 77
tonal motion 71–72
tonality 50; pitch 57–59
tones 182–183
topographical features of musical settings 116
Tramack, S. 124
transducers 203
triangle of listening 218, 227
Truslit, A. 5, 78–80
Twentieth century recording technologies, constraints of 196–198
Tyndall, J. 281

Ueno, K. 218, 223, 225
Uncanny Valley 289
Uncanny Wall 289
Ungerleider, L. G. 171
unproblematic perception 90

VAD (virtual auditory display), *Parisflâneur* 246–247
VAE (virtual acoustic environment) 222–223; performing in 225–229
Vamp.net 262
Van Dyck, E. xvii, 4, 13–28
Varela, F. J. 266
VAT (McGill Virtual Acoustic Technology) 221
ventriloquism effect 285
vertical spatial plane, pitch 51–52
*Vespers* 196
Vickers, P. xvii–xviii, 5, 89–109
Vienna Symphonic Library (VSL) 159
vigor of movement response, entrainment 20–23
Viola, B. 31
virtual acoustic environment (VAE) 222–223; performing in 225–229
virtual acoustic spaces, performing in 223–229
virtual acoustic technology (VAT) 219–223
virtual auditory display (VAD), *Parisflâneur* 246–247
Virtual Concert Hall 223
Virtual Haydn project 229
virtual hyper-realism 276
virtual reality: NMP (networked music performance) 271–272; *Parisflâneur* 246–247

Virtual Singing Studio (VSS) 222
visio-spatial intelligence 179
visuo-spatial neglect 168
Vocaltone 152
voices, classification of 123–124
von Bismarck, G. 156
von Helmholtz, H. 71, 151, 152
vowel tones 152
vowel-colour, timbre 152
VSL (Vienna Symphonic Library) 159
VSS (Virtual Signing Studio) 222

Walk Mate 19
walking 20–23
Waterworth, E.L. 286, 288
Waterworth, J.A. 286, 288
Weber, G. 150
Welles, O. 138
Wenger V-Room 221

what system 171
where system 171–172
Wii Remote Controllers 273–274
Willaert, A. 196
Williams, D. M. 22
Willis, R. 152
Windsor, W. L. xviii, 6, 113–128
Wishart, T. 242
Wittgenstein, L. 96
Wollheim, R. 96–97
Wöllner, C. xii, xviii, 1–10, 69–88
women, mental rotation 178–179
Woodruff, G. 268
Worrall, D. xviii, 102, 89–109

York Theatre Royal 229

Zatorre, R. 171, 182
Zimmermann, B.A. 73